The Cambridge Companion to the String Quartet

This Companion offers a concise and authoritative survey of the
string quartet by eleven chamber music specialists. Its fifteen carefully
structured chapters provide coverage of a stimulating range of
perspectives previously unavailable in one volume. It focuses on four
main areas: the social and musical background to the quartet's
development; the most celebrated ensembles; string quartet playing,
including aspects of contemporary and historical performing practice;
and the mainstream repertory, including significant 'mixed ensemble'
compositions involving string quartet. Various musical and pictorial
illustrations complete this indispensable guide. Written for all string
quartet enthusiasts, this Companion will enrich readers'
understanding of the history of the genre, the context and significance
of quartets as cultural phenomena, and the musical, technical and
interpretative problems of chamber music performance. It will also
enhance their experience of listening to quartets in performance and
on recordings.

Cambridge Companions to Music

Topics

The Cambridge Companion to Blues and
  Gospel Music
Edited by Allan Moore

The Cambridge Companion to Conducting
Edited by José Antonio Bowen

The Cambridge Companion to Grand Opera
Edited by David Charlton

The Cambridge Companion to Jazz
Edited by Mervyn Cooke and David Horn

The Cambridge Companion to the Musical
Edited by William Everett and Paul Laird

The Cambridge Companion to the Orchestra
Edited by Colin Lawson

The Cambridge Companion to Pop and Rock
Edited by Simon Frith, Will Straw and John
  Street

The Cambridge Companion to the String
  Quartet
Edited by Robin Stowell

Composers

The Cambridge Companion to Bach
Edited by John Butt

The Cambridge Companion to Bartók
Edited by Amanda Bayley

The Cambridge Companion to Beethoven
Edited by Glenn Stanley

The Cambridge Companion to Benjamin
  Britten
Edited by Mervyn Cooke

The Cambridge Companion to Berg
Edited by Anthony Pople

The Cambridge Companion to Berlioz
Edited by Peter Bloom

The Cambridge Companion to Brahms
Edited by Michael Musgrave

The Cambridge Companion to Bruckner
Edited by John Williamson

The Cambridge Companion to John Cage
Edited by David Nicholls

The Cambridge Companion to Chopin
Edited by Jim Samson

The Cambridge Companion to Debussy
Edited by Simon Trezise

The Cambridge Companion to Handel
Edited by Donald Burrows

The Cambridge Companion to Mozart
Edited by Simon P. Keefe

The Cambridge Companion to Ravel
Edited by Deborah Mawer

The Cambridge Companion to Schubert
Edited by Christopher Gibbs

The Cambridge Companion to Verdi
Edited by Scott L. Balthazar

Instruments

The Cambridge Companion to Brass
  Instruments
Edited by Trevor Herbert and John Wallace

The Cambridge Companion to the Cello
Edited by Robin Stowell

The Cambridge Companion to the Clarinet
Edited by Colin Lawson

The Cambridge Companion to the Organ
Edited by Nicholas Thistlethwaite and
  Geoffrey Webber

The Cambridge Companion to the Piano
Edited by David Rowland

The Cambridge Companion to the Recorder
Edited by John Mansfield Thomson

The Cambridge Companion to the Saxophone
Edited by Richard Ingham

The Cambridge Companion to Singing
Edited by John Potter

The Cambridge Companion to the Violin
Edited by Robin Stowell

The Cambridge Companion to

THE STRING QUARTET

············

EDITED BY
Robin Stowell

CAMBRIDGE
UNIVERSITY PRESS

PUBLISHED BY THE PRESS SYNDICATE OF THE UNIVERSITY OF CAMBRIDGE
The Pitt Building, Trumpington Street, Cambridge, United Kingdom

CAMBRIDGE UNIVERSITY PRESS
The Edinburgh Building, Cambridge, CB2 2RU, UK
40 West 20th Street, New York, NY 10011–4211, USA
477 Williamstown Road, Port Melbourne, VIC 3207, Australia
Ruiz de Alarcón 13, 28014 Madrid, Spain
Dock House, The Waterfront, Cape Town 8001, South Africa

http://www.cambridge.org

© Cambridge University Press 2003

First published 2003

Printed in the United Kingdom at the University Press, Cambridge

Typeface Minion 10.75/14 pt.   *System* LaTeX 2$_\varepsilon$ [TB]

A catalogue record for this book is available from the British Library

Library of Congress Cataloguing in Publication data
The Cambridge Companion to the string quartet / edited by Robin Stowell.
    p.   cm. – (Cambridge companions to music)
Includes bibliographical references and indexes.
ISBN 0 521 80194 X (hardback) – ISBN 0 521 00042 4 (paperback)
1. String quartet.   I. Stowell, Robin.   II. Series.
ML1160.C36   2003
785.7′194 – dc21   2003043508

ISBN 0 521 80194 X hardback
ISBN 0 521 00042 4 paperback

Contents

Illustrations

Contributors

Christina Bashford teaches at Oxford Brookes University, where she is Senior Lecturer in Music. She has published several articles and essays on chamber music and concert life in nineteenth-century London, and currently co-ordinates the *Concert Life in Nineteenth-Century London Database* research project. She was managing editor of *The New Grove Dictionary of Opera* (1992) and joint editor, with Leanne Langley, of *Music and British Culture, 1785–1914: Essays in Honour of Cyril Ehrlich* (2000).

Kenneth Gloag is a Lecturer in Music at Cardiff University. His research interests include twentieth-century British music, the music of Stravinsky, popular music, and general critical and theoretical issues. His principal publications include a Cambridge Music Handbook on Tippett's *A Child of Our Time* (Cambridge University Press, 1998) and contributions to *Tippett Studies* (Cambridge University Press, 1999) and *The Cambridge Companion to Stravinsky*. He has recently completed an essay on popular music and historical periodisation for the interdisciplinary journal *Rethinking History* and is currently writing a book on the music of Peter Maxwell Davies.

Stephen E. Hefling, Professor of Music at Case Western Reserve University, has also taught at Stanford, Yale and the Oberlin College Conservatory. He is the author of *Gustav Mahler: Das Lied von der Erde* (Cambridge University Press, 2000), and edited the autograph piano version of that work for the Mahler Kritische Gesamtausgabe (1989). He is also editor of *Mahler Studies* (Cambridge University Press, 1997) and *Nineteenth-Century Chamber Music* (1998), and has contributed articles and chapters to *19th Century Music*, *Journal of Musicology*, *Journal of Music Theory*, *Performance Practice Review*, the revised *New Grove Dictionary of Music and Musicians*, *The Nineteenth-Century Symphony* (1997), *The Mahler Companion* (1999), etc. Also a specialist in baroque performance practice, Hefling has performed extensively with early music ensembles in the northeastern US, and his book *Rhythmic Alteration in Seventeenth- and Eighteenth-Century Music* (1994) is widely regarded as the standard reference on that topic.

David Wyn Jones is a Reader in the Department of Music, Cardiff University and has written extensively on music of the Viennese Classical period. His publications include the *Oxford Composer Companion: Haydn* (2002), *The Life of Beethoven* (Cambridge University Press 1998), *Music in Eighteenth-Century Austria* (editor, Cambridge University Press, 1996) and *Beethoven: Pastoral Symphony* (Cambridge University Press, 1995). He is currently engaged on a research project supported by the Arts and Humanities Research Board, 'The symphony in Beethoven's Vienna'.

Colin Lawson has an international profile as a period clarinettist, notably as a member of the English Concert, the Hanover Band and the London Classical Players, with which he has recorded extensively and toured worldwide. He has appeared as concerto soloist at many international venues, including Carnegie Hall and the Lincoln Center, New York. His solo discography includes concertos by Fasch, Hook, Mahon, Mozart, Spohr, Telemann, Vivaldi and Weber, as well as a considerable variety of chamber music. He is editor of *The Cambridge Companion to the Clarinet* (Cambridge University Press, 1995), author of two Cambridge Music Handbooks (1996, 1998) and co-author of *The Historical Performance of Music: an Introduction* (Cambridge University Press, 1999). He has also written a book on playing the early clarinet and is editor of *The Cambridge Companion to the Orchestra* (Cambridge University Press, 2003). He taught at the Universities of Aberdeen, Sheffield and London prior to his current appointment as Pro Vice-Chancellor at Thames Valley University.

Tully Potter was born in Edinburgh in 1942 but spent his formative years in South Africa, where he grew to appreciate music. The human voice was his first interest and he studied singing in Johannesburg with Leah Williams; but he came to the conclusion that his place in music was as a listener. He has been collecting records seriously since he was twelve and has made a special study of performing practice as revealed in historic recordings. He has contributed to many international musical journals, notably *The Strad*, and since 1997 he has edited *Classic Record Collector*. His biography of Adolf Busch is due to be published soon and he is preparing a book on the great string quartet ensembles.

Jan Smaczny was educated at the University of Oxford and the Charles University, Prague. Well known as a writer, critic and broadcaster, he has written extensively on many aspects of the Czech repertoire, in particular opera and the life and works of Dvořák; his most recent book is a study of Dvořák's B minor cello concerto. Since 1996 he has been the Hamilton Harty Professor of Music at Queen's University Belfast.

Simon Standage read music at the University of Cambridge and studied the violin with Ivan Galamian in New York. After a period as a freelance violinist, which included four years as sub-leader of the English Chamber Orchestra, he became interested in the Baroque violin and he has been active in the field of historical performance, both as a violinist and director, since the early 1970s. Initially with the English Concert and the Academy of Ancient Music, and since 1982 and 1990 with the Salomon String Quartet and Collegium Musicum 90 respectively, he has made numerous recordings and played concerts worldwide. He currently plays as soloist, director and chamber musician in Britain and abroad. He has taught Baroque violin at the Royal Academy of Music since 1983 and at the Dresdner Akademie für Alte Musik since 1992.

Robin Stowell was educated at the University of Cambridge and the Royal Academy of Music, London, and is currently Professor and Head of Music at Cardiff University. Much of his career as a musicologist (author and editor) is reflected in his work as a performer (violinist/Baroque violinist). His first major book *Violin Technique and Performance Practice in the late Eighteenth and early Nineteenth Centuries* (Cambridge University Press, 1985) was a pioneering work in its field, and he has since published numerous chapters and articles in a wide range of books, dictionaries and journals. His most recent major publications include a Cambridge Handbook on *Beethoven's Violin Concerto* (Cambridge University Press, 1998),

The Early Violin and Viola: a Practical Guide (Cambridge University Press, 2001) and a co-authored volume (with Colin Lawson) entitled *The Historical Performance of Music: an Introduction* (Cambridge University Press, 1999), these last two publications forming part of a series of 'Cambridge Handbooks to the Historical Performance of Music', of which he is co-editor. He is music consultant for and chief contributor to *The Violin Book* (1999) and editor of and principal contributor to *The Cambridge Companion to the Violin* (Cambridge University Press, 1992), *Performing Beethoven* (Cambridge University Press, 1994), and *The Cambridge Companion to the Cello* (Cambridge University Press, 1999).

W. Dean Sutcliffe is University Lecturer at the University of Cambridge and a Fellow of St Catharine's College. He edited the volume *Haydn Studies* (Cambridge University Press, 1998) and is editor of the journal *Eighteenth-Century Music*, the first issue of which will appear in 2004. His book *The Keyboard Sonatas of Domenico Scarlatti and Eighteenth-Century Musical Style* has recently been published by Cambridge University Press.

David Waterman studied philosophy at Trinity College, Cambridge, where he was a Research Scholar and was awarded an MA and Ph.D. Simultaneously, he studied cello privately with Martin Lovett, William Pleeth and Jane Cowan. In 1979 he became a founder member of the Endellion String Quartet, which has played all over the world, broadcast countless times on BBC Radio and TV, and recorded for EMI, Virgin Classics, ASV, and Pearl. The Endellions are currently Quartet in Residence at Cambridge University, were given honorary degrees by MIT after residencies there, and in 1996 were given the Royal Philharmonic Society Award for Best Chamber Ensemble.

Waterman has also performed chamber music with many other musicians, including members of the former Amadeus Quartet, Joshua Bell, the Chilingirian, Vellinger, Stamic and Belcea Quartets, Michael Collins, Imogen Cooper, Ivry Gitlis, Lukacs Hagen, Erich Hobarth, Steven Isserlis, Daniel Phillips, Gábor Takács-Nagy, Mitsuko Uchida, Sándor Végh, Radovan Vlatkovic and Tabea Zimmerman.

Preface

From tentative beginnings, the string quartet has evolved for over 240 years, serving as a medium for some of the most profound and personal musical expression. At first it was a medium that allowed four gentlemen amateurs to converse musically, an aspect of its function that has retained its significance throughout the years. But this aspect has long been interconnected with a view of the genre as one that is appropriate for music of the deepest personal expression, as well as sophisticated humour and wit.

Sir George Dyson once remarked that probably the most ideal situation in which a musician can find himself is to be of equal gifts in a gifted string quartet. Sir Yehudi Menuhin, too, was of little doubt that string quartet playing constitutes the highest form of music making. 'The quality of listening, the quality of "teamwork", of adjusting to one another, of recognising the main voice wherever it may be, of reconciling the different accents and inflections, and the purity of the intonation', he claimed, 'is unequalled by any other ensemble, except perhaps human voices themselves.'[1] Certainly, some of the most musically rewarding periods of my life have been spent playing string quartets (whether as a professional violinist, as a student or in domestic music making), listening to them either as a critic or a devotee and writing about the medium which Edwin Evans described as 'the most perfect, concise, and self-contained combination in all music'.[2]

The principal aim of this volume is to provide a broad readership with a compact, authoritative survey of the string quartet in all its aspects. In so doing, it focuses on selected topics in the kind of depth that will interest and enlighten a more specialist student and scholarly audience. The carefully structured series of essays concentrates on four main areas: the social and cultural contexts which influenced developments in the string quartet, both as a genre and as a family of instruments; the most distinguished ensembles and their personnel, careers and significance; string quartet playing, including an inside view of the musical and interpretative priorities of a professional string quartet as well as perspectives on contemporary and historical performing practice; discussion of the string quartet repertory from its origins in the middle of the eighteenth century to the present, and consideration of 'mixed ensemble' works underpinned by the string quartet ensemble.

The task of covering such an extensive corpus of material within the limited space available naturally poses particular challenges for an editor and his contributors. Authors have thus been required to be selective in their essays; for example, the more detailed consideration has largely been reserved for what may be described as the 'cornerstones' of the repertory, while less significant works are introduced on a more *ad hoc* basis and in more general terms. Various works, composers, ensembles and other details have had to be omitted or summarised in what to some might seem to be a perfunctory manner. However, scholars who have devoted their lives to a single aspect of the genre and find that it gets only brief mention here should be reassured that thorough investigation of that aspect was necessary before even that brief mention could be properly contextualised. The writers' and editor's judgement on what is important is, of course, open to review, so no claim will be made for this volume as the definitive compendium on the string quartet. It is simply one attempt at making as comprehensive a survey as possible within the confines of this ever-expanding series of Companions. The outcome, I hope, will be considered as an indispensable guide for all serious chamber music lovers, amateur and professional, and one that will enhance our understanding of the performers' roles and objectives and enrich our experience of listening to quartets in live performance or on recordings.

The initial impetus for this book came from Penny Souster at Cambridge University Press, who envisaged yet another type of volume that might be embraced by the Cambridge Companion series. It would not have been possible for me to assemble a manual of such breadth without the help of a large number of people. Among these I wish especially to record my gratitude to the contributors, all of whom have stuck to their task and produced with varying degrees of promptitude commissioned chapters that fit with my original outline. Some contributors have requested that due acknowledgement be recorded elsewhere for the help and advice given by others in the compilation of their chapters. Thanks are due, too, to my good friend Dr Ian Cheverton for preparing the music examples, to Tully Potter for the loan of a number of rare photographs from his collection, and to Penny Souster, who has given support to this project beyond the call of duty. I am also indebted to my copy-editor, Lucy Carolan, for managing the typescript smoothly and efficiently through the publication process.

Robin Stowell

Acknowledgements

Some contributors wish to acknowledge the advice and assistance given by friends and colleagues in the preparation of their chapters.

Christina Bashford wishes to record her thanks to Cyril Ehrlich for reading an early draft of Chapter 1 and for much stimulating discussion.

Tully Potter is indebted to Richard Turner's comments on the drafts of Chapters 3 and 4.

David Waterman is extremely grateful for the wise and penetrating feedback on the draft of Chapter 5 from Steven Isserlis, Ruth Waterman, Jonathan Del Mar and Sara Fanelli, who are in no way responsible for any of its shortcomings. Above all, he records his indebtedness to his superb colleagues in the Endellion String Quartet, and also to his students and many other chamber music collaborators for sharing countless hours of illuminating and joyous music making.

Pitch

The Helmholtz system is employed throughout to indicate pitch. In this system middle C is indicated as c^1. Under this scheme the notes to which the instruments of the string quartet are normally tuned are represented as follows:

violin: g–d^1–a^1–e^2
viola: c–g–d^1–a^1
cello: C–G–d–a

1 octave below middle c

2 octaves below middle C

PART 1

Social changes and organological developments

1 The string quartet and society

CHRISTINA BASHFORD

We are 'living in a bad time for practising the intimate, introspective art of the string quartet'.[1] So writes a UK broadsheet journalist at the dawn of the twenty-first century. He is talking, be it said at once, about the difficulties of making a living solely as a professional chamber ensemble that plays the classical repertoire and, though despairing of dwindling public interest, and of string quartets selling out to razzmatazz and pop, he ends with an optimistic assessment of fresh ideas for drawing in new audiences. Be that as it may, his initial, nostalgic message is clear: it was not always thus. Indeed, times have changed as far as the string quartet's relationship with society is concerned: and like other types of music, the string quartet has a social and cultural history, well worth exploring.[2]

This chapter attempts to draw out some of the central threads in that history, by presenting an outline of the changing social function of the string quartet, along with fluctuations in cultural attitudes towards it, from mid-eighteenth-century central-European beginnings right up to the present. The main theme is the relationship between performers and repertoire on the one hand and audiences or 'society' on the other – at root demonstrating a shift from participation to listening. But there is counterpoint, too, not least in the intimacy of the quartet genre and in how, as the very epitome of the chamber music ideal, it has responded to the problems and challenges that external factors have brought.[3]

Music of friends

The story of the string quartet begins in the second half of the eighteenth century, with the newly emerging body of works composed for two violins, viola and cello – sometimes called 'serenade', sometimes 'divertimento', sometimes 'quartetto' (a consistent nomenclature had yet to crystallise) – and intended as 'real' chamber music: that is, music to be performed for its own sake and the enjoyment of its players, in private residences (usually in rooms of limited size), perhaps in the presence of a few listeners, perhaps not. Written by composers such as Vanhal, Gossec, Boccherini, Haydn and Mozart, these works followed on in a long line of music for domestic recreation that stretched back to the madrigals of the fifteenth century and earlier.[4] However, the special timbres and subtly variegated hues created by music spread among four string instruments gave the string quartet a particular purity that was a new departure for chamber music (English viol fantasias excepted); and this may well have marked out the quartet as something different in the minds of its players. At any rate, the quartet edged out the trio sonata as principal instrumental ensemble in the home relatively quickly: a less surprising change than we might at first imagine, given that this was an age when the contemporary and new were constantly sought after.

Quartet composition took off in a number of European centres, but there was by no means one homogeneous idiom, and works embodied differing levels of thematic development, equality of part-writing and concentration of expression – the qualities that later became the touchstone of the Classical quartet style. As it happened, those qualities were first enshrined in Vienna by Haydn and Mozart, who brought the quartet to a notable peak of artistic maturity around the 1780s. Sets of works such as Haydn's Op. 33 or Mozart's six quartets dedicated to Haydn produced, albeit unintentionally, the prototype against which the quartet repertoire was for a long time thereafter to be measured and even modelled, setting the genre apart from most other types of contemporary chamber music. This was the quintessential 'music of friends',[5] an intimate and tightly constructed dialogue among equals, at once subtle and serious, challenging to play, and with direct appeal to the earnest enthusiast. 'Four rational people conversing' was how Goethe would later see it.[6]

Wherever quartet-playing flourished in eighteenth-century Europe (for example in Austria, Germany, Britain, France and Russia), it was typically the province of serious music-lovers among the wealthy, leisured classes – the aristocracy and emerging bourgeoisie. Furthermore, in light of the social conventions then governing the playing of instruments in polite society, it was executed exclusively by men.[7] Women played the keyboard or the harp or sang for private recreation, but were never to be seen with limbs in ungainly disarray playing violins, violas or cellos. That, and the serious business of quartet music, was left to *cognoscenti* husbands, sons, brothers and fathers – though women were surely allowed to listen in, when the presence of a small audience was deemed appropriate.[8]

Reconstructing this musical world is not easy. The essentially private nature of quartet-playing renders documentation scanty, suggesting a less extensive activity than was almost certainly the case; but occasional accounts in diaries, letters and the like enable some glimpses to be caught. Writing from Vienna in 1785 Leopold Mozart recounted one gathering of five people (himself, his son, Haydn, and 'the two Barons Tinti'), at which four of them played three of Wolfgang's new quartets (K. 458, 464, 465); in England, a few years later, the gentleman composer John Marsh noted that he and his brother William had been 'to Mr Toghill's to meet Maj'r Goodenough & play some of Haydn's 2 first setts of quartettos [?Opp. 1 and 2] w'ch the Major play'd remarkably well' in spite of his quiet tone production.[9] Much of this sort of testimony blurs distinctions between *ad hoc* music-making by the players alone and organised play-throughs at which listeners were present, suggesting that many quartet parties doubled as informal, private concerts, or at least that gatherings with audiences were the ones most frequently documented. Take, for example, the memoir of the Muscovite Prince I. M. Dolgoruky, writing about chamber music at his home in 1791:

> Every week during Lent we had small concerts: Prince Khilkov, Prince Shakhovskoy, Novosiltsev, Tit [? composer S. N. Titov], passionate lovers of music and excellent exponents themselves, came over to us to play quartets.[10]

Likewise, the account by the singer Michael Kelly of a Viennese gathering at which quartets were played by Haydn, Dittersdorf (violins), Mozart (viola) and Vanhal (cello) and at which Paisiello and the poet Casti were, like him, among the audience. His oft-quoted remarks include the apt observation of Viennese quartet culture ('a greater treat or a more remarkable one cannot be imagined'), and remind us that the musical rewards of quartet-playing made professional musicians – almost invariably from lower social orders than the leisured classes – some of the most avid participants and enthusiasts.[11]

Key to the spread of quartet-playing in the late eighteenth century was the publication of parts, usually in Vienna, Paris or London, and dissemination to a range of urban centres. Although the market, in comparison with that for piano music, songs and other popular domestic genres, was relatively limited in size, and the music costly, there were enough wealthy *Kenner und Liebhaber* around to stoke a reasonable demand. According to one scholar's calculation, several thousand quartets by about 200 composers (both French and foreign) were published in Paris between 1770 and 1800.[12] Some of the repertoire – particularly Viennese quartets, namely Haydn's, Mozart's, and Beethoven's Op. 18 – was tough for any but the most highly skilled amateurs to get through, and while such players certainly existed (Wilhelm II, dedicatee of Mozart's three Prussian quartets, is a good example), many were surely less accomplished and may have sought more manageable fare. A number of French works, designated *quatuors concertants*,[13] by composers such as Vachon and Bréval were elegant, easy-to-play pieces which, lacking tightly wrought musical arguments *à la Viennoise*, boasted a democratic,

Figure 1.1 Quartet evening at the home of Alexis Fedorovich L'vov, *c.* 1845

if simple, sharing of material: aping French salon conversation, as another commentator has argued.[14] Other repertoire for quartet players included arrangements of large-scale works such as symphonies, operas and oratorios: these were a popular way of recalling and recreating pieces from the public arena. Operatic medleys, known as *quatuors d'airs connus*, were also favourites with French publishers and amateurs.[15]

Several amateur ensembles probably lacked skilled players, though wealthy and influential patrons could always buy their way out of difficulty. George IV, when Prince of Wales, delighted in playing the cello in quartets, alongside top London performers, in private.[16] In Vienna, *c.* 1795 Prince Lichnowsky hired Ignaz Schuppanzigh (later to become the great player of Beethoven's quartets) and others to entertain him and guests on a weekly basis.[17] On the other hand, many chamber music lovers surely relished laborious repeated attempts at a repertoire; and although the early nineteenth century was to see public concerts open up to the quartet, the practice of domestic quartet-playing persisted, with special keenness in German-speaking lands, where *Hausmusik* would be an important part of life for the professional and business classes for decades to come.

Figure 1.2 Quartet performing at the Monday Popular Concerts in St James's Hall, London; from an engraving in the *Illustrated London News* (2 March 1872). The players are Madame Norman-Neruda (violin 1), Louis Ries (violin 2), Ludwig Straus (viola) and Alfredo Piatti (cello)

Into the concert hall

As commercial concert-giving advanced in many European centres in the first half of the nineteenth century, chamber music and particularly string quartets became a familiar presence in the concert hall. A few precedents existed, in that quartets had typically featured in miscellaneous orchestral and vocal concerts, especially in England – Haydn famously writing in extrovert style for 1790s London in his Opp. 71 and 74; and around the turn of the eighteenth century a burgeoning, organised culture of private salon concerts, at which quartets were performed, had emerged in cities such as Vienna and Paris.[18] But it was in the early nineteenth century that a new type of 'public' concert, devoted exclusively to chamber music – very occasionally to string quartets alone – was born, with audiences formed initially around groups of enthusiastic amateur practitioners, and performances safeguarded financially by subscription lists. New initiatives included Schuppanzigh's quartet concerts at Count Razumovsky's palace in Vienna (begun in 1804–5), Karl Möser's quartet evenings in Berlin (in 1813–14) and Pierre Baillot's Séances de Quatuors et de Quintettes in Paris (in 1814). Other developments followed, with varying lifespans. In London a rash of innovations broke out in the 1835–6 season (the Concerti da Camera,

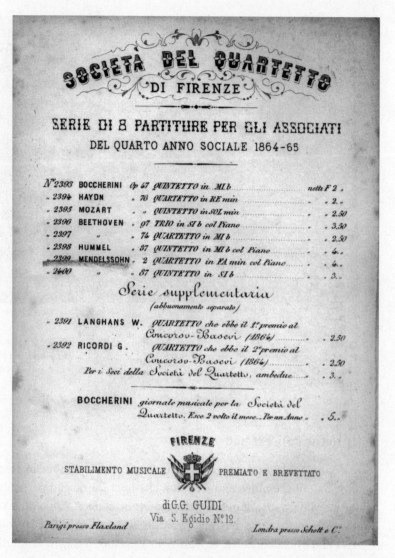

Figure 1.3 Title-page for the series of pocket scores specially published in Florence by G. G. Guidi for the Società del Quartetto di Firenze's concerts of 1864–5 [actual size 10 cm × 14.3 cm]

the Quartett Concerts, the Classical Chamber Concerts) and, later, institutions such as John Ella's Musical Union (1845–81; see Fig. 3.1, p. 43 below) and Chappell's Popular Concerts (1859–1902) came into being. Meanwhile, Vienna had its Musikalische Abendunterhaltungen under the auspices of the Gesellschaft der Musikfreunde (1818–29; 1831–40) and Joseph Hellmesberger's quartet concerts (established in 1849); and Paris witnessed a flurry of series such as those set up by Alard and Chevillard (1837–48), the Tilmant brothers (1833–49) and the Dancla brothers (1838–70), followed by the notable Société Alard et Franchomme (1847–70) and Société des Quatuors

Armingaud et Jacquard (1856–68). As the century unfolded, concert life continued to grow and diversify, with many quartet performances, in most European centres of population. New audiences were drawn in; concert-giving spread into countries such as Spain and Italy where operatic traditions had previously held sway; and first inroads were made into the USA. Among several notable newcomers were the Mason and Thomas Chamber Music Soirées in New York (1855–68), the Società del Quartetto in Florence (established 1861), the similarly named organisation in Milan (1864; Boito was a supporter), the Kammermusikforening in Copenhagen (1868) and the Kammermusikverein in Prague (1876).[19]

Chamber music succeeded in the concert hall partly because of the low costs and ease of rehearsal (in contrast to full orchestra concerts) that were involved, but it also entailed some aesthetic contradictions, especially for the string quartet. Formal halls, reverberant acoustics and sizeable audiences (the last an economic necessity for financial well-being) were decidedly at odds with the inwardness of quartet playing and the intricate details that Classical composers had intended to be heard; and public performance seemed the very antithesis of the idiom. Recognising this, some concert promoters in London made adaptations to the layout of the concert hall and seating arrangements in the hope of creating an aura of intimacy: Ella, apparently taking his cue from Prince Czartoryski's private quartet concerts in Vienna, placed the performers in the centre of the hall and had the audience sit around them, drawing listeners into the music and the music-making.[20] Performers learned to project the sound out rather than in, and by the turn of the century some purpose-built chamber music halls (Bösendorfer-Saal, Vienna, 1872; Bechstein Hall, London, 1901; both built by prominent piano firms) were offering more intimate surroundings. Composers reacted to the new environment too. Richly resonant writing, thicker textures and bold gestures – vocabulary for larger spaces – were fused with the conventions of tightly knit structure and concentration of expression in many a nineteenth-century quartet; and professional players rather than amateurs became the intended executants, with technical demands increasing accordingly, from Beethoven's Op. 59 (written for Schuppanzigh's ensemble) right through to Tchaikovsky's and Smetana's quartets.[21] By comparison, the domestic repertoire was only occasionally replenished – George Onslow was a notable exponent.

In many cities, quartets were played by local string players, usually the leading orchestral musicians in the area, who formed regular concert line-ups and gathered kudos for the musical advantages – unanimity of ensemble and phrasing, the blending of tone – this brought.[22] But visiting top-class performers, especially first violinists, could usually offer more, filling halls with listeners as well as sound; and at some concerts, particularly in the second half of the century, 'star' violinists were habitually slotted above three local players, rewarding box office and connoisseurs alike, though sometimes earning critical censure for loose ensemble. This practice was particularly common in London, concert marketplace *extraordinaire*, whose visitors included Vieuxtemps, Auer and Sarasate. There were also a few touring foursomes, often brothers, usually Germans. The Moralts (1800–?; 1830–40), the Müllers (two generations: 1831–55; 1855–73), and the Herrmanns (none of whom were brothers or called 'Herrmann'; 1824–30) all travelled Europe, capitalising on kinship as much as musicianship, and foreshadowing, in some respects, the 'professional' quartets that began to flourish around the turn of the nineteenth century. These included Joachim's Berlin-based quartet; the Brodsky Quartet in Manchester; and two touring ensembles: the Czech Quartet in Europe and the Kneisel Quartet in America.

Throughout the century, the shape and content of concert programmes was subject to a good deal of local variation. In Paris, Baillot's Séances (which lasted till 1840) comprised four or five string quartets or quintets – typically a range of works by Haydn, Mozart, Boccherini and Beethoven – topped off by a showy violin solo with piano accompaniment. Most concerts in London in the 1830s and 1840s, by comparison, were longer and their contents more mixed: chamber music with piano was virtually indispensable (the Beethoven piano trios and Schumann piano quartet and quintet were much performed), though string quartets occupied an important place (initially a broad range of Haydn, Mozart, Beethoven, Mendelssohn; later additions included Brahms, Tchaikovsky and Dvořák) and the instrumental items were invariably interspersed by songs.[23] Concerts of quartets alone, complete with 'logical', or chronological, programming, were something of a rarity until the early to mid twentieth century. Even then, adding a pianist or other instrumentalist(s) for quintets and so on was a common way of introducing contrast and broadening appeal.

More significantly, chamber music's arrival in the concert hall coincided with, and reinforced, the widespread preservation and enshrinement of the Viennese classics in the repertoire. In practice this meant that, from the outset, string quartets were at the heart of things, most especially the last ten works by Mozart, Haydn's Opp. 76 and 77 (and a few others, too) and Beethoven's Opp. 18, 59 and 74. While modern quartets were added to the 'favourites' list gradually – e.g. Mendelssohn's Opp. 12 and 44, Schubert's A minor and D minor, and some Brahms, Dvořák and Tchaikovsky – the old remained, anchoring the repertoire around a body of works that were fast taking on special status as exemplars of high musical art. This in itself was a 'new' thing. The Beethoven quartets represented the pinnacle of achievement and seriousness, and rapidly became central and canonic at all times and in all places; championing of the late quartets (occasionally broached but not yet fully assimilated) was undertaken by such institutions as the Beethoven Quartett Society (1845–52; London) and the Société des Derniers Quatuors (established in Paris, 1852). Meanwhile, pieces for other chamber music combinations – Mozart's G minor and C major string quintets, Beethoven's 'Archduke' piano trio, Schumann's piano quintet – became embedded in the repertoire too.

A diet of string quartets, even when mixed with piano trios and so on, was for many listeners something of an acquired taste, and palates almost always benefited from a little education. This was particularly the case for initiates to chamber music, but it was also true for those who were familiar with some quartets from their own domestic music-making, given that perceptions gained from playing, as opposed to listening, were very likely to differ; that new works were beyond many amateurs' performance capabilities anyhow; and that appreciation could always be deepened. Insightful critics, writing in the ever-growing print media, filled some of this need for enlightenment, at the same time celebrating the genre's inherent seriousness. Equally, at some concerts (starting with those in England) informative programme notes were provided, with a view to explaining formal and tonal structures and unlocking expressive content.[24] Musical literacy was taken for granted – these were the glory days of the pianoforte – and listeners were expected to work hard at gaining familiarity with the music in whatever way they could, including self-improvement at home. Miniature scores were one route to this sort of appreciation (they were on sale as early as the middle of the century); piano transcriptions, often *à quatre mains*, were another.[25] Domestic quartet-playing may have contributed to the process, especially in musical Germany, but evidence for the true extent of such practices is lacking. Nevertheless, the classic pieces for home erudition were the staple Viennese quartets – clearly essential reading for anyone aspiring to appreciate chamber music.

Back in the eighteenth century, a love of string quartets had been largely limited to two groups: interested amateurs with sufficient wealth to play them, or status to attend select, private renditions; and musicians and their families. In the nineteenth, the advent of chamber music concerts, often at modest prices, allowed the treasures of the quartet repertoire to be opened up to many who would hitherto have been excluded. Notably also, women became a significant part of the audience.[26] Wealthy connoisseurs remained keen advocates and several concert societies were supported by well-heeled, even aristocratic, listeners, while at the other end of the scale the doors were opened to aspirants to high culture and respectability among the lower orders. In Vienna, August Duisberg's quartet mounted low-cost subscription concerts on Sunday afternoons, aimed at lower middle- and working-class people; in London, there were the philanthropic and morally worthy South

Place Ethical Society's Sunday chamber concerts (1887–), to which admission was free.[27]

Enter technology

In the early twentieth century gramophone records and, later, broadcasting created a new environment for listening to string quartets, taking the music back into people's homes for private consumption. Anyone with sufficient interest (and initially, for records, spending power) could now experience what was generally deemed to be the finest art music, finely played, again and again in his/her own home. Although there were, by the mid-1930s, many types of music for gramophone listeners to choose from, chamber music, and *ipso facto* string quartets, on record always had the in-built advantage of verisimilitude, with which opera and orchestral music could simply not compete. To paraphrase Compton Mackenzie, founding editor of *Gramophone* magazine, it was tantamount to having one's own private string quartet and would likely become a real substitute. Of course, the technology was far from perfect, as Mackenzie freely admitted – 'the winding of it [the gramophone], the hiss of the needle, the interruptions caused by changing discs' amounted to a 'detestable handicap', and there was the loss of the live 'beauty of sound in motion' – but the '78' record nevertheless offered listeners to quartets the opportunity of hearing nuances and intricacies often missed in the concert hall, and of getting to know the repertoire through repeated sitting-room encounters. Mackenzie, for one, was in no doubt that for string quartets, the intensity of gramophone listening was preferable to concert-going, and in Walter Willson Cobbett's encyclopedia of chamber music (first issued in 1929) he proselytised accordingly.[28]

Even in the early days of acoustic recording (up to 1927) the string quartet had reproduced well, giving it a head start in the building of a repertoire. And with electrical recording, many 'standard' quartets (or at least movements from them) – some sixty-odd works from Haydn to Debussy – swiftly became available.[29] The number of professional string quartets with relatively permanent personnel was beginning to increase significantly, along with standards of playing, and groups such as the Rosé, Flonzaley, Léner and London quartets recorded several works. In the 1930s, Europe (in particular London) became the focus of activity; many notable recordings were made by the Busch, Léner and Budapest quartets. Records, however, were expensive, their bulk and fragility adding heavy distribution costs. Special interest groups were therefore encouraged to guarantee risky ventures by subscription: the Haydn Quartet 'Society', for example, was HMV's device for marketing the Pro Arte's cycle of twenty-nine of the quartets. Whether

Figure 1.4 The Budapest Quartet playing to the United States Army Air Forces Technical School in Colorado during World War II

by luck or by judgement, the record companies were making significant investments in much of the chamber repertoire; the range of music explored was considerably enlarged, reinforcing hierarchies of works (including, of course, quartets) and artists in the process.[30] And like concert-givers before them, record companies found that ensembles were relatively cheap to hire, and usually came pre-rehearsed. Besides, the music itself would endure.

From the late 1920s onwards, broadcasting, of recordings or studio concerts, gave string quartets access to an immense and broadly based audience. Government-funded stations such as the BBC carried a good deal of carefully chosen serious music, including quartets, on mainstream channels.[31] The medium could also, as in the case of the BBC's Light Programme 'Music in Miniature' – a half-hour compilation of single, appealing movements from chamber works, put out during evening slots, 1945–51 – do a little evangelising. By this time, a sizeable music appreciation literature based around recordings of what were considered the 'classic' quartets had grown up, and much wisdom and elucidation by Percy Scholes and others awaited any neophytes.[32]

The long-playing record arrived at the end of the 1940s, removing the constraints of the '78' format and reducing costs and, ultimately, prices. During the 1950s and 1960s the market expanded to become truly international,

Japan, the USA and Australasia being significant growth areas. As new labels appeared and ensembles jostled for contracts, the repertoire also took off. Enthusiasts could now purchase all the quartets of Haydn, Mozart and Schubert (Beethoven had long stood alone in the catalogues in this respect), explore a range of nineteenth-century repertoire (and additionally many works for enlarged ensembles – the Brahms string quintets and sextets, a range of piano quartets and quintets, and so on) or discover modern newcomers (most crucially, the six Bartók quartets). Multiple recordings of the same piece could be compared, with help from a new industry of published and broadcast journalism.[33] From the players' perspective, there were three principal sources of employment: recording, broadcasting and 'live' concerts – and a lifetime's worth of music too.

The aftermath of World War II saw the number of professional ensembles expand further, and with unprecedented vigour. This was the period when quartets such as the Amadeus, the Fine Arts, the Juilliard, the Hollywood and the Quartetto Italiano came forward. Many groups, particularly in the USA, were formed from the pool of top-quality string-playing Jewish refugees who had fled Nazi Europe in the 1930s. These were people with a strong, vibrant tradition of quartet-playing, and some brought extraordinary talent and much experience. The Budapest and Amadeus quartets, to name just two, had members from such a background.[34] A shared training was also fairly common and helped groups create distinctive stylistic and sonorous identities: the members of the Pro Arte were all former students of the Brussels Conservatoire; those of the Léner were from the Hungarian Royal Academy of Music; and the upper Austro-German strings of the Amadeus had all learned with Max Rostal.

Contrary to what Compton Mackenzie had believed or even hoped, chamber music concerts did not fade out in retreat from technological innovations. Concert life continued throughout the twentieth century, though in Europe it was twice ruptured by world wars. Social change made its mark, too. In the decade before World War I, professional quartets with women players – some, famously, staffed by women alone (e.g. the Norah Clench and Langley–Mukle ensembles) – had come into existence in England. This reflected economic realities as well as changing social attitudes: for although gender taboos on string instruments had been broken and advanced training opportunities increased during the late nineteenth century, orchestral chairs were in the pre-war decade still largely occupied by men. The self-regulating nature of string quartets enabled many capable female ensembles to enjoy prominence into the 1930s. Thereafter these groups fell away, though a few women took up places in reputable quartets: it would nevertheless be some decades more before quartets with significant international reputations would regularly contain or comprise women.[35]

By the 1960s the quartet recital had become an established concert type worldwide, with a piece for larger or mixed ensemble often prominent in a programme. Air travel, a world market and punishing schedules became commonplace for some groups. Chamber music societies, which were growing aplenty, booked ensembles, as did American universities – the so-called campus circuit – and specialist summer festivals. Wide availability of records and radio broadcasts meant that an ensemble's reputation literally could go before it, securing ticket sell-outs in countries where it had never given a live performance.[36] The chamber music scene in both the USA and Britain was particularly strong in the decades after World War II, audiences having benefited from a sizeable pre-war influx of music-lovers with central European cultural values, which regarded the string quartet as the highest of high musical art.[37]

Beethoven remained at the apex of the quartet repertoire, in concert hall and on disc, with Brahms and later Bartók becoming rightful heirs. As a genre, the quartet retained its hold over composers as a repository for their most intimate thoughts and close working-out, and a steady supply of fresh works came forth, often tailored to particular ensembles. Shostakovich composed many works for the Beethoven Quartet, Bartók's Fourth was written for the Kolisch, Britten's Third for the Amadeus, Tippett's Fifth for the Lindsay. Several groups proved keen to explore new quartets alongside the standard repertoire, and a few developed close working relationships with composers.[38] Technical standards were reaching unprecedented levels, and composers responded, making acute, often highly imaginative, demands of the players.

Private patrons also stimulated quartet composition and performance, most notably in the early decades of the century. In Britain, the dictionary-making ex-businessman Cobbett supported chamber music in several ways. His most celebrated act was the establishment in 1905 of a number of prizes, including one for 'phantasy' chamber works (inspired by Elizabethan viol fantasias), which gave rise to a discrete repertoire of English chamber music, including the phantasy quartets of Hurlestone and Howells.[39] The USA had the benefactress Elizabeth Sprague Coolidge, herself the winner of one of the Cobbett Medals for services to the art. Among her many grand gestures were the patronage of the Berkshire Festivals of Chamber Music, 1917–24; the establishment of a trust fund at the Library of Congress in Washington in 1925, principally to fund concerts and award composition prizes for new works; and the sponsorship of the library's Coolidge Auditorium, specially designed for chamber music at a cost of more than $90,000.[40] Also noteworthy for her munificence and imagination was Gertrude Clarke Whittall, who donated her five Stradivarius instruments to the Library of Congress and came up with the idea for a quartet residency there, tied to performances on the Strads, in 1938.[41] The Budapest Quartet was the first incumbent.

In Europe, international festivals, including those at Donaueschingen and Baden-Baden, and a series organised by the International Society for Contemporary Music, played their part in supporting quartet composition in the inter-war years. Later (1950s and 1960s onwards), universities in the UK and USA instituted residencies for string quartets, providing groups with valuable subventions and environments for artistic renewal. Around the same time summer schools at Dartington and Prussia Cove (UK) and the Marlboro' Festival (USA) created special training grounds, at which emerging student quartets could learn from veteran chamber musicians such as Sándor Végh and Pablo Casals. Quartet writing continued to be encouraged through the prevalence of chamber media in international composition competitions, the coexistence of composer and quartet residencies in universities, and commissioning programmes, for instance the one established by Chamber Music America (1983).

Shifting cultural values

By the 1970s it looked as if, in the space of a little more than two centuries, the quartet had secured an audience which, though smaller than most listening publics, was far wider than eighteenth-century musicians and nineteenth-century concert-goers would have believed possible. A core repertoire had also been created, preserved and later extended, and had taken on a seemingly unassailable canonic position. There had, admittedly, been a transformation in the nature of string quartet consumption, as the activity changed from one based around participation to one largely constituted of listening and, in the cases of more earnest audiences, knowledgeable appreciation; yet, in spite of occasional performances in large venues and new works that challenged the genre with theatricality and other heterodoxies, the vital ingredients of the quartet 'experience' typically remained intimacy and inwardness.

But change was again imminent. During the century's last two decades, the certainties and values that had for so long been attached to classical music underwent fundamental reassessment, affecting the string quartet as much as any genre. Hierarchies of taste based on value and authoritative judgements came into question, relativism became widely expounded, the dominance of the musical 'canon' was challenged, and quartets that had been gathering dust were recovered and rehabilitated.[42] The recorded repertoire, in particular, broadened dramatically, and niche labels for unfamiliar works became common. Re-mastered recordings on CD opened up the string quartet's performance history for all to hear, but the idea that there was a set of 'gold standard' string quartets that the music-lover ought to get to know was fast becoming a thing of the past.

Meantime, popular and world musics staked their claim to the serious consideration that classical repertoires had always enjoyed. There were creative gains here, as cross-fertilisation took place. The albums and activities of the Kronos Quartet, which plays works by composers emanating from non-European cultures and juxtaposes different styles in pursuit of extra-musical connections and new types of insight, are a case in point and have been followed by groups such as the new Brodskys and the Soweto String Quartet. But set against this has been a seeping away of widespread serious interest in classical music. (The popularisation of a few orchestral or operatic 'classics' – admittedly a sizeable phenomenon – is something else, often treating classical music as material for relaxation, rather than for stimulus and engagement.) The string quartet, in particular, has become tarred with the brush of elitism, on account of its inherent cerebrality as well as its historical associations with wealth and middle-class consumption (Adorno, it should be recalled, famously discussed chamber music's 'bourgeois' identity).[43] It is not surprising, then, that imaginative, accessible packaging of both performers and music is a major concern for agents and publicists, and that techniques for attracting new audiences in the first place, and engaging them thereafter, are constantly being tried, some with notable success. The education of newcomers has been a recurring theme in this essay, but given the climate outlined above – not to mention the essence of the quartet genre, conventionally understood, as 'musicians' music', and the fact that *widespread* familiarity with musical notation has disappeared during the century – the challenge has at no time been greater than at the present. And since the prevailing image is 'highbrow and elitist', a live string quartet has become an almost obligatory *chic* trimming for wedding services and receptions – symbol of high culture and social refinement for consumer-driven ceremonial. The musical content, it should be noted, typically centres around arrangements of popular instrumental classics and jazz and show tunes.

Amidst such cultural change and uncertainty, serious lovers of music continue to support their favourite ensembles and repertoires, and to taste new works, different styles of playing and débutant groups. The choice is great: quartets range from those playing only highly contemporary works (e.g. Arditti Quartet) to those making a virtue out of historical awareness and period performance (Salomon, Quatuor Mosaïques), with many occupying the central, 'traditional' repertoire, or exploring curious backwaters. Women, it may be observed, have become an unremarked presence in professional quartets; but making a successful livelihood is tough for all, and winning an international competition, such as the one founded in Banff (1983), can launch an ensemble career. On the domestic front, quartet-playing for its own sake is still pursued by professional musicians seeking recreation and by highly-trained 'amateur' string players, the latter presumably forming an important slice of the quartet-listening public, able to connect with performances in the concert hall in uniquely privileged ways. The music of friends still has its friends.

2 Developments in instruments, bows and accessories

ROBIN STOWELL

Few of the world's top string players perform in public nowadays on instruments made by contemporary luthiers. Most opt instead for antique instruments, especially examples by Antonio Stradivari (1644–1737), Bartolomeo Giuseppe Guarneri del Gesù (1698–1744) or other Italian master luthiers, which they are either sufficiently wealthy to own or fortunate to have on extended loan. This is no recent trend. Rightly or wrongly, it has long been believed that the sound potential of most violins will mature with age and playing.[1]

There is naturally good reason for the esteem in which both Stradivari and Guarneri have been held, even though during their lifetime the tonal qualities of the highly arched models of the Amati family and the Austrian Jacob Stainer (?1617–83) generally held favour.[2] The instruments developed by Stradivari, Guarneri and their contemporaries began to reign supreme only after they, in company with most other extant instruments of the violin family, had been subjected to various external and internal modifications towards the end of the eighteenth century, to make them more responsive to changes in musical style and taste.[3] These modifications occurred between c. 1760 and c. 1830 as a response to the demand for greater tonal sonority, volume and projection, resulting from the increasing vogue for public concerts discussed in Chapter 1.[4] Developments in bow construction at about the same time led to the standardisation (c. 1785) of bow design, measurements, weights and materials by François Tourte (1747–1835).

The exterior body outline of instruments of the violin family remained substantially unaltered during the Romantic era despite attempts at 'improvement'[5] and the introduction of new designs such as François Chanot's guitar-shaped violin, Félix Savart's trapezoid violin, Hermann Ritter's *viola alta*, Michel Woldemar's *violon-alto* and Jean-Baptiste Vuillaume's enlarged violas.

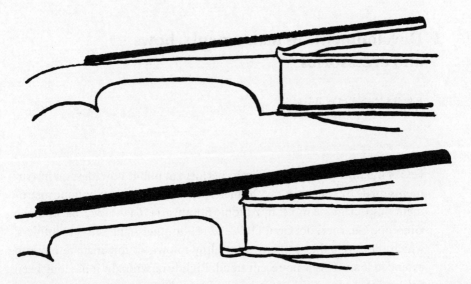

Figure 2.1 Diagram showing the respective angles of the neck and fingerboard of a 'Baroque violin' (above) and a 'modern' instrument

The violin

The late-eighteenth-century desire for a more brilliant, powerful sound was met chiefly by subjecting stringed instruments to considerably greater tensions. The fundamental exterior shape of the violin and its normal body-length (typically *c.* 35.6 cm) remained essentially unchanged. However, makers substituted a longer (by 0.64–1.27 cm to the present standard of 12.86–13.02 cm) and thinner (by *c.* 3.18 mm) neck and set it at an angle of 4–5 degrees from the body of the instrument (with the level of the nut just below that of the table),[6] thus eliminating the need for an impossibly cumbersome wedge between fingerboard and neck, in order to enable the fingerboard closely to follow the angle of the strings for clear tone production (see Fig. 2.1). This modification also offered an increase in the playing length of string (by up to 1.25 cm) and resultant tonal benefits.

The typical neck of most original Baroque and early Classical violins protruded from the instrument roughly at right angles to the ribs; it was generally glued to the body and secured by three nails driven from inside the block. The new neck conformation enabled the full range of the instrument to be exploited. In most cases it involved retaining the original head and grafting it on to a new neck which was then attached through a mortise into the top block in order to provide additional strength to withstand the increased tensions on the instrument; these latter were often exacerbated in many cases by the need for a slightly higher, thinner and more steeply curved bridge, the design of which was variable but gradually standardised.

The position of the bridge may also have been standardised as late as the second half of the eighteenth century. In many seventeenth- and eighteenth-century paintings and engravings of violins, for example, the bridge is depicted much closer to the tailpiece end of the instrument than nowadays.[7] This is too common a feature to be dismissed merely as artistic licence or representational inaccuracy, especially since bridge 'footprints' indicating a variety of playing lengths of string are commonly found on instruments of that period. However, no firm deduction can be made as to its verity without more positive information about the relative situation of the soundpost. If the bridge placement had been even roughly as depicted, it would have been practically impossible for the soundpost to be positioned in anything like its modern relationship.[8] Indeed, it seems likely that some performers may have played on instruments whose bridges were positioned behind the soundpost, a conformation which would doubtless have produced a warm, mellow tone, but without the volume and potential for projection required by late-eighteenth-century performers.

To support old instruments against the greater pressures to which they were subjected – and the more so when pitch standards began generally to rise – bass-bars were lengthened and made considerably more substantial. Comprising a piece of pine perfectly split and fitted longitudinally to the underside of the bass side of the instrument by the left foot of the bridge, the bass-bar provided the requisite strength to oppose the downward pressure of the strings on the bridge feet. It was of no fixed dimensions for any instruments in the seventeenth and eighteenth centuries, different schools advocating different sizes.[9] Surviving examples and available evidence suggest that the average bass-bar dimensions used by Stradivari for his violins were:

length: 50 mm away from the upper and lower ends of the belly
height: 6–7 mm under the bridge
width: 5 mm

These measurements are small when compared with the standardised dimensions of the 'modern' violin bass-bar, as introduced from *c.* 1800:

length: approximately 39.5 mm away from the upper and lower ends of the belly
height: 10 mm
width: 5.5 mm

The soundpost, a small rod of pine wood which links the table to the back, was also made more substantial in order to perform more effectively its structural and acoustical functions.

The longer, narrower neck of late-eighteenth-century violins in turn affected the shape of the fingerboard. By that time increasingly of ebony rather than veneered hardwood, the fingerboard was also narrowed at the peg-box end; it was also broadened somewhat towards the bridge and made more markedly arched throughout in keeping with the typical sweeping curve of the modified bridge. Furthermore, it was lengthened by approximately 5.08–6.35 cm to an average length of 26.67 cm,[10] thus extending the range of the instrument well beyond seventh position and affording players greater facility in the high registers.

It is difficult to establish who actually instigated these modifications to most extant violins. The impetus appears to have been provided by makers resident in Paris,[11] of whom Nicolas Lupot (1758–1824) and François-Louis Pique (1758–1822) were especially prominent. The French example was evidently followed by makers in Italy, and German luthiers were also implementing similar changes at about the same time.[12] However, some Gagliano violins made as early as the 1780s combine original necks of almost modern dimensions with fittings of eighteenth-century lightness, and the necks of some English violins *c.* 1760 were already of approximately modern length.

During this wind of change, particular interest was shown in the 'classical' model of Stradivari's 'golden period', whose relatively flat (low-arched) table and back were probably inspired by the compact, powerful instruments of Brescian Giovanni Paolo Maggini (*c.* 1581 – *c.* 1632). Stradivari's 'flat' model violin was found to respond best to the modifications and soon began to gain tonal supremacy over the instruments of Stainer and the Amatis. The Italian violinist Giovanni Battista Viotti (1755–1824), the principal inspiration behind the celebrated nineteenth-century French violin school, was influential in establishing Stradivari's instruments in the favoured position they still occupy today.[13] His tone evidently had a beauty, breadth and power that his contemporaries regarded as new, and it is probably no coincidence that a reviewer for *The London Chronicle* (1794) attributed these qualities to his 'changed violin structure' which offered greater sound projection. The violins of Guarneri del Gesù, notable for their massive build, powerful tone and a certain ruggedness of character and workmanship, achieved their prominent position somewhat later, thanks largely to Nicolò Paganini (1782–1840), Henri Vieuxtemps (1820–81) and Henryk Wieniawski (1835–80), while Ole Bull (1810–80) and Charles-Auguste de Bériot (1802–70) championed the cause respectively of the Brescian makers Gasparo da Salò (1540–1609) and Maggini.

The viola

Early in its history, the viola was available in various sizes, larger models normally being described as 'tenor violas' and smaller ones as 'alto violas' in keeping with the registers most commonly exploited within their range.[14] Some 'tenor violas' were so large as to be almost unplayable on the arm, notably the Andrea Amati tenor viola (1574) in the Ashmolean Museum, Oxford, which has a body length of 47 cm. Antonio Stradivari's enormous 1690 'Medici' instrument (48.3 cm long) contrasts with his smaller contralto models (41.3 cm long), while the length of Jacob Stainer's violas (1649–70) evidently varied between 40 cm and 46.3 cm.[15]

Makers continued to produce large and small violas throughout the seventeenth and early eighteenth centuries, but most larger models were later 'cut down' for ease of playing. Smaller models predominated thereafter until the early twentieth century, suggesting makers' response to technical advances and demands.[16] In the interim, instruments underwent similar (but proportionate) modifications of the neck, fingerboard and internal fittings to the violin in order to increase string tension, tonal brilliance and left-hand facility. Further experiments at acoustical improvement in the nineteenth century turned the instrument's evolution full circle and involved lengthening or enlarging the body,[17] culminating in the 'Tertis' model (with an average body length of 42.5 cm) developed by Lionel Tertis and Arthur Richardson in the 1930s.

The cello

The oldest surviving cello, by Andrea Amati (1572), was made as part of a group of instruments for Charles IX, King of France 1560–74. Along with the rest of Andrea Amati's cellos, this instrument's peg-box was probably made to accommodate only three strings (tuned F–c–g);[18] it underwent modification later to accept a fourth peg. After Agricola, most descriptions of the cello cite four strings tuned B♭[1]–F–c–g, a tone below modern tuning; the latter was introduced in early-seventeenth-century Italy but spread only slowly, the old 'B♭[1]' tuning continuing to appear in England into the eighteenth century.

The early cello was also made in a wide range of sizes. The first instruments made in Cremona by Andrea Amati and his family were large, *c.* 79 cm in length of back. Almost contemporary with these were smaller cellos made in Brescia, with a corresponding back measurement of *c.* 71 cm. These two sizes seem to have persisted as alternatives well into the eighteenth century, but Cremonese makers' preference for the larger model unfortunately re-sulted in the majority of seventeenth-century cellos made by the most revered violin makers being 'cut down' for modern use and thereby los-ing the original integrity of their design.

The standard back length in use nowadays is approximately 75 cm, a me-dian measurement between the two earlier sizes which was first employed in Cremona towards the end of the seventeenth century. Stradivari had al-ready made several instruments of the larger pattern when Francesco Rugeri began to work to a 75 cm model. Stradivari's revised pattern on that size, the 'B' form introduced after 1707, did much to gain for the cello its cur-rent status in music, offering fuller tonal projection and a greater range of expression.[19]

Many other aspects of the cello's background history were the subjects of wide variation and experimentation well into the eighteenth century. Most of the Cremonese makers made instruments of hybrid form, designs in-corporating characteristics of both the cello and bass viol. Stradivari made at least two cellos before 1700 with a flat back, while other luthiers, in-cluding Amati and Joseph 'filius Andrea' Guarneri, made bass viols in cello form, illustrating the common ground between the two instruments and indicating the quest for a design which incorporated the agility of the viol and the sonority of the cello.[20] Other hybrid models include the five-string cello, the *harmonicello* of J. C. Bischoff, the *heptacorde* devised by Raoul and Vuillaume, and Johann Staufer's *arpeggione*.

While the design of the cello reached its ideal with Stradivari's 'B' form, changes in detail and fittings, many in common with the violin and viola, have continued until the present day. The short, stocky eighteenth-century neck has been increased in length by *c.* 2.5 cm and made slimmer to facilitate playing in the upper positions, and the old system of nailing the neck to the body, or setting the ribs into slots cut in the side of the neck, has been aban-doned in favour of mortising the neck into the upper block. The fingerboard has been lengthened to extend the range on each string, but it is now made of solid ebony rather than veneered wood in order to resist the wear caused by metal-covered strings. The bass-bar has increased in length and depth to provide more support for the lower-register strings. The bridge is now generally lighter and its delicate form has evolved into two basic designs: the French, which is the more common, and the even lighter Belgian model, which is used in the interests of greater volume rather than tonal breadth. A further refinement to the fingerboard was introduced by Bernhard Romberg (1767–1841), who flattened it beneath the length of the C string to provide increased clearance for the wide vibration of that heavy string when played *forte*, and thus avoid its grating buzzes and rattles against the fingerboard surface. Romberg's recessed fingerboard, adopted by his protégé Dotzauer and by Spohr for the violin at the beginning of the nineteenth century, was never universally accepted.

Perhaps the most important development for the player was the adjustable endpin, introduced by Adrien Servais in the mid-nineteenth century to give the instrument greater stability during large shifts of the left hand.[21] Fitted directly to the cello, its metal spike can be stored inside the body of the instrument during transportation and be extended to the required length to raise the cello into a comfortable playing position. It only gradually became accepted as a standard fitting but it has played a significant part, in its various forms, in the development of left-hand technique and tonal quality.

Accessories

Strings

Silk, steel, brass and copper strings were available during the seventeenth century but do not appear to have been widely used by string players of the violin family. From its inception until into the eighteenth century, the violin was normally equipped with strings of gut.[22] By the early eighteenth century, gut (or silk) strings wound with silver (or copper) began to gain preference in many countries for their superior tonal potential for the violin's g and the viola's c and g strings and the cello's C and G strings, allowing for an increase in mass without an increase in diameter and a consequent loss of flexibility.[23] Emanating from Bologna, they are mentioned by Playford as sounding 'much better and lowder than common Gut Strings, either under the Bow or Finger'.[24] Their gradual adoption led to the eventual demise of the tenor-size viola.

Despite the increased loyalty to overspun strings and the well-publicised disadvantages of gut – notably the need to keep them moist, their tendency to unravel, their sensitivity to variation in atmospheric temperature, the common incidence of knots and other imperfections – the combination of plain gut e^2, a^1, d^1 and a g with copper, silver-plated copper or silver round wire close-wound on a gut core was the violin norm throughout the nineteenth century.[25] Nevertheless, Gunzelheimer was still a strong advocate of all-gut violin stringing in 1855, while Alberto Bachmann recorded (1925): 'The fourth or G string is the only covered string used on the violin.'[26] A few performers, most notably Fritz Kreisler, persevered with a gut e^2 until at least *c.* 1950; however, gut was gradually replaced by a steel (so-called 'piano-wire') variety, championed in particular by Willy Burmester and Anton Witek, which was accompanied by its metal adjuster for greater facility in fine tuning.

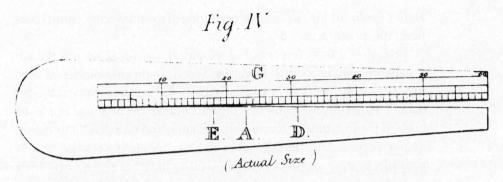

Figure 2.2 String gauge: Louis Spohr, *Violinschule* (Vienna, [1832])

Available evidence regarding pitch, string tensions and string thicknesses
is so conflicting, and circumstances were so variable, that it is impossible
to draw definitive conclusions.[27] Some scholars believe, for example, that
eighteenth-century strings were generally thinner than their modern counterparts, in keeping with the lower string tension and generally lower playing
pitch of that period;[28] others disagree, some quoting Sébastien de Brossard's
statement (*c.* 1712) that the contemporary silver-wound d^1 and g violin
strings were thinner than their counterparts made simply of gut.[29]

Clearly, string thicknesses differed considerably according to considerations of pitch (thicker strings were employed for the lower pitch standards),
the size of the instrument employed, the situation, national or individual tastes regarding string materials, and many other variables. Italian and
German violinists generally used thicker strings, strung at greater tension,
than the French, presumably with greater brilliance and volume in mind.
However, Quantz acknowledges the use of thick and thin strings and Leopold
Mozart recommends, for optimum tonal results and reliability of intonation, the use of thick strings for 'flat pitch' and large-model violins and thin
strings for 'sharp pitch' and small models.[30]

Paganini evidently used very thin strings, whereas Spohr claims that
optimum string thicknesses for any instrument can be determined only by
experiment, with equal strength and fullness of tone from each string as
the ultimate goal.[31] Spohr employed the thickest strings his violin could
bear, so long as their response was quick and easy and their tone bright. He
employed a string gauge to ensure the uniformity of his string thicknesses.[32]
This device comprised a metal plate of silver or brass with a graduated slit,
lettered for each string, and with regular markings from 0 to 60 (see Fig. 2.2).
The scale unit of Spohr's gauge is not stated, but the thickness of each string
was ascertained at the point where it became lightly wedged in the gauge
(e^1 = 18; a^1 = 23; d^1 = 31; g = 25).[33]

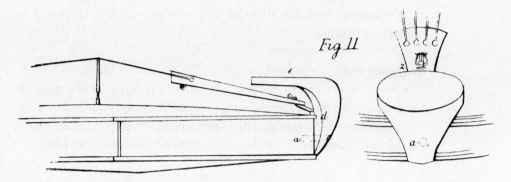

Fig II

Figure 2.3 Spohr's chin rest and its position on the violin: Louis Spohr, *Violinschule* (Vienna, [1832])

Chin-rest

The chin-rest (*Geigenhalter*: literally, 'violin holder') was invented by Spohr in about 1820 to ensure the greater stability required for increased mobility of the left hand and greater freedom in violin bowing.[34] Spohr's model was made of ebony and was placed directly over the tailpiece, not to the left side as is usual today (see Fig. 2.3). It only gradually achieved general approbation, but it was probably fairly widely used in violin and viola playing, together with the various models it inspired (e.g. the low, ebony ridge employed by Sarasate and others), by the mid nineteenth century. Nevertheless, many leading players, among them Wilhelmj, evidently rejected utilising such equipment.

Mute

Use of the mute was gradually extended from ensemble to solo playing during the eighteenth century. This device, generally of wood or metal (Quantz states wood, lead, brass, tin or steel, but dislikes the growling tone produced by the wood and brass varieties),[35] underwent no fundamental change in design until the mid nineteenth century, when the inconvenience of manually applying or removing a mute during performance prompted Vuillaume to invent his *Sourdine pédale*.[36] However, this latter, enabling violinists to apply the mute by means of gentle pressure with the chin on the tailpiece, gained, like Bellon's invention, only ephemeral success.

Shoulder pad

Pierre Baillot (1835) was one of the first writers to recommend the use of a shoulder pad to facilitate the correct and comfortable support of the violin. He suggests that 'a thick handkerchief or a kind of cushion' might be used to fill in any gap between the player's left shoulder and the instrument, particularly in the cases of children, youths and women.[37] However, dress codes were often such that shoulder pads were not regularly employed by violinists or violists.

Wolf(-stop) mute

This device is attached to the G string behind the bridge of the cello. Its function is to eliminate or suppress the 'wolf' note or notes on an instrument. These are notes which, owing to that instrument's structure, are too loud or too soft or difficult to play precisely in tune compared with other notes.[38]

The bow: history and development

The use of a bow to draw sound from a stringed instrument has been traced back almost six centuries before the violin family's evolution; not surprisingly, string players at first adopted the types of bow employed by players of other stringed instruments such as the rebec and viol. These bows were unstandardised as regards weight, length, form and wood-type but had certain general characteristics in common. Many early-seventeenth-century models were probably quite short, but evidence points to an increase in length by the end of the century.[39] They were usually convex and the narrow skein of horsehair was strung at fixed tension between the pointed head (in some cases there was no distinct head, the hair merely meeting the stick in a point) and the immovable horn-shaped nut at the lower end of the stick.

Few examples of seventeenth-century bows have survived, but icono-graphical evidence suggests that fashions in bow-types related directly to musical tastes and requirements. Short, light and fairly straight bows were ideal for dance musicians and were especially popular in France, while the increased cultivation of the sonata and concerto in Italy encouraged the use of longer, straighter (but sometimes slightly convex) models capable of producing a more singing style with a greater dynamic range. Solid, con-vex bows of intermediate length tended to be favoured by German players, probably because they offered greater facility in the execution of the German polyphonic style.[40]

The gradual interaction of national styles during the eighteenth century and the demand for increased tonal volume, cantabile and a wider dynamic range (met also by developments in instrument construction), prompted the production of longer and straighter bowsticks. Straightening of the stick required modifications in the height and curvature of the so-called pike's (or swan's) head, in order to allow sufficient separation of the hair and the stick; and when, towards the mid eighteenth century, makers began to anticipate the concave cambre of the 'modern' stick, further changes in the head-design were required for optimum hair/stick separation at the middle,

Table 2.1 *Weights (in g) and measurements (in cm) of violin,*
viola and cello bows (c. 1700 – c. 1780)[41]

		Violin	Viola	Cello
Overall length	minimum	70.5	69.5	67.2
	medium	72.5	71.5	70.9
	maximum	73.9	74.0	74.3
Diameter of stick at frog	minimum	0.85	0.88	0.85
	medium	0.88	0.95	0.99
	maximum	0.91	1.00	1.09
Diameter of stick at head	minimum	0.51	0.58	0.56
	medium	0.57	0.60	0.66
	maximum	0.70	0.62	0.75
Hair to stick at frog	minimum	1.55	1.60	1.85
	medium	1.77	1.77	2.07
Width of hair in frog	minimum	0.62	0.85	1.00
	medium	0.82	1.03	1.16
	maximum	1.05	1.15	1.45
Bowing length	minimum	60.1	59.9	56.7
	medium	62.5	62.5	59.6
	maximum	64.2	64.7	62.2
Weight	minimum	47.0	59.0	65.0
	medium	51.5	64.0	76.0
	maximum	58.0	71.0	86.0

marking the demise of the pike's head in favour first of the various hatchet
head models and finally the bows of substantially 'modern' design, which
closely resemble the model standardised by François Tourte (?1747–1835)
during the 1780s.

Bow-lengths varied considerably, but the eighteenth-century trend was
towards bows with a greater playing length of hair, especially in Italy. Sir
John Hawkins confirms (1776): 'The bow of the violin has been gradually
increasing in length for the last seventy years; it is now about twenty-eight
inches [i.e. 71.12 cm overall length]. In the year 1720, a bow of twenty-
four inches [60.96 cm] was, on account of its length, called a sonata bow;
the common bow was shorter; and . . . the French bow must have been
shorter still.'[42] By *c.* 1750 the average playing length of violin bows measured
approximately 61 cm, although Tourte *père* produced some longer models.
Table 2.1 provides a general overview of weights and measurements of extant
violin, viola and cello bows *c.* 1700 – *c.* 1780.

Many early-eighteenth-century bows were fluted in all or part of their
length. They were generally lighter than modern models, but were nevertheless strong, if somewhat inflexible, and their point of balance was
generally nearer the frog, owing to the lightness of the head. Most types
tapered to a fine point at the pike's head and were commonly of snakewood
('specklewood'), but pernambuco, brazil wood and plum wood were

certainly known and pernambuco was increasingly used as the century progressed.

The type of nut employed for regulating the hair tension varied from a fixed nut to the crémaillère device (comprising a movable nut, whose position was adjusted and secured by a metal loop locked into one of several notches on the top of the stick) and, generally by c. 1750, the 'modern' screw-nut attachment. This latter device was probably invented in the late seventeenth century, David Boyden citing a bow in the Hill collection (London), in original condition and date-stamped 1694 on its movable frog, which is adjusted by a screw.[43] The frogs of this period were completely unmounted and were of ebony, rosewood or ivory.

Few seventeenth- or early eighteenth-century makers stamped their names on their bows. Instead, bow-types became associated with distinguished performers. Both Fétis (Fig. 2.4) and Woldemar (Fig. 2.5) illustrate four eighteenth-century bow types, named respectively after Corelli, Tartini, Cramer and Viotti,[44] while Baillot (Fig. 2.6) illustrates six varieties (Corelli, Pugnani, two unnamed transitional types, Viotti and Tourte).

The term 'Corelli bow' appears to have designated the common early eighteenth-century Italian sonata bow with its straight or slightly convex bow and pike's head, while the 'Tartini bow' (Baillot's 'Pugnani bow' looks very similar) seems to have referred to a straight, apparently longer bow of more streamlined design, which, according to Fétis, was constructed from lighter wood and fluted at its lower end in the interests of lightness and greater manual control.[45] This would appear to be the bow type illustrated in the violin treatises of Leopold Mozart and Löhlein as well as in numerous iconographical sources of the period up to roughly the last quarter of the century. The 'Cramer bow', one of the many transitional types between the various Italian models and the Tourte design, was in vogue between c. 1760 and c. 1785, especially in Mannheim, where Wilhelm Cramer (1746?–99) spent the early part of his career, and in London after he had settled there in 1772. Longer than most Italian models but slightly shorter than Tourte's eventual synthesis, it was also distinguished by its characteristically shaped ivory frog (cut away at both ends), the slight concave cambre of its stick, and its bold, yet neat 'battle-axe' head (with a peak in the front matched by a peak in the back of the head proper).[46]

Michel Woldemar records that the 'Viotti bow' 'differs little from Cramer's in the design of the head (although this is more hatchet-like with a peak in the front only), but the nut is lower and brought nearer the screw attachment; it is longer and has more hair; it looks slightly straighter when in use and is employed almost exclusively today'.[47] It is possible that Fétis's and Woldemar's 'Viotti bow', with its fully developed hatchet head, is actually the Tourte bow in all but name. Certainly Tourte would have been

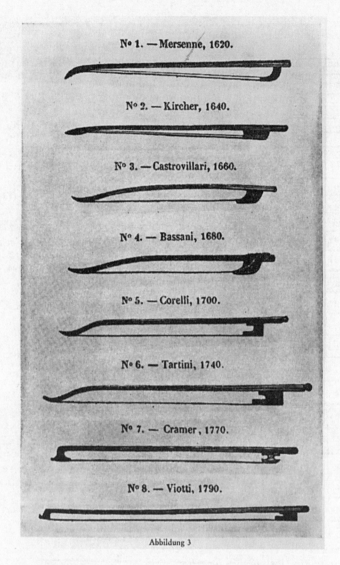

Nº 1. — Mersenne, 1620.

Nº 2. — Kircher, 1640.

Nº 3. — Castrovillari, 1660.

Nº 4. — Bassani, 1680.

Nº 5. — Corelli, 1700.

Nº 6. — Tartini, 1740.

Nº 7. — Cramer, 1770.

Nº 8. — Viotti, 1790.

Abbildung 3

Figure 2.4 Violin bows *c.* 1620 – *c.* 1790: François-Joseph Fétis, *Antoine Stradivari, Luthier Célèbre* (Paris, 1856)

influenced by those performers who frequented his workshops either to suggest ideas and improvements or simply to inspect and play examples of his work. Fétis implies that there was some collaboration between the two personalities, but Baillot's illustration of the 'Viotti' and Tourte bows as two distinct models, the 'Viotti bow' for the violin (*c.* 72.39 cm) being slightly shorter than the Tourte (*c.* 74.42 cm), suggests otherwise.[48]

François Tourte initially served an apprenticeship as a clock maker, only later joining the family bow-making business as his father's pupil and assistant. He experimented with various kinds of wood in order to find a

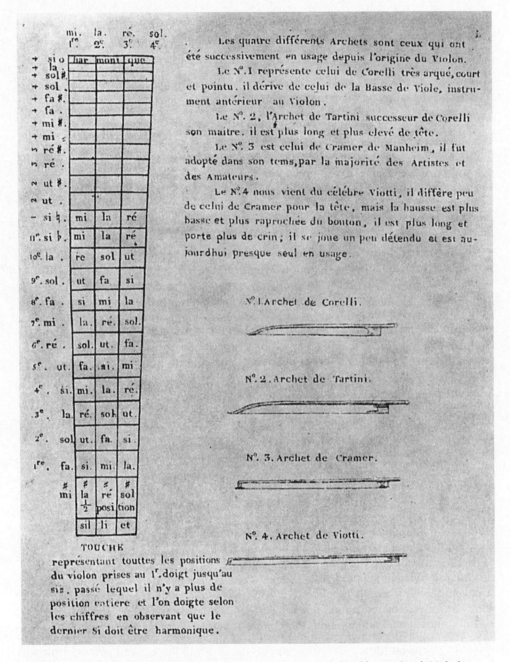

Figure 2.5 Violin bows of the seventeenth and eighteenth centuries: Michel Woldemar, *Grande Méthode ou étude élémentaire pour le violon* (Paris, c. 1800)

variety which offered those qualities of lightness, density, strength and elasticity demanded by string players of his day. He eventually concluded that pernambuco wood (*Caesalpinia echinata*) best satisfied these requirements. According to Fétis, he further discovered that, after thoroughly heating the stick, he could bend (rather than cut) it to the desired concave cambre, thus

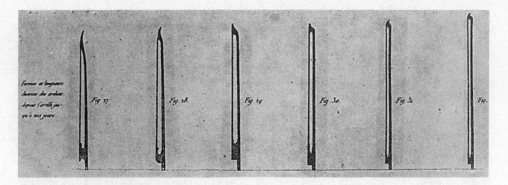

Figure 2.6 Violin bows of the seventeenth, eighteenth and early nineteenth centuries: Pierre Baillot, *L'art du violon: nouvelle méthode* (Paris, 1835)

preserving the wood's natural resiliency.[49] Tourte's sticks tapered gradually to the point, the diameters of violin bow-sticks measuring about 8.6 mm throughout the 11 cm length of their lower ends and decreasing evenly by 3.3 mm to their tips.[50]

Tourte also standardised the length and weight of bows of the violin family, determining the ideal length of the violin bowstick to be 74–5 cm (providing a playing length of approximately 65 cm and a balance point about 19 cm above the frog) and the optimum overall weight as about 56–60 g, somewhat lightweight by modern standards. Viola bows were slightly shorter (*c.* 74 cm) and heavier and cello bows shorter (72.2–73.6 cm, with a hair length of 60.3–61 cm) and heavier still. The pronounced concave cambre of the Tourte bow necessitated changes in the design of the head to prevent the hair from touching the stick when pressure was applied at the tip. The head was consequently made higher and heavier than before, Tourte opting for a hatchet design and facing it with a protective plate, generally of ivory. He redressed the balance by adding the metal ferrule and inlay to the frog, and any further metal to the back-plates and the screw button (see Fig. 2.7).

From about the middle of the eighteenth century, the amount of hair employed in the stringing of bows was gradually increased (from about 80–100 to in excess of 150 individual strands, according to Spohr),[51] presumably with the contemporary demand for greater tonal volume in mind. To counteract the irregular bunching of the hair, Tourte increased the width of the ribbon of hair (to measure about 10 mm at the nut and about 8 mm at the point),[52] and he was one of the first makers to keep it uniformly flat and even by securing it at the frog with a ferrule, made originally of tin and later of light-gauge silver. A wooden wedge was positioned between the hair and the bevelled portion of the frog so that the hair was pressed against the ferrule by the wedge and the ferrule itself was prevented from sliding off.

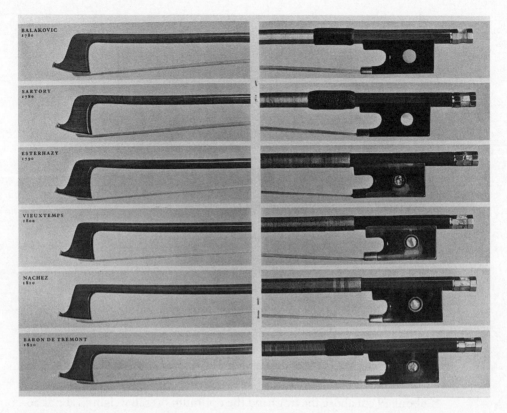

Figure 2.7 Violin bows (*c.* 1780 – *c.* 1820) by François Tourte

A mother-of-pearl slide (*recouvrement*) was also fitted into a swallow-tail groove in the frog in order to conceal the hair fastening and enhance the bow's appearance. The metal heel-plate on the frog is also believed to have been added by makers during the last decade of the eighteenth century; François Tourte was one of the first to use it with some consistency. Of variable dimensions, its principal function was to strengthen the back of the frog, but it also brought to the frog the additional weight desired by many players of that time.

The Tourte-model bow enabled performers to produce a stronger tone and was especially well suited to the sustained cantabile style dominant in the period of its inception. Its ability to make smooth bow changes with the minimum differentiation, where required, between slurred and separate bowing brought the later 'seamless phrase' ideal nearer to reality. A normal straight bow stroke, with the index-finger pressure and bow speed remaining constant, produced an even tone throughout its length because the shape and flexibility of the stick enabled the index-finger pressure to be distributed evenly. Variation of this pressure, bow speed, contact point, type of stroke and other technical considerations provided the wider expressive range so important to contemporary aesthetic ideals, in which the element of contrast, involving sudden changes of dynamic or long crescendos and diminuendos, played a significant role.

The hair of most pre-Tourte bows was generally capable of considerably less tension than that of Tourte models. Thus, it yielded rather more when brought into contact with the strings and produced, according to Leopold Mozart, 'a small, even if barely audible, softness at the beginning of the stroke'.[53] A similar 'softness' was also perceptible at the end of each stroke, thus resulting in a natural articulation of the bow itself. The concave bow stick of the Tourte model, on the other hand, yields very little when pressed on the string and thus affords a more or less immediate attack. Furthermore, its quicker take-up of hair, greater strength (particularly at the point) and broader ribbon of hair also contributed to a considerable widening of the vocabulary of bow-strokes.

Universal approval of the Tourte bow was only slowly won. Michel Woldemar claims (1801) that the similar 'Viotti' model was exclusively used,[54] but many French makers continued to make bows modelled on pre-Tourte designs, and Baroque transitional and Tourte models co-existed in most orchestras and in solo spheres, as did violins with Baroque transitional and/or modern dimensions and fittings, well into the nineteenth century.[55] Nevertheless, Spohr, who is known to have purchased a Tourte bow in Hamburg in 1803, records that Tourte's bows, though expensive, are 'the best and most sought after' and 'have won for themselves a European celebrity' on account of their 'trifling weight and the elasticity of the stick, the . . . graduated cambre . . . and the neat and accurate workmanship'.[56]

The full potential of the Tourte bow was probably not realised until the early years of the nineteenth century, when its inherent power and its expressive and other qualities could be implemented on an instrument modified to fulfil similar ideals. Apart from a few minor nineteenth-century additions, refinements and unsuccessful attempts by others to improve the bow, it has been imitated universally as the virtual blueprint for all subsequent bow makers of the nineteenth and twentieth centuries, particularly by Jean Grand-Adam (1823–69), Jacob Eury (1765–1848) and J. P. M. Persoit (?1782 – c. 1855). François Lupot (1774–1837) is normally credited with the addition (c. 1820) of the underslide (*coulisse*), a piece of metal affixed to the part of the frog that comes in sliding contact with the bowstick and designed to prevent any wear on the nut caused by friction with the stick, while the indentation of the channel and track of the frog and the combination of rear and upper heel plates into one right-angled metal part are normally attributed to Vuillaume.[57] Otherwise, few of Vuillaume's inventions in bow-making survived the test of time.[58]

Although the inventor of the metal thumbplate is unknown, the device was championed by Etienne Pajeot (1791–1849), whose bows are generally more elegant in the profile of the head than those of Tourte. Dominique Peccatte (1810–74) developed a more robust, more heavily wooded stick, generally with a rounded cross-section and a higher frog than his predecessors,[59] while François Nicolas Voirin (1833–85) produced a lighter, slightly longer and more delicate-looking bow in his mature years. Particularly characteristic is the slimmer profile of the head (with a notable thinning of the two faces), which is also markedly less square than that of Tourte's design, and the different cambre, the progression of which has been moved closer to the head for additional strength and suppleness in the stick. The balance of the bow was redressed by a reduction in the diameter of the lower end of the stick, where the frog was appropriately in proportion. A similar design also achieved some popularity with makers such as Alfred Joseph Lamy (1850–1919), the Thomassins and the Bazins but never seriously challenged the Tourte model's supremacy.

English bows tended to be made more with functional durability than artistic craftsmanship in mind, as is generally borne out by their square heads, roughly planed shafts and block-like ivory frogs. Nevertheless, these ungraceful bows generally possessed fine playing qualities. John Dodd (1752–1839) was probably the first English maker to adopt similar modifications to those introduced by Tourte. Whether he actually copied Tourte or arrived at a similar design quite independently has never been proven.[60] However, Dodd was less consistent than Tourte, experimenting widely with various weights, shapes of head, lengths and forms of stick and mountings on the nut. Close examination of his bows generally reveals cruder and more primitive craftsmanship. Many are slightly shorter (in both the stick and the playing length) and lighter than the average Tourte model; and their frogs lack a metal ferrule. Indeed, Dodd is believed to have produced full-length Tourte-model bows only late in life; those earlier sticks that have survived underwent later 'modernisation', their plain ivory mountings being either adapted or jettisoned.[61]

Aside from any repair, restoration or general maintenance that they will inevitably have undergone over the years, most members of the violin family made before c. 1800 have thus been subjected to a substantial transformation process.[62] If the various accessories used by players nowadays that were not part of seventeenth- or eighteenth-century string playing are also added to the equation, the instruments used by our modern quartet players are far from being the authentic products of their makers. In truth, those who have paid inflated prices at auction or private sale for a Stradivari, Guarneri or an instrument of equivalent status set up for modern concert use have purchased one that is arguably barely more than half 'original'. However, that the instruments of Stradivari and Guarneri continued to prosper many years after their deaths speaks wonders for these makers' vision, foresight and expertise and may provide justification enough for the present-day veneration and valuation of their creations.

The development of historical performance in theory and practice to form a significant part of mainstream musical life in the twentieth century has occasioned a second reversal in the set-up of some old instruments.[63] The scarcity of genuine period stringed instruments of good quality has obliged performers either to have a good seventeenth- or eighteenth-century instrument converted from its modified state of *c.* 1800 back as closely as possible to its original condition, or to commission an historically accurate modern copy of an original instrument by a master craftsman. Many have taken the first option, despite a common view that tampering with a valuable instrument may prove unwise for both tonal and investment reasons. Nevertheless, the Stainer and Amati models, which suffered most from the late eighteenth-century conversion process, have proved prime candidates for such re-adjustment. One London-based restorer and expert on historical instruments, Dietrich M. Kessler (b. 1929), recalled with some amusement how he spent the first twenty-five years of his career converting instruments from their original to modern specifications, only to devote an equal period thereafter to returning others to their original condition![64]

Modern experiments and the infiltration of electronic and computer techniques into the quartet repertory have placed further demands on the equipment and accessories required by participating ensembles. Modern developments have included Carleen Hutchins' new family of violins,[65] comprising eight instruments constructed on the basis of mathematical design, acoustical theory and classical violin-making principles, and electric violins, violas and cellos. Although Hutchins' instruments have attracted new compositions, they have scarcely been exploited in the string quartet genre; nor has Kagel's requirement of prepared instruments for his Quartet (1974), discussed in Chapter 7. But the development of electronic instruments has equipped players with a new flexibility and versatility for the third millennium.[66] It has opened up an almost limitless sound-world with the potential for amplification (with or without filters/boosters), modification (through tremolo or vibrato, ring modulation, 'wah-wah' etc.) and alteration ('fuzz-box', envelope shaping, echo and reverberation effects with time delay and echoes, and distortion) at the flick of a switch.

PART 2

Celebrated ensembles

3 From chamber to concert hall

TULLY POTTER

Although the first full-time professional string quartet ensemble did not emerge until 1892,[1] the nineteenth century saw a steady improvement in the standard of quartet playing. Several trends can be seen running through the century as a whole: a gradual strengthening of the actual sound emitted by the players; the emergence of Beethoven as the recognised king of quartet composers; and the espousal of the heritage or museum-style concert in which music of a previous age was presented. The last two of these developments were largely precipitated by Joseph Joachim (1831–1907), whose giant personality cast its shadow over the second half of the century.

The sound of the quartet

It is possible to make an informed guess at the kind of sonority produced by a typical string quartet ensemble at the start of the century. With rare exceptions, quartets were played in large rooms rather than halls, and there was no need to strive for a powerful sound. The tone of even the top violin soloists was not large. Bows had reached their evolutionary peak but most instruments still had their original shorter necks and the fingerboards ran more parallel with the bodies, so that the gut strings were under relatively light pressure.[2]

Full-time violists were unknown, although the Stamitz brothers both played the instrument to a high standard, and the viola in a quartet would invariably be played by a violinist who would adapt violin technique to a smallish instrument and would therefore make a quite narrow, nasal sound. The cello had no endpin and the cellist held it resting on his lower legs, partially muffling the tone. Although there is not complete agreement on how much vibrato was generally applied, it is likely that, especially in quartet music, the effect was used sparingly, like an ornament, and never in chordal passages. We therefore have in our mind's ear a quite small, delicate, 'straight' sonority which various twentieth- and twenty-first-century period-instrument groups have striven to reproduce, with varying success.[3]

As the nineteenth century progressed, orchestral music was heard in larger halls and string soloists needed to make more sound. So, as described in Chapter 2, instruments were strengthened and placed under greater tension by the lengthening and tilting back of the neck and fingerboard and the tautening of the strings. As the same instruments were used for playing quartets, and as chamber music also moved into larger venues, the sound of the ensemble strengthened, although in other ways it remained fairly constant through the century until the introduction of more or less constant vibrato by such players as Ysaÿe. The second half of the century also saw the introduction of the endpin, which freed the cello to some extent from the embrace of the player's legs, allowing a more unfettered resonance. The violist had to respond to the challenges of such works as Smetana's E minor Quartet by playing with more weight. Lightness and grace still predominated, however.

The leader dominated the quartet, unless it was one of the all-star ensembles which arose from time to time. One famous Viennese group headed its programmes: 'Hellmesberger Quartet with the assistance of Messrs Math. Durst, Carl Heissler, Carl Schlesinger'. The role of the *primarius* was often blatantly superior musically, as such composers as Spohr and Rode favoured the *quatuor brillant* in which the other three parts provided little more than a background for the first violin. If the players in professional quartets gradually became more equal, this change was due as much to the kind of music being written as to any democratisation of the musical profession.

The sight of the quartet

The classic nineteenth-century seating arrangement for quartets was to have the violinists facing each other at the front, with the cellist on the leader's left at the rear and the violist on the second violinist's right. A contemporary drawing (Fig. 3.1) shows Vieuxtemps leading a group in London; he and Alfredo Piatti, who unusually sits opposite him at the front, are seated on high stools while the players of the inner parts (Deloffre and Hill) are on ordinary chairs. A few ensembles stood to play; and Baillot in Paris stood to lead his group, while his colleagues were seated. But in general string quartets were played in public in a seated position.

Vienna and the Beethoven phenomenon

Beethoven's music was intimately bound up with the development of the string quartet ensemble and from 1804 it was closely connected with the career of Ignaz Schuppanzigh (1776–1830). Born and bred in Vienna, this fine fiddler led a number of privately sponsored groups, including one for Prince Lichnowsky from 1795 and another for Count Razumovsky from 1808. More importantly, perhaps, he started a series of public subscription quartet

G. Haddock. Milne. Vieuxtemps.

Delottre. Hill. Piatti. John Ella.

Vieuxtemps. H.R.H. the Duke of Cambridge

THE MUSICAL UNION. 1846

Figure 3.1 A string quartet performance at John Ella's Musical Union in London (1846) featuring Henri Vieuxtemps as first violinist

concerts in Vienna in 1804, at which Beethoven's 'Razumovsky' Quartets, Op. 59, were premiered (1806). In this respect Schuppanzigh was ahead of his time, as the public concert did not catch on; but his ensemble continued to work with Beethoven under the auspices of Count Razumovsky – who sometimes took the second violin part, as the group's membership was fluid. Similarly, Prince Lobkowitz sometimes played viola.

Stories of the composer's dissatisfaction with Schuppanzigh and his colleagues are well known, but we should not be hard on these players. One has only to hear a student or young professional quartet struggling with Beethoven's music to realise that, even in Op. 18, he was asking a great deal. The notes do not always lie easily under the fingers and Beethoven is always demanding a higher degree of expression than any other quartet composer. Being faced with such music when it was new was a fearsome challenge. And however much he may have grumbled, Beethoven clearly depended on Schuppanzigh: it is possible that he would never have written his late quartets, had the violinist not returned in 1823 after a six-year spell in St Petersburg (the Razumovsky palace had burnt down in 1814 and the quartet had more or less disbanded in 1816). The knowledge that this faithful servant was once again available was undoubtedly a stimulant to Beethoven, who always had performance in mind for even his most advanced music, and the ensemble's second violinist at that time, Karl Holz, was a close friend of the composer.

The Schuppanzigh Quartet duly introduced Op. 127 and although Beethoven virtually dismissed the leader after a rather disastrous premiere, giving the next performance to Josef Böhm, Schuppanzigh was back for Opp. 132 and 130. Böhm, a more secure but less improvisatory leader, gave the first private performances of Op. 131, which Schuppanzigh never played; and it was Böhm who led the single movement of Schubert's G major Quartet that was played in public in that composer's lifetime. Schuppanzigh had, however, given the first public performance of Schubert's A minor Quartet (D. 804), in 1824, as well as private readings of his D minor Quartet (D. 810) and performances of his other chamber music.

Two important spin-offs from the Schuppanzigh Quartet were the ensembles led by Joseph Mayseder (1789–1863), who had been its second violinist from 1804 to 1816, and Leopold Jansa (1795–1875). The Mayseder Quartet ran from 1817 to 1860, while the Jansa Quartet (1834–50) more or less followed on from Schuppanzigh and at first included two members of his circle, Holz and Joseph Linke. The city also saw influential visits by such charismatic quartet leaders as Vieuxtemps (1842–3) and Ferdinand Laub (1863–5); but the dominant Viennese quartet of the second half of the century was that led first by Joseph Hellmesberger (1828–93) and then, for four seasons from 1887, by his son Joseph Jnr (1855–1907). Founded in 1849, it was the first regular ensemble – the personnel stayed pretty constant until the mid-1860s – and the first to be named after its leader. Its period in the limelight coincided with the first great decades of the Vienna Philharmonic, whose parent body, the Court Opera Orchestra, was led by Joseph Snr from 1855–79, and the codifying of what we think of as the Vienna string style – Joseph Snr's father Georg had been a pupil of Böhm and himself an influential teacher. The cellist David Popper (1843–1913) was a member of the Hellmesberger Quartet from 1868 to 1870 and two other members later played in the group's successor, the Rosé Quartet.[4]

The Rosé Quartet's chief rival in its own time was another group from the Court Opera, the Fitzner, which gave a complete Haydn cycle in the city around the time of the Great War. Up to the war, the city could also boast the second of Marie Soldat-Roeger's all-female groups, which was sponsored by a member of the Wittgenstein family and commanded such guest artists as Nedbal and Casals; its violist was Mahler's friend Natalie Bauer-Lechner.

Germany

Berlin was not far behind Vienna in the quartet revolution, thanks to the violinist-composer Karl Möser (1774–1851), who began his chamber music career in Friedrich Wilhelm II's house quartet. In 1812 he became concert-master of the Court Opera and by the next year he was organising quartet concerts. He was one of the first to offer Beethoven's Op. 132, in 1828; and his series, which lasted until 1843 and included orchestral concerts, was influential. A later high point in Berlin's quartet life was the period 1856–63 when the Bohemian virtuoso Ferdinand Laub (1832–75) led an excellent group. Otherwise the city was dominated by Joachim.

The best-known German violinist of the first half of the century, Louis Spohr (1784–1859), was important in the development of ensemble playing; and although his quartet compositions were of the *quatuor brillant* type, his string quintets show that he was capable of a more restrained style. In fact, his own playing, while brilliant, was not unrelievedly virtuosic – he disdained bounced-bow effects and the use of vibrato, which he considered strictly an ornament. Spohr led a quartet in Gotha from 1805 to 1811 and after moving to Vienna in 1812 he got to know Beethoven. Although he never came to terms with that master's mature works, he was a champion of the Op. 18 quartets, which he was the first to perform in Berlin and Leipzig. Spohr can be considered a 'star' leader of the old school, as can the Polish virtuoso Karol Lipiński (1790–1861), who was already an experienced quartet player when he settled in Dresden in 1840. The quartet he led there until 1860 played all the late Beethoven except the *Grosse Fuge*. On the other hand someone such as Ignaz Lüstner, who led various ensembles in Breslau throughout his career, from 1816 to 1872, must be considered the prototype of the local musician content to serve a particular audience. At one stage Lüstner's colleagues comprised his sons Ludwig, Otto and Karl.

The most sensational group in Germany before the rise of Joachim was another family affair, composed of the brothers Karl Friedrich (1797–1873), Theodor (1799–1855), Franz (1808–55) and August (1802–75) Müller. Hailing from Brunswick, the Müllers clearly gained from playing together all the time; and they gained an early scalp when in their first year of public performance, 1828, they gave the public premiere of Beethoven's Op. 131 in Halberstadt. A Berlin reviewer of an 1833 concert, at which they played a Spohr work and Beethoven's Third 'Razumovsky', described their performances as 'one bowing, one accent, one breath, one soul'. From 1830 they were based in Meiningen, where their patron Duke Bernhard I liked to hear them play Onslow's music; but they toured assiduously throughout Germany and were the first truly itinerant quartet players. From 1855 they were succeeded by Karl Friedrich's sons, under the leadership of Karl Jnr, who from 1860 to 1868 was replaced by Leopold Auer (1845–1930) when the group toured. This second Müller Brothers ensemble was not as successful as the first and ceased in 1873, although the cellist, Wilhelm, later played in the Joachim Quartet.

More or less contemporary with the elder Müllers was Hamburg-born Ferdinand David (1810–73), a pupil of Spohr, who organised a private quartet in Dorpat from 1829–36 at the behest of Baron von Liphart. Initially it included the cellist Bernhard Romberg (1767–1841). From 1836 David was a colleague of Mendelssohn at Leipzig, where he led the Gewandhaus Orchestra and took over from Heinrich Matthäi – who had headed an ensemble there from 1809 to 1835 – the tradition of forming a quartet from the string principals. As a result David's ensemble had a bewildering turnover of personnel – Joachim played second violin in 1847 and again in 1849 – and was not rigorously rehearsed. The group's chamber concerts in the 400-seat Old Gewandhaus became famous and sometimes David ceded the leadership to a visiting celebrity – Heinrich Ernst (1814–55) in 1844 and Hubert Léonard (1819–90) in 1846. David himself was a transitional player and his editions indicate that he was among the first to employ 'expressive portamento'. His last years coincided with the beginnings of the Russian violinist Adolf Brodsky's first quartet, which was based in Leipzig and flourished from 1870 to 1891. Jean Becker was the original second violinist, Hans Sitt was the violist, Otakar Nováček played second violin and then viola in the 1880s and Julius Klengel was the cellist. One of the group's warhorses was Tchaikovsky's Third Quartet.

Frankfurt was a great centre for chamber music and its famed Museum Quartet was led by Hugo Heermann from 1865 until he was ousted by scandal in 1906 and went to the USA. A graceful player trained entirely in the Franco-Belgian school, Heermann (1844–1935) made solo records but none with the quartet, which from 1890 to 1905 included Hugo Becker. One of the cellist's last performances with the group was its most famous premiere, of Reger's D minor Quartet Op. 74.

Two quartettists who led restless lives were Henry Schradieck (1846–1918) and Willy Hess (1859–1939). Although neither man stayed in one place for long, Schradieck – who reputedly could play all the Beethoven quartets from memory – left his mark in his native Hamburg, Moscow, Leipzig, Cincinnati, Philadelphia and New York, while Hess had quartets in Manchester, Cologne, London, Boston and Berlin. Hess's successor in Cologne as leader of the Gürzenich Quartet was the Dutchman Bram Eldering (1865–1943), who arrived in 1903 and not only sustained the impetus built up by Gustav Hollaender and Hess but made the group famous throughout the Rhineland. Known as the 'Quartet of Professors' because its members taught at the Conservatoire, the ensemble had its best period in the decade before the Great War when the line-up was Eldering, Carl Kürner, Josef Schwartz and Friedrich Grützmacher the Younger. Its repertoire included the new music, by Reger, Straesser and others, as well as the works of Brahms – whom Eldering had known well – and the Viennese classics.

Eldering's pupil Adolf Busch was much influenced by the group's style and even played viola in it a few times when Schwartz was ill. Later Emanuel Feuermann was a member and it is sad that the Gürzenich made no recordings.

The age of Joachim

The dominant figure in the nineteenth century was Joseph Joachim, who counted Böhm among his teachers, and his influence spilled over into the twentieth century. During his Leipzig years (1843–50), he took part in chamber music performances and *Hausmusik* with his mentors Mendelssohn and David, and he played more chamber music than anything else on his extended first visit to London in 1844. At Radley's Hotel in Blackfriars, for instance, three weeks before his thirteenth birthday, he opened an evening in Mendelssohn's honour by leading Messrs Case, Hill and Hancock in Mozart's D minor Quartet and closed it with Beethoven's C major 'Razumovsky'. He thus had a good deal of quartet playing with *ad hoc* groups behind him when he moved to Weimar as concertmaster at Liszt's behest in 1850. With Karl Stör, Johann Walbrül and Bernhard Cossmann he instituted quartet evenings, either in his own rooms or at the Altenburg, which were so successful that from the 1851–2 season they were opened to the public. Liszt charged such high prices, however, that only the cream of music-loving society was present. Hans von Bülow joined the group in the Schumann Piano Quintet and one concert featured Beethoven's Op. 18 no. 5, Op. 74 and Op. 131 – Joachim would always plan his Beethoven programmes in this 'historical' progression. In 1853 he moved to Hanover and there he formed an ensemble with the brothers Theodor and Carl Eyertt and the cellist August Lindner.

In his Hanover quartet activities one can see Joachim's programming ideas in a fully developed form. On 28 April 1855 he and his colleagues opened their account with Beethoven's Op. 18 no. 5, Op. 59 no. 1 and Op. 131. Mendelssohn's Octet was played the following January and on 10 April 1856 they began a regular series at the Künstlerverein, in a tiny hall which has recently been restored. First came two private soirées and then a public series of three concerts. Of the eight concerts given in the first two years, four started with a Haydn work, although this composer's C major Quartet, Op. 76 no. 3, ended another evening. Three concerts ended with a string quintet – Mozart's K. 516 or K. 593 or Beethoven's Op. 29 – and Schubert's 'Death and the Maiden' was used as a closing piece in both years. Every concert included a work by Beethoven. Three quartets by Mozart were performed and one by Mendelssohn. Schumann's A minor was played in

Figure 3.2 Joachim Quartet (1897–1907): (left to right) Joseph Joachim, Robert Hausmann, Emmanuel Wirth, Karel Halíř

both years; his death on 29 July 1856 came between these performances, and in his memory his other two quartets were played at a special concert. From the 1863–4 season the Joachim Quartet gave its public series in the acoustically superior Aula of the Lyceum.

When the kingdom of Hanover ceased to be independent in 1866, Joachim annulled his life contract. By this time he was engaged regularly as a quartet leader in London – this sphere of his activity is dealt with below – but after his move to Berlin in 1868 he was not long in forming the ensemble with which his name is now most closely associated. The Joachim Quartet, which existed from 1869 until his death in 1907, was a foursome of soloists and went through changes of personnel; but by nineteenth-century standards it was well integrated at any one time and was thought to be nonpareil in vigour of attack in fast movements, spiritual *Innigkeit* in slow movements, trueness of intonation and precision of ensemble. Among the second violinists were Heinrich de Ahna, Johann Kruse and Karel Halíř, among the violists were de Ahna and Emmanuel Wirth, while the cellists were first Wilhelm Müller and then Robert Hausmann. The most celebrated formation was the last: Joachim, Halíř, Wirth and Hausmann (Fig. 3.2). The violist was a dry player and the cellist was not really a virtuoso – a passage in one of Beethoven's Razumovsky Quartets bothered him so much that when he knew he had to perform it, he would get his students to play it to him on the day of the concert. Nevertheless, even when Joachim was old and no longer playing as accurately as of yore, the ensemble made a remarkable impression. Today its programmes have a comfortably conservative look, but among the works it premiered were three by Brahms and three by Dvořák; and the quartet music by Mendelssohn and Schumann was relatively new when Joachim began playing it.

Great Britain

The nation which had embraced the viol consort from the Tudor age to the time of Purcell could be expected to appreciate the string quartet. As early as Haydn's tours to England in the 1790s, Johann Peter Salomon's (1745–1815) public quartet performances in London were attracting attention. Haydn wrote his Opp. 71 and 74 for these concerts at the Hanover Square Rooms but the quartets were interspersed with other works – as they were at Philharmonic Society events. Some forty years after Haydn's visits, in 1835, quartet concerts really took off in London when the violinist Joseph Dando (1806–94) organised a benefit for a distressed colleague (expanded to a series, by popular demand). He led an excellent ensemble in programmes of Haydn, Mozart, Beethoven, Spohr and others at the Horn Tavern in Doctors' Commons. After two years these Quartett [sic] Concerts shifted to the Hanover Square Rooms, Dando taking the viola part and Henry Blagrove (1811–72; a pupil of Spohr) leading, with Henry Gattie as second fiddle and Charles Lucas as cellist. They had seven or eight rehearsals for each concert and were asked to play for the Philharmonic Society. In 1843 Blagrove started his own series (with his brother Richard on viola) and Dando moved to Crosby Hall in Bishopsgate, resuming the leader's role with John Loder as violist. This ensemble continued until Gattie and Loder died in 1853; among the works Dando introduced to Britain were Haydn's Seven Last Words, Mendelssohn's Eb and Schumann's A minor. Meanwhile Thomas Alsager of *The Times*, wealthy *éminence grise* of the Queen Square Select Society which had been giving British premieres since 1832, was developing the interest in Beethoven which had led to airings of the Op. 18 quartets in 1834. Spohr and Camillo Sivori (1815–94) led ensembles for him in the early 1840s, and in 1845 his Beethoven Quartet Society began its series at 76 Harley Street with the world's first cycle of the composer's quartets. The society would hijack any notable string player who was in town: Bernhard Molique was one leader, and in 1847, the year after Alsager's death, Piatti appeared at a soirée given for Mendelssohn. Also important were the morning recitals of The Musical Union, led by the Philharmonic Society violinist John Ella from 1845 (see Fig. 3.1) and the first to issue analytical programme booklets.[5]

But the most illustrious quartets were those which appeared at the Chappell Brothers' Popular Concerts from 1859. The venue was the 2,200-seat St James's Hall, small enough for intimacy but large enough to hold a viable audience – one thousand of whom paid only one shilling. The 'Monday Pops' were held in the evening, the 'Saturday Pops' in the afternoon, and their varied programmes opened and closed with major chamber works. The first event featured a line-up of Wieniawski, Louis Ries, C. W. Doyle and Piatti, with Schreuss joining them in a Mendelssohn quintet; other eminent leaders were Blagrove and Prosper Sainton; and later a typical line-up might be Ludwig Straus (a Viennese pupil of Böhm), Ries, J. B. Zerbini and Piatti.

A keen quartet player was the Moravian virtuoso Vilemína Neruda (?1838–1911; Lady Hallé) (see Fig. 1.2), who often deputised for Straus as leader. Perhaps because of her example, women played a more prominent role in quartets than in some other branches of British music. In Victorian times Emily Shinner (Mrs A. F. Liddell) led an all-female foursome – the other players being Lucy H. Stone, Cecilia Gates and Florence Hemmings; later Gabrielle Wietrowitz acted as leader. And the Lucas Quartet, a foursome of sisters good enough to play octets with the visiting Rosé ensemble, flourished in the decade or so before the First World War. The tradition of all-female groups has survived in Britain to this day. Shinner's teacher was Joachim, who had an enormous influence on British music-making. On his first visit in 1844 he played in Alsager's concerts and in 1859 he was second fiddle to Ernst at one of these events, with Wieniawski on viola and Piatti on cello. He frequently led the quartet at the Popular Concerts (Straus, Doyle, Zerbini or Benoit Hollander playing viola) and later this loosely organised group included more local players, such as the violinist and violist Alfred Gibson or the cellist Arthur Williams.

In 1896 Joachim began to bring his Berlin ensemble to Britain, first for mixed programmes at the 'Pops' and then, from 1901 to 1906, for out-and-out chamber programmes under the auspices of Edward Speyer's Joachim Quartet Concert Society. The scandalous replacement of the St James's Hall with a hotel in 1905 meant that the series transferred to the elite 600-seat Bechstein (Wigmore) Hall for three seasons: a Brahms festival was held in 1906; Halíř substituted for the ailing leader in 1907; and Joachim's death that summer brought a further change of emphasis. Speyer's Classical Concert Society continued the series until the Great War, but quartets were only a part of its remit.

From 1874 to 1893 a select London audience could hear chamber concerts organised by Edward Dannreuther at his home in Orme Square, Bayswater – late Beethoven quartets were played there – and from 1887 a more democratic assembly of Londoners could enjoy the Sunday Evening Concerts at the South Place Institute, which introduced works by Dvořák and Brahms; their Quartet was led by John Saunders with Charles Wood-house, Ernest Yonge and J. Preuveneers (later Charles Crabbe). Nor were the regions left out. Gibson led the quartet at Oxford University Musical Club, while in Manchester the Hallé Orchestra acquired Adolf Brodsky as leader in 1894; he organised a Quartet (with Rawdon Briggs, Simon Spielman and Carl Fuchs) which lasted almost three decades. Glasgow and Edinburgh had flourishing chamber music seasons in which the best groups of the late Victorian and Edwardian eras were heard. Encouragement to native performers and composers came from that doughty champion of chamber music Walter Willson Cobbett (1847–1937).

London had several serious quartets at the turn of the century: Lionel Tertis (1876–1975) took part in those led by Willy Hess, Johann Kruse and the Viennese-born Hans Wessely, while Frank Bridge (1879–1941) played for nine years in the English Quartet. But the first British ensemble of international reputation was the London Quartet, discussed in Chapter 4.

France and Belgium

The reputation of Paris as a centre of Beethoven interpretation was hard won. Pierre Baillot (1771–1842) formed his quartet in 1814 specifically to perform the Op. 18 works but when he essayed Opp. 131 and 135 in 1829, all hell broke loose; Berlioz, who was present, was one of only a handful of people who appreciated the music. Baillot had more success with the works of Cherubini (which he premiered), his teacher Viotti, Mendelssohn, Haydn, Mozart, Boccherini and Onslow. He gave 154 public chamber mu-sic concerts before disbanding his ensemble in 1840, by which time his audience had increased from around fifty to several hundred. His pupil Delphin Alard (1815–88) continued the Beethoven campaign from 1835 with the Quatuor Alard–Chevillard and then from 1849 with the Société Alard et Franchomme, groups organised with the cellists Pierre Chevillard and August Franchomme. The first, which played under the auspices of the Société des Derniers Quatuors de Beethoven, mostly gave private concerts until 1849, when it was headed by Jean Pierre Maurin (1822–94), an even more remarkable figure who kept the quartet going until 1894 – during the Franco-Prussian War it decamped to London. With Chevillard in his group until 1865, Maurin made a great reputation in the late Beethoven quartets and passed the torch on to his pupil Lucien Capet (1873–1928). Some, how-ever, including Clara Schumann, preferred the group led from 1855 by Jules

Armingaud (1820–1900); it had Edouard Lalo taking both inner parts at different times and played at least three of the late Beethovens, although its stocks-in-trade were Schubert, Mendelssohn and Schumann. The credit for giving the first popular, inexpensive Parisian chamber concerts must go to the Quatuor Lamoureux, formed in 1860, which played at the Salle Herz and Salle Pleyel.

Brahms enjoyed the way the Quatuor Geloso played his music but this group was actually the resident quartet of a new Beethoven Society, founded in 1889 by Pierre Chevillard's son Camille with Charles Lamoureux, Chabrier and d'Indy. Given the task of playing the late quartets every season, it was led by the Spaniard Albert Geloso; Lucien Capet was second violinist for a time; and it had a succession of brilliant violists including Louis van Waefelghem, Pierre Monteux and Louis Bailly.

Indeed, while it was in Paris that the iniquitous practice developed of naming a quartet after its leader and cellist, the city saw the emergence of the first specialist violists: Chrétien Urhan (1790–1845), who played the obbligato in the first performance of *Harold in Italy* and participated in the Baillot, Bohrer and Tilmant Quartets, and the enigmatic 'Casimir-Ney' (Louis Casimir Escoffier, 1800–77), who also played in various ensembles and for more than twenty years was a member of the Quatuor Alard–Chevillard. The viola parts of the Debussy and Ravel quartets bear witness to the raising of standards which culminated in the career of Maurice Vieux (1884–1957), a member of the Quatuor Parent and the Quatuor Firmin Touche in the early years of the twentieth century and founder of the modern French school of viola playing.

Belgium boasted one of the pre-eminent quartets of the late nineteenth century, led by the virtuoso Eugène Ysaÿe (1858–1931) from 1886. Each member was a soloist: second violinist Mathieu Crickboom led his own quartet at various times and toured performing Mozart's *Sinfonia concertante* with the violist Léon van Hout, father of modern Belgian viola playing, while Joseph Jacob was a leading Belgian cellist. The ensemble seems not to have rehearsed overmuch, even for premieres, of which it gave a good number including works by Debussy, Fauré and D'Indy. Ysaÿe's gigantic personality and the excellence of his colleagues always won the day, however. In 1899 Crickboom was replaced by Alfred Marchot. Having already stopped performing together, three of the players regrouped with a new second violinist, Edouard Deru, for the premiere in 1906 of Fauré's First Piano Quintet.

César Thomson (1857–1931) led an excellent ensemble in Liège from 1898 and from the turn of the century to the First World War the Brussels Quartet flourished, touring widely; as it was composed of two Germans and two Belgians, it did not survive the invasion of Belgium by Germany.

Italy

Having produced the world's first all-star quartet, plus a succession of charming music from two of its members, Cambini and Boccherini, as well as Paganini and the opera composers Paisiello and Donizetti, Italy was far from devoid of chamber music. But only in the 1860s was a concerted effort made to propagate it, as societies sprang up in Bologna, Milan, Florence and Naples. It took a while to accustom listeners to such fare, as Ottocento opera, with its shortish arias or ensembles and frequent moments of relaxation, was not conducive to concentrating over even a single sonata-form movement. When Antonio Bazzini's 35-minute String Quintet, which had won a prize offered by the new Società del Quartetto di Milano for such a work, was first played at the Società in 1866, many of the audience left the hall before the performance was over.

In contrast, a slightly earlier performance in Florence had gone well. And it was in Florence that Italy's only international quartet was formed, that very year. Even then, it was led by an Alsatian, Jean Becker (1833–84), and it never included more than two Italians. Nor did the Florentine Quartet consistently perform in its city of origin – it was more faithful to Vienna, where it appeared every season. It toured throughout Europe and was famed for its playing of the central repertoire. Indeed, along with the Müller Quartet, it was the closest approximation to a modern professional ensemble before the rise of the Czech Quartet. Among its commissions was Dvořák's E♭ major quartet, which it played a good deal, although it could not give the premiere. In 1875 Becker's illness and a change of cellist brought a hiatus; but in the 1876–7 season the Florentine gave 149 concerts in seventeen locations across Europe. A change of violist owing to an accident to Luigi Chiostro in the 1878–9 season foreshadowed the end, which came in 1880. An all-Italian group founded by a recovered Chiostro did not reach the eminence of the first one.

Russia

Although public concerts were known in St Petersburg from 1746, at the start of the nineteenth century chamber music was largely heard in the great houses of the nobility and the *nouveaux riches*. Rode was active in the city as a quartet player from 1802 to 1805, as were Baillot from 1803 to 1805 and Schuppanzigh from 1816 to 1823. Lipiński was there in 1825 and again in 1838, the year that Böhm visited from Vienna. Vieuxtemps was much in evidence as a chamber music player from 1846 to 1852. Count Mathieu Wielhorski, who organised the first Russian performances of Beethoven symphonies at his palace, had a quartet from 1810 in which he played the cello; his brother was also a noted patron. Prince Nikolas Galitzin generally played the cello in his private quartet, which was in existence from at least 1822 – when, at the suggestion of the violist Zeuner, he commissioned from Beethoven the quartets we know as Opp. 127, 132 and 130.

The accomplished amateur violinist and composer Alexey L'vov (1798–1870) led a famous quartet from 1824 to 1865 which gave no public performances, as he held a high rank both in society and in the army – and in 1836 succeeded his father Feodor as director of the Imperial Court Chapel; the recitals were generally held at his own home, Count Kushelyov-Bezborodko's or Count Wielhorski's and the latter often played cello. Late Beethoven was not tackled but new music by such as Mendelssohn was presented; and when Robert and Clara Schumann were in St Petersburg in 1844, L'vov put on a performance of Schumann's Piano Quintet in their honour. In 1849 L'vov visited Leipzig, where he gave his only public concerts – Schumann was impressed by his leadership of Mozart and Mendelssohn quartets. Best remembered today as composer of the Tsarist national anthem, L'vov wound down his activities in the 1860s, suffering from deafness.

Aficionados of chamber music in Moscow were equally dependent on wealthy private sponsors, but from 1817 the Silesian teacher and composer Franz Xaver Gebel (1787–1843) was a potent presence. From 1829 to 1835 Gebel organised concerts at which his own agreeable quartets and quintets (for string quartet plus double bass) were performed, as well as music by Beethoven and the other Viennese Classical masters. The quartet, drawn from the Bolshoi Theatre Orchestra, was led by the concertmaster I. Grassi and included the outstanding cellist Heinrich Schmitt.

The Imperial Russian Musical Society, founded in St Petersburg in 1859, had an excellent but loosely organised quartet, using whatever players were available. Early leaders were Johann Pickel, Wieniawski, Ferdinand Laub and August Wilhelmj. The year 1868 saw the arrival of the Hungarian Leopold Auer, who generally led the group until 1906. Pickel was now often the second violinist. Hieronymus Weickmann was the usual violist from the beginning until 1889 and the cellists included Carl Davidov and Alexander Wierz-bilowicz. The repertoire took in works by Arensky, Borodin, Cui, Glazunov, Rimsky-Korsakov, Rubinstein and Tchaikovsky, frequently played from the manuscripts. Towards the end of the century there were complaints about poor performances, either through lack of rehearsal or because the players were getting on in years. In 1871 Eugen Albrecht, who had often played second fiddle in this quartet, formed a Chamber Music Society in which he led the quartet with his brother Constantin-Carl as cellist.

The quartet of the Moscow branch of the Russian Music Society was run on equally *laissez faire* lines from 1860 to 1900. The leaders were Karl Klammroth, Ferdinand Laub – who led the premieres of Tchaikovsky's first two quartets – Ludwig Minkus and I. Grummann. Second violinists included Klammroth, Grummann, Hanuš Hřimalý and Mikhail Press; among the violists were Vasily Bezekirsky and Minkus; and the last three cellists were Bernhard Cossmann, Wilhelm Fitzenhagen and Alfred von Glehn.

The first really professional Russian ensemble was active in St Petersburg from 1900 to 1922. Known at home by the name of its sponsor the Duke of Mecklenburg, it toured as the St Petersburg Court Quartet. From 1905 to 1918 it was led by the finest Russian violinist of the pre-Elman era, Karol Gregorowicz (1867–1921), the other members being Naum Krautz, Vladimir Bakaleinikov and Sigismund Butkevich. The group had the use of a set of Guarneri instruments and toured all over Europe, often coming to Britain. After 1917 its members fell on hard times. Gregorowicz ended his life teaching at the Vitebsk Conservatory and no one knows if his death in 1921 was caused by imprisonment, starvation or being shot while trying to flee the country – all three fates have been suggested. Bakaleinikov played for a few years in the Stradivarius Quartet, led first by David Kreyn and then by Alexander Mogilevsky (1885–1953) and including the cellist Viktor Kubatsky. In 1927 Bakaleinikov moved to the USA, where he was influential as a player and teacher as well as a conductor. Mogilevsky emigrated in 1930 to Japan, teaching at the Tokyo Conservatory from 1937 and passing on the secrets of his own teacher Auer.

Another significant group of the early Communist period which did not make records was the Lenin Quartet, comprising Lev Zeitlin, Abram Yampolsky, Konstantin Mostras and Gregor Piatigorsky. Zeitlin went on to set up the Persimfans conductorless orchestra and to become a notable teacher at the Moscow Conservatoire, its head of strings from 1930. His colleagues also had rewarding separate careers.

Bohemia and Hungary

Chamber music in Prague tended to be dominated by a few players, such as the violinist Friedrich Pixis the Younger (1785–1842), a Mannheim-born pupil of Viotti who came to the city of his ancestors in 1807 as leader of the Opera Orchestra and was professor at the Conservatory from 1811. His quartet played Haydn, Mozart, Beethoven, Spohr, Mendelssohn, Onslow and music by the Bohemian composer Veit. Pixis's pupil Moric Mildner (1812–65) was his second violinist – the other members being Vincenc

Bartók and František Hüttner – and took over from him as Prague's unofficial chamber music leader. Meanwhile the shortlived virtuoso Josef Slavík (1806–33) led a notable family quartet in which his father and brothers joined him.

Mildner's pupil and second violinist Antonín Bennewitz (Benevic) (1833–1926) succeeded him as leader and in 1876 was among the founders of the Kammermusikverein, whose nationalist ideals stimulated Smetana to start his famous E minor Quartet ('From my life'). Ironically the piece was at first thought too difficult and 'orchestral' and was not even tried out properly until April 1878, when Antonín Dvořák tackled the fearsome viola part. It finally reached the public in March 1879, performed by an *ad hoc* group led by Ferdinand Lachner at a Society of Arts concert, and proved a watershed in Czech chamber music.[6] Lachner, a friend of Dvořák, was often leader of the quartet at the Kammermusikverein, which, as its name suggests, was dominated by German-speaking music-lovers. In 1894 the Czech Society for Chamber Music was set up as a Czech-speaking counterblast and it quickly became known as a venue for even better performances. Visiting quartets would often play for the German and Czech societies on consecutive evenings. But by then Prague had its own professional quartets.

Some of the best Czech quartets of the early twentieth century were expatriate groups; in fact the Ševčík and Prague Quartets started that way. In 1907–10 Jaroslav Kocian led a group in Odessa which became legendary, the other members being František Stupka, Josef Perman and Ladislav Zelenka. In the 1920s the New York Quartet, founded in 1919 by Mr and Mrs Ralph Pulitzer, achieved a rare standard but sadly was never invited to make recordings. Its members were Otakar Čadek, Jaroslav Siskovský, Ludvik Schwab and Bedřich Váška.

Hungary also exported many players but wonderful chamber music could be heard in the great country houses and in the salons of the twin cities on the Danube, especially Pest. In 1886 the now-unified city acquired the Budapest (or Hubay–Popper) Quartet led by Jenö Hubay (1858–1937), who had just returned to teach at the Academy. Although this pupil of Joachim has gone down in history as an arch-conservative, because of his directorship of the Academy from 1919, he was more of a radical in his youth: he and his cellist colleague, David Popper, laid the foundation of the Hungarian quartet tradition. The other original members were Victor Herzfeld and Bram Eldering; the latter did not stay long but took away priceless experiences of performances with Brahms – who thought the group the best he had heard.

In contrast to the refined playing of Hubay and Popper, the violist in the quartet from 1898, Gustav Szermy, had a booming tone and was the first Hungarian to make a real impression on the instrument – Popper said of him: 'He is a string-trombone player!'

The USA

One comes across evidence of chamber music in late eighteenth-century America – for instance, the set of six string quintets written in 1789 by the Dutch-born John Frederick Peter (1746–1813), a member of the Moravian sect. As for public performance, research by Karen A. Shaffer has turned up a series of six subscription concerts given in New York – probably in 1792 – by a quartet from London led by the English violinist James Hewitt (1770–1827).[7] But it was in Boston that the first regular group, the Mendelssohn Quintette Club, was formed in 1849. Its two violists were able to double on other instruments, Edward Lehmann on flute and Thomas Ryan on clarinet. August Fries was the leader until 1858, when Wilhelm Schultze took over, and his brother Wulf Fries was the cellist throughout the ensemble's existence, until 1898. Tours were made as far afield as California, Hawaii and the Antipodes. The violinists Sam Franko and Gustav Dannreuther (younger brother of Edward of London fame) were among many musicians who played or toured with the club.

New York was not far behind, with its Mason and Bergmann Chamber Concerts begun by the pianist William Mason and the cellist Carl Bergmann in 1855. After a slight hiatus they resumed in 1857–8 with the violinist Theodore Thomas, German-born but American-trained, joining Mason as organiser. Although it continued only until 1868, this group was influential, giving some six concerts a season. Thomas (1835–1905), best remembered as a conductor, was an outstanding fiddler; and he persuaded his sometimes reluctant colleagues to play late Beethoven quartets as well as Schumann, Schubert, Franck, Volkmann, Brahms, Rubinstein and Berwald. The second violinist was Joseph Mosenthal, the violist George Matzka and the cellist Bergmann until 1861, when Frederick Bergner replaced him. The altruistic Mason made up the inevitable financial shortfall of the concerts himself.

Gustav Dannreuther (1853–1923), who though Cincinnati-born had studied with Joachim and De Ahna, ran the Buffalo Philharmonic in upstate New York from 1882 and started his Beethoven Quartet in 1884 – taking the name from the Beethoven Quintette Club of Boston, in whose quartet he had played. His ensemble, which eventually gave concerts under his name, was highly influential as it toured a good deal until 1917.

Two pupils of Schradieck and Joachim who led excellent quartets were Maud Powell (1867–1920) – thought to be the first woman to head a group otherwise composed of men – and Theodore Spiering (1893–1905), who racked up more than 400 concerts and toured Canada as well as the USA. An important all-female quartet was led by Olive Mead (1874–1946) from 1902 to 1917.

Figure 3.3 Kneisel Quartet: (left to right) Hans Kneisel, Alwin Schröder, Louis Svečenski, Otto Roth

Apart from the Mendelssohn and Beethoven Quintettes, Boston could boast an all-female quartet, formed in 1878 by pupils of Julius Eichberg and named after him. Lillian Shattuck led it for some fifteen years but her colleagues changed several times, owing to the usual pressures on female players in those days. The group studied with Joachim in Berlin in 1881–2.

But the most celebrated ensemble to emerge from Boston was also the top American group of the late nineteenth and early twentieth centuries. The Kneisel Quartet (Fig. 3.3) was formed when the Bucharest-born fiddler Franz Kneisel (1865–1926), a pupil of Grün and Hellmesberger Snr in Vienna, became leader of the Boston Symphony in 1885. Henry Lee Higginson encouraged the young man to start a quartet; and Kneisel and the Croatian violist Louis Svečenski were to stay in place for thirty-two years. They and their colleagues were friends of both Brahms and Dvořák, giving many important local premieres as well as the world premieres of Dvořák's 'American' Quartet and Quintet – they were also virtually the first to perform his Op. 105. They would spend their summers back in Europe, so that they kept in touch with musical developments there; and in 1896 they toured there to acclaim. Later summers were spent in Blue Hills, Maine, which developed into an artists' colony. The Kneisel Quartet gave subscription series in Boston, New York, Washington, Baltimore, Hartford and the universities. Beginning in the small Chickering Hall, Boston, by the mid-1890s they had to move to the Association Hall, with double the seating capacity. Kneisel devoted himself entirely to the quartet from 1903 and from 1905 he taught at the Institute of Musical Art (later the Juilliard School) in New York, where he was a potent influence. A number of superb players filled the second violin and cello chairs at various times and the last second violinist, Hans Letz, started his own ensemble after Kneisel's final concert in 1917.

4 The concert explosion and the age of recording

TULLY POTTER

In the last years of the nineteenth century, the prototype of the modern string quartet ensemble emerged: democratic, virtuosic, well rehearsed and no longer tied to one locality but willing to travel in search of work. It was necessary to embrace the work ethic because concert fees had to be split four ways: a front-rank violinist such as Adolf Busch would receive as much for playing one concerto as his entire quartet would earn for playing the equivalent of three concertos in an evening. Summer festivals were virtually unknown in 1900 and artists lived for the whole year on what they could make in the winter season. Only a fortunate few ensembles had wealthy sponsors; hence the members of many quartets supported themselves partly by teaching or by orchestral playing – and it was common for the string principals of an orchestra to appear as a quartet, whether they matched well or not.

The almost obsessive perfectionism that would mark twentieth-century ensembles was still unknown; but before long, it was beginning to take shape in response to the demands of the new music. As with most developments in the history of string playing, technical progress was patchy and sporadic. However, two countries in particular, Bohemia and Hungary, consistently led the way in advancing standards. The emergence of the gramophone record, the proliferation of chamber music societies and the ease of modern transport, which made touring by professional quartets a viable proposition, all played their parts in these developments; and the two World Wars acted as watersheds for the introduction of new generations of ensembles. By midway through the century, festivals were beginning to spring up all over the world in the summer months; and the idea of having a resident quartet in an educational institution was catching on.

The last quarter of the century witnessed the development of 'period-instrument' ensembles, and it is now possible to see that the playing of string quartets has come full circle in the past one hundred years. For much of that time, the main story was the steady development of vibrato; but now quartets are making a good living by playing in a way that would have given the players of the 1940s and 1950s a severe toothache. Even the cello's endpin, which was not universally adopted until well into the century, is being banished again by these 'period-instrument' groups.

Recording has had a vast influence on the quartet medium; it has disseminated the work of famous ensembles to millions of people who have never heard them in concert and has enabled great players to live on after their deaths in an eerie immortality. It has thus already been invaluable to students of performance practice. But recording, too, has come full circle. In the first half of the century, all recording was live and unedited, even if it was done in the clinical environment of a studio and in five-minute sections to suit the old 78rpm discs. The advent of tape machines and eventually digital technology enabled artists, in collaboration with technical staff, to achieve a level of perfection in their recordings which they could rarely, if ever, match in the concert hall. Significantly, many ensembles have reacted against this emphasis on perfection in recent years and have released live recordings, warts and all. The digital recording medium is now ubiquitous, as the cost of producing compact discs has steadily fallen. Young quartets can use CDs as visiting cards and can often submit tapes as their initial entries to competitions. They can record their rehearsals and performances as an objective check on their progress.

Film, television and video have still not been sufficiently exploited for bringing string quartets to wider audiences, although major ensembles such as the Alban Berg and Smetana have had videos released of their performances. The string quartet is ideally suited to presentation on television, and it can only be the fear of elitism that has restricted its appearances. The use of such media as teaching aids is also in its infancy and will surely increase.

Bohemia, Moravia and Hungary

The nursery of the modern string quartet movement was not Berlin, Paris, Vienna or even London but that part of central Europe taking in Hungary and the Czech lands, Bohemia and Moravia. By common consent the first quartet ensemble that was both democratic and virtuosic was the Czech Quartet, founded in Prague in 1892 by four brilliant students. The cellist, Otto Berger, soon withdrew owing to a fatal illness and for the first two decades of the group's career his teacher, Hanuš Wihan, played in his stead. The other members were the violin soloist Karel Hoffman and the composers Josef Suk and Oskar Nedbal, both pupils of Dvořák. Although they premiered only one work by Dvořák, they were very close to him – Suk was his son-in-law – and they were all central figures in Czech musical life. In the 1890s they already toured widely and made a deep impression with Smetana's E minor Quartet 'From My Life': several writers have left us

Figure 4.1 Czech Quartet: (rear) Josef Suk, Ladislav Zelenka; (front) Karel Hoffmann, Jiří Herold

impressions of Nedbal turning over the first pages of his part, then swiv-elling round to the audience to deliver the searing viola fanfares that open this work. With Nedbal, who quickly became a leading specialist violist, the viola in the string quartet finally came of age. He quit the group in 1906 in scandalous circumstances, but it continued with a first-rate substitute, Jiří Herold – leader of both the Czech Philharmonic and an eponymous quartet – and later with Ladislav Zelenka in Wihan's place (Fig. 4.1). The Czech Quartet was best known for its Czech interpretations but played a vast repertoire and, from 1909, enjoyed a close rapport with the German pianist and composer Max Reger, premiering one of his quartets. Among its many other first performances, Janáček's First Quartet – which it commissioned – stands out.

The Czech Quartet made numerous recordings; those it set down for Polydor in 1928 have had a particularly wide currency. By then it was clearly not rehearsing much, but the verve and musicality of its interpretations of works by Smetana, Dvořák and Suk himself make the records still worth

Figure 4.2 Ševčík Quartet (1911–13): (left to right) Bohuslav Lhotský, Karel Moravec, Ladislav Zelenka, Karel Procházka

hearing. By coincidence, virtually the same repertoire was recorded around the same time by the Ševčík Quartet (Fig. 4.2) – which, although its members were only slightly younger, already represented a new generation. Named after the pedagogue who taught three of its members, the Ševčík did not play such a vital role in Czech musical life as the Czech Quartet but it did significantly advance the technique of quartet playing. Its records show broadly the same characteristics as the older group – a light, airy violin tone, sparing use of vibrato and liberal portamenti – but everything is tighter in ensemble and better organised.

The death of its leader Bohuslav Lhotský in 1930 cut off the group's career prematurely after less than three decades, but by then there were several other superb groups working in Prague and touring. Of these, the most exceptional was the Prague Quartet, which was founded just after World War I, played a leading role in bringing forward new music – such as the works of Schulhoff – and petered out in the early 1950s. Leaders and cellists came and went, but the players of the inner parts, Herbert Berger and Ladislav Černý, remained constant virtually throughout. The violist Černý, a contemporary of Busch and Szigeti, was one of the most extraordinary musicians of the century. Not above retouching scores to suit his own ideas, he was a friend of Hindemith and an inspiration to generations of Czech chamber musicians. The records of Dvořák, Schumann and Janáček made by the Prague Quartet are exceptional, especially Dvořák's G major, Op. 106,

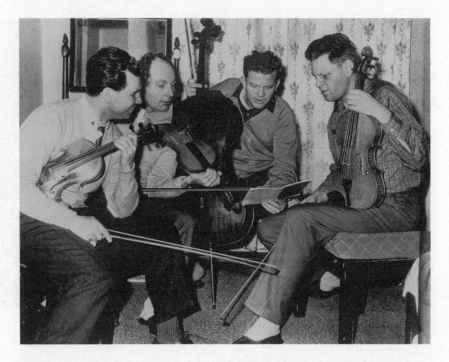

Figure 4.3 Smetana Quartet (*c.* 1960): (left to right) Jiří Novák, Lubomír Kostecký, Antonín Kohout, Milan Škampa

with the original leader, Richard Zika, and the outstanding cellist Miloš Sádlo. Soon after that recording was made in 1933, Zika defected to the rival Ondříček Quartet, which as a result became almost as good as the Prague for a time. It made some beautiful records.

After World War II the finest of all Czech ensembles emerged in Prague. The Smetana Quartet came to play the same role in its country's musical life as the Czech Quartet once had, premiering many Czech works and securing the places of Smetana's D minor and Janáček's two quartets in the international repertoire. More than that, it became the first Czech group to make a worldwide reputation in the Viennese classics. Its *spiritus rector* was the cellist Antonín Kohout, and the other founder to remain constant was the second violinist Lubomír Kostecký. The conductor Václav Neumann was an early member. For many years the group played all its repertoire by heart and to the end of its days, it retained a central core of Czech warhorses which it performed from memory. By 1955 the personnel was finally settled, with Jiří Novák as leader and Dr Milan Škampa – a pupil of Černý – as violist. During the next three decades the Smetana Quartet (Fig. 4.3) played to a standard not surpassed before or since. All the Beethoven quartets were recorded, some more than once; and the ensemble's Mozart, which included all the quintets with the younger Josef Suk as first viola, was superb. In the music of Smetana, Dvořák, Janáček, Novák, Suk, Martinů and Eben it had no peer, even though Prague boasted other fine ensembles such as the Vlach, which was attached to Czech Radio and thrived on large-scale works such as Dvořák's G major, Suk's Second and Stenhammar's Fourth.

The main Moravian centre, Brno, also produced a superb ensemble after World War II. The Janáček Quartet played its own part in disseminating the works of its name composer; and, taking its cue from the slightly older Smetana Quartet, – with which it often performed Mendelssohn's Octet – it played from memory. The death of its leader Jiří Travníček in 1973 sent it into partial eclipse, but it is again playing superbly, having evolved into a completely different line-up.

In the 1970s and 1980s Prague had another splendid classical ensemble in the line of the Smetana. This was the Talich Quartet, which sometimes sounded too refined in its native repertoire but made an international reputation in Mozart and Beethoven, especially through its recordings. A rather brutal reorganisation in the late 1990s resulted in a complete change of membership within a few years, however. The example and the teaching of the Smetana Quartet have led to the emergence of a hugely talented new generation of ensembles. Among these the senior, and the most refined, is the Panocha, named after its leader. For some years it has played as well as any in the world and its tours have taken it to all major centres. Its series of Dvořák recordings has set the standard for the twenty-first century, but in Janáček it has perhaps been surpassed by the more pungent, powerful artistry of the Pražák Quartet.

Hungary

The work of the Hubay Quartet acted as a stimulus for chamber music in Budapest, as did the teaching of its members; but two decades elapsed before its successor emerged. The Hungarian Quartet – known at home by the names of leader Imre Waldbauer and cellist Jenö Kerpely – was a seminal twentieth-century ensemble, and it is tragic that it left no recordings. It came into existence to perform the works of Bartók and Kodály and the two concerts it gave in Budapest in March 1910 – after more than ninety rehearsals – ushered in a new era in Hungarian music overnight. The players were all major personalities: the second violinist János Temesváry, who stayed with the group throughout like Waldbauer and Kerpely, was a fine player and the first two occupants of the viola chair, Antal Molnár and Egon Kornstein, were musicologists. After the latter moved to America in the early 1920s (changing his name to Kenton) the Hungarian Quartet had several violists and lost its focus slightly, although it still toured. By the

Figure 4.4 Budapest Quartet (1920–6): (left to right) Emil Hauser, Imre Pogany, Istvan Ipolyi, Harry Son

time it petered out in the late 1930s it had given the world or Budapest premieres of most of the important Hungarian chamber music of the era and its members had contributed to the superb education available at the Budapest Academy between the wars.

After the First World War several groups emerged from the orchestra at the Budapest Opera and left Hungary to make their fortunes, the most important being the Budapest and Léner. All eight men were pupils of Hubay or Popper. The Budapest began with a line-up of three Hungarians and a Dutch cellist but was bedevilled by personnel changes. By 1926 it was being infiltrated by a Russian, and a decade later it had metamorphosed from an athletic Magyar group to a rather solid Russian one (Fig. 4.4). The Léner, on the other hand, kept the same personnel for more than two decades. It played with a good deal of the wide 'Hubay vibrato', making a sound very different from the light, brilliant Budapest, and Jenö Léner's own style could be a little soupy. Its ensemble could also be sloppy but its natural flair and warmth won it many friends. It was the first quartet to record extensively, taking advantage of the superior technology available in London, and by the mid-1930s it had sold more than a million 78rpm discs, an astonishing feat even though many of its performances required several discs. The backbone of its repertoire was the Beethoven cycle, which it recorded complete, even making two versions of some works. Its Beethoven cycles were important occasions, especially in London, until the Busch Quartet arrived on the scene. Like the Budapest, the Léner did not make a great effort to play modern music, but its series devoted to the history of the string quartet were influential at the time. Its playing style quickly became dated and its recordings were virtually ignored for the latter half of the century. Fortunately some of these performances have recently been revived and, with all their faults, have much to offer an informed listener.

In the mid-1930s the first really modern Hungarian ensemble was formed by students of the Budapest Academy. The New Hungarian Quartet made its name by collaring the local premiere of Bartók's Fifth Quartet, which it studied with the composer. In 1937 early teething problems were solved by bringing in the virtuoso violinist Zoltán Székely as leader; and for a year his predecessor Sándor Végh played as second fiddle. During the war the group was trapped in Holland, in conditions of some privation; but it emerged in 1945, having learnt the Beethoven cycle and dropped the New from its name, to become one of the world's leading quartets. A purist might complain that the violins were not well matched, as the second, Alexandre Moskowsky, was Russian and played in a different style; in addition the cellist Palotai, older than the others, was too dominant. Nevertheless, the group made a profound impression in the central repertoire and its interpretations of twentieth-century music were excellent. Changes in the second violin and cello positions ushered in its best decade, the 1960s. Playing in a more homogeneous but also more relaxed style, the Hungarian Quartet was as successful in its adopted home the United States as in Europe. The recorded cycles of the Bartók and Beethoven quartets that it made then will be heard with respect for years to come. Its members remained influential even after its dissolution.

Bartók and Beethoven were also the specialities of another expatriate Magyar group that Sándor Végh formed in 1940, not long after leaving the New Hungarian Quartet. He was able to keep his eponymous quartet together for more than three decades, even though his colleagues disliked him intensely. Végh himself could be an infuriatingly sloppy player – live recordings made as early as 1950 reveal him playing excruciatingly out of tune – and the group often sounded as if its members had not met before coming on stage (they lived in four separate cities). Végh's outsize personality generally got them through, however. Records made in the 1950s and 1960s were variable and sometimes surprisingly dull; but in the early 1970s the players pulled themselves together long enough to make fine Bartók and Beethoven cycles. After the group fell apart, Végh soldiered on with two different formations, but with mixed success.

At home in Hungary, the post-war scene was dominated by the solid ensembles led by Vilmos Tatrai and Péter Komlós. The Tatrai Quartet, founded in 1946, lasted almost half a century. It will probably be remembered mainly for its sturdy Haydn performances; it achieved one of the first complete recorded cycles, although the recordings of the earlier works, done last, inevitably showed some deterioration in technique. Komlos's group, founded in 1957 and known as the Bartók Quartet from 1963, has been highly effective in the works of Beethoven, Brahms and its name composer, all of which it has recorded with success.

The younger Hungarian quartets have mostly flattered to deceive, either failing to keep consistent personnel or lacking charisma; and yet the teaching of Andras Mihály has produced one promising group after another. The Takács, which in the late 1970s and early 1980s played very beautifully, always suffered from a rather laid-back cellist; and the acquisition of a major recording contract in the late 1980s coincided with a drastic loss of form. The leader resigned and the violist died; and since 1995 the group has consisted of two Hungarians and two Englishmen, a most unsatisfactory mixture.

The best hope for the Hungarian school is the Keller Quartet, which emerged in the late 1980s. At its best it plays with both brilliance and flair; and at the time of writing it seems to be getting over a period of upheavals. To the Viennese classics and the native classics of Bartók and Kodály it has added such specialities as Tchaikovsky and Dvořák; and in concert it has daringly juxtaposed the gnomic utterances of Kurtág with the counterpoint of Bach's *Art of Fugue*.

The Joachim tradition

By the time Joseph Joachim died in 1907, the string quartet recital had taken root in the concert hall in a way that the sonata recital had not – that development would take several more decades. Joachim himself had been largely responsible for the trend and, were he alive today, he would find things much as he left them. Recitals tend to be based on historical principles, so that a mature Haydn or Mozart quartet will often be placed at the start, to be followed by inferior music. It is still all too likely that the 'modern' work in the concert – placed just before the interval, in the approved Joachim way – will be the Ravel F major, written before Joachim's death. Of course the literature has been expanded by a century's worth of music – in particular Janáček, Bartók, Berg and Shostakovich – but our knowledge of Haydn and Mozart, relatively few of whose works were common currency in 1900, has also increased. Thus, exposure of the twentieth-century repertoire is still restricted to one work per programme, except on special occasions.

One suspects Joachim would not have objected. Certainly those who followed in his footsteps, before the German tradition was fractured by Hitler's insane aberrations, were content to follow his lead. The situation they inherited in Germany was a healthy one. A big network of chamber music clubs thrived, and the major centres such as Berlin, Munich and Frankfurt supported large numbers of concerts every season. In addition there was work to be found in Austria, Switzerland and Italy. Five quartet leaders in particular could lay claim to the Joachim succession: Edgar Wollgandt in Leipzig, Karl Klingler in Berlin, Carl Wendling in Stuttgart and two Dutchmen, Henri Petri in Dresden and Bram Eldering in Cologne. Petri died fairly soon himself and did not make records. Wollgandt's recordings are interesting mainly because his Gewandhaus Quartet could call on a vast array of experience. He himself was Nikisch's son-in-law and for many years the Quartet's cellist was Julius Klengel, a friend of both Brahms and Joachim – it is possibly more important that this ensemble recorded a single Brahms movement than that it made one of the first complete sets of Beethoven's Op. 131. The playing on all the Gewandhaus discs is old-fashioned – light in tone and vibrato, replete with portamenti – but deeply moving in its dedication.

Klingler and Wendling were active into the 1930s and left records which are probably the closest we can come to hearing the Joachim Quartet. Indeed, the cellist of the first Klingler formation (1906–14), the Welshman Arthur Williams, followed his teacher Hausmann in playing without an endpin. Apart from Karl Klingler himself, the mainstay of the Quartet was his elder brother Fridolin, who played the viola throughout the group's career. The early Klingler records, of individual movements, are musically excellent, but one notes the rather spongy attack, soft-grained sound and lavish portamento. These traits are still in evidence in the one major work the ensemble recorded in the 1930s, Beethoven's Op. 127. The *sforzati* are lacking in drama and it is the probity of the playing, rather than its excitement, that impresses. The slow movement of Haydn's Op. 76 no. 5, done as a separate item, is interpreted with immense breadth. Wendling's records are also mostly of individual movements, but they include the entire Mozart Clarinet Quintet and part of Reger's Clarinet Quintet, dedicated to him, as well as the Adagio of Schubert's C major Quintet. Again, it is the honesty of the artistry that hits home. Perhaps it is significant that both Klingler and Wendling behaved admirably in the Hitler era.

Bram Eldering, leader of the major ensemble in the Rhineland, the Gürzenich Quartet, made no records but, like Banquo, was destined to have many heirs – among his pupils at the Amsterdam and Cologne Conservatoires were innumerable quartet leaders, principally Adolf Busch, Willem de Boer, Ria Queling, Max Strub and Wilhelm Stross. Of these the most notable – indeed, the greatest quartet *primarius* of all time – was Busch (1891–1952). He gave an enormous number of concerts and managed to be Europe's busiest soloist while devoting much of his time to chamber music. His Quartet, which performed from 1912 to 1951 with only two brief interruptions, was always composed of soloists, and if Busch himself dominated a little in the nineteenth-century manner, that was due to his gigantic personality. The Busch Quartet was recognised as the first in the German-speaking lands to rehearse exhaustively and democratically. Its first few years were spent in Vienna and it always had a Viennese violist – until

Figure 4.5 Busch Quartet (1930): (left to right) Adolf Busch, Gösta Andreasson, Herman Busch, Karl Doktor

1944 Karl Doktor. The cellists were Paul Grümmer and then, from 1930, his pupil Herman Busch. From 1920 to 1944 the second violinist was the Swede Gösta Andreasson, from the same Joachim tradition as Adolf Busch (Fig. 4.5). Although considered Joachim's successor, Busch departed from his pattern in certain ways. For example, he liked to place the Op. 18 quartets in the centre of the programme in Beethoven cycles, as points of relief from the heavier fare, and he often started with a late quartet; whereas Joachim would place an Op. 18 first, with a middle-period quartet second and a late quartet last. In general Busch liked to vary his programmes as much as possible, so that even if he were playing three cycles concurrently in three different cities, all three would be ordered differently. From 1921 he had his future son-in-law Rudolf Serkin as the Quartet's resident pianist; and he would programme a duo, trio, quintet or sextet among the quartets to lend variety.

The Busch Quartet toured indefatigably, basing its programmes on the Viennese classics and playing more Haydn than any of its peers, but also programming a certain amount of conservative modern music, including the leader's own excellent compositions. Busch's hero was Reger and we are fortunate that a radio recording of Reger's E♭ Quartet Op. 109 survives. It is also almost as important that Busch's recordings of Beethoven's late quartets exist as that the music itself exists, as Busch alone plumbed their full depths. He believed this rarefied music had to be taken to extremes and he possessed both the technique and the power to do it. His interpretations, for all their occasional tiny inconsistencies, are fit to be taught in music colleges and, once such institutions have caught up with the significance of historic recordings, perhaps they will be. Busch was hardly less effective in Haydn, Mozart, Schubert, Brahms and Dvořák. In the 1940s the Busch Quartet was based in the United States, where it was not fully appreciated; even there, however, Busch was responsible for bringing a leavening of the Old World to the New by founding the Marlboro Summer Music School. He has not yet had a German successor, but both the Strub and Stross ensembles left important records of Reger. Strub's second of his three line-ups included Walter Trampler and Ludwig Hoelscher but collapsed in 1939 on Trampler's emigration.

It is necessary, for historic reasons, to mention the Amar Quartet, which had Paul Hindemith as violist and played much new music in its short life (1921–9). Unfortunately its records are of almost negligible musical interest; and although those of Hindemith's own works give certain clues as to how he may have wished the music to go, they have been surpassed many times over. The contrast with the other group in which he was involved, the string trio with Szymon Goldberg and Emanuel Feuermann, could hardly be greater. The Amar Quartet's playing is almost shockingly direct and unnuanced, and one wonders what the players thought they were doing, essaying the piece by Verdi.

After the 1939–45 war Germany – by now split in two – was unlucky. In the West the excellent Schäffer Quartet, which played late Beethoven well, received little publicity and the Barchet Quartet, which commanded a fair amount of tonal colour, was eclipsed by its leader's early death. Similarly, the Drolc Quartet from the Berlin Philharmonic, which changed three of its personnel halfway through its career, died prematurely with its leader. In the Eastern sector, polished ensembles flourished in Berlin, Leipzig and Dresden, often as adjuncts to the great orchestras. Among those who led notable groups were Karl Suske – who worked in Berlin and then Leipzig – and the Dresden concertmaster Rudolf Ulbrich; but their concerts and even their records had to be heard in situ. So the German flag has mostly been flown internationally by the terminally dry Melos Quartet of Stuttgart and, in more recent years, by the Brandis, the Auryn and the younger Petersen, Vogler and Leipzig.

More interesting than any of these worthy ensembles is the Orpheus Quartet, a polyglot group (a Frenchman, a Dutchman and two Romanians) based in Düsseldorf and already, after little more than a decade, of world class. The Orpheus has brought forward interesting repertoire such as the Malipiero cycle and has shown itself equal to all styles from the classics to Bartók and Dutilleux. A recording of Schubert's C major Quintet with Peter Wispelwey displays remarkable freshness and originality.

Figure 4.6 Rosé Quartet (in the late 1920s)

Vienna and Salzburg

Although Vienna has produced many marvellous quartets, nearly all of them have been tied to the city's orchestras. Only with the emergence of the Alban Berg Quartet in the 1970s did it become possible to run a full-time ensemble. The towering figure in the closing years of the nineteenth century and the first four decades of the twentieth was the Romanian-born Arnold Rosé (1863–1946), whose group performed from 1882 to 1945 (Fig. 4.6). Although it always played to a high standard, it suffered innumerable personnel changes and Rosé, whose word was law in Viennese string-playing circles, was dominant. The Rosé Quartet gave six to eight subscription concerts every season in Vienna and toured Europe when its members could get leave from their work in the Court/State Opera. Its most famous concerts, for which it rehearsed assiduously, were those at which it introduced Schoenberg's early chamber music. The Second Quartet in particular caused a scandal and Rosé made no attempt to export the music to other centres. He also rejected Wolf's powerful D minor Quartet. He did have curiosity about new music, however; and in the early 1940s, when he had been forced to emigrate to England and reconstitute his ensemble in London, he played Shostakovich's new First Quartet. Most of his ensemble records featured single movements, but in the late 1920s he set down three Beethoven quartets, one early, one middle-period and one late. At this point his group was well worn in, having changed only its cellist since the early years of the century; and, although the violist suffered from Parkinson's disease – as can be heard at his first entry in Op. 131 – all four men were playing to a high standard. What we hear is virtually nineteenth-century style, with many slides and modest use of vibrato, but the way the players tear into the development of the first movement of the 'Harp', Op. 74, proves how well the nineteenth-century approach could work in Beethoven.

The next big name to emerge – in the early 1920s – was Rudolf Kolisch (1896–1978), who played the violin left-handed and therefore sat on the right wing of the quartet, an ideal solution for classical works and for disseminating the sound in all music. The first occupant of the chair opposite him was Fritz Rothschild, a former member of Busch's ensemble, and at first the two shared the leadership; but too much democracy has never been good for quartets and Rothschild soon departed. Other Kolisch innovations, such as rehearsing from scores and playing from memory, lasted longer. Kolisch was Arnold Schoenberg's brother-in-law and unlike Rosé was bent on propagating music of the Second Viennese School beyond Vienna. With his various colleagues he presided over the world premières of many works, including Berg's *Lyric Suite*, Schoenberg's last two quartets and Bartók's last two.

By the late 1920s the group, by then named after its leader, had settled down with a Viennese second violinist, a Hungarian violist and a Russian cellist (Fig. 4.7). This mélange did not make for ideal balance, as the cellist patently played in a different style from everyone else and inner parts were weakly projected. Once one has heard such groups as the Busch, the Kolisch approach to Schubert sounds feeble. Nevertheless, enough sound documents have survived to show that the group, in its very Viennese way, had something to say. Recordings of Wolf's *Italian Serenade* and Mozart's *Musical Joke* are almost ideal in their lightness and airiness. The legendary records of the Schoenberg quartets were made in Hollywood, under less than ideal circumstances, and should be heard with an awareness of the limitations of the group's style in other music; they are still of historical interest; indeed, the recording of the Fourth Quartet was either the world première or the second performance. Soon after, in 1939, the group disbanded and the two violinists found new partners who were better attuned to their style. Sadly, for various reasons, this line-up did not prosper, but it did make a recording of Mozart's 'Dissonance' that is the best souvenir of Kolisch's musicianship (an uneven account of Bartók's Fifth was not issued until the CD era). Kolisch later led the Pro Arte Quartet in its American incarnation and taught many chamber musicians.

The real successor to the Rosé as an echt-Wiener ensemble was the Konzerthaus Quartet, founded in 1934 by four members of the Vienna Symphony

Figure 4.7 Kolisch Quartet: (left to right) Felix Khuner, Eugen Lehner, Benar Heifetz, Rudolf Kolisch

Orchestra – who were soon taken into the State Opera Orchestra and the Philharmonic. This group has come down to us as the Haydn quartet *par excellence*, because of its many commercial and radio recordings; but its Mozart, Schubert and Beethoven are hardly less striking and it has left important records of Bruckner, Schmidt and Pfitzner. Here is the pliant, yielding Viennese style at its best. The Konzerthaus Quartet kept its original members for almost a quarter of a century and even in its dying years, in the early 1960s, it was capable of good things.

Of short duration but of seminal influence was the career of the Galimir Quartet, composed of Felix of that ilk and his sisters. Intent from the first on seeking the approval of the composers whose works they played, the Galimir made recordings in the late 1930s of the Ravel F major and Milhaud Seventh, both supervised by the composers, and Berg's Lyric Suite – of immense importance because, although Berg was dead by then, they had studied it with him relatively recently. The Milhaud, of less worth musically, was superbly played, as was the Ravel, although the first movement was taken too fast. Galimir made an immense impact on chamber music in the United States, not least through the Marlboro Summer School, and sporadically led quartets, although no longer with his sisters. Significantly, when he came to record the Berg and Ravel works again half a century later in America, the former was much the same in outline but the latter featured a more relaxed opening movement.

Rosé was succeeded by other leaders of the Opera orchestra who played quartets to a high standard. Under Wolfgang Schneiderhan, Walter Barylli and Willi Boskovsky the ensemble was more or less the same, with Otto Strasser as the second violinist from the late 1930s into the 1960s and few changes in the other positions. Another leader of the orchestra, Walter Weller, also had an excellent quartet and the tradition continues to this day with Rainer Küchl and Werner Hink. But none of these ensembles has made a mark at the highest level – the Schneiderhan Quartet, which might have done so, had the misfortune to lose vital years to the war and its aftermath – although worthwhile recordings have been made of all of them.

The emergence of the Alban Berg Quartet in the early 1970s made a huge difference to the Viennese scene. Here was a group of the highest quality, dedicated not just to playing the classics well but also to propagating twentieth-century music. The original four players signalled their intentions immediately by studying for a year with the LaSalle Quartet in Cincinnati. Two personnel changes since then have not affected the Quartet's quality, although they have changed its personality in subtle ways: having started as a marvellous Mozart ensemble, the Alban Berg Quartet has become a strong Haydn one. The Beethoven cycle, central to its career, has been recorded twice, the second time live, like most of the group's more recent recordings. Berg, of course, has been vital to these players as well as Webern and Schoenberg. The more exotic central European fare such as Bartók and Janáček has not suited them so well; but many premieres have been given – Berio, von Einem, Leitermeyer, Haubenstock-Ramati, Rihm, Schnittke, Urbanner, Wimberger et al. – and the group has been prepared to keep its new music in its repertoire. It is still playing with massive command.

The Alban Berg Quartet's lead has been followed to an extent by the Artis Quartet, a decade younger, which has made a speciality of exhuming good music by such composers as Weigl and Zemlinsky. Its performances of the classics have sometimes exhibited a certain stiffness but it has made a positive contribution to expanding the Viennese repertoire.

The Viennese ensemble that has created the most stir in recent years is the Quatuor Mosaïques, founded in Paris in 1984 as an offshoot of a chamber orchestra. It purports to play on period instruments but in truth only its French cellist, Christophe Coin, approaches a real period technique. The other three players, all Viennese, play in a sort of halfway-house style; in fact the leader, Erich Höbarth, uses exactly the same instrument when he leads the 'modern instrument' Vienna Sextet – the only change is that he uses gut strings for the quartet. It is the innate musicality of the group, rather than any doctrinaire approach to style, that has won it so many plaudits. Its recordings of the Viennese classics have been extremely successful, as have its concert tours.

Salzburg has had a great ensemble for twenty years in the Hagen Quartet, which began as a group of siblings. Three still play in the Quartet but two changes of second violinist have brought about subtle differences, and the arrival of the German violinist Rainer Schmidt in 1987 was decisive in lifting the ensemble's standard even higher. Lukas Hagen is one of the few leaders to play consistently in tune and the group's stylistic sensitivity in Haydn and Mozart is exemplary. Its Beethoven is almost too lean and hungry, and one feels that much development is still to be made in this composer's music. A good part of the Quartet's activity is given over to twentieth-century music, in which it is very effective, thanks to its strong intellectual grasp of musical structures.

Recently Thomas Zehetmair has headed a remarkable group which has exhibited the pros and cons of playing from memory in the most vivid way. Some of its performances of the classics have been mannered beyond belief, but in the music of such composers as Bartók and Hartmann its technical prowess has been revelatory.

The Franco-Belgians

Few French or Belgian composers have written more than one token string quartet, so it is not surprising that native ensembles have largely looked elsewhere for their repertoire. As far as style goes, it is interesting to reflect that in the decade between the composition of the Debussy and Ravel quartets, now considered the cornerstones of the French school, the way of playing string instruments underwent a seismic revolution. The two works should therefore not be played in the same way, although they have outward similarities – and they both continued the trend of freeing the viola part. Because string teaching has always been basically conservative, the innovations of players such as Ysaÿe and Kreisler, with their continuous vibrato, took some time to spread, so that in Paris up to around 1930 one could have heard a gamut of playing styles.

Lucien Capet (1873–1928), the great French quartet leader of the last years of the nineteenth century and the first quarter of the twentieth, was identified above all with Beethoven. He was a master of bowing whose ideas influenced many later players; and if his use of the left hand was rather nineteenth-century in effect, with little or no vibrato and pronounced

Figure 4.8 Quatuor Capet: (left to right) Camille Delobelle, Henri Benoît, Maurice Hewitt, Lucien Capet

portamenti, he played with much stylistic awareness. Capet led four different formations over the years, all with excellent players including two members of the Casadesus family; but the Quatuor Capet which chiefly concerns us is the last, which performed from 1918 until the leader's sudden death at the end of 1928 (Fig. 4.8). Beautiful records of Beethoven, Haydn, Mozart, Debussy, Ravel and Franck – the Quintet, with Marcel Ciampi at the piano – were made in the electrical era and, had Capet lived only a year or two more, we should have had others. The violist and cellist played on, under other leaders, and the second violinist, Maurice Hewitt, became a conductor. The Quatuor Capet's recordings are obligatory listening for their courtly musicality and the window they provide into late nineteenth-century performance practice. The sound made on the gut strings is very pure, almost chaste, and yet the interpretative vision is both probing and powerful.

More modern in its approach and less dominated by the leader was the Flonzaley Quartet, founded in 1902 as the private ensemble of the Swiss-American banker Edward J. de Coppet. Its name came from his villa in Switzerland. Although only the cellist was Belgian, the other three members – Swiss second violinist, Italian leader and violist – were pupils of César Thomson at Liège and the ensemble hewed to the light Franco-Belgian style. It soon transcended its origin as a rich man's plaything and forged an important career, with one foot permanently in the United States and the

Figure 4.9 Ernest Bloch (standing, left) with the Flonzaley Quartet: (left to right) Adolfo Betti, Alfred Pochon, Iwan d'Archambeau, Ugo Ara

other in Europe; de Coppet continued to sponsor it, however, until his death about halfway through its lifespan. The Flonzaley gave some high-profile premieres, including Enescu's and Bloch's first quartets and Stravinsky's *Three Pieces* and *Concertino* (Fig. 4.9); but its importance lay more in the way it disseminated chamber music through its tours and records. After 1917 it had a series of substitute violists and its famous electric recordings of the piano quintets by Brahms (with Harold Bauer) and Schumann (with Ossip Gabrilowitsch) were made with the ubiquitous Russian player Nicolas Moldavan, who rather diluted its homogeneity of style. In 1928 it dissolved in a flurry of lawyers' letters and writs – neither the first nor the last ensemble to perish in that way.

The real heir to the Belgian tradition of the Quatuor Ysaÿe was the Quatuor Pro Arte, which was founded in Brussels in 1912 but did not really get going until after the Great War. Its 'Three Musketeers' were the violinists Alphonse Onnou and Laurent Halleux (who alternated as leaders in the early days) and the violist Germain Prévost. They stayed with it throughout. When it was reconstituted in 1918 the cellist was the composer Fernand Quinet; he was replaced in 1922 by Robert Maas and the group's classic formation was complete. The Pro Arte was the foremost contemporary music group of the inter-war years, introducing countless works through its own concert series in Brussels and Paris. It was also taken up by America's leading patron of new music, Elizabeth Sprague Coolidge, who sponsored many of its tours and its university concerts. In the 1930s the Pro Arte had a summer residency at Mills College in California and it was the first quartet to be given a university residency, at the University of Wisconsin, Madison. Maas became separated from the others by the war and Onnou soon died; the two others soldiered on at Madison for a time with other players and in theory the quartet still exists – but its great days ended in 1939. The Pro Arte was wonderfully comprehensive in its interpretations of Franco-Belgian music – Franck, Debussy, Ravel, Fauré – which it played with a light touch typical of its roots; fortunately it recorded the major works. In the classics it was sound but not special, so it is ironic that it should be remembered mainly for its series of Haydn records. It gained the contract by a bare-faced lie and had to sightread several of the performances in the studio. The interpretations are fine in their way but one longs for real Haydnesque grit occasionally. Of the Pro Arte's contemporary repertoire little was recorded.

From the Paris Conservatoire two outstanding groups emerged after the First World War, playing in a very French manner but with a warmth that would be recognised by today's audiences. The Quatuor Krettly was at its best in the late 1920s, when it consisted of three Frenchmen and a Belgian, and it left some unsurpassed recordings, notably of Fauré's Quartet. The Quatuor Calvet began to hit its stride in 1928 when Daniel Guilevitch joined as second violinist. During the 1930s it toured throughout Europe and made sublime records of Debussy, Ravel, Mozart, Beethoven and Schubert. In 1940 it disbanded and a post-war formation did not last long, but its members were hugely influential: Joseph Calvet taught generations of French chamber musicians; Guilevitch (under the name Guilet) had his own quartet in the USA and founded the Beaux Arts Trio; and violist Léon Pascal had his own eponymous quartet from 1940 through the 1950s, making many fine recordings, including a Beethoven cycle.

After the war the major French quartet was the Quatuor Parrenin, which played a great deal of contemporary music but also excelled in the mainstream repertoire. It ran from 1942 for five decades but its best days were in the 1950s and 1960s. Its records of Debussy, Ravel, Fauré and Bartók were notable. The Quatuor Bernède, which performed from 1963 to 1991, also kept up a high standard and at various times three refugees from the Parrenin migrated to it.

In recent years an enormous amount of time, money and effort has been invested in propagating the string quartet medium in France, but no remarkable ensemble has established itself. The Ysaÿe, the Parisii and the Castagneri (which boasts a left-handed second violinist, enabling it to adopt the ideal seating formation) are the younger groups which look most likely to succeed; and the Quatuor Turner, playing on period instruments, has renewed the Parisian Beethoven tradition.

The Belgian tradition also flagged after the war, although the Paganini Quartet kept it alive for twenty years in the USA. Now a mainly French ensemble, the Quatuor Danel, has settled in Brussels and taken on a Belgian violist. This group, with the Danel brothers at the top and bottom of the range, has a dedicated outlook and is conscious of the Franco-Belgian tradition. It plays interesting repertoire such as the quartets of Vainberg and although it is capable of performances of profundity, its concerts and recordings have included lighter fare by the likes of Gounod and Rosenthal.

The Netherlands

Holland has produced only one great quartet, perhaps because it has exported so many of its best string players. The Netherlands Quartet, which grew out of the earlier Amsterdam Quartet in the early 1950s, was composed of four outstanding personalities. The leader Nap de Klijn was a superb stylist, happiest in the classics; the second violinist Jaap Schroeder, younger than the others, later became a guru of the period-instrument movement; the violist Paul Godwin had been the leading light music player in Berlin until the advent of the Nazis in 1933; and the cellist Carel van Leeuwen Boomkamp was a cultivated player who also excelled on the viola da gamba. Through the 1950s and 1960s the Netherlands Quartet made extensive tours and its records, especially those of Haydn and Mozart, were greatly appreciated – some have been reissued on CD. A change of cellist in 1962 hardly affected the group but it unravelled in the late 1960s.

Its only notable successor has been the Schoenberg Quartet, which has specialised in the Second Viennese School; in 2001 it marked its silver jubilee by issuing new recordings of all Schoenberg's string chamber music, including a transcription by its violist Henk Guittart of the wind quintet. The polyglot Orlando Quartet has been based in the Netherlands since 1976 but, apart from a brief period under its first leader, has been more successful in its teaching than in its playing.

Switzerland

Although native Swiss such as Alphonse Brun in Berne did valuable work in organising quartets, Switzerland gained most from becoming a refuge in the inter-war years for such outsiders as Adolf Busch and Stefi Geyer. The Dutchmen Willem de Boer (Zurich) and Joachim Röntgen (Winterthur) were devoted quartet leaders as well as orchestral concertmasters. Röntgen's successor at Winterthur, Peter Rybar, brought the ensemble there to a high standard in the 1940s and 1950s and the group's recordings – including a Brahms Piano Quintet with Clara Haskil – are still sought after.

In more recent times the New Zurich Quartet, which flourished in the 1970s and 1980s, the Quatuor Sine Nomine, founded in Lausanne in 1975, and the Carmina Quartet, formed in Zurich in 1984, have all played to a high standard.

Italy

The inter-war period saw Italy beginning to fend for itself, with such fine ensembles as the Quartetto Poltronieri and Quartetto di Roma touring and recording. The breakthrough was made after World War II, however, with the emergence of the Quartetto Italiano. Playing from memory for the first decade, these players consciously strove to be known not just for Boccherini, Cambini, Donizetti and Verdi – which they played beautifully – but for the Classics, the Romantics and a discriminating choice of repertoire from the twentieth century. Beauty of tone, matching of vibrato, precise ensemble and cultivated musicianship put the Quartetto Italiano among the greatest of string quartets, and it was still playing superlatively when a succession of unfortunate incidents led to its dissolution in 1981. Its Achilles heel was rhythm but its best recordings have already stood the test of time.

In 1954 the ensemble's illustrious teacher, the cellist Arturo Bonucci – who had played trios with Casella and Poltronieri before the war and was also a member of the Quintetto Boccherini – founded the Quartetto Carmirelli with his wife Pina Carmirelli. This group, whose interpretations had infinite humanity, left precious recordings of Ravel, Prokofiev and Italian music. The best tribute to the Quartetto Italiano's playing and teaching has been the large number of excellent successor groups, from which it would be invidious to single any out. The part-time ensemble of soloists led by the great violinist Salvatore Accardo is a special case, however; its recordings include magnificent accounts of Mozart's quintets and Schubert's G major quartet.

Romania

Although one would like to eavesdrop on some of the *ad hoc* ensembles which once flourished in Romania – such as those led by Carl Flesch or George Enescu – until recently it was difficult to think of any ensemble from this country of fine string players which had risen above the 'excellent' level. During the Communist era several expatriate groups did good work without setting the world alight; and at home the Voces Quartet's music-making has been patchy. Now, however, the Ad Libitum Quartet is playing to the highest standard – its interpretations of Enescu's quartets, which have been recorded, are definitive – and other groups such as the Contempo are showing real promise.

Britain

The British string style, unshowy and conducive to a good blend, has always been suited to quartet playing. The first notable professional group to make records was the London Quartet, founded in 1908 with Albert Sammons (1886–1957) as leader. His records with the ensemble, which included Mozart's G minor Quintet with Alfred Hobday as guest, were all set down in the acoustic era. In the early electric days, under other leaders, the Quartet continued to do good work and make records; but its famous violist William Primrose, who joined in 1930, was documented on only one recording. The London Quartet ended up in America, where it found wealthy sponsors.

In the 1920s there were several fine groups such as the Spencer Dyke Quartet, which made good recordings. But towards the end of the decade a really dedicated foursome emerged, trained by Lionel Tertis at the Royal Academy of Music and led by a young man who, like him, had been raised in the slums of east London – Sidney Griller (1911–93). This ensemble was beautifully balanced and its members were determined to live by quartet playing alone. Through the 1930s the Griller Quartet forged a fine reputation and a number of works were written for it by British composers. It was polished in the classics, especially Mozart, but perhaps it will be remembered chiefly for its connection with Ernest Bloch, whose favourite ensemble it became, premiering several of his works. Its Bloch First is one of the great quartet recordings. After the war the Griller accepted a university residency in California and although it returned from time to time before its disbandment in 1963, it left the field at home open for other contenders.

Chief beneficiary was the Amadeus Quartet (Fig. 4.10), which would have had a good career in any case. As it was, this group composed of three Austrian refugees and an English cellist of immigrant stock got off to a flying start in 1947 and never looked back. In the 1950s and 1960s the Amadeus garnered international acclaim, fuelled by its numerous tours and

Figure 4.10 Amadeus Quartet: (left to right) Norbert Brainin, Siegmund Nissel, Peter Schidlof, Martin Lovett

recordings, while at home its members – Norbert Brainin, Siegmund Nissel, Peter Schidlof and Martin Lovett – became national figures.[1] Its strengths lay in the music of such bourgeois composers as Mozart, Schubert and Brahms. In the earthier Haydn and Beethoven its response was often too smooth. Although it did not play much new music, its interpretation of Britten's Second Quartet, which was recorded, showed off its bronze tone to advantage; it was no surprise when his Third Quartet was dedicated to the group. The shockingly sudden death of Schidlof brought the end after exactly forty years.

Not that the Amadeus had things all its own way. The Allegri, founded in 1953, was impressive for a quarter of a century; and the Aeolian – which as the Stratton Quartet had won Elgar's admiration with its records of his music in the early 1930s – had its finest hours in the 1970s under the leadership of Emanuel Hurwitz. Here was a *primarius* who could rise to the heroic challenges of Beethoven while also doing justice to the spiritual side. Happily the Aeolian's interpretations of the late quartets – which it played memorably on television – were recorded; and the ensemble was the first to complete a cycle of the Haydn quartets.

Two ensembles formed in 1966 had differing fortunes. The Gabrieli Quartet kept up a high standard for more than twenty years but lost impetus after a change of leader. The Lindsay Quartet, on the other hand, is still making news with interpretations of daring and penetration. In Peter Cropper it has one of the best leaders – musically speaking – since Busch. Its first recording of Beethoven's Op. 130 would alone entitle it to immortality and a Schubert C major Quintet (with Douglas Cummings) is almost as good. If the group's technical address equalled its imagination it would be even better thought of. Perhaps, like most British ensembles, it tries to play too wide a repertoire.

As the number of music clubs willing or able to hire a quartet has declined, too many British quartet players have had to do other work in order to earn a decent living. Or, like the Brodsky Quartet, they have been driven to desperate ploys to attract publicity – this foursome's ventures into 'crossover' have been questionable and their insistence on playing standing up has not aided audience concentration. The residencies available to British ensembles have also been few and not as munificent as those in America. Small wonder that in the past two decades, although such groups as the English String Quartet have made valuable contributions and the Fitzwilliam had a decade of glory with Christopher Rowland leading, only one British ensemble – the Endellion Quartet (Fig. 4.11) – has consistently met international standards. This superb classical quartet is playing as well as any in the world at present and its interpretations have a rare intellectual penetration.

Many hopes are invested in the young Belcea Quartet, British trained but with a Romanian leader and Polish violist, which has already displayed much accomplishment. Britain is also the base for a remarkable international ensemble, the Arditti Quartet, which in a quarter of a century has given innumerable first performances of new music. Its leader, Irvine Arditti, has been in place since the beginning and in 1985 the group acquired the distinguished Sri Lankan cellist Rohan de Saram. Its past and present members have all had the reputation of being fearsome sightreaders and fortunately many of the quartet's interpretations have been recorded. One can forgive the gimmickry of the Arditti's party piece, Stockhausen's *Helikopter* – where each member plays in a separate helicopter – when so much of its work has been so dedicated. Its activities, along with those of the Kronos Quartet in America, have helped to revitalise the quartet medium for the twenty-first century. In Britain its challenge has been taken up by the young Kreutzer Quartet, which has already given many astonishing performances of new scores.

The Nordic lands

Denmark has consistently produced expert professional quartets, and two groups with their roots in the 1930s, the Erling Bloch and the Koppel (named

Figure 4.11 Endellion Quartet: (left to right) Andrew Watkinson, David Waterman, Garfield Jackson, Ralph de Souza

after its violist and led by his wife), made important recordings, especially of the works of Nielsen. The Danish Quartet, which ran from 1949 to 1983, was at its peak in the 1960s and 1970s. But the jewel among the Danish ensembles was the Copenhagen Quartet, formed in 1957, which had a close relationship with one of the century's great quartet composers, Vagn Holmboe, and toured worldwide. Apart from its discs of Holmboe, Nielsen, Gade, Kuhlau et al., the Copenhagen recorded a worthy set of the late Beethoven quartets and excelled in a wide repertoire of classic and romantic music. Its leader Tutter Givskov is still passing on her insights to younger generations.

In recent years the Kontra Quartet, led by the Hungarian Anton Kontra, has set the tone for Danish quartet playing. In fact the contribution of Hungarian violinists to Scandinavian music has been considerable. In Sweden, the group led by Carl von Garaguly was the first to perform the Beethoven cycle, in 1948. That country, like Norway, has had many quartets of excellent quality without producing any of international calibre until recently. However, the Norwegians now have the characterful Vertavo Quartet, composed of two pairs of sisters.

In Finland the Jean Sibelius Quartet, led by the Japanese violinist Yoshiko Arai, has been performing and recording with cultured elegance since 1980; while the Helsinki Quartet has given promise of a vital younger generation.

Russia and Eastern Europe

No ensemble has been more closely connected with a composer than the Beethoven Quartet with Shostakovich. Founded in 1923 in Moscow, this group comprised four major personalities: Dmitry Tsïganov was among the leading violinists of his era, Vasily Shirinsky a composer and musicologist, Vadim Borisovsky one of the main figures in the viola's development, and Sergey Shirinsky, brother of the second violinist, a nonpareil quartet cellist. The four stayed together for more than forty years, an amazing record in itself. During that time – and in a further dozen or so years with new players of the inner parts – they gave innumerable premieres, including all of Shostakovich's chamber works except his first and last quartets (Sergei Shirinsky died while they were preparing for the first performance of the Fifteenth). They rehearsed every premiere under the composer's meticulous supervision; and their recordings are still the benchmarks against which Shostakovich performances must be measured.

More or less contemporary with the Beethoven was the Glazunov Quartet of Leningrad, which premiered Shostakovich's First Quartet and left a few valuable records, including a fine Borodin Second.

After World War II the Soviet state machine interfered more and more in concert life. Only favoured ensembles were allowed to make trips abroad, while those in disfavour were condemned to tour the most remote regions. Despite the restrictions, some elite ensembles made decent livings. The violist Rudolf Barshai was involved in two noted ensembles, the second being the Tchaikovsky Quartet, whose career was ended by the untimely death of its leader Yulian Sitkovetsky. The first, which became known as the Borodin Quartet after Barshai's departure, has now been going for more than half a century and includes no founder member, although the cellist Valentin Berlinsky has been aboard since its early days. He is perhaps responsible for the way this quartet – which admittedly plays to a superlative standard – hands its interpretations down from generation to generation like holy writ. Much of its music-making is mannered and unspontaneous, with its trademark *senza vibrato* overused. Capable of memorable performances on a good day, the Borodin Quartet is far from deserving the iconic status it enjoys in some quarters – its Shostakovich interpretations have been wildly overpraised. Some of the problems stemmed from its founder leader Rostislav Dubinsky, a preening, narcissistic player. His successor Mikhail Kopelman brought a more human face to the ensemble, and his successor is perhaps the best violinist *per se* that the group has had. So it continues to evolve.

Shostakovich's own second choice of ensemble was not the Borodin but the Taneyev Quartet of Leningrad, which in a long career starting in 1946 was always capable of profound statements. Its recorded cycles of Shostakovich, Myaskovsky, Beethoven and Schubert are all worth hearing – Schubert's C major Quintet, with Rostropovich assisting, has claims to be the greatest performance of that work ever set down.

The Shostakovich Quartet, which has recorded the cycle by its name composer twice, is also to be taken seriously. Its concerts can be inspirational and its recording of Haydn's *Seven Last Words* – a brave choice of repertoire at the time it was made – is among the finest.

Various ensembles from the regions of the old USSR were of good quality but the Komitas Quartet of Armenia – founded in 1925 and still going, with different players – stood out for its luscious tone, fine balance and committed musicianship. An old recording of the Grieg is fit to be placed alongside the Budapest Quartet's version; and in the 1950s its superb Tchaikovsky and Borodin records were issued in the West.

Bulgaria has had one quartet of the first rank, the Dimov, founded in 1956 and at its peak in the 1960s and 1970s. Poland did not find ensembles equal to the challenges of Szymanowski's two quartets until the Wilanow Quartet appeared in the 1960s. A decade later its violist and cellist joined up with the Bruczkowski brothers to form the outstanding Varsovia Quartet. And recently the Karol Szymanowski Quartet has emerged with distinction. A problem common to all fledgeling quartets, but especially to those from Eastern Europe, is the difficulty of finding decent instruments. Considering the obstacles placed in their way, many ensembles have worked wonders.

Israel

Many important quartet players – Emil Hauser, Harry Son, Felix Galimir, Lotte Hammerschlag among them – spent at least some time in pre-war Palestine, and the earliest generation of Israeli string players adhered to their Central European tradition; but in a country of individualists, few quartets developed. Only the splendid Tel Aviv Quartet, which flourished especially in the 1960s and 1970s, made an impression internationally. Since its heyday a vast influx of Russians has changed the complexion of Israeli

music-making and some vibrant young groups such as the Jerusalem and
Aviv Quartets reflect this sea-change in playing style.

North America

Economics have ruled chamber music in the USA even more than in other
countries. Although some societies have long and distinguished records,
there has never been a network of clubs to compare with that in Europe.
This lack of infrastructure and the vast distances involved made it almost
impossible to keep a professional quartet going in the first half of the twentieth century, without sponsorship. The Flonzaley Quartet was subsidised
by a banker in its early years. In the inter-war period, the Perolé Quartet was
sponsored by the Perera, Robson and Leventritt families, hence its name,
while the Musical Art Quartet spent most of its time performing in the
great houses of the rich; both groups were of premium quality, to judge
from their few recordings. Mrs Coolidge, the 'Lady Bountiful of chamber
music' in Cobbett's phrase,[2] made several attempts to found a successful
ensemble and came closest with the Coolidge Quartet, which she started in
the mid-1930s. She also made it possible, through her festivals and subventions to various foreign ensembles, for much new music to be heard; and
she was one of the major figures behind the musical activities at the Library
of Congress. She was also the instigator of the residency idea, by which
a quartet was supported by a school or university in return for a certain
amount of teaching. Despite all this activity, and the various schemes which
followed Mrs Coolidge's lead, no quartet written on US soil has yet followed
Dvořák's 'American' into the repertoire; and the many composers churning
out music on university campuses have failed to match the excitement of
American popular music (yet when the black jazz pianist and composer
James P. Johnson wrote to Mrs Coolidge asking for help in promoting his
string quartet, she did not even reply; the work is now lost). With rare exceptions, US quartet ensembles, for all their technical skills, have also failed
to get to grips with the grand European tradition, especially the works of
Beethoven. This lacuna is strange when one reflects that the Austro-German
ethos, as exemplified in quartets by the Kneisel ensemble, ruled music in
the US until after the First World War and continued to be influential
thereafter.

By 1920, the waves of immigration from Russia in the previous forty
years were beginning to have an effect on string playing; indeed, through
the rest of the century the dominant style in American string circles was to
be 'Russian American'. All the more credit, then, to the Flonzaley Quartet,
which during the first three decades of the century managed to confound all

the norms. It was in essence a Franco-Belgian ensemble, as already noted; it toured assiduously throughout the country, playing anything from the classics to 'Turkey in the Straw'; it became successful enough to do without sponsorship in the latter part of its career; and it was a front-rank recording organisation.

The first residencies in the US went to foreign groups, the Quatuor Pro Arte and the Budapest, which from 1939 to 1962 held the plum post at the Library of Congress, with the use of a set of Stradivarius instruments. It filled the position admirably, playing a good deal of American music. By this time the group was wholly Russian in make-up; but all the members had also received German training and so their playing of the classics, especially Mozart, was first-rate. In Beethoven they projected a massive competence, without the heartstopping moments that made the Busch Quartet's performances so memorable; but generations were introduced to the Beethoven cycle by the Budapest. The group was at its best when Alexander Schneider was its second violinist. During the decade when he was absent, 1944–54, it was not quite the same force, and after his return it was sometimes technically fallible as old age encroached.

The quintessential American ensemble did not emerge until the late 1930s and its early years were disrupted by the war. As a result the Hollywood Quartet, founded by the husband and wife Felix Slatkin and Eleanor Aller, had an effective career of only a decade. It was re-formed in 1947 with two other leading players from the Hollywood studio orchestras and owed its success to a unique combination of factors. As it was a spare-time activity, the players plunged into it with joy and dedication. Being used to working in the movie studios, they were great recording artists from the start – in fact, although the group toured a certain amount and gave regular concert series, as far as most of the world was concerned it was a record phenomenon. It also came along at precisely the right time to exploit tape recording and the long-playing disc. The second violinist Paul Shure was good enough to have led the group and both violists, Paul Robyn and then Alvin Dinkin, were superior artists. The Hollywood Quartet combined an eclectic taste in music and an awesome command of technique with an almost perfect judgement of tempo, evident in its recordings which have been reissued on CD to acclaim. It even made a brave shot at the late Beethoven quartets and came close to success.

Three major quartet leaders emerged after the Second World War. Broadus Erle and Eudice Shapiro were destined to be largely overlooked, but Robert Mann received his due from critics and public. He led the resident quartet at the Juilliard School, New York, from its inception and during his fifty years in the chair saw numerous colleagues come and go. As if in recompense for their compatriots' having let Béla Bartók virtually starve in

New York, the members of the Juilliard Quartet focused intensely on his six works for the medium; it has since been possible to speak of an American Bartók style. Their other major project was the Schoenberg cycle and they premiered many American works. They proved themselves superb Haydn players and were effective – if unnecessarily expressive – in Mozart, but never came near an authentic Beethoven style. The group, which has become a little more romantic in outlook over the years, is still going under new leadership.

Erle led the avant-gardist New Music Quartet, in which his colleagues included the violist Walter Trampler and the cellists Claus Adam and (later) David Soyer. This group disbanded in 1956 when Erle moved to Japan, where he was highly influential. On his return in 1960 he went to teach at Yale, where he led a superb resident quartet with, over the years, two Japanese second violinists, the violists David Schwartz and Trampler, and the cellist Aldo Parisot. In 1967–71 the Yale Quartet recorded the most probing set of Beethoven late quartets to have come out of the USA so far, but its great days ended with Erle's death in 1977.

Shapiro has been a vital force in West Coast music since the war years. She and her husband, the cellist Victor Gottlieb – who had played in the Coolidge and Pro Arte groups – formed the American Art Quartet with the violist Virginia Majewski in Los Angeles in 1945, and it became a mainstay of the legendary Concerts on the Roof. The two occupants of its second violin chair were both dedicated artists and its records of modern music show it to have been a top-flight, flexible ensemble.

The USA has seen some yeoman groups, such as the Fine Arts, Vermeer and Guarneri Quartets, but many of them have had a rather heavy playing style, symptomatic of performing overmuch in halls too large for intimate music. The Guarneri, a particularly beefy quartet, has even had a book written about it,[3] and one wishes its members played as profoundly as they talk. Several ensembles in the land of the free have carried democracy to the absurd lengths of having co-leaders, forgetting the lesson of the Kolisch Quartet. For the connoisseur, it is irritating to hear what are, in effect, two different quartets tackling a Beethoven, Bartók or Shostakovich cycle. In the case of the Orion Quartet, having two brothers as the violinists has slightly mitigated the violence of the change from one leader to the other; but the work of the Emerson Quartet has been fatally flawed, especially as one leader has shown himself to be a better fiddler and interpreter than the other. The Emerson has also consistently failed to find the right style or even the right sound for Beethoven.

Two notable classical quartets of recent years have been the Cleveland Quartet – now disbanded – which evolved from a rather overheated group to an *echt* Beethoven ensemble under its latter-day leader William Preucil Jnr, and the American Quartet, which is still playing as well as any in the world. Its complete recording of the Mozart quartets is wonderfully stylish. On the West Coast the Angeles Quartet acquired an enviable reputation, not least through its fine complete recording of the Haydn quartets, but disbanded at its peak in 2001.

Since 1973 the Kronos Quartet, based first in Seattle and then in San Francisco, has given hundreds of first performances and has done much to attract a younger audience with its imaginative programmes. Among its successes, George Crumb's *Black Angels* is beginning to sound old hat, but Steve Reich's haunting *Different Trains* will probably stay in the avant-garde repertoire.

Over the border in Canada, the Hart House Quartet of Toronto was of good repute for most of its 1923–46 career; but the string quartet immediately gained a higher profile when the violinist Kathleen Parlow returned to her native country in the early 1940s. Her group, also based in Toronto, played the classics well but did much, through its many broadcasts and occasional tours, to propagate Canadian music.

The first Canadian ensemble to gain an international reputation was the Orford Quartet, which flourished in Toronto from 1965 to 1992, toured widely and made excellent recordings of the Beethoven cycle. The all-female Lafayette Quartet, founded in 1985, has been based at the University of Victoria since 1991.[4] Its solution to the usual problem faced by female ensembles – two members have families – has been to restrict its touring; but eventually it will have the world-wide fame it deserves.

Canada has suddenly started to produce young quartets, thanks to initiatives such as the scheme at Banff, and three to watch are the Alcan, the St Lawrence and the Claudel, another all-female ensemble.

South and Central America

The South American continent has been something of a *terra incognita* for the major international ensembles, although the Busch Quartet was touring there in the mid-twentieth century. Three members of the Léner Quartet settled in Mexico City in 1941 and had a profound effect on music-making there. It was therefore no surprise that, when a world-class native group arose in 1981, it came from that city. The Cuarteto Latinoamerica – which includes three brothers – now has two residencies, in its home town and Pittsburgh, and has made definitive recordings of the quartet music of Revueltas, Ginastera, Villa-Lobos et al.

The Far East

Japan had its first notable ensemble as early as June 1928, when the Suzuki Quartet was founded in Nagoya. It was a family affair, led by Shin'ichi Suzuki (1898–1998), who had just returned from eight years of study with Klingler in Berlin. He and brothers Kikuo, Akira and Fumio – a pupil of Heinrich Werkmeister in Tokyo and Julius Klengel in Leipzig – played together until 1945 and left a handful of records, including a suite with tenor voice composed by Fumio Suzuki. Not surprisingly the group's style was reminiscent of the Klingler ensemble. It was during one of its rehearsals that Shin'ichi Suzuki had the inspiration for his Talent Education system.

Japan was a refuge for a number of fine Western quartet players, such as Alexander Mogilevsky, who led a group with three local players; and Ryuhtaroh Iwabuchi founded the all-Japanese Pro Musica Quartet in 1953. But the first outstanding Japanese quartet did not emerge until the mid-1960s.

The Mari Iwamoto Quartet should be known the world over, especially as it has a large discography of rare quality; but its leader, a distinctive artist trained by a Russian pupil of Auer, took some time to persuade her family that chamber music, not solo work, was her real vocation. After this late start she had not much more than a decade of success with her Quartet before her death from cancer in 1979. The ensemble, which from the evidence of its records could pass for a Central European quartet of the first rank, gained much from the artistry of its cellist Toshio Kuronuma, a profound player whose influence on Japanese chamber music continued after Iwamoto's death.

Iwamoto was half American, and both she and Kuronuma had spent short periods in America; the cellist had also played in Broadus Erle's Japanese group. And the one Japanese ensemble to make a world-wide reputation so far, the Tokyo Quartet, was largely an American creation, trained at the Juilliard School and heavily influenced by Robert Mann. Over the years it has been diluted by personnel changes. Just one founder remains and the group inevitably lacks that edge which comes from all members of a quartet sharing a common heritage.

China has not yet recovered from the ravages of the Cultural Revolution, and the only group to make any headway has been the distinctly medium Shanghai Quartet, which for some time has been based in the United States, with an American cellist. The Vega Quartet, of Chinese origin but American trained, is very promising.

It is possible that Korea will become a growth area for quartets. At least one excellent ensemble, the Virtuoso Quartet, has emerged in Seoul in the late 1990s and has recorded some stylish Mozart.

Australia

One can find mentions of string quartets in Australia as far back as 1905. More recently Musica Viva has done amazing things for Australian chamber music and is probably the largest such organisation in the world. For many years, however, this huge country depended on visiting ensembles for real quality. The man who turned the tide was Hungarian-born Robert Pikler (1909–84), who began as a front-rank violinist but turned to the viola when he settled in Sydney after World War II. He founded several ensembles including, in the mid-1960s, the outstanding Sydney Quartet, in which he played.

In 1985 the Australian Quartet was formed under the equally inspirational leadership of William Hennessy. This group has had its ups and downs, for the usual economic reasons, but among its many recordings is one of the most profound accounts of Mozart's G minor Quintet ever heard by this writer.

The Goldner Quartet, composed of two married couples, came to the fore in the 1990s and is of unquestionable world class. Among its finest interpretations and recordings are quartets by the nation's leading composer Peter Sculthorpe. The audience for chamber music in Australia's major centres is committed and informed; and although touring from such a distant corner of the world is not easy, the local players have good support at home.

PART 3

Playing string quartets

5 Playing quartets: a view from the inside

DAVID WATERMAN

Introduction

This chapter is not primarily intended as a manual for playing quartets; nor is it a description of what actually transpires in the privacy of any particular rehearsal room. Rather, it aims to describe the main issues which ensembles, in their own way, have to resolve in preparing their performances. After a brief exploration of the notion of a collective interpretation, the main body of the chapter deals with some important aspects of rehearsing, principally in relation to facets of ensemble playing such as voicing, blend, intonation, rhythm, tempo, articulation, phrasing and structure. There follows a discussion of different strategies for coping with residual disagreements, and then some concluding thoughts.

First movement: interpretation

The concept of musical interpretation

Any musician preparing a work of classical music for performance faces the challenge of developing an interpretation which reveals the soul of the work with conviction and freshness. Such a challenge is amplified for a string quartet, because the players have the additional task of reaching their interpretations collectively.

Even without the problem of collective decision-making, what does 'interpretation' involve? Just as Shakespeare's *The Tempest* can seem to be a multitude of extraordinarily different plays in the hands of different theatre companies (especially from various cultures and centuries), so there can be a comparable variety of readings of, say, Mozart's 'Dissonance' Quartet (K. 465), even if each group is aiming simply to be 'true to the score'. This is because it is impossible for a composer to notate for musicians any more precisely than a playwright can for actors. Mozart cannot show us exactly what tone of voice or sonority to use at any one moment, let alone every subtle passing inflection as the music unfolds through time; nor can he show us clearly how to shape and phrase – how, where and how much to breathe and to stress; and how, where and how much to make the tempo ebb and flow; nor, indeed, what the tempo should be. Even the overall character or mood of a piece is impossible to indicate in words except through necessarily cryptic sign-posts for those performers who can understand. Mendelssohn perceptively wrote that 'music I love does not give me ideas that are too vague to be expressed in words, but too definite'. He added that words are 'so ambiguous, so vague, so capable of misinterpretation in comparison with real music . . .'[1]

Of course, composers have tried to be more prescriptive and specific, but to no avail. For example, composers as contrasted as Elgar and Webern both crammed their scores with directions, but it is doubtful whether the resulting performances are better for it, or even 'truer to the score' in any meaningful sense. On the one hand, the markings are too dense, which can lead to nuances becoming fussy and exaggerated, or can induce a stiff adherence to instructions, without the understanding that would make the markings organically part of the music. On the other hand, if these composers were really hoping to define a performance, then even their copious markings are quite insufficient. For instance, every time string players draw the bow across the string, they are making choices (often unconsciously, instinctively or carelessly) as to the speed of bow used (constantly varying), the position and angle of the bow (how near the bridge it is, and how much bow-hair is used) and the bow pressure (also subject to variation through time). These factors all affect the dynamic and tone-quality of the sound at any one moment, and the shaping or phrasing of the line as it develops. Simultaneously a multitude of 'choices' are made for the left hand through the speed and amplitude of vibrato and the selection of fingerings, including the placement of glissandi, harmonics, open strings etc. These choices, which are the corollary of the broad gaps in notation referred to earlier, are neither purely technical nor purely interpretative but lie at the intersection between the two – the point of integration where a musical intention becomes realised physically.

Furthermore, the interpreter's choice of every detail must relate to his conception of the meaning or character of the whole work as its structure unfolds. There is a constant two-way interaction between detailed nuances and whole structures in building an interpretation. The overview is not necessarily built from the details, but rather the details are derived from the overview, just as an architect's plan determines where the walls should go; and bricks cannot be placed intelligently in ignorance of his plan. On the other hand, the overall plan may be modified or even invalidated by stubborn details at ground level.

This image also suggests a basic flaw in the (apparently sensible) procedure of some interpreters and teachers who prepare a piece by first sorting out detailed technical problems, and then pasting on an interpretation. It should be clear that this dichotomy is false. If every choice of fingering and bowing – in fact, every sound drawn from the strings – has an interpretative significance, there can be no neutral learning of notes as a prior stage to interpretation, without 'practising in' features of a performance which may be senseless from an interpretative point of view.

Given the inevitable latitude left by notation, it is possible for a performance to diverge considerably from the spirit of a composition, without ostensibly contradicting anything in the printed text. A performer's 'instinct', however powerful, is almost certainly not enough even to *suggest* answers to every interpretative problem. Moreover, those answers that instinct does suggest cannot always be trusted, because instinct is all too easily distorted by the peculiarities and passing fashions of one's musical environment and upbringing. Consequently, it is important for a performer not to rely on instinct alone, but to reinforce his interpretations with evidence from analysis (harmonic, motivic etc.) of the score, together with a historical understanding of its meaning, and an informed empathy with the poetic imagination of the composer. This sets some boundaries within which any interpretation needs to be placed, but it gives the performance a genuine authority and conviction; furthermore, within the limits of those boundaries, an infinite variety of approach is possible. It is notable that recordings by composers performing their own works (e.g. Shostakovich, Britten, and Stravinsky) demonstrate that their own performances varied greatly over time. However, they never strayed from the discipline imposed by their sense of the fundamental nature and structure of their compositions. When this discipline is fully understood and deeply absorbed, spontaneity, far from being constrained, is immeasurably enhanced.

Collective interpretation – unity and diversity

For an individual, the problems of interpretation are challenging enough, but for a quartet grappling with some of the most profound, intimate, and heartfelt compositions in the music literature, the communal nature of the decision-making is often even more testing than the decisions themselves.

There are, no doubt, as many approaches to collective decision-making as there are string quartets. The simplest approach is for one dominant personality (often the first violinist) to take, or to be given, the role of interpreter as if he were the all-powerful conductor of an orchestra. Through both his dominance in rehearsal and his playing, he controls, as much as possible, every aspect of the group's performance. This deals with the problem of integrating four conceptions of a work by reducing them to the one conception of the 'leader'. A solo pianist playing a Beethoven piano sonata experiences the power (and the corresponding loneliness) of single-handedly (or rather, single-mindedly) playing all of the several voices or roles characteristically co-existing in the music. Similarly, the dominant quartet leader tries to be fully in charge of the whole performance, with the six other hands, as it were, all extensions of himself.

This image raises a fundamental question about the nature of string quartets and chamber music in general. Is such music *essentially* for shared, communal performance with dialogue and interaction between deliberately distinct individuals? Or is it only an accident of instrumental limitations that more than one performer is involved? In other words, imagine that one person could miraculously play all four string instruments simultaneously – would that eliminate something vital from a Beethoven quartet performance? If it would, then would it be preferable for a Beethoven piano sonata to be played by four different pianists, each playing one voice like a 'piano quartet' in a new eccentric sense of a quartet of four pianists? If not, then is it the case that whenever Beethoven wrote for string sonorities, he always conceived the music as an interaction between distinct individual players, whereas for piano sonorities he always limited himself to music requiring a single interpreter? What, then, are we to make of his own arrangements of the E major Piano Sonata Op. 14 no. 1 for string quartet, and the C minor Piano Trio for string quintet?

The most natural answer to these questions is that both piano sonatas and string quartets demand from their performers a capacity for both unity *and* diversity. The overall conception of the architecture, character and dramatic progress of the piece, as well as many specific textures such as chorale, cadential chords, and most rhythmic unisons, need unity. However, the voices of different characters, which often appear simultaneously, need diversity whether they are in dialogue or competing for our attention. Consequently, pianists (whilst not having to confront the challenges of collective decision-making) need to learn to divide themselves, both technically and emotionally, sometimes into four or five diverse voices; whereas quartets, with their natural capacity for diversity, need to strive for unity.[2]

Historically speaking, there has been a trend in the latter part of the last century against leader-dominated quartets, which possibly has sociological or political roots rather than musical ones. The leader concept was so strong in Joachim's time that that great musician-violinist (admired for his integrity and instinctive intelligence by Brahms, Schumann, Mendelssohn and virtually every serious musician of his time) often happily played quartet concerts in different parts of the world with an *ad hoc* group of three 'supporting' local players. The first two-thirds of the twentieth century witnessed several quartets dominated by gargantuan personalities such as Végh, Dubinsky and Kolisch, but today this is most exceptional. The rejection of dictatorial, controlling personalities in small groups is no doubt a result of liberal emancipations throughout society; and even if it were musically desirable, it is hard to imagine today three highly trained and skilled musicians being able to tolerate absolute power in a 'leader' through their long years of existence. The remainder of this discussion will therefore rest on the assumption that quartets are not one-person dictatorships and consequently need to find a more complex route to collective decisions.[3]

Second movement: rehearsing

The 'quartet-personality' and individual criticism

In a quartet without a dictator, everyone's voice will be heard. While this can cause confusion, exhaustion and fury, it is also stimulating and enlightening to have the benefit of four viewpoints. This is not only because they come from four different people, but also because each person has a particular angle of vision derived from the perspective of his own role in the quartet.

A good quartet player, of course, needs to be a fine musician and instrumentalist but he also needs a personality suited to being in a small group. He needs to be able to balance assertiveness and flexibility; to speak clearly and strongly whilst at the same time listening carefully and with sympathetic understanding. This applies equally to playing and rehearsing. If the player is insufficiently sensitive to his colleagues, his lack of awareness will make him unresponsive in performance and uncomprehending in rehearsal. If, on the other hand, he is very sensitive but insufficiently assertive and confident, his colleagues will have nothing to 'bounce off' in performance and will not benefit from his views in rehearsal. This balance of qualities develops with experience until, for example, in performance, the player can play with full commitment and intensity, yet remain aware of every nuance of all his partners.

Another vital part of a quartet player's constitution must be an ability to give and to take criticism gracefully. This requires a self-confident and secure ego with no need to prove itself or to be unduly bolstered, or delicately handled, by the others. It also involves a willingness to look dispassionately at oneself – hopefully with humour and tolerance. All this is necessary because quartet rehearsals do not stop at collective suggestions or interpretative discussions, but inevitably include individual criticisms between player and player with the others sometimes piling in, too. These criticisms may range from tiny instrumental details to the overall interpretation of a solo passage. Since quartet players have each devoted decades of their lives to their training and development, and usually love intensely the pieces they perform, they feel very strongly about how those pieces should sound. Consequently, it might be tempting to fudge and avoid all potentially 'dangerous' individual criticisms, with the result that they are repressed or made mealy-mouthed. If this happens, not only do standards become mediocre, but subterranean resentments simmer. Conversely, there is an obvious danger that individual criticisms can become destructively hurtful, personal and bitter. If criticisms are voiced too harshly and personally, no-one ends up in a fit state to play. Virtually all playing requires complete physical ease and relaxation, even (or especially) in music of great intensity and ardour, and in music which is rapturous, celebratory and joyous. Hence, suggestions or criticisms barked at someone with an anger bordering on hatred are likely to be counter-productive, and are preferably avoided if at all possible (not always easy!).

This suggests an important duality of function in the voicing of criticism. On the one hand, it is an attempt to change or improve something in the quartet's performance; on the other, it is a letting off of steam. (The two functions may easily conflict, though not necessarily so. Sometimes an angry outpouring can have a salutary effect on the player at the receiving end.) Naturally, if a criticism is mainly a letting off of steam *and* likely to have a negative effect, it is best for it not to be voiced immediately before a concert, or when a player is already feeling attacked and vulnerable, is ill, or is having a crisis in his personal life.

Most criticism, however, should be aimed at improving something – though whether it succeeds is another matter. Quartet players have to learn to monitor the effectiveness of what they say. They will notice what language and what approach their colleagues respond to. For instance, some players like a very precise, clear, analytical criticism of what is wrong, for example, 'you are stressing the barline too much because your vibrato is much faster on that note than on the others'. Other players get tied up in knots by detailed suggestions about bow-distribution, phrase-stresses, exact rubatos etc. and prefer an image or metaphor, a gesture, a facial expression, a demonstration, or any other oblique guide which leaves it to them how exactly to realise the idea, for example, 'it sounds too hot', 'it's lumpy', 'it should be a gently lapping sea', even 'this sounds unconvincing to me'. A good critic must expand his repertoire of criticism to embrace all these possibilities; and a good receiver of criticism must try to understand any language in which the criticism is couched.

Communal rehearsing and problem-solving

Individual criticism is one element of rehearsal, but quartets also have to deal with many issues communally, and they must try to resolve problems without reaching a position of deadlocked disagreement.[4]

As a prelude to discussing how quartets resolve disagreements, I shall make three general points. First, trying out everyone's suggestions is a fun-damental rule of good rehearsing, and not only trying them out, but doing so to the satisfaction of the person making the suggestion. This rules out both 'going-through-the-motions-of-trying-out-but-with-bad-grace', and trying out without really understanding the suggestion. Very often, af-ter a series of attempts to try someone's idea, the idea gets so modified,

or the understanding of the idea is so modified, that what was initially scep-
tically received becomes enthusiastically adopted. If substantive discussion
happens before any trying out, then there can be a lot of arguing at cross-
purposes and entrenching of positions, either because the idea is not fully
formed or clearly expressed, or because it is misunderstood.[5]

The second general point is that when players disagree about a passage,
there is a broad distinction that can be made between whether they are
aiming at a different goal and need to settle what the goal should be; or
whether they are aiming at the same goal, but are hearing differently when
they play because they are not equally attentive. Rhythmic, intonation and
ensemble irregularities, as well as unintended differences of phrasing, colour
and character, can easily occur without everyone being aware of them, and
it is often enough to direct someone's attention to some unnoticed detail
for the fault to be acknowledged and corrected. Disagreements when the
goals themselves are different are clearly more intractable.

The third general point to note is that in many disagreements there is
a danger of 'pendulum rehearsing'. For instance, if the tempo of a piece is
at issue, the group may swing back and forth between playing it faster and
more slowly without everyone (or anyone) being wholly convinced by *any*
of the tempi. A way must be found through such dilemmas by finding a
new dimension of possibilities – relocating the problem in a new context
where it may dissolve. In other words, the problem needs to be redefined
in a way that a solution becomes possible and a synthesis found between
the apparent opposites – one which is acknowledged to be a genuinely
positive synthesis with which everyone is happy, rather than a 'compromise'
which disgruntles everyone. In the happiest examples, the synthesis leads
to a solution universally agreed to be better than either of the originally
promoted versions.[6]

Balance or voicing

In the accepted canon of great string quartets until the middle of the twentieth century, the normal or basic texture involves some hierarchy of voicing.
The roles within this hierarchy are constantly being redistributed between
the players. According to the widely used, over-simplistic schema, there is
characteristically a primary voice, often a subsidiary voice or two, and often
a voice or two of accompaniment – rhythmic ostinato or harmonic filling,
for instance. A quartet player must recognise his role in the texture at each
moment.

The primary voice is simply the one that draws the ear most readily to
itself, usually because it carries the most compelling motivic or melodic
material.[7] A subsidiary voice may also carry melodic or motivic material
and it sometimes has its own character and phrasing. The accompanying

voices are often more in the background, and in terms of phrasing they usually mirror one of the other voices.

Primary voice

The above schema is, of course, rough and ready, and often fails to apply to the more complex reality of actual pieces.

(a) For instance, two primary voices may overlap rather than hand over the baton. In Berg's *Lyric Suite*, for example, where the voicing is explicitly indicated in the score, there are often overlapping '*Hauptstimmen*'.

(b) Where there are successive canonic entries, sometimes the ear should stay with the first entry and the next entries are better presented as subsidiary voices; sometimes it is better to draw the ear to each entry in turn; but sometimes each voice of the canon is equally and simultaneously important, and then it becomes artificial to nominate a primary voice.

(c) Turning from canons to textures where two simultaneous voices are very distinct, there is again often no point in designating one of the voices as primary. Both can be heard clearly, as in the opening of the main section of Beethoven's *Grosse Fuge* where the angular, leaping, dotted rhythm of the initial figure contrasts sharply with the basic motif of the movement – which is also distinctly lower in register.

(d) Variations also present complexities of voicing. Frequently, the theme, having been stated as a clear primary voice at the outset in the highest register, is then repeated in a lower register whilst an interesting decorative filigree is played above it. For example, in the Andante of Haydn's Op. 77 no. 2, should the cello, which has the melody, be heard as the main voice, or should the ear be directed more to the violin decoration (Ex. 5.1)? Again, this question shows the limitations of the concept of a primary voice, because neither the cello nor the first violin line needs to be dominant. What is important in such a variation is that each voice should clearly fulfil its own distinctive role. The cello should play melodically, enjoying the contrast between his open, easy A-string sonority and the sonority of the same melody as it is heard at the opening of the movement on the warm and intimate lower strings of the first violin. The viola provides the bass, which needs to be rhythmically steady and clearly phrased around the structural harmonies of the theme. The second violin makes little comments and interjections, and the first violin (whilst always playing with awareness of the melody he is decorating) should play with fantasy, rhythmic freedom and spontaneity, and certainly not take a back-seat role. This variation would be pointless without the violin decoration; the listener hears the decoration in an inseparable relationship with the repeated theme. Moreover, at the end of the variation, the music is propelled forward by developing not the theme, but rather the decorative line of the first violin.

Example 5.1 Haydn: Quartet in F major Op. 77 no. 2, iii, bb. 74–81

Once the players agree on their roles in this variation, the question of choosing a 'primary voice' is dissolved rather than solved, and all the clearly differentiated voices become audible.

In this example the reiterated theme has added importance in the texture, because the movement is not a set of variations but a hybrid between variations and sonata form, and so the return of each version of the theme has more significance than in 'normal' variation form. Similarly, although the slow movement of Beethoven's Op. 127 is a genuine set of variations, the theme is so disguised and altered that its reappearance in almost its original form feels like a recapitulation, so (as in the Haydn) the 'recapitulated' (or easily recognisable) theme has particular significance in the texture, and is not overshadowed by its violin decoration. By contrast, in Schubert's 'Death and the Maiden' variations (D. 810), we never lose sight of the theme, so by the time we reach the violin decoration in variation 4, the violin attracts by far the greatest attention.

To summarise, where there are two possible candidates for primary voice, they tend to be either of very distinct character and therefore easy to keep clearly separate and audible, or part of a passage whose densely woven texture is its main feature.[8]

Subsidiary voice

The subsidiary voice must not dominate the texture, but must be phrased and characterised convincingly and sometimes differently from the main voice. A voice may feel subsidiary despite its motivic nature if it is in a lower register, or more fragmented, than the main voice, if its entry starts later, or simply if it has less distinctiveness.

Accompaniment

Accompanying is an art in itself. Whilst never overshadowing the main lines, the accompaniment needs sometimes to support and join in fully, and sometimes to remain po-faced and unmoved by the surrounding emotions. There are also occasions when what is clearly an accompanying line makes the largest contribution to the mood, perhaps by being out of character with the melodic or motivic material it is accompanying, as in the cello drum-beat accompaniment in the fifth variation in the slow movement of Mozart's K. 464 in A major. Similarly, a subtle change in an accompaniment may radically alter the character of the primary material it is accompanying. For example, in the finale of Britten's Third Quartet, a simple change from *marcato* to *legato* in the cello's passacaglia line transforms the overall mood quite magically.

Probably the most subtle problems in relation to accompaniment concern rhythm (see pp. 113–15).

Quartet players clearly need the ability to switch roles with ease, one moment taking on the main voice with all the freedom and energy that it might demand, the next moment supporting, or accompanying discreetly or otherwise. As for disagreements about voicing, these tend to be more often about how to achieve the agreed objectives than what those objectives should be. Hearing what the voicing *actually* sounds like (whatever the intentions of the group) is a skill that has to be developed, and it is naturally very useful for one of the players to listen to the others from a considerable distance – especially in a concert hall. Improving the balance is often not simply a matter of playing louder or softer; this can lead to unsatisfactory pendulum rehearsing until more subtle solutions are found. The primary voice may capture the attention better if it is more aptly phrased or characterised; the other voices may need to sustain their longer notes less, attack them more gently, release the sound more quickly, or vibrate less, none of which is the same as playing more softly. In classic quartet textures, clarifying the voicing leads to everyone being heard clearly. It is not a question merely of highlighting the main voice with the others lumped together inaudibly in the background.

Sometimes, of course, unsatisfactory balance does have to be remedied simply by adjusting the relative dynamics within the group. With few exceptions, it was not until the late nineteenth century that some composers tried to balance ensembles and orchestras by differentiating dynamic markings for the ensemble in the score. More usually, balancing is left to the players, and the dynamics refer to the overall, collective level of the group. When the players' individual parts are copied out of the score, the dynamics are transferred to each part, and this can mislead. Sometimes, an individual needs to play *mf* in a *ff* passage so as not to overwhelm the main voice which might be in a much muddier register or heavily outnumbered. Similarly, an individual may need to play at least *mp* in a *pp* passage if he is the main voice in danger of drowning in a thick and complex texture. Since dynamic markings are as much character markings as indicators of decibel levels, it is possible to fulfil the expression required whilst balancing clearly.

Blend

The concept of blend relates to the totality of the sonority of the players. Earlier, I compared a quartet with a solo pianist and concluded that to respond to the demands of the music, pianists need to cultivate diversity, and quartets, unity. In the playing of some groups, the striving towards unity has gone so far that one is aware of a strong tendency to submerge individuality of sound into one (often very rich) collective sonority; in others, the players keep their individual identities more separate. This individuality is by no means simply a matter of sonority, but sonority is certainly an important factor.

Provided that it has not submerged the individuality of its members, a quartet is naturally suited to musical textures in which the voices are deliberately separated. In such cases, each of the voices may have its own role as if the players were four characters on an operatic stage singing simultaneously in their different ways – perhaps a love duet at one side of the

Example 5.2 Mozart: Quartet in B♭ major K. 458, iv, bb. 291–300

stage, the enraged, thwarted father at the other end, and a comic figure in-
terjecting comments in the middle. The delightful passage forty-four bars
before the end of Mozart's K. 458 ('The Hunt') is a good example of such
separation of voices (Ex. 5.2). At the other textural extreme is writing in
unison, chorale writing (such as can be found in the slow movements of
Beethoven's Op. 132 and Schubert's 'Death and the Maiden' D. 810), and
most cadential and opening chords (Ex. 5.3). Even where the characters are
strongly individualised, there are ways of executing this which make a satisfying whole – blending the disparate – and ways that do not. This blending
and balancing of colours is similar to painting; not all colours combine
harmoniously.

It is vital that each player should stick to his own role and not assume
someone else's. For instance, if one player's part consists of a bland, inexpres-
sive, rhythmic drumbeat, he must not be tempted to make it over-expressive,
perhaps in compensation for his feeling that the main voices are not expressive enough. Equally, he may be inspired to join in an *espressivo*, so as

Example 5.3 Schubert: Quartet in D minor D. 810 ('Death and the Maiden'), ii, bb. 1–8

Example 5.4 Schubert: Quartet in A minor D. 804, ii, bb. 53–7

to turn his spear-carrying role into a co-starring one. An example may be found in the slow movement of Schubert's 'Rosamunde' Quartet (D. 804). Here, at the second occurrence of the main theme, the viola's essentially rhythmic role must maintain its relentless insistence, and forgo the freedom and delicacy of the first violin (Ex. 5.4).[9]

Example 5.5 Mozart: Quartet in E♭ major K. 428, i, bb. 1–4

Quartet intonation

The first thing to say about excellent quartet intonation is that it is founded on the excellent intonation of the four individual players. There can be no weak links in terms of individual abilities, because they cannot be hidden. Even if we assume, however, consistent and impeccable individual intonation, it does not follow that the quartet's intonation will be faultless. Although a necessary condition, the individuals' excellence is by no means sufficient.

There are many reasons for this. The most fundamental is that string intonation is more expressive and sensitive than equal-tempered piano intonation. This expressive advantage enjoyed by the strings comes at a price: different degrees of stretching or bending of notes are possible. So, even in a unison (where no 'vertical' or harmonic complications arise) quartet players must learn to unify what might be their different, but equally valid, systems of intonation. For example, in the opening of Mozart's Quartet in E♭ K. 428, the unison phrase has five semitone intervals which will not necessarily be exactly the same distance apart. For instance, the B is likely to be felt to be close to the C which follows it – but to what degree (Ex. 5.5)? When harmony is added, contradictory pulls arise between the vertical and horizontal requirements of a note, especially notes on the third, sixth and seventh degrees of the scale. Whereas one may often wish to push up the major third for melodic reasons, for vertical reasons it often needs to be kept low. The leading note in a melody will almost certainly beg to be sharpened; if it makes a major seventh with the bass it may often be very sharp indeed, but when the bass is playing the dominant, the leading note (a major third above the dominant) will not tolerate as much stretching – even less so if the chord includes a seventh.

The best balance between the vertical and horizontal needs of the music is a matter of fine judgement, which has to be communal and requires constant awareness of one's role in the harmony. General rules such as always tuning to the bass, or always tuning to the principal voice, tend to be insufficiently flexible, unduly favouring the harmonic or melodic dimension.

Quartets often face the danger of becoming obsessive about intonation and being paralysed by its problems, but there *are* benign ways of improving it. One idea is to practise unison scales slowly and carefully with a clear, focused sonority and no vibrato. The intonation can rest on, or adjust to, one nominated member of the group, each taking his turn. This highlights differences in the melodic urge between the different players, as does slow, careful practice of unison passages selected from the repertoire, for example, the unison bars, already mentioned, at the opening of Mozart's K. 428.

Another useful exercise is to practise basic cadences in different keys: chord sequences such as IV, V, I, distributing the voices variously; or to work at examples of problematic cadences from the literature. Such practising trains the quartet to be aware of the vertical harmonic pull and how to play chords in tune.

Naturally, it is also useful to play slowly any passages from the literature which are troublesome. It is often better not to stop and correct every note but to keep going, slowly registering what is wrong, and allowing it to improve gradually. If there is too much stopping and criticising, no clear pitch gets established and the intonation does not settle. However, sometimes a note or a bar may require a special, very slow examination if it is not improving and if the problem is hard to diagnose.

It is important that in slow practice the players should not play mechanically or unmusically, but rather that the slow playing should be a slow-motion version of the up-to-speed playing, so that the tone-colours, phrasing and other interpretative features are retained as much as possible in the slow version. This is for two reasons. One is that if, when practising slowly, the group learns to play accurately only when it is being mechanical and too uninvolved, it could easily lose that accuracy, not because of the speeding up, but because the players have not learned to be accurate whilst making music with commitment. A second reason is the supremely important fact that whether the intonation sounds convincing or not depends not only upon where exactly the finger of the left hand is placed but also on many contextual factors such as tone-colour, vibrato, balance, blend, tempo and acoustic.

This gives a tool for understanding and solving those intonation problems which may be causing bewildering pendulum rehearsing. It may often happen that a chord sounds out of tune, but no-one can quite diagnose why. The apparently offending note in the chord is raised and lowered by moving the finger up and down, but neither move satisfies anyone and a fruitless to-and-fro may ensue. In all probabilities, the diagnosis is wrong;

tuning needs to be improved not in the left hand but in the right hand. I have already remarked that quartet players need to make blending colours. Sometimes they may need to make the same colour, and sometimes contrasting colours are required, but they must be the *right* contrasts. In passages where players should make similar sonorities the intonation will never sound right if someone is playing with the bow near the bridge and someone else on the fingerboard; if someone is near the bridge and pressing and another player is near the bridge but just using bow-weight; or if someone is using a very contained bow-stroke (slow-moving and only using part of the bow-span) and someone else spending the bow freely. Similarly, if one player is vibrating widely, and another is vibrating narrowly, or not at all, or at a very different speed, the intonation will be affected as it will be also by incompatible choices of fingerings and string-colour. In passages where the players' colours may need to differ – for example, where the main voice but not the bass should use vibrato – then the fingers may need to be placed slightly differently from where they would be if both players were playing *senza vibrato*.

A closely related factor is the balance within a chord. Within the same colour one can play a little more or less, and often intonation can be improved by altering the balance. For instance, the third of the chord in the inner parts should rarely be stronger than the bass. This gives the impression of the third being too high. So instead of adjusting the placement of the left hand (which may make it sound too flat, however slightly it is done), a softening of the third in the balance may be necessary. On other occasions the bass may need to be stronger. Sometimes, one of the middle parts may need to be stronger to bridge the gap between the treble of the first violin's E string and the inevitably less focused bass notes of the cello C string (as well as the cellist focusing his sound and the violinist softening his sound as much as possible). Other intonation problems may be resolved through the realisation that the stretching of expressive notes at one tempo might not work at another. This may be a hazard of slow practice. At speed, intervals can register differently; for example, the faster a whole-tone trill is, the wider it may need to be.

In addition to illustrating how pendulum rehearsing can give way to satisfying resolutions of problems, the field of intonation also gives an excellent example of the necessity for a quartet player to be able to balance flexibility and assertiveness with a sure judgement. If he adjusts his own note every time he hears something awry, it is just as unhelpful as if he never adjusts his own note and assumes it is someone else who is 'wrong'.

Another issue is the tuning of the instruments. To begin with, what pitch should be taken for the A? Naturally, this needs to be agreed. Cellists, and sometimes violists, need to resist the temptation to push the pitch up to make their instruments clearer and easier to articulate; violinists sometimes may be tempted to push the pitch down if they feel that their instruments sound too shrill and insufficiently warm. The best way is to agree on a tuning fork pitch preferably at a′ = 440.[10]

Because of the gap in sonority and pitch between the top of the violins and the bottom of the cello, cellists (and often violists) tend to tune their fifths down from the A narrowly, particularly making the C string as sharp as is tolerable. Sometimes the gap between D and G is very narrow as well. The violins may similarly tune the E as low as possible. It is not usually advisable for each instrument to take the A from the tuning fork, as the pitch of the fork (because of its unique sonority) is harder to match than the pitch of another string; traditionally, therefore, the quartet takes the A from one player, who takes it from the fork. However, again because of sonorities, it may be better for the player to give his D, because D is a central string on each of the instruments and not on the outside of the instrument, where the sonority may be more idiosyncratic.

Ensembles have to learn how to tune up, especially in concerts. They should be pragmatic about what works best for them – whether to tune quietly at the same time or one at a time, how much adjusting to do between movements, how to tune backstage etc. However, a most important ability is to play in tune when the strings are out of tune, because there will be plenty of occasions when they will be – notably where the temperature on the platform is very different from the temperature backstage, where there has been a string-break, or where the instruments are not acclimatised or settled, after a long journey.

Rhythm and ensemble

One of the most crucial issues relating to accompaniment concerns rhythm. When accompanying, one needs to judge convincingly how far to accommodate the free rubato of the principal voice. Pendulum rehearsing is a danger here. If the principal voice and an accompanying ostinato are played with 'perfect' ensemble – completely together at every instant – then playing the principal voice freely will make the ostinato sound like a limping or sea-sick traveller, whereas playing strictly metronomically will make the main voice sound as if in a straitjacket, with no space in which to move or to breathe.

The solution is for the two lines *not* to play absolutely together but to meet only at certain vital points in the phrase. Even if the ostinato is played with almost metronomical rhythm, the main voice can nevertheless be very free within the bar or phrase. For example, in the middle section of the slow movement of Haydn's Quartet Op. 64 no. 6, the first violin's stormy, rhapsodical outburst requires great rhythmic freedom and a sense of improvisation, whereas the semiquaver ostinato of the three lower strings

Example 5.6 Haydn: Quartet in E♭ major Op. 64 no. 6, ii, bb. 32–40

must be disciplined and severe. The first violin needs to coincide with the ostinato only at stronger beats or harmony changes (Ex. 5.6). In fact, the more the accompaniment is stable, the more the main voice is likely to feel free. Sometimes, it may be a secondary voice which is free, such as the frolicking of the first violin in the first movement of Schubert's 'Death and the Maiden' D.810 (bb. 102ff.). This sort of freedom within disciplined boundaries, called 'rubato in tempo', was clearly being referred to in Mozart's letter from Augsburg to his father Leopold: 'Everyone is amazed that I always keep strict time. What these people cannot grasp is that in tempo rubato in an Adagio, the left hand should go on playing in strict time. With them the left hand always follows suit'[11] – a perfect description of the cello's role in rubato in tempo. Or nearly perfect! In practice, the 'metronomical' playing of the accompanying ostinato often sounds unsatisfactory if it is absolutely mechanical. Instead, it should give the *impression* or *illusion* of being metronomical. Tiny adjustments may be necessary to make this sort of passage work, but any such accommodation should be so discreet as to be unnoticed by the listener.

These tiny adjustments may be necessary in an ostinato even where it is accompanying a main voice which is apparently being played virtually strictly in time. The accompanist needs to judge where, and where not, to accommodate the minute deviations from the pulse which may happen with, say, a strong *sforzando*, a huge leap in pitch, or a significant harmony, as in the opening of Beethoven's Op. 18 no. 4 in C minor, where the cello ostinato may need to accommodate discreetly the first violin's *sforzandi*. The cellist cannot just switch on his inner metronome at the beginning and play on regardless, but must remain constantly alert. Too much accommodation is unsettling, but none whatsoever will probably be equally unsatisfactory. Another example of the imperceptible flexibility required of an ostinato accompaniment is to be found in the viola's demisemiquaver accompaniment to the melody in the recapitulation of the slow movement of Beethoven's Op. 59 no. 1 (Ex. 5.7). Compare the opening of Beethoven's Op. 18 no. 6, where the middle voices should not deviate at all. The clockwork energy is part of the intention here, which the quartet players may infer from the sharing of the ostinato between two instruments, its sheer speed, and its relative lack of harmonic subtlety or development.

Notwithstanding the necessary freedom of tempo rubato, quartet players must nevertheless be able to play together perfectly if they want to, and this often requires rehearsal. Some persistent ensemble problems (which may, if misunderstood, lead to pendulum rehearsing) are symptomatic of unacknowledged disagreements about phrasing and characterisation. Once these are resolved, the ensemble corrects itself.

Quartet-players often need to give compact and clear 'leads' or visual indications to each other, for instance, at the start of a piece, or after an unmeasured rest. Leads may need to indicate the beginning of the note, and also, very often, the tempo which is to follow. They may also help the ensemble during accelerandi and ritardandi and at changes of tempo, which in twentieth-century music may be very frequent. Leads should not

Example 5.7 Beethoven: Quartet in F major Op. 59 no. 1, iii, bb. 84–8

interfere with the playing of whoever is leading, and they should also be in the character of the music to be played. A dreamy Adagio should not be led with a short, sharp breath or the preparatory beats of a band-master; conversely, a tense Allegro should not be led with a limp, vague upbeat.

Whenever a lead is necessary, it should be decided who should give it. Often it should be the player of the main voice, because he, above all, needs to be absolutely confident about the tempo and attack (for example, in the opening of Beethoven's Op. 59 no. 1, the cello should lead despite having the slower-moving notes) (Ex. 5.8). However, sometimes it works best for an accompanying ostinato to lead (especially if it is shared by two or three players), if, for instance, the main voice glides in with an anacrusis starting with a very still up-bow. An example occurs in the sixth of Haydn's Seven Last Words (b. 14), where it may be preferable for the second rather than the first violin to lead. Sometimes if two players are in rhythmic unison it can help if, as far as possible, they lead together as well as play together, as at the start of Haydn's Op. 54 no. 3.

Example 5.8 Beethoven: Quartet in F major Op. 59 no. 1, i, bb. 1–4

Example 5.9 Beethoven: Quartet in C major Op. 59 no. 3, iv, bb. 108–12

Leading in twentieth-century music is often particularly vital because of the aural complexity of the music and the constant fluidity of tempo; moreover, different time-signatures and spacing of barlines may co-exist in different parts, which, nevertheless, may be required to be played with accurate ensemble.

Chords in rhythmic unison may need special attention, particularly at a piece's openings and endings. Problems can be caused by the different spreading of four-part chords in individual parts. Will the spread be before or on the beat? As a rule, if anyone is heard first he will capture the ear and become primary. This may be desirable if his is the primary voice; and sometimes a spread from the bass works, too, if the harmony is very important; but if the spread is in the middle of the chord, it usually sounds unsatisfactory.

Another difficulty for ensemble lies in the accurate timing of notes which follow tied notes and rests, for instance throughout the finale of Beethoven's Op. 59 no. 3, where the problem lies in the timing of the first of the quavers to follow the first note of the fugal theme, especially in those instances when it is accompanied by quavers or in canon (Ex. 5.9). The danger is usually that the note after the tie or rest starts too late and the subsequent notes are hurried.[12] Sometimes, it may be a natural rubato slightly to extend long notes and bunch the following shorter ones (which may work even against an ostinato). However, it is often just an unintentional rhythmic fault.

Fast passages in rhythmic unison can be quite easy to play together (for example, the end of Beethoven's Op. 59 no. 3) but can sometimes be very difficult, as in the finale of Bartók's Fifth Quartet (bb. 440ff.). This passage is so complex that it is hard to know how to correct it if it begins to wobble in its rhythm, which it all too easily can. Such a passage may require some ongoing visual leading until the players get used to it. This shows that even amongst an experienced group of players, a communal pulse breaks down very quickly unless it is based on constant auditory confirmation. That is to say, playing the passage from Bartók's Fifth Quartet is not just a matter of playing one's own part exactly in time, hoping to come out together with the others in the end.[13]

Finally, when trying to improve ensemble-playing, there is often a danger of stressing increasingly frequent small beats, and emphasising those beats, or the bar-lines, with monotonous regularity. This is even more pointless than practising intonation mechanically, and often leads to difficult passages sounding like 'passagework' rather than music.

Tempo

Tempo is one of the prime battlefields in rehearsal, as it is so interlinked with the music's character and mood. As remarked earlier, pendulum rehearsing is more than likely here. There are various ways of trying to break down the simple dichotomy of 'slower' or 'faster'. Whether a passage feels fast or slow is dependent not only on the metronome speed but on many other factors, and these other factors need examination when changing the speed is not helping.

Whether the group is thinking in large or small beats is one vital corollary to the speed. Sometimes it can be helpful to think in beats each lasting a bar or even two bars. Conversely, some passages benefit if the players think in much smaller beats. A frequently fluctuating 'pulse' within the same tempo is an important compositional device and players need to feel these variations collectively. Too small (or frequent) a beat leads to playing that sounds laboured or sluggish; too large a beat has the opposite effect. The freedom of rubato within a tempo is another vital factor to the feel of that tempo. Sometimes a phrase may sound 'arthritic', not because it is too slow, but because it needs a more fluid rubato within the tempo. The texture can also be important. A hurried feel may be relaxed by making the texture clearer. The acoustic is relevant, too; a 'bathroom' acoustic needs a slower tempo than a very dry acoustic. Sometimes, the tempo seems too fast only because the playing is unjustifiably breathless or hurried (perhaps because long notes and rests are being clipped), and passages which are intensifying are rushing rather than feeling the friction of growing intensity within a fixed tempo. Sometimes, a tempo seems too slow or too fast simply because the music is not characterised or phrased enough; again, the basic tempo may not be to blame. It can help to practise at a slowish tempo, concentrating on making the music flow and the lines as long as possible; and then playing the same passage at a maximum tempo, concentrating on making the music breathe and relax without hurrying. The clarity of motivic details is a limiting factor on how quick a tempo can be, and the clarity of the structure of the phrase (and possibly the whole movement) is a limiting factor on slow tempi.

Tempo, then, is not a starting point. It is a culmination, or function, of all these other details of phrase-length, articulation, rubato, colour, texture, rhythm, and, above all, the overall mood; and there needs to be a fitting marriage of all these features.

Finally, a group must decide how much variation in tempo there should be within a movement. Composers such as Janáček, Berg and Bartók explicitly ask for frequent tempo changes; but in music of the Classical era, in which changes of tempo are rarely marked within the main body of the movement, how much variation of speed should there be? The tempo can be one important unifying factor in a Classical movement and, arguably, it should not fluctuate widely. But there may be subtle sides to the tempo; one may play slightly to the back of it or slightly looking forward, like a tempo rubato, but spread over the length of the whole movement. Schubert, with huge differences of character within movements such as the first of D. 887 in G, tempts performers towards very different tempi within the movement, but many think that unity is easily destroyed by giving in to these temptations. Clearly, such issues need to be communally resolved.

Articulation

What sort of attack or beginning should a note have? How long should it be held? What should happen during the life of the note? Should the sound be released or grow, or a combination of both? Each passage in music poses these questions, and provides its own various answers.

These questions of articulation are rarely settled through reference to the score, because in Classical repertoire, and often in that of the nineteenth century and beyond, it was quite normal for notes not to be held for their full written length. Also, in the Classical era, it was often taken for granted that the sound of a long note would be released (as well as the note shortened) unless some special intensity was required. How much, and in what way, to do this (and where the exceptions are) are matters for the players to determine.

There are very few occasions where a long note should be held absolutely evenly with no growth or release. Very legato, joined-up, and evenly sustained notes are generally inappropriate to the Classical and pre-Classical eras, and to any music with folk roots or roots in dance or speech (*parlando*). For example, in the opening theme of Haydn's Op. 76 no. 1 in G, the slurs in the first bar should breathe and the crotchets in the third bar should dance, and not be 'glued together'. In the opening of Mozart's K. 387 in G, the accompanying crotchets should be *marcato* in contrast to the first violin's legato, thus clarifying the texture and enlivening the character.

Problems about how a note should end are frequently resolved by finding the right gesture for the *beginning* of the note. The start of a note is often the seed which determines the eventual shape of that note.

Phrasing

Classical articulation does not mean that phrases need to be broken into small segments of equal value. Players can shape phrases into long lines even if they are releasing (diminishing) on each note and separating notes, as any fine pianist can demonstrate. By varying the degrees of attack and release, notes can be graded (i.e. increased or diminished in significance) and this is enough to create a sense of line. Indeed, in music of the Classical era, string articulation and phrasing can often usefully be modelled on that of the piano. Of course, notes may blossom and grow as well as diminish and they then lead easily to the next note.

Very often in quartet writing, the same phrase is passed around the group and the players will need to phrase in a similar way – there should at least be a family resemblance – unless differences in the harmony, texture or structure give a reason to vary the phrasing. Pendulum rehearsing can often occur in relation to the question of whether something is over-phrased or under-phrased. This may not be a disagreement about the shape of the phrase, but a question of how the phrasing is realised technically. For example, there is an important difference between achieving the decay or growth of a note by, on the one hand, varying the bow pressure and contact point, and, on the other, by accelerating or decelerating the bow without changing the contact point, i.e. phrasing through 'bow distribution'. If done well, the latter can be more subtle and allow continual nuancing and shading without drastic changes of basic colour. When bow speed is even, the unhappy alternatives can seem to swing between a deadly lack of nuance, or an excessive range of colour change at every moment, which destroys all sense of structure and proportion. Quartet players need a strong grasp of these phrasing techniques to be able to match each other.

Players with independent lines need to be aware that the main stresses of their phrases may not coincide. For example, in the coda to the finale of Beethoven's Op. 95, in the four bars of duet between violin and viola, the violin clearly has a pair of two-bar phrases, each stronger on the first of the bars; whereas the viola has a four-bar phrase with no stress needed on the third bar. In general, the expressive and rhythmic climaxes of a phrase may not coincide with the barlines or strong beats. Indeed, there is in nearly all classical writing a constant syncopation between the barlines and the positioning of the phrasing stresses. The barlines are like the regular reference lines on an Ordnance Survey map, and the music is the actual landscape with all its irregular contours and shapes. Phrasing which has too many unwanted accents and over-regular stresses quickly sounds intolerably dull.

Structure

Often, there may be agreement about, say, what a characterisation or a colour should be, but a dispute arises as to 'how much?' To the ears of one player, the group may be overstating or labouring the point, imposing itself on the music, and lecturing or hectoring the audience, whereas for another, the group may be understating, not responding to what is happening in the music – a modulation, a new direction for the phrase, a new texture, etc. The players need to develop a communal view so as to get things in proportion, distinguishing between immensely significant structural moments and passing nuances, in order that the progression of the music is intelligible and dramatically convincing. Composers' dynamic markings often give no help with this, and interpreters, often with the aid of analysis, need to be aware of the drama of a work developing so that the appropriate importance is given to each event. Once the group is happy with the structure, there may still be questions about the overall scale of a movement and its range of characters. The appropriate emotional temperature and scale of contrast is clearly different in, say, Haydn and Janáček – which is not a remark about the profundity of the music.

Third movement: in the event of total disagreement

Having examined some of the most important aspects of quartet playing and suggested how some disagreements may be resolved, I would now like to consider how quartets can cope if deadlock is reached. Even if this occurs, it might help for everyone to 'sleep on it', where this is practical. The next day, new ideas may emerge and the problem be swept away. However, it is more than likely that even after copious discussion and trying out of ideas, there will still be some residual matters of unresolved disagreement. If these are too frequent and too important, it is probably a signal that the group should not be playing together and should find more compatible partners. However, to some extent they are probably inevitable, and if a concert is imminent, a group needs to decide what to do. In practice, if groups are *asked* what they do (it is a favourite interviewers' question) they usually have a party-line: the official version. This may be consciously believed by the members, or some of the members, of a group, but it is not necessarily what actually happens. That can only be established by observation. One good vantage point is as a guest playing quintets with a group, although quartets, like families, are liable to behave differently with guests.

In the absence of a fixed dictator, there are alternative ways of settling things. One possibility is for the mantle of dictator to shift around the group. In other words, for a particular issue, one member of the group asserts himself so forcefully or powerfully that the others defer to him on that issue; and then a different member takes charge at another juncture. This may stem from an especially strongly felt response to a particular issue. Equally, it may occur because one person has exceptional energy in one rehearsal whilst the others are tired out. Related to this is the useful device (already mentioned) of nominating one of the group to stop playing during a disputed passage, in order to go to listen from some distance to the others playing that passage. This distance gives the listening player a perspective from two points of view. First, because he is no longer playing himself, he can listen all the more sharply to the others. Secondly, because he goes to a point sufficiently distant from the group to hear the overall effect of the remaining players blended (or not) by the acoustic, he hears something much more difficult to judge from inside the group. The person nominated to listen will often be whoever has the least important part at that moment, and he is often granted a temporary magisterial authority because of his brief separateness from the group.

The other extreme to these approaches is democracy, each issue being decided by majority vote (for this, quintets have the edge over quartets). Major problems result. One is that strength of feeling counts for nothing as everyone counts for one vote. Another is that one player with an important melody or main voice (with secondary accompanying material in the rest of the group) may find himself being forced by democratic vote to play in a way he finds awkward or distasteful, with the result that he cannot do it convincingly.

A different approach is to accord a final say on an issue to whoever has the primary voice in the passage under discussion. The advantage of this is that the main voice will always be played with maximum conviction. Also, everyone in the group gets his turn, and understands on what basis his temporary authority is determined (*not* force of personality). Of course, this means that in much music the first violin is the final arbiter for the majority of the time, but not always, and only through the justification of his having the main voice.

This method also has drawbacks. I have already remarked that sometimes it is not obvious that there is a primary voice, or it may be that two overlap. Strength of feeling is again not taken into account (although one is likely to feel most strongly about an important voice one is playing oneself). Above all, there is a drawback that applies to all the methods I have mentioned, except for one-man dictatorship: namely, that whilst they settle local disputes about particular passages, this may lead to a fragmented interpretation with no coherent structural unity. Ideally, all the 'local' disputes should be discussed in relation to the overall conception. But their resolution by different people may result in incoherence. Once again, the quality of a group, and whether, ideally, it should play together, will be partly determined by the coherence of the totality of its decisions. Some committees design a camel instead of the intended horse; but it was a committee that produced the unsurpassed King James' Authorised Version of the Bible. In reality, most groups are probably not consistent in exclusively applying one approach to all their disagreements – on different occasions they settle their disagreements in different ways, and rightly so.

Fourth movement: concluding remarks

Performance

The chemistry of a group in performance is different from its chemistry in rehearsal. Performance is the crystallisation and focus of all its musical preparations. The excitement and concentration of live performance need to be shared and reacted to in consistent ways by the group. Mutual awareness needs to be heightened (hearing oneself accurately is hard enough, but simultaneously hearing three others is harder still, especially in an unaccustomed acoustic). The happiest groups encourage and support each other during the concert. The palpable sense of living the drama and enacting the characters of the music can be enhanced for each individual by sharing it with his colleagues, as can the sheer enjoyment radiated in performance.

What is remarkable is how many quartets function reasonably effectively, well after their members have come to loathe each other (which sadly, from what I hear, happens all too often). Whilst it is regrettable that this happens, it is food for thought that such an intense and necessarily co-operative relationship as a string quartet can survive at all, despite the personal feelings of its members.

Verbal, analytical description and actual, holistic practice

The entire discussion so far may well lead to a false impression, which should now be redressed. A quartet is not a debating society, and although its members need to 'negotiate' solutions to interpretative problems and find a collective interpretation, this does not mean that the whole process need be, or should be, verbal, analytical or even conscious. The *description* of all the issues involved in quartet playing is inevitably long and complex. After all, quartet playing is an artistic and social activity which, ideally, wholly integrates the body, brain, heart and soul within each of the players, as well as involving them in teamwork of the highest order. However, in contrast to description, *playing and rehearsing* quartets does not involve laboriously ploughing through each aspect of interpretation one by one. The poetic imagination and interpretative gifts of the group may well be realised holistically, and without over-tedious analytical discussion.[14]

Probably all quartets begin by verbalising a lot in rehearsal, and with time and experience they talk less and play more. This is because the players usually discover that many problems can be solved over time by their silent awareness of inconsistencies of approach and their creative response, whilst playing, to any unjustifiable differences.[15] At the outset of a new piece the players are likely to have different experience and knowledge of the piece and some players need time to 'catch up'. Some players, on the other hand, need time to shed a preconceived view of the piece too rigidly held as a result of previous encounters. Another reason why groups talk less as they develop together is that a lot of basic issues have been dealt with in previous rehearsals on different pieces. A group develops its style or approach, and has no need to discuss, say, its use of vibrato, how to attack a certain sort of chord, or how to interpret a Beethoven *subito piano* at each occurrence.

Alternative forms of rehearsing

There are ways of rehearsing which encourage non-verbal and non-specific communication, and which may 'loosen up' the players. It may be helpful to play from memory, to play without looking at each other, to play in different seats from the accustomed ones, to switch parts, to play with the players of the three upper instruments standing up (or walking around), to listen together to recordings of the group, and to recordings and concerts of other performers, to play to an outside adviser, and so on. All these can help to sharpen the hearing, and to expand or shift the point of view from which each player hears the piece.

In practice, not all rehearsals are devoted to the leisurely building of an interpretation of a piece new to the quartet. Some rehearsals are preparations for a programme of pieces already performed hundreds of times. These rehearsals may involve radical re-thinking of part or all of a piece, refreshing some stale parts of it, or fine-tuning some details. Again, this may be achieved with or without much discussion.

Changing a member of a quartet

There is a strong mystique surrounding the idea of a long-lived quartet which never changes its membership. This stems from the assumption that fine quartet playing can result only from an unchanging group growing together for decades.

What is actually far more important is that four quartet-players should be fine musicians and instrumentalists, natural and experienced chamber musicians and team players, and compatible with one another.[16] With these ingredients, four players playing through together, for the first time, a work familiar to each of them individually, may perform it excellently.[17]

Very often, a change of one player in a quartet can be refreshing and healthily disturbing, and part of the growth of the group. Provided that the new grouping of players is a good one, it need not take more than a few months to settle down.

The interpreters' personality

In the opening discussion of interpretation, I emphasised the latitude that any notation leaves to its interpreters. Subsequently, I have stressed the extent to which interpretative questions can be addressed through an ever closer understanding of what lies behind the written notes of the score. The individuality or personality of the interpreters lies in the uniqueness of their relationship with the score, rather than in their treating it with a cavalier disregard and using the notes merely as a platform to show off their beauty of sound, instrumental brilliance and ability to shock or amaze. The latter approach tends to make all pieces sound alike, and becomes boring to a discriminating listener.

From the performers' point of view, after devoted study of a piece with both a microscope and a telescope, a conception evolves, which for the time being is 'how the piece goes'. They lose themselves in performing the piece and the music plays itself through them. Nevertheless, the same piece refracted through another group equally 'lost in the music' will sound different; and that difference is due to the players' personalities. A listener may be completely drawn to hear the work through the ears of one set of performers, but may also be aware of the individuality of that version, or its distinctness from other versions. This individuality is probably best if it is unconscious on the performers' part – which was easier, no doubt, before the increased globalisation of interpretation since the days of recorded sound and international academies.

Finally, great interpreters may override little faults of ensemble playing through the strength and validity of their convictions and powers of communication. The opposite is not true. Ensemble playing which is perfectly polished in intonation, blend, balance and other such facets will not amount to a great performance in the absence of artistry in characterisation, colouring and the communication of structure.

6 Historical awareness in quartet performance

SIMON STANDAGE

String quartet performance might at first seem an unpromising area for the practice of historical awareness.[1] After all, there is no mystery about the instruments required and the musical texts are so explicit that there can be little room for radical re-interpretation. Yet the huge amount of music written in the first seventy or so years of the string quartet's existence was played on instruments substantially different from their modernised twentieth-century successors. The Classical repertory from Haydn to Schubert and the even more numerous contributions from their lesser contemporaries were written for instruments and bows whose construction reflected their historical position midway between the late Baroque and the early nineteenth century.[2] And although the opportunities to decorate or alter the notes on the page became increasingly rare as the eighteenth century progressed, the manner in which these notes were played was also far removed from conventional twentieth-century practice.

The early quartets

An indication of the historical and stylistic location of the early quartets of the mid eighteenth century is given by the fact that several of their composers also produced collections of trio sonatas, a Baroque form then on its last legs. The variety in this early quartet repertory is reflected in its range of titles, from 'quartetto' to 'cassatio'. The content of these works ranged from straight fugues through simple sonata forms to light divertimento movements. Two sets stand out. One of the earliest references to a quartet party is in the autobiography of Dittersdorf, where he recalls tackling 'six new quartets by Richter'.[3] Published in London in 1768, but written ten years earlier if Dittersdorf's memory is to be trusted, these quartets are remarkable for the equality of their part writing and particularly their liberation of the cello from its bass role, over a decade before Haydn's Op. 20 no. 2. The second set worthy of special notice is Boccherini's Op. 2, entered in his own catalogue for 1761, when he was eighteen years old. These are the first serious (non-divertimento) quartets that were composed in Vienna. The first, in C minor, has a ferocious last movement and antedates Haydn's first minor-key quartet (Op. 9 no. 4 in D minor) by seven years.

Haydn settled on 'Divertimento a quattro' as the title for his first ten quartets, when he entered them in his personal catalogue and he continued to use this term until 1785 (Op. 42), when he adopted 'Quartetto' in its place. The term for Haydn, therefore, is firmly connected with the string quartet proper and does not in itself suggest any other form of performance. One of the arguments put forward to support the use of a double bass in these early works is the incidence of overlapping parts, which result in momentary second inversions. James Webster significantly notes that they recur throughout Haydn's output and are not restricted to the ten early quartets.[4] Regarding the possible use of keyboard continuo, he suggests that continuo practice had been abandoned in Austrian secular chamber music by 1750. Altogether he makes a convincing case for simple quartet performance of these works.

Although Haydn told his Viennese publisher Artaria that he wanted his quartets to be remembered as starting with Op. 9, which dates from about ten years later, these first quartets can already be seen as a part of his life-long exploration of the form. The first movement of Op. 1 no. 3 in D, which was probably his first (the opus numbers and order come from Pleyel's edition (1801) and are no indication of chronology), is still half in the world of the trio sonata. For much of the time the two violins are in dialogue over the purely harmonic support of the lower parts. The other slow movements are simply dominated by the first violin, whose occasional virtuosity will be developed further in Opp. 9 and 17; however, as Reginald Barrett-Ayres observes, 'From the first quartet . . . to no. 10 in F (Op. 2 no. 4), Haydn makes some progress towards a real quartet style.'[5] The galant idiom of these early quartets is just a step away from the Baroque. Their generally light and pleasant air, short phrases and articulated language hardly make any demands on the instruments or style of performance beyond those of the late Baroque.

One quartet composer, however, Gaetano Pugnani (six quartets, 1763), had a very different playing style, one which, through his pupil Viotti, makes him the grandfather of the modern violin school of the Paris Conservatoire. Pugnani used a bow that was longer and straighter than the norm, and he employed thick strings. His grand bowing manner and powerful tone were recalled by Spohr when he visited Italy in 1816. Spohr wrote: 'my playing reminds them of the style of their veteran violinists Pugnani and Tartini, whose grand and dignified manner of handling the violin has become wholly lost in Italy'.[6] Pugnani's debut at the Concert Spirituel of 1754 created a sensation. That of Viotti in 1782 was even more fêted and had a more profound influence. Viotti's playing was characterised by a big full tone in addition to a powerful singing legato and a highly varied bowing technique. It was 'fiery, bold, pathetic and sublime'.[7] This substantially different playing style, notable for its power and legato, cried out for a new model of bow. The design that François Tourte perfected towards the end of the century was associated with Viotti, although, apart from Woldemar's *Grande méthode* (1800), where it appears as *L'Archet de Viotti* with the comment that it is 'almost solely in use today' (see Fig. 2.5), little evidence exists of a direct personal connection;[8] even so, Viotti's bow may not have been of quite the full modern length. Complementing the bigger bowing style (*arco magno*) of Pugnani and Viotti were the extended demands on left-hand technique and fingering.

Fingering

In Haydn's three sets Opp. 9, 17 and 20 such advances in technique included playing *una corda*, a technique more often associated with the nineteenth century and particularly Paganini. *Una corda* indicates playing from bottom to top on one string (usually the G) instead of crossing over to higher strings. These violinistic challenges were probably inspired by the presence of Luigi Tomasini, leader of Haydn's orchestra and considered by Haydn to be the most expressive player of his quartets. The slow movement of Op. 17 no. 2 could be regarded as an operatic duet between the mezzo soprano (A string) and tenor (G string), in the same category as the overtly operatic slow movements of Op. 9 no. 2, Op. 17 no. 5 and Op. 20 no. 2. However, Haydn's use of *una corda*, which appears in all his sets of quartets from Op. 17 onwards, is never merely virtuosic. It is employed for colour, to ensure portamenti, or simply for broad humour, as in the trio of Op. 33 no. 2. This last example, which is very explicitly fingered, is quoted by Baillot, who rather bowdlerises it by reducing the slide to a minimum.[9] In all these cases *una corda* remained for Haydn a special effect, whereas for later writers it became part of a string player's general technique and style.

Already in 1756 Leopold Mozart recommends playing *una corda* for equality of tone and a more consistent and singing style.[10] Around the turn of the century the theorist and violinist Galeazzi suggests, for expressive passages, never using two strings for music that can be played on one, and avoiding open strings, with their harder sound, for the same reasons.[11] Baillot (1835), however, considers the use of *una corda* as a matter of personal preference; according to him, Viotti almost always played in one position, whereas Rode and Kreutzer often played up and down the string.[12] At the turn of the following century Maurice Hayot was untypical of his time in that he avoided position changes and portamenti and played wherever possible in the first position. Flesch was particularly impressed by his performances of Mozart quartets.[13] But more typical of nineteenth-century practice were the fingerings of Ferdinand David and Andreas Moser, which produce frequent and casual portamenti and, by generally avoiding second and fourth positions, involve large movements of the hand. Leaving aside the personal preferences of particular players, it seems that *una corda* playing and its associated portamenti were treated as special effects in the late eighteenth century but became an integral part of violin technique in the nineteenth.

With the increasing use of portamento, a variety of portamento types became distinguishable, of which some were considered more acceptable than others; and, as with vibrato, there were always those who condemned its overuse in general. The most practised model was that in which, when sliding between two notes, the slide is made with the starting finger; sliding with the finger of arrival was generally disapproved of, as was gratuitous sliding when descending to an open string. Slides of different speeds, leaping, anticipating, changing finger on the same note, sliding to a harmonic, and various personalised combinations of all these, accumulated through the nineteenth century. Andreas Moser in 1905 still does not recognise the slide with the arriving finger and advocates restraint; Carl Flesch recognises both kinds, but advises discretion in the use of the latter, and discrimination in the use of either.[14]

Bowing

The comparison of the string quartet with a stimulating conversation between four intelligent people is particularly apt in the case of Haydn.[15] Such conversation took on a weightier and more intense tone from Op. 9 onwards. *Sforzando* markings appear in increasing numbers and are often associated with disruptive syncopations. These were complemented by *cantabile*, *sostenuto* and *tenuto* markings, all calling for a more 'muscular' bowing style, which in turn demanded the newer models of bow (Cramer and Viotti), with their heavier heads and wider ribbon of hair.

The need for the 'modernised' violins and bows is even stronger in the case of Mozart's mature quartets. His early quartets began their evolutionary journey, as had Haydn's, from a trio-sonata-like movement – the Adagio which opens K. 80. When, after a gap of nine years, Mozart wrote the six quartets dedicated to Haydn, he adopted a full-blown operatic style, whose long singing lines simply cannot be adequately played without the longer bows and the more powerful instruments, built or modified according to the latest developments of the time. The cantabile character of Mozart's quartets is part of his personal style, but emulation of the human voice, in both its singing and speaking capacities, has been standard advice to violinists from Telemann to Galamian. Now, on the threshold of the nineteenth century, the scale of that voice was bigger. Although reference is still made to speech and punctuation in writings of the time and continued to be so throughout the next century, it is the singing element which is in the ascendant. Even Haydn, whose language is most speech-like, stretches it to the limit. The opening bars of the Adagio of his penultimate complete quartet (Op. 77 no. 1) have a breadth of line that overrides the bar lines, and a sostenuto indicated by slurs that can no longer be simply equated with bowing; they are, as László Somfai suggests, indications of phrasing in the nineteenth-century sense.

An even more seamless effect seems to be intended in the variations movement of the 'Emperor' Quartet (Op. 76 no. 3), and in the Trio of Op. 77 no. 2, where their purpose appears to be to conceal any break of articulation and to bypass the bar lines (Ex. 6.1). A similar feeling of the music bursting out of its metrical jacket is present from the beginning of Mozart's first mature quartet (K. 387). The restless effect of the frequently changing dynamic markings is compounded by the crescendos at bars 8 and 10 which go against the metrical order and the natural shape of the phrase. The broad approach which this music calls for accords with Mozart's own preferred playing style. The grand and singing bowing of the Italians was admired by his father Leopold, who advises playing 'with earnestness and manliness'; this respect for legato playing was shared by the son, whose quartets abound in slurs that are often too long to be bowing marks.[16]

The hierarchical system which these long legato lines override, and which is violated by the offbeat *sforzandi* and crescendos of the type just mentioned, is described in detail in writings of the time.[17] It is a system in which units of all sizes – phrase, bar and beat – are in a state of diminuendo; so the first part of a phrase, bar or beat is by rights stronger than the second. This fundamental order, against which other claims for musical emphasis were pitted, was being proposed until well into the nineteenth century. Nevertheless, a less respectful attitude towards the bar line developed around the turn of the century and the novel ideas of the Belgian theorist Jérôme-Joseph de Momigny were in keeping with this new thinking.[18] Momigny related music to the human walking pace and reduced all music to a series of *cadences*, pairs of notes consisting of an upbeat and a downbeat which were 'mariées cadençalement'. This marital analogy was carried through to the extent that a phrase which began on a downbeat was considered to start with a note in a state of widowhood. The bar-line between these two notes was, according to Momigny, a sign of union and not of separation. His theories are elaborately illustrated in a ten-stave score of the first movement of Mozart's D minor Quartet K. 421. This shows the melodic and harmonic *cadences*, and sets the entire first violin part to Dido's speech to the departing Aeneas, which he considered to be the best way to express the true feeling of the piece (Ex. 6.2).

Example 6.1 Facsimile of the autograph Ms. of Haydn's Quartet in F major Op. 77 no.2, iii (Trio)

Example **6.2** Facsimile of Mozart: Quartet in D minor K. 421, i, bb. 1–8, as presented in Jérôme-Joseph de Momigny, *La Seule Vraie Théorie de la Musique* (Paris, 1821)

Example 6.2 (*cont.*)

This emphasis on connection rather than articulation is indicative of the nineteenth-century movement away from metrical restraint and towards an increasingly *sostenuto* ideal of tone production. Liszt called for an end of 'playing tied to the bar lines', and Hugo Riemann (1883) wanted musical shape determined by phrase structure alone.[19] Wagner considered 'tone sustained with equal power' as the basis of all expression, and Andreas Moser (1905) described the imperceptible bow change, and hence the seamless legato, as 'a violinistic virtue, which cannot be too highly extolled'.[20]

When playing the quartet repertory in which the metrical structure is still alive and well, the features which challenge that structure only achieve their full force and gain their proper significance if that order is itself recognised and respected. For string players this metrical order is made audible through the exercise of the so-called 'rule of down-bow'. This system was given its most extensive exposition by Leopold Mozart who, in the opening paragraph of the Preface to his *Versuch* (1756), describes his concern when he heard 'fully-fledged (*gewachsene*) violinists . . . distorting the meaning of the composer by the use of wrong bowing'.[21] In following this principle, the string player actually has a more complete experience of the conflict between metrical and other accents than is possible for woodwind or keyboard players. Because bowing consists of two contrary physical actions, which the force of gravity naturally divides into strong (down) and weak (up), playing an off-beat stress with an up-bow is not only a different physical sensation from playing it with a down-bow; it also gives that stress its proper significance and full emotional weight. Playing stressed upbeats with a down-bow, as proposed by Moser in the Peters edition of Haydn's Quartets, misses the point, and loses the tension and forward movement which result from an up-bow execution.

François Tourte's new bow model was created in response to the demands of players and contemporary musical tastes and performing styles. The full range of its capabilities was detailed by Baillot in 1835, but it was already in widespread use around 1800. Its increased length answered the need for greater singing power, and the wider ribbon of hair, held flat by the metal ferrule, gave a fuller tone and a sharper edge to the attack; but the feature most relevant to the new bowing style was the head which, balanced by a heavier frog, converted the upper half of the bow into a distinct area capable of producing a series of strokes of a brand-new type. The muted (*mat*) and dragged (*traîné*) strokes described by Baillot had a longer contour than the organically shaped notes of the previous century, and the specialised strokes illustrated by Woldemar (1798), each named after the violinist who had coined it (Viotti, Kreutzer, Rode etc.), mostly exploit this new area.

In contrast with these on-the-string bowings, the jumping bow-stroke associated with Wilhelm Cramer was also the product of a new bow model, that associated with his name. Similar to the Viotti/Tourte model but with a narrower band of hair, a shorter stick and a higher frog, it makes a clearer, slighter tone. It was later used by Paganini, whose light playing style also stood outside the Viotti mainstream. But it was the heavier Tourte bow, and the style associated with it, which prevailed. The jumping strokes, which did not even get a mention in the tutors of Baillot, Rode and Kreutzer (1803) and Spohr (1832), were considered by the latter to be flashy (*windbeutelig*) and unworthy of serious art, and it was only later in the century that such bowings were considered an indispensable part of a violinist's technique. Thus, Clive Brown suggests that, in playing music of the earlier nineteenth century, where the present inclination might be to play faster notes in the middle or lower half, violinists of that time were more likely to have used the upper-half bowings mentioned above.[22]

Intonation

In baroque music the almost constant presence of a fixed-pitch instrument in any ensemble put constraints on the intonation of the other instruments with more adjustable tuning. The fixed-pitch instruments were tuned in a chosen temperament and the others had to fit in with it or ignore it. With the disappearance of the continuo in later music, ensembles were free to play in whatever tuning system they fancied, and the string quartet was perhaps the freest of all. Excepting the open strings, all its pitches were 'bendable'.

The main influence on intonation then was the language of the new classical style itself, which, as Charles Rosen points out, depends on the system of equal temperament.[23] Whereas in the older unequal temperaments D♯ and E♭ were two distinct pitches, in equal temperament they share one compromise pitch. A striking demonstration of the tacit assumption of the newer system can be seen in the slow movement (Fantasia) of Haydn's Op. 76 no. 6 (bb. 35 and 36). In this crafty transition from B♭ major to B major, the inner parts for two bars are notated in the sharps of the up-coming key while the outer parts are simultaneously written in the flats of the key of origin. Haydn makes his apologies for the notational inconsistency with the marking of 'c.l.' (cum licentia) on the second violin and viola parts at the point of deviation (Ex. 6.3). In a similar modulation from E♭ minor to E minor in the first movement of Op. 77 no. 2, Haydn is even more specific. Between the cello E♭ in bar 92 and its D♯ in bar 93 he writes 'l'istesso tuono' ('the same note').

Even before the creation of the classical style there were advocates for equal temperament, notably Rameau;[24] and with the increasing harmonic

Example 6.3 Haydn: Quartet in E♭ Op. 76 no. 6, ii, bb. 31–9

freedom exemplified by the above examples it came to be regarded as a virtue as well as a necessity. Momigny calls the twelve equal semitones the 'élémens inaltérables de la musique', and Spohr refers to the 'theory of the absolutely equal size of all twelve semitones'. For him, 'pure' intonation means equal temperament 'because for modern music no other exists'.[25]

Balancing all this enthusiasm for equal temperament, many players and writers have been more concerned with tunings which produce either more true intervals (particularly thirds and sixths) or more expressive ones (particularly raised leading notes) or both together, the former as 'harmonic' and the latter as 'melodic' intonation. Robert Bremner's 'Some thoughts on the Performance of Concert-Music' (London, 1777), which he published as a preface to a set of string quartets by J. G. C. Schetky, contains a series of exercises in double stopping for refining the ear in judging pure intervals, and learning the physical feel of major and minor semitones, a salient feature of just and meantone tunings. Another aspect of such tunings is the pitch distinction between enharmonic pairs (C♯/D♭ etc.) where the D♭ is higher than the C♯. In 1829, Melchiore Balbi wrote that 'even the most ordinary violin player, when unaccompanied customarily preserves a *sensibilissima*

Example 6.4 Extracted from Joseph Joachim and Andreas Moser, *Violinschule* (3 vols., Berlin, 1902–5)

syntonic distinction between two enharmonically equivalent notes'; and in 1876 the music historian Cornelio Desimoni wrote of the 'armonia pura del quartetto' in contrast to the piano's equal temperament.[26]

This preference for a more just intonation was shared by Viotti and Baillot,[27] and in the following century Joachim, a descendant of this Viotti school (through Rode and Böhm), also showed his sensitivity to just intervals. However, both Baillot and Joachim tuned their open strings in pure fifths, which gave rise to the problem demonstrated by Joachim in his *Violinschule* (1902–5), namely the discrepancy between the pitch of the E required to be in tune with the G string in the first chord (Ex. 6.4a) and that needed to fit with the A in the second (Ex. 6.4b). The first finger on the E, having played chord (a) in tune, has to move up a syntonic semitone to be in tune for chord (b). This test is almost identical with the one in the *Traité de Musique* (1776) by the French theorist Anton Bemetzrieder. Joachim did, however, distort intervals in certain cases, namely augmented and diminished intervals, which require 'characteristic' intonation, also semitones in fast scale passages. In this reversal of just intonation, F♯ is placed *higher* than G♭, G♯ *higher* than A♭ and so on.[28]

Carl Flesch took this reversal still further.[29] He divided violinists who play in tune into two categories: the many who are content with the tempered tuning of the piano, and the few who, in a melodic context, raise the leading note $f\sharp^2$ to about a quarter tone's distance from the g^2, so that $f\sharp^2$ is 12 vibrations higher than $g\flat^2$. Already as a young man he was criticised for making his semitones much too small. But even Flesch confines this reversed tuning to melodic contexts. This co-existence of 'melodic' and 'harmonic' tuning standards had already been proposed by Bemetzrieder: 'The Virtuoso raises the sharp sometimes more, sometimes less; he plays the same flat note differently according to whether it is the minor 6th or the tonic.' The same flexible approach is echoed by the cellist Bernhard Romberg (1840), who claimed to play the leading note higher in minor keys than in the major.[30]

The tuning of the only fixed notes, the open strings, is critical. If in a string quartet all four fifths from the cello's bottom C to the violins' top E are tuned pure, the C–E interval will be uncomfortably large (Pythagorean). This was overcome either by avoiding open strings, or by tempering their fifths. This second and more practical solution, already proposed by Quantz (1752),[31] may have been practised more than it was ever openly proposed.

The theorist Luigi Picchianti suggested in 1834 that to avoid having over-sized (Pythagorean) intervals when using open strings, 'it is essential that the three (open string) fifths must be made a little smaller, and this is the way violinists tune them in practice, the majority of them without knowing why'.[32]

Playing with good intonation in a string quartet is an even greater challenge with the relatively lean string sound of the eighteenth and nineteenth centuries – the sound of gut strings and sparse vibrato. Tuning the fifths about a sixth of a comma small is a good solution not only for making those big cadential chords sound good, which inevitably combine the cello's open C with the violin's open E. The reduction in the size of the fifths, although a fraction more than in equal temperament, is still small enough to be easily accepted and it makes a good framework for 'harmonic' tuning, particularly for the eighteenth-century repertoire, where open strings are still part of the normal tonal palette. An aid to achieving this 'harmonic' tuning in chromatic passages is the use of the fingering widely used in the eighteenth century, and which persisted into the nineteenth. As described by Leopold Mozart and others, the basic principle is that of sliding the same finger between notes of the same letter (C/C♯, F/F♯) but using two different fingers for notes with different letters (C♯/D, F♯/G). In this way the smaller sliding movement is matched with the minor semitone, and the larger space made by the use of two fingers with the major semitone. There is a speed above which this fingering can sound smudgy (which is why Geminiani rejected it) but, that apart, the application of this principle can greatly assist good 'pure' intonation, just as the use of bowing which is consistent with the down-bow principle can of itself ensure rhythmic and musical clarity.[33]

Tone colour

Of all the factors which influence tone quality in string instruments, vibrato is the most decisive and the most closely related to the player's personality. Since 1545 when Martin Agricola mentioned it as a sweetener of violin tone, most subsequent descriptions have been accompanied by advice to use it in moderation. Its overuse has been compared to a variety of physical and nervous ailments as recently as 1921, when Leopold Auer described the use of continuous vibrato as 'an actual *physical* defect'.[34] He found that certain of his pupils were 'unable to rid themselves of this vicious habit, and have continued to vibrate on every note, long or short, playing even the driest scale passages and exercises in constant vibrato'. However, this very practice was considered by Carl Flesch to 'ennoble faster passages' and to be one of Kreisler's positive contributions to modern violin technique.[35] Support for the older tonal ideal represented by Auer was nevertheless still in evidence in 1935. In the fifty-fifth edition, 'entirely revised', of Wm. C. Honeyman's *The Violin: How to Master It*, Honeyman finds 'the close shake' (i.e. vibrato) 'a most effective ally of the solo player, but . . . one which is greatly abused, and often introduced where it has no right to appear. Indeed, with some solo players it appears impossible to play a clear, steady, pure note, without the perpetual tremola coming in like an evil spirit or haunting ghost to mar its beauty.'[36] Early recordings give us evidence of this shift of taste from a relatively straight nineteenth-century tone slightly coloured by a narrow vibrato, to a twentieth-century tone in which an intense vibrato penetrates every corner of the sound.

Written advice on the application of vibrato generally proposes logical and unexceptionable principles: e.g. using it only in appropriate places (Spohr and Joachim/Moser) or never on successive notes (Baillot and Auer); and even Carl Flesch, a proponent of the twentieth-century approach, offers a balanced picture of the ideal vibrato as 'one differentiated in the highest possible degree, one which . . . is able to traverse a gamut of emotions'.[37] In practice, however, its application is much more arbitrary and less well defined. Its perception is also highly subjective. Menuhin as a young man found the tone of the Capet Quartet intolerable on account of its playing, as he thought, without vibrato.[38] In fact, recordings show that all four players used a more or less continuous vibrato, which was constantly fast and varied in width from narrow to zero. The crux was that by comparison with his teacher George Enescu's vibrato, which was wider, the relatively straight sound of the Capet Quartet did not match up to the modern idea of violin tone. Similarly when, in the first years of the twentieth century, the composer Eric Coates heard Joachim play, he was disappointed and found his playing cold. He thought 'a little more vibrato might well have covered up (his) lack of intonation' – perhaps a legitimate criticism of the ageing Joachim's intonation but maybe also a modern taste for more sweetener in the tone.[39] Perhaps the best recorded evidence of the nineteenth-century string quartet sound is offered by the Rosé Quartet. Flesch judged Arnold Rosé's style to be of the 1870s, 'with no concession to modern tendencies in our art'.[40]

If early recordings do give us an idea of the string tone quality characteristic of the nineteenth century, only writings and instruments can be used to attempt to rediscover the sound of the later eighteenth century. A violin in pre-modern condition played with a lighter transitional bow already defines the tonal palette to some extent, and the lighter set-up also circumscribes the extent and nature of vibrato use.

Another influence on tone quality is the material of the strings. Gut strings were in general use until the 1920s. Until then the combination of plain gut E, A and D, with the G of gut wound with silver, was the norm. Flesch noted that in the interval between the first (1923) and second (1929) editions of his *Die Kunst des Violinspiels* the metal E string had 'completed its victory throughout the violin-playing world and the gut E is hardly used any more these days by professionals'.[41] The aluminium D and the steel A followed, to complete the transition from gut to metal. But there were players who continued to play on gut against general practice, and the early resistance to steel was upheld by supporters of the old aesthetic. In 1935 Liza Honeyman, daughter of the now deceased author of *The Violin: How to Master it*, wrote: 'Primarily, the violin as we know it was not designed to be strung as a banjo or mandoline. Pupils of the late Prof. Ševčík used a set of steel strings for practice hours, and the well-known violinist Příhoda does so on the platform; but, as his violin is an old and apparently thin-wooded one, it is a nightmare to look at and listen to!'[42] Her preference was for silk.

The reliability of metal strings was a great comfort to violinists who had previously had to play in constant fear of strings going wildly out of tune, squeaking and breaking. In the age of gut, though, violinists did know how to cope with these likely accidents. Dittersdorf was taught to learn to play all his concertos on three strings in anticipation of breakage. The same teacher also advised him to check and change his strings before going to bed so that they could stretch overnight.[43] Breaking strings could even be turned to dramatic advantage. Alexandre-Jean Boucher (1778–1861), the charlatan virtuoso who bore a striking resemblance to Napoleon, suffered a broken E string while playing his own quartet. 'I quickly caught the remains of the string in my mouth to prevent it from interfering with the other strings and continued as if nothing was amiss . . . You should have seen the musicians gaping in admiration, and all the audience who came closer in order to hear better and to see if I would slip up.'[44] Joachim, aged twelve, at his debut in Leipzig, 'had hardly begun when his E string snapped. With the greatest sangfroid he put on another and continued to play, every now and then tuning the new string in the tuttis, as calm and secure as if nothing had happened.'[45] Flesch said that he would never allow a pupil to appear in public unless he were assured that he could adjust his strings in the manner shown in Ex. 6.5.[46] Flesch also offers emergency measures to deal with squeaky strings, including accented bow attack, greater bow pressure with reduced amount of bow, and avoidance of all light strokes and jumping bowings. 'The jumping bowings are to be replaced by a small détaché. As you see, a completely altered playing style quite against the basic principles of violin playing, and so substituting a lesser for a greater evil, inferior tone production instead of squeaks – nevertheless a real improvement.'[47]

Today's players on gut strings may have some advantage over their predecessors. Whereas in 1935 'even the best of gut E strings are a

Example 6.5 J. S. Bach: Chaconne (Partita No. 2 in D minor) extracted from Carl Flesch, *The Art of Violin Playing*, i, p. 11

lottery – sometimes breaking immediately they are tuned up',[48] today we have a choice of easily available strings of a consistently high quality. Better still, the use of varnished strings, which are less susceptible to changes in humidity, further reduces the element of risk involved in playing on gut.

Tempo

Finding the right speed for a piece of music is as much a gift as a skill. It will not be said of many players, as it was of the Dresden concertmaster Pisendel, that 'he never – not even once – made a mistake in the choice of tempo'.[49] But this natural sensitivity, with which Pisendel was said to be so richly endowed, needs to be coupled with skill acquired through experience. This skill includes assessment of internal features of the music such as note-values and harmonic density, the character of or occasion for the piece, the size of the hall, the choice of time signature and the movement headings. These last, in the hands of Haydn and Mozart, were ordered into a multi-layered and subtly nuanced palette of speeds. In his mature quartets Mozart uses sixteen different movement headings, and Haydn's quartets contain close on forty. 'Allegro' alone appears with seven different qualifying words or phrases. Beethoven continued this expansion of the vocabulary, but in the meantime Maelzel had produced his metronome and in 1817 was promoting it in Vienna. This device made it theoretically possible for the composer to fix the speed of his music precisely; although it was generally recognised that in practice it could only give a general idea, this was at least some safeguard against a variety of interpretations, which could depend on national style, school of playing, or merely fashion, aside from the personality and judgement of the performers themselves.

Beethoven was the first significant composer to issue metronome marks for his own works – in 1817 for the first eight symphonies and in 1819 for the quartets up to Op. 95. About half the marks in the quartets are surprisingly fast, mostly by an increase of two or three metronome notches, but in some cases more, even to the extent of complete incompatibility with the movement headings.[50] Several attempts have been made to explain this, including the suggestion that by the time he came to supply the marks perhaps 'his ear had grown impatient with some of his old music'.[51] Two theories seem plausible. At quartet performances Beethoven was too busy beating the time to be able to make a record of it.[52] He therefore probably made his judgements either at the piano or in his head. As Brahms pointed out to Clara Schumann, who was about to set metronome marks for her husband's music, 'on the piano . . . everything happens much faster, much livelier and lighter in tempo'. And estimates made in the head against a ticking metronome, as Tovey observed, are likely to err on the fast side.[53] But these markings, if they need to be taken with a pinch of salt and may even include actual errors, nevertheless give a strong indication of Beethoven's intentions. They are also consistent with the slightly later markings which Czerny attached to the piano music of Beethoven,[54] whose pupil and close associate he was, and which Hummel and Czerny added to their piano arrangements of Haydn and Mozart.[55] Mendelssohn's and Schumann's metronome marks for the fast movements of their quartets also tend sometimes to the unfeasibly rapid, but it is the faster tempi of their slow movements which indicate a more radical difference of musical approach. Even Dvořák, whose metronome marks do not stretch credulity, indicates relatively flowing slow movements. The contrast is particularly striking between the turgid or sentimental renderings of slow movements in some early-twentieth-century recordings and the fleeter, lighter conception implied by these composers' own markings.

In the same year in which Beethoven published the metronome markings for all his quartets to date, Spohr's Op. 45 quartets also appeared, with both pendulum and Maelzel marks. The speeds are in general as practical as one would expect from a performer/composer, but the slow movements are truly slow.

Although tempo instructions originating from the composers themselves naturally carry most authority, those from other sources can be significant. For the pre-Maelzel quartets of Haydn and Mozart, the source closest in time is Czerny's four-handed arrangement of Mozart's quartets, from the late 1830s. Having made allowance for the increase in tempo associated with the transference to the piano, it is the slow movements and Menuets which are notably faster, whereas the outer movements mostly conform to present-day expectations.

Further removed in time, in 1854 the Polish violinist Karol Lipiński added Maelzel marks to all of Haydn's quartets, in an edition based on Pleyel's Paris publication of 1801, for which Baillot, himself famous as a quartet player, was partly responsible. In general Lipiński's slow movements are very slow and his first and last movements mostly moderate, but his minuets are almost without exception very fast. This approach to tempo could be seen as an aspect of his playing style, which was in the solid tradition of Viotti and Spohr; on the other hand it tallies in part with the report, in 1811, that Mozart and Haydn 'never took their first Allegros as fast as one hears them here. Both let the Menuetts go by hurriedly.'[56]

In search of the right tempo, the quartet player still needs to exercise musical judgement in combination with serious consideration of the historical evidence, always keeping the mind open to new ideas.

Text

'The modern practice . . . of "editing" recognised classical and standard works cannot be too severely condemned as a Vandalism', wrote Moser in 1905.[57] He cites Spohr as having particularly suffered from this treatment. Spohr's quartets are certainly marked in great detail: fingerings, bowings, articulation, metronome marks and even vibrato, leaving no room for doubt as to his intentions. Yet, less than fifty years after his death, his works were being reworked, due partly to 'an utter lack of knowledge regarding certain peculiarities in his style of composition and treatment of the violin'. The scope for such misinterpretation is even greater in music which is further removed in time and with fewer performance directions.

Moser produced editions of Haydn, Mozart and Beethoven quartets, outlining his editorial policy in the Preface to his collection of thirty celebrated Haydn quartets (1918).[58] Although this policy shares some of the aims of a modern critical edition, it differs mainly in its declared representation of the 'then current practice of the Joachim Quartet'. This was suitable in the case of Beethoven's quartets. Joachim was taught by Joseph Böhm who, during the 1820s in Vienna, was closely associated with the new chamber music of Beethoven and Schubert. Both Böhm and Beethoven had their connections with the new style of the Paris Conservatoire, Böhm as a pupil of Rode and Beethoven through his association with Kreutzer and Rode. So the fingerings and bowings of the Joachim/Moser editions, which reflect Conservatoire practice, may also represent the intentions of Beethoven and Schubert. In the case of the editions of eighteenth-century works, however, this is obviously not appropriate.

A modern critical edition attempts to remove such third-party interference between the performer and the composer. It also takes on the task of tracing the often tortuous history of the sources and assessing their relative significance in the attempt to reveal as closely as possible the composer's intentions. Attractive as it may be to play from facsimiles of early printed editions or hand-written copies, these are unlikely to contain the whole truth and will probably have a fair share of omissions, ambiguities and actual mistakes. They are, though, unlikely to have as many impossible page turns as supposedly practical modern editions (which are also prone to misprints); and in the case of works which exist in only one source, or for which the best source is a printed one, playing from an old source can combine authority, practicality and good looks. In any case, with the increasing availability of facsimiles of autograph scores and first editions, there are ever more opportunities to follow Moser's suggestion that before accepting the given text, we can consult the original.

Ornamentation

Attitudes towards alteration of the notes on the page have, as in the case of vibrato, generally ranged from written pleas for moderation to reports of excessive or inappropriate practice. Moser wrote (1905) that to prevent their music being drowned in embellishments, composers had been forced to give such precise instructions that 'it has now become a point of honour to make no alteration of any kind in a composition'.[59] The players responsible for this situation were such as Boucher, whom Spohr heard in 1818 when he 'played a quartet of Haydn, but introduced so many irrelevant and tasteless ornaments, that it was impossible for me to feel any pleasure in it'.[60] In fact Boucher was so renowned for his gratuitous additions that when he agreed to play a piece 'textuellement', i.e. sticking to the written notes, his audience who 'feared that he would not hold to his promise ... was agreeably surprised' when he did.[61] Ferdinand David, pupil of Spohr, friend of Mendelssohn, and admired quartet leader, was also accused, particularly in later life, of making tasteless additions to Classical quartets. Baillot, on the other hand, was admired for his quartet playing in which there was 'no departure from the character of the piece and no alteration by parasitical embroideries'.[62] Spohr's own advice in the case of what he calls the 'true quartet', as opposed to the leader-dominated *quatuors brillants* written by himself, Viotti, Rode and others, is that ornamentation should be limited to those sections which are clearly solo, with the other parts mere accompaniment.[63] Such opportunities are to be found in the slow movements of early quartets of Mozart and Haydn, notably Haydn's Opp. 9 and 17 where, in addition, cadenzas are frequently called for at cadential pauses.

The complexity and quality of the music is also a guide as to whether embellishment is appropriate. Music which is the result of long and hard work ('frutto di una lunga e laboriosa fatica')[64] by Mozart is unlikely to be improved by the spontaneous ideas of even the most inspired quartet player, whereas the baser metal of his lesser contemporaries may well benefit from a bit of gilding; and an awkward compositional corner can sometimes be more smoothly negotiated with the help of some well-chosen additions. As an example of the first situation, Baillot quotes the opening of the slow movement of Mozart's 'Dissonance' Quartet as a case of 'Chant Simple', which 'must be played as the composer has written it'.[65] The reason becomes clear at the theme's second appearance, where Mozart gives his own ornamented version. The second situation is illustrated by Spohr, whose description of his teacher Franz Eck playing a quartet by Krommer praises 'the tasteful fioriture by which he knew how to enhance the most commonplace composition'.[66]

Pitch

At the time of the emergence of the string quartet pitch varied not only from town to town but, within each town, between the different churches, theatres and chambers. Broadly speaking, though, pitch levels rose in the course of the eighteenth century and this rise accelerated in the early part of the nineteenth. In 1860, in a footnote to an updated English edition of Otto's *Treatise on the Structure and Preservation of the Violin*, the translator described 'the excessive rise in the musical pitch which has taken place since the commencement of the eighteenth century'. He reckoned that from Tartini's time (1734) to 1834 pitch had risen a semitone, and during the next thirty years another semitone, creating increased pressure on 'the masterpieces of the great violin makers . . . which they were never constructed to bear; and hence, also, another argument in favor [sic] of a reduction of the musical pitch'.[67] Several attempts were made in the first decades of the nineteenth century to lower pitch again and standardise it. In 1813 the London Philharmonic Society produced a tuning fork at $a^1 = 423.5$Hz, and in 1825 George Smart, who had been one of the four members to approve this pitch, went on a tour of Europe testing his Philharmonic fork against every orchestra, organ, piano and string quartet that he encountered. Half of his readings were 'exact to my fork', but in Vienna the pitch was generally 'rather above my fork', as it was when he was present at the first performance of Beethoven's Op. 132 at the lodgings of the music seller Schlesinger, who published the work two years later.[68]

Pitch continued to rise through the century in the interests of instrumental brilliance but to the detriment of singers' health. In France a 'diapason normal' of $a^1 = 435$Hz was established by law in 1859, but decisions made at a conference in Vienna in 1885 led to the acceptance of $a^1 = 440$Hz, a decision confirmed again in the next century. The practical desirability of having a standard pitch, recognised in the mid eighteenth century, became even more acute with the increase in recordings in the 1970s and in the use of ever more sophisticated splicing techniques. The compromise pitch of $a^1 = 430\text{Hz}$ adopted then for classical repertoire would appear to be very near that of Beethoven's Vienna, and although possibly lower than that of the later part of the century, also makes a good median pitch for a quartet programme with a broad range of repertoire.

Seating plan

There is scant evidence of how the players were arranged in an eighteenth-century quartet, but iconography suggests that just about every possible seating permutation seems to have been tried in the nineteenth century.[69] Evidence can be divided into two broad categories, according to whether the two violins are side by side or opposite each other. Two of the most popular arrangements were represented by Joachim, when playing with his Berlin quartet, and when playing with Ries, Straus and Piatti in London. In the former the violins sat facing each other (Fig. 3.2). This pattern, reflecting standard orchestral seating, was the most favoured during the nineteenth century, particularly in Germany. In Joachim's London quartet, on the other hand, the violins sat side by side, an arrangement which rivalled the Berlin pattern in popularity at that time and became standard in the twentieth century, with either the viola or the cello sitting opposite the first violin. For performance of quartets in the more conversational style of Haydn, Mozart, Beethoven and their imitators, the seating with antiphonal violins has the advantage, both for the violinists themselves and for the audience, of separating the two treble lines and so clarifying the texture.

Conclusion

A string quartet wanting to get closer to the spirit of the composer and his times certainly needs a reliable and transparent edition. It would be assisted by the use of instruments, bows and fittings contemporary with the music, but stylish playing need not depend on this, any more than it is guaranteed by their use.

The most striking element of any playing style is sound quality, which is determined principally by the type of strings, the model of violin and bow employed and the application of vibrato. Of these, vibrato is the most decisive and personal. Although appropriate articulation, accentuation and phrasing are easier to achieve with a 'period' bow and violin, they can be emulated with 'modern' equipment. Tempo selection is hardly affected by the choice of instrument or bow, and intonation, although closely linked with sound colour, needs independent consideration.

It is, therefore, the extent to which players are prepared to modify their performance style, with or without period instruments, and how far audiences will go along with them, that will determine how closely one can approximate the composer's original conception. In the late twentieth century, a range of new performing styles for early music was heard. The elements they had in common, in particular their leaner sound, were generally accepted, indicating a shift in musical taste. Whether any future shift in popular taste will take the historical performance of string quartets further along this road remains to be seen, but there is no doubt that an increased awareness of past performance practice can demonstrate how much there is to discover in any such attempt to get closer to the heart of this rich repertory.

7 Extending the technical and expressive frontiers

ROBIN STOWELL

This chapter can give only a flavour of the myriad ways in which twentieth-century composers extended the frontiers of string playing in their quartets and, hence, the timbral palette of ensembles. Restrictions of space allow only a general overview, together with some detailed discussions of specific trends, techniques and expressive effects, with pertinent examples from the repertory. In many respects the weight of Classical tradition and the perceived limitations in the technical possibilities of stringed instruments initially resulted in the genre resisting radical change to a greater extent than most other media. Despite the extraordinary variety and concentration of texture and timbres in Webern's *Bagatelles* Op. 9, for example, performers are consistently required to pursue their traditional roles of hearing and feeling as a unified ensemble, interpreting each note as belonging to a single melody of timbres.

This is in sharp contrast to the more individualistic roles encouraged later in the century, when the genre became a vehicle for remarkable experiment and radical compositional thought. Bartók's quartets, with their wide range of pizzicato effects, vibrato indications, *col legno* and micro-tones, provided the most significant spark to those composers seeking to expand the vocabulary of available sounds and timbres. The chromaticism, the rhythmic and metrical devices and the colouristic and textural use of glissandi in Bartók's Third Quartet, for example, were all highly unusual for the sometimes retrogressive 1920s; furthermore, Hindemith's contemporary Second Quartet (Op. 16) requires the second violinist to reiterate a figure without regard to the pulse of the other parts (finale, bb. 458–511), a technique tentatively foreshadowing the development of aleatory devices such as appeared in, for example, Gunter Schuller's First Quartet (1957), with its opportunities for improvisation.

As discussed further in Chapter 14, some of the most radical re-thinking of quartet composition emanated from Poland, where, in common with other European countries, a flirtation with twelve-note techniques was followed by a reaction against them. In his two quartets (1960, 1968), Penderecki extended the sound-world of the ensemble by using, for example, quarter tones and indeterminate pitches, notes produced between the bridge and tailpiece, bowing on the tailpiece itself, and the drumming effects of the open hand, the finger-nails, or the frog of the bow either on the strings or on the table of the instrument. Irregular glissando and controlled vibrato effects were also employed. Such extreme effects were indicated by customised notational symbols and copious written directions.

Twentieth-century composers tended to concern themselves less with the practicalities of composition and often opted for rapid changes from one textural, timbral and/or dynamic extreme to another, as powerfully illustrated by the opening of the quasi-development of the first movement of Webern's Op. 5, the sharply contrasting and extremely detailed dynamic and performance markings in Sculthorpe's Eighth Quartet (1969), Xenakis' *ST/4-1,080262* or Ligeti's Second Quartet, or the *pppppp* ending of Schnittke's Quartet No. 2 (1980). Furthermore, some of Villa-Lobos' writing for the medium is, to say the least, awkward, his violin and viola parts involving some precise playing in the stratospheres and tempting some ensembles to revoice the lines.[1]

The exploitation of micro-intervals and other such challenges for the left hand lessened the significance of traditional scales and finger patterns. Effects such as harmonics, pizzicato, glissando and vibrato underwent a marked expansion in their range and usage, and scordatura and *con sordino* also offered additional timbral variety. The vocabulary of the bow was also extended to exploit its various components' sound potential in a wide range of strokes and contact-points. Vocal effects and the use of electronic and other new technologies altered the relationship between composer and performer, as well as performer and listener, and opened up new colours and compositional styles; and performance problems were sometimes further compounded by literary, narrative and other extra-musical factors that players were duty-bound to 'research' and faithfully to realise.

These radical changes in performing techniques and styles and consequent modifications of compositional style, form, rhythm, colour and harmony increased in scope and intensity as the century progressed, requiring performers to re-think strategies of individual technical practice, ensemble rehearsal, concert programming, interpretation and general musical communication. Some composers even required the performers to assume some of the compositional decisions. Sometimes this requirement was highly structured within the work; sometimes it was trusted more freely to the performer's fantasy and taste. Boulez's *Livre pour Quatuor* allows the performers to select which movements they play, while Gunther Schuller resorts to free improvisation on relevant notes selected from his twelve-note series in the finale of his First Quartet. While the second violinist plays tremolandi at a specified tempo, the first violinist is required to improvise on five notes in fast legato runs (not necessarily continuously nor in the notated order); the violist is required to improvise on four notes, tremolo (normal or 'ad lib. pont.') and in any order or speed; and the cellist is asked to improvise on four notes in any order or speed but always at the prescribed dynamics. Henry Cowell's *Mosaic Quartet* also calls for free improvisation and presents musical segments which the performers may order at will.

Some works have tested players to the limits of their mental, aural, physical and technical potential. Among performers' numerous challenges is that of familiarising themselves with new musical notation, the unstandardised nature of much of which has led to considerable confusion.[2] Other challenges are purely technical, often demanding of players an aggressive virtuosity (as in Penderecki's First Quartet). Broadly speaking, rhythm and metrical considerations have become more complex, sometimes involving tempo being indicated in seconds, so many seconds to each passage marked off by a barline (without metrical significance, as in Penderecki's First Quartet); dynamic, timbral and articulation requirements have become more exacting and extreme and, as independent compositional strands, are required to be observed scrupulously; and the exploration of harmonic effects and of the different overtones and timbres produced with various, more precisely defined contact points of the bow on the string have resulted in the rapid play of changing timbres, as demonstrated in Penderecki's Second Quartet. Furthermore, performers' and audiences' ears have had to be educated to appreciate atonality and microtonality as well as new methods of sound production – the complex amalgam of colours in Xenakis' *Tetora* (1990) or *Ergma* (1994), for example, creates significant problems of reproduction – and performers have been required to appreciate and realise in their performances the extra-musical inspiration of several works and undertake modes of performance (act, sing, or play percussion instruments) which take them far beyond their specialist musical training into theatrical and other spheres.

The professional string quartet

Although the marked increase in compositional diversity and technical complexity has not, as well it might have, resulted in the demise of the medium, it has certainly moved the string quartet away from its original social function and intimate chamber context firmly into the professional environment of the concert hall. The technical and interpretative requirements of most twentieth-century works are well beyond the capability of amateur musicians and require highly skilled, versatile and specialist performers. Bartók's quartets, for example, have no place in the domestic environment, while works such as Elliott Carter's Second Quartet (1959), with its deliberately ostentatious first violin part, strain the technical resources of most professional players; and only the most dedicated and seasoned professional ensemble would possess the commitment and stamina to perform Morton Feldman's epic *String Quartet II*, lasting continuously for at least five hours, or his two-hour *Violin and String Quartet* (1985). Feldman's works reflect his 'pre-occupation with scale over form and his interest in enveloping environments, in which listeners experience music from "inside" a composition'.[3]

The virtuoso physical and mental demands of Heinz Holliger's *Quartet* (1973) and the new techniques it encompasses also test performers to the extreme. Each player is required to read two staves, one for each hand, and is even given detailed instructions as to how to breathe. 'Fatigue from unaccustomed lengths of respiration should', Holliger notes, 'manifest itself in the tone' (for example, in a shaky bow; or in tense, halting bowing).

Individualisation

Along with the increasing trend of transforming the string quartet into a medium for specialist professional performance, many twentieth-century composers have treated it as an ensemble of four different and individual personae. Charles Ives was arguably one of the first to start such a trend. His Second Quartet (1907–11) also allots each part greater independence and freedom, each reaching extremes of expression and often sounding unrelated to one another. As H. Wiley Hitchcock has commented:

> One hears virtually every kind of melody, harmony, rhythm, phrase structure, plan of dynamics, scoring, and writing for the instruments . . . The wildly varied materials succeed each other abruptly, sometimes violently; sometimes they literally co-exist. Alongside the most radical sort of jagged, wide-spanned, rhythmically disparate, chromatic melody is melody of the simplest stepwise diatonicism. Triadic harmony alternates with fourth- and fifth-chords, chromatic aggregates, and tone clusters. Canons without any harmonic underpinnings follow passages anchored to static harmonic-rhythmic ostinatos. 'Athematic' writing is set side-by-side against passages quoting pre-existent melodies in almost cinematic collage.[4]

The titles for the work's three movements ('Discussions', 'Arguments' and 'The Call of the Mountains' respectively) provide the impetus for the juxtaposition of contrasting musical styles, involving amongst other aspects whole-tone scales, rhythmic pedals and the quotation of numerous well-known tunes. A note on the first page of Ives' manuscript explains his intended scenario: 'S.Q. for 4 men – who converse, discuss, argue (in re

'Politick'), fight, shake hands, shut up – then walk up on the mountain side to view the firmament.'[5] Furthermore, his numerous marginal notes outline how the various discussions and arguments develop.

Later in the century, Elliott Carter's Second Quartet (1959) concentrated on the superposition of distinctive types of expression in the four instruments. Each instrument has a particular vocabulary of musical intervals (melodic and harmonic) and rhythms and is played in the character indicated in the score's preface: the first violin should exhibit the greatest variety of character, but plays mostly in a bravura manner; the second violinist's contribution is regular and often witty; the viola's role is predominantly expressive; and the cellist's rubato and accelerando playing looks towards a temporal world beyond the chronometric. The various sections of the work are linked by cadenzas for the first violin, the viola and the cello – a ploy also used by Britten (in the Chacony of his Second Quartet) and other composers – and the players are spatially separated to clarify the different characteristics of the music allotted to each.

Carter's Third Quartet (1971) is similarly concerned with the interaction between contrasted material, though the parts are grouped here as two duos: first violin and cello; and second violin and viola. Carter explains that: 'The two duos should perform as two groups as separated from each other as is conveniently possible, so that the listener can not only perceive them as two separate sound sources, but also be aware of the combinations they form with each other.'[6] In similar vein, his Fourth Quartet is also characterised by 'a preoccupation with giving each member of the performing group its own musical identity'.[7]

Among other composers who similarly 'individualised' the ensemble in the twentieth century have been Milton Babbitt, George Perle, Ruth Crawford Seeger and Pascal Dusapin (*Time Zone*), each of whom has treated the medium as four different voices or characters engaged in musical discourse but united only by commonality of instrumental family. Sculthorpe, too, cultivated independence, his indication 'Liberamente' in his Eighth Quartet (1969) referring to his desire 'that players should be rhythmically independent of each other'. Lutosławski also writes of his String Quartet (1964):

> Within certain points in time particular players perform their parts quite independently of each other. They have to decide separately about the length of pauses and about the way of treating ritenutos and accelerandos. However, similar material in different parts should be treated in a similar way.[8]

While Ligeti's quartet writing often emphasises the individuality of the four parts, he is quick to signal the need for precision of ensemble. In the third movement of his Second Quartet he demands: 'very precise: the demisemiquaver motion is simultaneous in all 4 instruments'.[9] For composers such as Shostakovich and Schnittke, however, individual contributions were very much for the corporate cause. The quasi-recitative solo passages for each player in Shostakovich's Quartet No. 14 are cases in point, while 'Cadenza', the third and final movement of Schnittke's String Quartet (1965/66), distributes its material among the four players 'in the manner of a "collective solo", in such a way as to create, when performed, the impression that a single, super-dimensional string instrument is playing'.[10]

Notation

Some twentieth-century composers dispensed, partly or wholly, with conventional notation and presented performers with a whole new and unstandardised language of performance directions (and hence sounds) to recognise and realise. Henze's Fourth Quartet, for example, includes an opening movement written in proportional, and sometimes graphic, notation and a finale whose indeterminacy is manipulated to a great extent by the first violinist, while Betsy Jolas exploits space-time notation to excellent effect in her Second Quartet (1966).

The cello part of Carter's Second Quartet incorporates various kinds of indicated rubati. In one example, a dotted arrow line extends from the first note-value (a crotchet tied to a quaver), which is to be played for its full length, to the final note of the group (a semiquaver), which is also to be played for its full length. Carter explains: 'The intervening notes are to be played as a continuous *accelerando* (in other cases, where the notation indicates it, a *ritardando*), the notation indicating approximately whether the *accelerando* (or *ritardando*) is regular, or more active at the beginning or the end of the passage. In all cases, however, the first note-value, over which the arrow starts, and the last, to which it goes, are to be played in the metrical scheme in which they occur.'[11]

Penderecki employs graphic notation in his First Quartet, conventional barlines being replaced by individual sections of one second's duration that determine the actual tempo. Each period of five seconds is clearly demarcated, tempo deviations from 0.8 to 1.4 seconds being permitted within each period, depending on the first violinist's choice. More fluid still with regard to tempo is Penderecki's Second Quartet – there is no strict division of bars into seconds. This work also uses an adventurous system of customised notational symbols that represent performance instructions (involving indeterminate pitches, vibrato specifications, microtones etc.), as explained in his preface.

Similarly, Sculthorpe's Eighth Quartet (1969) incorporates symbols to indicate unorthodox performance directions, ranging from the requirement for 'any very high note' to an 'harmonic played between [the] bridge and tailpiece on [the] string indicated', a 'sustained sound, duration indicated by [the] length of [the] ligature', and the rapid repetition of a given figure. Ferneyhough's music is also formidable in its intricate notational demands, which, together with his characteristic choice of small note values in his Second and Third Quartets, for example, seem deliberately intended to create a tension and energy in the players that is then translated into their performance.[12]

Rhythm and metre

Composers' fascination with folk and multi-metrical music, the syncopations of modern jazz, ostinato motor-rhythms, complex polyphony and mathematical patterns and formulae has contributed to the emergence of rhythm as a potent structural element in twentieth-century music. Rhythms and metres reminiscent of Bulgarian folk music had a far-reaching influence on Bartók's works, particularly in the Scherzo of No. 5 and in the complex compound metres exploited in the equivalent movement of No. 4 (Scherzo: 4+2+3/8; trio: 3+2+2+3/8). However, the performing problems posed by such compound metres are negligible when compared with those raised by, for example, the rhythmic oppositions of Ives' Scherzo 'Holding Your Own' (1903–14) for string quartet from *A Set of Three Short Pieces*,[13] the algorithmic forms and new sonorities of Ruth Crawford Seeger's Quartet (1931), the indeterminacy of Lutosławski's String Quartet (1964), the freedom of interpretation so vital to the first, third and fifth movements of Sculthorpe's No. 8 (1969), or the interpretation of movements in which some or all of the quartet members are required to conform to different metres. In Boulez's *Livre pour Quatuor* (1948–9), for example, the first violinist is required to play in triple time, without accents, while occasionally 'conducting' with his violin in duple time, in which the others play.

Perhaps the greatest rhythmic challenge for performers stems from so-called irrational (in the arithmetic sense) rhythms, indicated by proportional notation. Carter, for example, superimposes independent melodies in polymetrical relationships as complex as 3 against 7 against 15 against 21 in his First Quartet (1950–1), achieving a constant change of pulse by overlapping tempi.[14] Furthermore, in Nancarrow's Third Quartet, all four instruments play the same material in a tempo ratio of $3:4:5:6$, while Ferneyhough's *Sonatas* abounds in irrational rhythms, reference points being provided in the relevant other parts to aid synchronisation. A striking freedom is given to the concluding bars; while the viola and cello proceed 'in tempo giusto al fine', the two violins are directed 'to proceed to the end in complete rhythmic independance [sic]'.

Quartet seating

The distribution of the string quartet has only rarely come into the composer's domain, most opting for the traditional semi-circular arrangement of (from left to right as one looks 'front-on'): Violin 1, Violin 2, Viola, Cello. However, those works with theatrical objectives have naturally challenged such a convention, as have some quartets involving amplified sound and/or extra-musical influence.[15] No musical reason is offered by Ferneyhough for his suggestion that 'it may be to the advantage of the musical presentation' if players were to position themselves as follows for performance of his *Sonatas* (from left to right as one looks 'front-on'): Violin 1, Viola, Cello, Violin 2. He adds: 'a more conventional layout is acceptable if preferred. The distance between the players is immaterial, provided that a tight, homogeneous ensemble sound be produced.'[16] Interestingly, Michael Finnissy requires the first violinist to be seated separately from the rest of the ensemble in his *Multiple Forms of Constraint*.

Prepared instruments

Mauricio Kagel's String Quartet I/II (1965–7) requires the instruments to be 'prepared' (in the sense of John Cage's prepared piano) by means of the use of, amongst other things, adhesive tape, strips of paper and pieces of cloth on the fingerboard. In addition, the first violinist is instructed to wear a thick leather glove on his left hand, and the cellist is required to wedge knitting needles between the cello strings, along with matches, coins, xylophone beaters and a strip of paper, in order to alter the instrument's pitch, timbral and dynamic responses. Kagel illustrates graphically how the various objects are to be employed. In the second movement the preparations are fewer but the range of effects no less wild, including bowing with notched pieces of wood and drumming with fingers on the strings, as well as exploiting a wide variety of more conventional techniques. Among other composers who prescribe unconventional materials to set the string vibrating is Crumb, whose *Black Angels* calls for the use of glass rods to strike or slide along the strings (in 'Ancient Voices'), a metal plectrum for a particular pizzicato effect and thimbles on the right-hand fingers for a thrummed tremolando (in 'Threnody III: Night of the Electric Insects').

Techniques and special effects

Scordatura

Many twentieth-century quartet composers took advantage of scordatura, but the device was employed more as a timbral and colouristic resource than for tonal brilliance, notably by Scelsi (Quartets Nos. 3 and 4) and Kagel. Penderecki exploits the physical winding down of the string in his Second Quartet, while Xenakis takes this to extremes, requiring the cellist to retune his lowest string for every note. In the last section of his First Quartet ('Between the National and the Bristol'), Gavin Bryars requires the lower pair of strings of each instrument to be tuned down a semitone. The resultant contrasts between eight normally tuned strings and eight scordatura strings produce a striking effect.

Con sordino

The use of the mute was intensified in the twentieth century. It was particularly exploited by Shostakovich, especially as a timbre with which to conclude many of his quartets. Furthermore, like the second movement of Bartók's Fourth Quartet, the equivalent movement of Britten's Second Quartet is muted throughout. However, this particular Bartók example is unusual, in that its dynamic prescriptions extend to *fortissimo* and much of the movement comprises scurrying, *prestissimo* quavers. Composers generally opted for instant timbral contrasts within movements and gained a whole new range of tonal colours. Webern's *Bagatelles* Op. 9, for example, incorporate sonorities varied strikingly by muted effects; Berio even introduces a notational symbol to indicate *con sordino* and *senza sordino* in preference to the verbal instruction, possibly to facilitate the performers' realisation of an already complex score.[17]

Among the unusual demands of Michael von Biel's First Quartet is the requirement for the cellist to place a double bass mute on the strings between bridge and fingerboard and play alternately above and below it. Furthermore, Scelsi goes so far as to specify the use of a heavy copper mute for the relevant sections of his Third Quartet.

The manner of holding stringed instruments

The wide diversity of compositional influences and styles in the twentieth century led to the development of a corresponding variety of techniques and expressive effects. These have involved both left and right hands and have even extended to the manner of holding certain instruments. 'Excentrique', the second of Stravinsky's *Three Pieces*, for example, includes one figure to be played by the second violinist and violist with their instruments held like cellos, while two movements of Crumb's *Black Angels* require the violins

and viola to be held like viols, with the players bowing up near the pegs on
the 'wrong' side of the left hand. Sculthorpe also directs the first violinist
to hold the instrument in a vertical position for *col legno* effects, as in the
fourth movement of his Eighth Quartet (1969).

Fingering

The extended harmonic language of many twentieth-century composers
has led to players' liberation from traditional technical values and diatonic
fingerings and the increased exploitation of unfamiliar, often awkward non-
diatonic fingering 'patterns' (involving chromatics, whole tones, quarter
tones and other micro-intervals), and extensions and contractions that often render impossible the recognition of a definite concept of positions. High
position-work on all strings, sudden leaps between extremes of register and
non-consonant combinations of double and multiple stopping are also frequently encountered. Players have therefore been called upon to master new
fingering patterns, many of which may justifiably be considered unnatural,
ungrateful, non-uniform and downright unviolinistic, while demands for
sudden leaps and unusual intervals have necessitated the development of an
acute aural proficiency in anticipating and confirming the notes to which
shifts are required.

Interest has also been heightened in the particular sonorities and timbres
that stringed instruments are capable of producing. In addition to the standard fare of harmonics, pizzicato, glissandi and vibrato, composers have
distinguished timbres requiring the use of specific parts of the stopping
finger. In his Second Quartet, for example, Carter explains: 'The markings
①, ②, ③, indicate that the first, second, or third finger of the left hand is to
stop the note so marked by pressing the fingernail vertically on the string,
thus producing a ringing, guitar-like sound. The player may use another
fingering than that given if it produces the desired sonority more satisfacto-
rily. All notes without this marking are to be stopped in the usual way with
the fleshy tip of the finger.'[18]

Quarter tones and other micro-intervals

In 1895, the Mexican Julián Carrillo's experiments with the division of
a string into multiple parts led to the development of microtonality
and the various theoretical and musical systems derived from it: scales,
melodies, harmonies, metres, rhythms, textures and instruments. Carrillo
subsequently composed eight quartets using microtones, their accurate
performance involving a radical departure from traditional ear-training
and their mastery requiring both a new mental discipline and physical
precision. Ives also became involved in micro-interval composition, his
Quarter-Tone Chorale for Strings (1903–14) supposedly being inspired by

his father's experiment to build a quarter-tone keyboard instrument to imitate the ringing of bells which contained notes 'in the cracks between the piano keys'.

Ivan Vishnegradsky and Alois Hába both contributed string quartets in quarter tones from the 1920s and early 1930s. Himself a violinist, Hába was inspired by microtonal usage in Moravian folk music and he founded a Czech School of Microtonal Music at the Prague Conservatoire. He used quarter tones systematically as an integral part of the compositional material in his String Quartets Nos. 2–4 inclusive (1919–22), No. 6 (1950) and Nos. 12 and 14 (1959–60; 1963), as well as sixth tones in Nos. 5, 10 and 11 (1923; 1952; 1957) and fifth tones in Nos. 15 and 16 (1964; 1967), all notated according to his system. In the preface to his Second Quartet Op. 7 Habá wrote: 'It is my concern to permeate the semitone system with more delicate sound nuances, not to abolish it . . . to extend the possibilities of expression already given by the old system.'[19] Hába's microtonal quartets contrast markedly with his Quartets Nos. 7, 8 and 9, which are characterised by 'a greater simplicity of harmony and form and a less sophisticated expression'.[20]

Of course, Bartók also introduced quarter tones in the Burletta of his Sixth Quartet (iii, bb. 26 and 28); and Penderecki (No. 2), Karel Husa (Quartet No. 3 (1968), iv, bb. 8–9), Scelsi (Quartets Nos. 3 and 4) and Crumb (*Black Angels*, no. 13, beginning) have since exploited quarter tones as a means of bending pitches up or down for expressive effect. Scelsi based many of his compositions on the subtleties of slowly permutating microtone glissandi around a central pitch-mass, as in his String Quartet No. 4 (1964). This work's successor (1984) was based on recorded and microtonally inflected improvisatory material which was then transcribed and realised in score. Penderecki's Second Quartet also employs microtones, sometimes in double stopping, while Sculthorpe's performance directions in his Eighth Quartet include symbols to indicate 'quarter-tone trills'.

The Italian composer-cellist Pietro Grossi employed third-, quarter- and sixth-tones in his two string quartet works of the early 1960s (*Composizione* Nos. 6 and 12), and American computer-music buff Lejaren Hiller's Fifth Quartet (1962) is aptly titled 'In Quarter-Tones'. Maurice Ohana exploited microtones in his works for the medium, especially thirds of a tone, and Nicola LeFanu has developed a highly expressive use of microtones in her two quartets.

American composer Alvin Lucier (*Navigations*, 1991) has exploited 'an organization of "beating" and "interference" patterns that result from the exploration of many intervals between two pitches a minor third apart'.[21] This exploration is systematised by numbers beneath the notes indicating cents above (+) or below (−) the notated pitch and numbers in parentheses indicating the number of beats per second between adjacent pitches (indi-cated by diagonal lines); it is combined with a gradual deceleration of the pulse, a graduated diminuendo from *mp* to *pp*, and *senza vibrato* through-out. As Lucier explains: 'During the course of the performance, audible beats are heard, at speeds determined by the closeness of the tunings. As the in-tervals between the pitches grow smaller, the speed of the beating gradually slows down, from 14, 13, and 12 beats per second – the number of cycles per second between the original semitones – to zero beats at unison.'[22]

Microtonal music has largely lost its significance, not least because elec-tronic music can produce any and all sounds synthetically and only a low-pitch stringed instrument such as the cello can successfully establish a regular system of fingering to realise quarter-tones effectively.

Glissando

Although some theorists have attempted to differentiate between the terms portamento (involving a continuous slide) and glissando (a sliding effect articulating each semitone), twentieth-century composers have tended to use the two terms interchangeably, with glissando the more common.[23] The glissandi in Bartók's Fourth Quartet (i, bb. 51–2, 75, 79, 81, 103–4) are most effective, while the quasi-glissando in the same composer's Third Quartet (b. 4 of *Seconda Parte*, viola) eventually develops into full-scale glissandi in all instruments at the climax of the section (bb. 353ff.) and then again in the recapitulation of the first part, transforming this formerly unnotated expressive ornament almost into an integrated structural feature.

Kurtág's First Quartet mirrors some of Bartók's contrasting timbres, articulations and effects; other notable examples through the century in-clude the opening fifteen seconds of Penderecki's First Quartet and the double-stopped glissandi in the same composer's Second Quartet, along with quarter-tone glissandi in chords and harmonics and copious written directions such as that for the cellist slowly to unwind the peg in order to extend a downward glissando beyond the normal range of the instrument. In his *Tetras*, Xenakis prescribes an unusual effect formed by an amalgam of small glissandi interspersed with sustained pitch, while Gerhard exploits glissandi in harmonics (No. 2, cello, i, b. 96), and in pizzicato, in addition to the nail-glissandi in pizzicato mentioned below. Furthermore, Crumb makes effective use of the trilled glissando at the beginning of 'Threnody II Black Angels' in *Black Angels*.

Lutosławski (String Quartet, 1967) prescribes an extended glissando and specifies above it rhythms and bowings that are to be realised during its course. In his Second Quartet, Elliott Carter carefully notates the duration of each glissando, which is indicated by the length of the note-value from which it originates; and Earle Brown's graphic notation in his String Quartet prescribes variations in the speed and width of the glissando, as well as approximate pitches and annotated dynamics during its realisation.

Harmonics

Natural and artificial harmonics were increasingly exploited for their colouristic potential. While Schoenberg incorporated them only relatively modestly, and principally in the Scherzo of his First Quartet and the 'Langsam ein wenig bewegter' section of the first vocal movement of No. 2, Webern introduced them profitably in his *Bagatelles* Op. 9, sometimes *con sordino* to vary further the rich range of sonorities tapped. More recently, composers have incorporated harmonics even more freely, using them with or without vibrato, in double stopping and incorporating them in trills. Examples of this freer approach are plentiful in the first movement of Ligeti's Second Quartet, while one passage in Penderecki's Second Quartet calls for 'very high natural harmonics on all four strings', and the opening of Panufnik's Second Quartet ('Messages') is striking in its exploitation of harmonics. Remarkably, Villa-Lobos wrote, as early as 1916, a complete movement with left-hand pizzicatos and double harmonics, effects only rarely tapped before in the medium. His subsequent exploitation of harmonic effects in his Third Quartet is remarkable, as are, on paper at least (because they rarely sound!), the *ponticello* harmonics required by Berio in his *Sincronie*.

Ferneyhough uses different kinds and combinations of harmonic with striking virtuosity and variety of colour in his *Sonatas for Quartet* (1967), while Jonathan Harvey's Third Quartet inhabits an ethereal world which splits individual notes into slides, harmonics and partials. Furthermore, much of Gavin Bryars' First Quartet ('Between the National and the Bristol') is in the high register and makes extensive use of harmonics (natural and artificial). In the last of its four sections, from the point where the players are required to tune their lower pairs of strings down a semitone, only harmonics are used – natural on the detuned strings, artificial on the 'naturally' tuned ones. Bryars later revised the ending for a performance in London where the Arditti Quartet played electro-acoustic instruments, to enable the high harmonics more easily to be realised.

Vibrato (including *senza vibrato*)

The role of vibrato changed dramatically during the twentieth century, becoming more than simply an integral part of the player's individual tone quality and serving as an intensifying device, an ornament and an independent expressive technique occasionally separate from traditional musical phrasing. Customary usage of vibrato was often reversed, with demand for an intense, fast vibrato in soft passages, a wide slow vibrato in loud passages, or even a requirement for *senza vibrato* for contrast or special effect.[24]

Some composers have expressly indicated their desired gradations of vibrato. Penderecki (String Quartet No. 1) juxtaposed a rapidly oscillating vibrato (*molto vibrato*) with a very slow one extending to a quarter tone's breadth. Other composers go further, Schnittke's 'starkes Vibrato' in his String Quartet (1965/66) approximating to a semitone and Donatoni's in his Fourth Quartet equating to a whole tone.

Other extreme applications of vibrato have also been prescribed, among them the ornamental vibrato-glissando. Instead of keeping the finger in place and rolling it as with ordinary vibrato, the player allows it to slide up and down the string, creating a siren-like effect. The effect can be produced in wide and narrow slides, and in fast or slow oscillations, a wavy line normally indicating its width and speed along with the written term *vib. gliss.* or sometimes just *gliss.* In Penderecki's First Quartet, for example, the wavy line is explained as 'a very slow vibrato with a quarter tone interval produced by sliding the finger'.

Many twentieth-century composers exploit the *senza vibrato* effect. In some cases this was a reaction against the excesses of an older style; in others it was intended to emphasise steady-state pitch precision for contrast or other effect. Scelsi's experiments with the phenomena of wavering single-note surfaces created a palette that included acoustic beating tremolos (both slurred and reciprocating bowing), microtonal trills, different vibratos, and in certain cases, scordatura. Notable examples appear in his Quartets Nos. 3 and 4, while at the beginning of the third movement of Bartók's Fourth Quartet the violins and viola build up a cluster at first played without vibrato and then with vibrato colouring added. Among other notable examples of *senza vibrato* are those incorporated in the first movement of Ligeti's Second Quartet, Cage's *String Quartet in Four Parts* and the second movement of Husa's Third Quartet (bb. 34–6). Xenakis' *Tetras* and Takemitsu's *Landscape I* (1961) are played without vibrato throughout. Takemitsu's terse phrases alternate with tense pauses, the work's clustered, sustained chords suggesting the ethereal sounds of the Japanese reed-pipe mouth-organ, the *sho*. Furthermore, in his *Adagissimo*, Ferneyhough contrasts the two violinists, who play *senza vibrato* throughout, with the viola and cello players, who are required to vary the degree of vibrato in accord with the phrasing.

Pizzicato

Along with the powerful use of 'traditional' pizzicato in the second movement of Ravel's String Quartet (1902–3), in the Largo desolato of Berg's *Lyric Suite* and in Webern's *Bagatelles* Op. 9 and Quartet Op. 28, a wide variety of pizzicato effects has been developed, with demand for various pizzicato locations (e.g. midpoint of string, three-quarter distance between fingerboard and bridge, at bridge, behind bridge), specific plucking agents and other specific instructions such as pizzicato 'without holding the bow' (Carter No. 3) and pizzicato holding the violin like a mandolin, using a paper clip as a plectrum and sliding a glass rod along the strings to produce the notated pitches (Crumb, *Black Angels*). The 'snap pizzicato', where the string is pulled away from the fingerboard by the plucking agent and allowed to snap back on to the fingerboard with a percussive noise, was popularised by Bartók; perhaps Bartók's most notable exploitation of the device occurs in the fourth movement of his Fourth Quartet (bb. 48–51), a movement which requires all four protagonists to play pizzicato throughout and taps a range of pizzicato proficiency, whether of the 'snap' or 'brush' varieties, or in *sul ponticello* or glissando.

'Snap pizzicato' was taken up by numerous later composers, among them Sculthorpe (e.g. Quartet No. 8), Schnittke (String Quartet (1965/66)), Gerhard (Nos. 1 and 2), Dutilleux (*Ainsi la nuit*), Carter and Ferneyhough. Carter is particularly explicit about the employment of this effect in his Fifth Quartet. He prescribes that 'All snap pizzicati should not only produce the pitch but also an audible attack on the fingerboard. On open strings the snap should be as near the nut as possible. On high notes, the pitch should be produced so that the snap occurs over the fingerboard.'[25] Ferneyhough's *Sonatas* (1967) employs freely various kinds and combinations of pizzicato in an intricate web of colourful and virtuoso effect.

In addition to 'snap pizzicato', Ferneyhough prescribes different agents, including pizzicato with the fingernail (as, for example, in the second movement of Husa's Quartet No. 3 and in Carter's No. 2), various contact-points of pizzicato execution (e.g. *tasto* for the viola at the opening and *sul pont.* for the cello at bb. 225 and 258), *pizzicato subito sforzando*, pizzicato combined with upward or downward glissando and/or vibrato, spread pizzicato in double and multiple stopping, and pizzicato with other descriptors such as *sec*, *marcato* and *distinto*, *pizzicato con sordino*, and pizzicato effects that acknowledge the full range of dynamics. Among Ferneyhough's unorthodox requirements in this piece is pizzicato behind the bridge (indicated by an x) on a prescribed string, and he regularly requires players to change rapidly between pizzicato and *col arco*.

Some pizzicato usage suggests a kind of strumming effect, as in the *pizzicato tremolo* with the loose first finger in Bartók's Fourth Quartet (iv, bb. 78–9, first violin and viola) and in the middle section of the Marcia of the same composer's Sixth Quartet (ii, bb. 84–93), when the viola, playing in guitar position, imitates the banjo underneath tremolandi in the two violins. Penderecki introduces pizzicato effects, thrummed guitar-style across all the strings at an undefined pitch, in his Second Quartet. Left-hand pizzicato has been less readily adopted by twentieth-century quartet composers – although Bartók used it in 'snap' form in his Sixth Quartet (iii, b. 101, first violin and cello) and Britten adopts it in his First Quartet (viola, bb. 601ff.).

Many composers have taken considerable care to prescribe particular plucking agents for specific desired effects. In addition to the percussive flicking or 'picking' (Carter's No. 2) of the string with the fingernail, noted earlier, examples include Britten's prescription of pizzicato with two fingers for the cello double stopping in the opening movement of his First Quartet and his *quasi arpa* requirement for the cello pizzicato towards the end of the first movement of his No. 2. Furthermore, the pizzicato chords in the third movement of Bartók's Sixth Quartet (b. 98, all instruments) are normally executed with the thumb of the right hand.

Varieties of pizzicato involving legato slurs (Bartók No. 6, iii, bb. 99 and 101) and glissando have also been used. Some glissandi involve simply sliding up or down with the stopped finger; others require stopping the string with the fingernail, in order to produce a louder, clearer tone during the glissando (e.g. Gerhard No. 1, ii). Xenakis' *Tetras* requires a pizzicato in which the nail of a left-hand finger stops a note while a right-hand fingernail slides up or down the string. Schnittke's String Quartet (1965/66) includes a specific instruction for the cello: 'Zweimal pizz. gliss. bis zum höchsten Ton: zuerst auf gewöhnliche Weise (rechte Hand zupft *unter dem Griffbrett*, der Finger der linken Hand rutscht nach unten, d. h. in Richtung von Wirbelkasten zum Steg) dann auf umgekehrte Weise (rechte Hand zupft *auf dem Griffbrett*), der Finger der linken Hand rutscht nach oben, d. h. in Richtung von Steg zum Wirbelkasten)'.

Although the full potential of pizzicato may not have been tapped within the genre, composers have nevertheless promoted a wide range of sonorities using the technique. It has even been combined with *col legno* (Xenakis, *ST/4-1,080262*) and also with harmonic effects, generally of the natural variety, as in Crumb's *Black Angels*. Carter's instruction pizzicato 'sul tasto – secco' in his Second Quartet indicates 'A plucking position very near the L. H. finger stopping the string',[26] while pizzicato and vibrato have formed an effective partnership in numerous instances.

Bowing

Changes in compositional taste and style during the twentieth century led to the development of a wide range of challenges in bow management for string players. Such challenges included awkward string crossings, rapid changes and specific prescriptions of contact-point, speed and pressure, sudden or gradual changes in dynamic, often to extreme levels, irregular slurrings and a variety of complex bowing patterns, explicitly indicated (for example, Berio's symbol for 'in one bow stroke, from frog to tip' in *Sincronie*).

The increased rate of dynamic change and the enlarged timbral vocabulary in twentieth-century music impacted significantly on matters of bow control, particularly when realising sudden changes from dynamic extremes or dynamic changes on almost every note, as, for example, in Webern's Four Pieces Op. 7 (1910). The frequent dynamic indications in Milton Babbitt's Third Quartet (1970) have particular significance for bow control in respect of the inter-relationship of bow-speed, bow-pressure and contact-point and often point to shifts in metrical stress relative to the bar. The detailed dynamics and *sempre legatissimo* prescription in the third movement of Ruth Crawford Seeger's Third Quartet also impact significantly on bow control, the dotted ties indicating 'that the first tone of each new bow is not to be attacked; the bowing should be as little audible as possible throughout'.[27]

The more precise and exaggerated use of relatively familiar prescriptions such as *sul ponticello* and *col legno* (discussed later) accounted for many of the developments in twentieth-century bowing technique. However, composers also invented new sounds, often requiring the use of unconventional parts of the instrument and bow and techniques that ran contrary to traditional habits. Demand for asynchronism between the left and right hands, for example, reversed the traditional goals of preserving absolute coordination and synchronisation of fingering and bowing. Some of the fruits of composers' labours, such as the grating, high-pitched sounds produced on the strings behind the bridge or the ghostly, gravel-like tone resulting from playing with loosened bow hair, would previously not have merited description as musical.

Variable contact-point

The range of contact-points of the bow on the string seems boundless. *Sul ponticello*, favouring the reproduction of the upper partials over the fundamental pitch, was increasingly exploited by twentieth-century composers such as Bartók (e.g. No. 4, iii, bb. 41ff.), Schoenberg (No. 2, i, bb. 90–1), Webern (*Bagatelles* Op. 9) and Gerhard. Many composers contrasted the effect in the texture with *sul tasto* (e.g. Bartók, Quartet No. 3, rehearsal number 30).

Ferneyhough (*Sonatas*) uses various kinds and combinations of *sul tasto* and *sul ponticello* with virtuosity and freedom, while Aulis Sallinen's single-movement Fourth Quartet ('Quiet Songs') is based largely around the interplay of introverted *unisono* melodies and *sul ponticello* rhythmic repetitions on a single note. Takemitsu exploits a complex range of textures in his *A Way a Lone* (1981), ranging from lush string chords to spectral *sul ponticello* whispers, effects similarly demanded (via extremely light playing on the bridge) in Berio's *Sincronie* (1964). Berio uses special signs to indicate *sul tasto*, a contact-point near the bridge and over the bridge and, like Berg (*Lyric Suite*, iii, bb. 1–3), combines the effect with *con sordino*, explaining that the performer should press the bow hair against the mute as closely as possible. He also uses a symbol to indicate 'bowing at the frog across the bridge'.

In his Quartet (1970), Fortner seeks the soft, thin and distant sound produced by a bow contact-point above (i.e. on the 'wrong', peg-box side of) the left-hand fingers. Crumb uses a similar technique (and 'sempre senza vibrato') in the sixth movement of his *Black Angels* to recreate the sound of a viol consort (even suggesting that the violin or viola be held upright between the knees while sitting, in the manner of a gamba or cello). Michael von Biel also uses this technique to produce an unusual glissando effect in his Quartet (1965), and he differentiates between a *sul ponticello* played near the bridge and one played on the bridge. Meanwhile, Leon Kirchner, in his Second Quartet (1958; ii, bb. 115–16, and iii, bb. 240–1), uses the term 'quasi pont.' to indicate that some degree of *ponticello* tone colour is desired, but that the pitch of the note is to dominate.

Some twentieth-century composers prescribe bowing behind the bridge (between the bridge and the tailpiece), yielding a high-pitched, flute-like tone with a thin, ethereal quality. Such bowing has been combined with tremolo, 'thrown' strokes (the *jeté col arco* on the strings between the bridge and the tailpiece in Gerhard's Quartet No. 2), arpeggiation of all four strings (e.g. Penderecki's First and Second Quartets and Crumb's *Black Angels*), and improvisation according to the composer's instruction. Changing back and forth from normal playing to playing behind the bridge is a feature of the viola part in the 'Quasi "Trio"' of the fourth movement of Britten's Third Quartet; and near the end of the slow first section of Penderecki's Second Quartet, the viola plays *sforzato* with the bow on the tailpiece, before the first violin contributes tremolandi 'auf dem Resonanzkörper' and the second violinist indulges in finger-tapping 'on the soundboard'.

Other unorthodox sounds include the unique scraping effect produced from bowing on the tailpiece, as in Penderecki's quartets, playing 'with the bow on the right short side of the bridge' (e.g. Penderecki's Second Quartet), or tapping the tailpiece with the bow stick (Gerhard's Quartet No. 2).

Bow pressure effects
Among the unconventional bowing effects introduced by twentieth-century composers were those relating directly to strong bow pressure. The resultant sounds could retain some semblance of pitch, become an ugly, 'grinding' noise (as required in Penderecki's Second Quartet or sometimes in Crumb's *Black Angels*) or include a 'pedal tone' (as in Crumb's *Black Angels*).

'Pitched' sounds were cultivated by starting with normal tone and adding more pressure and/or reducing the speed of the bow, with a contact-point close to the bridge, to create a scratchy, scraping tone quality, yet with pitch still discernible. Penderecki's 'grinding' effect involves the combination of great bow pressure, slow bow speed and a contact-point away from the bridge; a difference in tone-quality is discernible as the bow's contact-point varies, the tone deepening as the bow is moved away from the bridge. Crumb's 'pedal tones' (in the 'Devil-Music' section of his *Black Angels*) comprise notes produced on the violin (mostly on the G string), which, when strong pressure is applied with a slow bow-speed and a contact-point close to the fingerboard, sound actually lower in pitch (by as much as an octave) than the open string or stopped note.[28]

Whole bow gliding and other bowing effects

The phenomenon of whole bow gliding begs a specific sound quality, obtained only by drawing the bow for its full length on every note or every small group of notes, as in Stravinsky's Three Pieces (i, b. 3 and iii, bb. 27–9) or Bartók's Third Quartet (Seconda parte; 'con tutta la lunghezza dell'arco'). The prevailing dynamic largely determines the resultant tone quality.

Other twentieth-century bowing techniques that were contrary to conventional practice included the exploitation of irregular bow changes for timbral effect (as in Penderecki's Second Quartet), *gettato*, for which, as Ferneyhough explains, the bow is bounced 'on the string (single bows) as fast as possible, while the left hand fingers the main notes as indicated', and the effect known as 'brushing'. This latter involves literally brushing along the string rapidly to and from the bridge to the fingerboard with the bowhair at the point. Sculthorpe's Eighth Quartet exploits a 'whispering sound, produced by lightly rubbing bow up and down on open strings'. Playing with loosened bow hair also creates a uniquely soft and ethereal effect.

Tremolo

Tremolo usage expanded considerably in the twentieth century. It could be measured or unmeasured, but such a differentiation was not always indicated with any consistency. Early in the century Bartók used the technique to excellent effect, notably in his Fourth Quartet (iii, bb. 42–54), where the first violin, viola and cello play tremolo double stops *sul ponticello* which alternate with *sforzandi* played in the normal bow position, and at the opening of the second movement of No. 6. By contrast, Penderecki exploits a 'very rapid, non rhythmicalized tremolo' in his First Quartet and the last movement of Crumb's *Black Angels* calls for a very fast tremolo on the strings with two fingers capped with thimbles.

Col legno

Two fundamental varieties of *col legno* stroke co-existed in the twentieth century: *tratto* (drawn), during which the bow-stick is drawn across the string; and *battuto* (hit), usually indicated by a wedge above the note, in which the stick is made to strike the string. The *battuto* effect is dependent upon the stick's point of contact with the string. A contact-point over the fingerboard produces a loud, clicking percussive sound, which results from the bow-stick causing the string to strike the fingerboard. Although the actual pitch of the written note does not change, the percussive clicking becomes higher in register the nearer the contact-point is to the bridge and lower the further it is from the bridge, thereby adding a further dimension to the sound. Notable examples of the effect occur in Bartók's Fourth Quartet (v, bb. 333–4, 336–8), Berg's *Lyric Suite* (iii, bb. 96–8), the second and third of Webern's Four Pieces Op. 7, and Xenakis' *ST/4-1, 080262*, the latter using the term *frappé col legno*.

More unusual *col legno* effects appear in Britten's Third Quartet (iv, trio), Schnittke's Quartet (1965/66), which combines *col legno* and glissando, and Gerhard's quartets, which exploit various *legno* and *sul tasto* effects in sharp contrast. Penderecki (Quartet No. 1) and Brown (String Quartet) prescribe the use of *col legno battuto* behind the bridge (with the tip of the bow), while Sculthorpe directs the first violinist to hold the instrument in a vertical position for the *col legno* strokes in the fourth movement of his Eighth Quartet (1969) and Crumb instructs the player to 'strike with bow near pegs for a more percussive effect' in a *col legno battuto* in *Black Angels* (fourth movement).

Crumb's use of the pure *col legno tratto* stroke in the 'Sounds of Bones and Flutes' section of *Black Angels* is rare in the string quartet repertory. Even Ferneyhough qualifies his instruction 'c.l.t.' in his Third Quartet to allow 'a small proportion of bow hair to remain in contact with the string'. He claims that this 'is especially important when playing in upper registers'. However, some composers specify a combination of stick and hair contact with the string, Karel Husa's Third Quartet (1968) including the direction 'half *col legno*, half *arco*' and Ferneyhough explaining (Third Quartet) that the player should 'turn the bow on its side in order to use the wood and hairs simultaneously and equally'.

Percussive effects using left and/or right hands

Some twentieth-century composers incorporated into their vocabulary sounds produced on areas of the violin other than the strings. The guitarist's tricks of knocking and tapping on the body of the instrument or tapping on the strings with a wood, metal, glass or plastic beater, for example, gradually entered into the string player's equation. Such knocking might be attempted in various places: on the table of the three lowest instruments with the tip of the bow (Shostakovich No. 13); on the table of the instrument with the knuckle of the right thumb (Gerhard No. 2); on the back of the instrument with either the bow-stick or a padded drumstick (Cowell No. 4); on or next to the saddle (near the peg-box) at the end of the fingerboard; on the strings over the fingerboard with the open palm of the hand or fingers (*sul tasto*, as in Penderecki's First Quartet); on the bridge producing a loud rapping sound with no pitch; behind the bridge, producing indeterminate pitches, higher and lower in accordance with the strings employed; on the fingerboard with the fingers of the left or right hands, or with the knuckles of the right hand (as in Crumb's *Black Angels*, no. 5), or with the frog or screw of the bow (Penderecki, String Quartet No. 1); on the tailpiece with the bow-stick or with the fingertips of the right hand (Gerhard No. 2); finger-trilling on the wood of the instrument (David Bedford, *Five*); on the strings with the left-hand fingertips (*senza arco*), releasing faint pitches; or, as prescribed in Penderecki's First Quartet: '*senza arco*: set string in vibration by pressing it strongly with the finger with simultaneous trilling'. Evidently this attempt to make a string vibrate without bowing 'by stopping it with a powerful application of the finger while trilling' was one of Penderecki's few miscalculations.[29]

Percussive effects using other instruments

Some twentieth-century composers incorporated into their string quartets sounds extraneous to the violin family entirely. Percussion instruments such as bells, drums or suspended cymbals and bowed effects on tam-tam, saw and similar 'instruments' have entered their agenda, as well as sounds such as floor stamping or scraping, finger-snapping, -tapping or -sliding and hand-clapping.

In Crumb's *Black Angels*, for example, the four string players are required to play 'traditional' percussion instruments such as the maracas, tam-tam (both struck and bowed, at its edge with a bass bow, as in the fifth movement), and 'non-traditional' percussive instruments such as two metal thimbles and seven crystal glasses (as 'glass harmonicas' filled to certain heights with water and then bowed to produce specific pitches).

Extra-musical influences on interpretation

By and large the quartet has remained staunchly a vehicle for abstract musical thought. However, the decision of a small number of composers to be swayed by extra-musical influences places extra responsibilities on executants fully to investigate, examine and realise that inspiration in their performances. The autobiographical nature of Shostakovich's Eighth Quartet and its numerous self-quotations is a particular case in point; and no ensemble should attempt to play Janáček's 'The Kreutzer Sonata' and 'Intimate Letters' or Berg's *Lyric Suite* without a knowledge of and empathy for the specific circumstances associated with them – those in Tolstoy's novel, Janáček's relationship with Kamila Stösslova and Berg's secret programme (addressed to Hanna Fuchs-Robettin, with whom he was in love). Furthermore, the significance of other factors such as the Berg work's direct quotations from Wagner, the Suite's highly mathematical system of rows, its numerical symbolism (the significance of the number 23 in the metronome markings and number of bars in each movement except the second) and the fact that the last movement, Largo desolato, is a 'setting' of Baudelaire's poem 'De profundis clamavi' ('From the depths I have cried to you') from *Les fleurs du mal*, with the 'vocal' lines (that is the melodic lines to which Berg subscribed the words of the poem) divided variously among the four instruments, should also be assimilated.[30]

Texts from Hölderlin assist performers in their interpretation of Nono's *Fragmente – Stille, an Diotima* (1979–80). Hugh Wood's Third Quartet (1976–8) has a similar skein of poetic superscriptions from John Donne's 'A Nocturnall upon S. Lucies Day' and George Herbert's 'The Flower'; furthermore, these are not small snippets but complete phrases and sentences, speaking of spiritual negation and rebirth.

The breathtaking land- and sea-scapes of Peter Sculthorpe's native Australia have always been central to his musical output. Quartet No. 11 'Jaribu Dreaming' (1990) is rooted in the Kakadu National Park, while No. 13 'Island Dreaming' (1996), which features a soprano soloist, was inspired by the Australian far north as well as the islands in and around the Torres Straits. By contrast, his Eighth Quartet reflects his interest in Balinese music in the late 1960s.

In his *Hambledon Hill* (for amplified string quartet and tape), Tim Souster sought an approach which grew out of some fundamental archetype of the quartet medium. Contemplating the relationship between the instruments' acoustic sound, amplified sound, and their sound as modified and extended on tape, he stumbled on his 'basic shape', or archetype: three concentric circles. Souster equated this with the basic layout of ancient structures which still haunt the British countryside, the iron-age hill forts, of which Hambledon Hill in Dorset is one of the most imposing, even if its sinuous contours are by no means exactly circular. In his work, the concentricity governs not only the layout of the players, who form a closed circle surrounded by a ring of loudspeakers, but also determines the harmonic and melodic structure (three symmetrically expanding sets of intervals), rhythmic structure (inter-related metres), instrumental groupings within the quartet (monophony, duophony, triophony) and in a sense, too, the overall registration of the work (a circular progression from high to low and back).

The titles and arrangement of the thirteen continuous sections of Crumb's *Black Angels*, written in response to the Vietnam war, hold programmatic significance as the stages of the 'voyage of the soul' that Crumb invoked. Performers will also benefit from familiarity with this work's arch structure, within which numerological relationships occur in terms of durations, groupings of certain notes and patterns of repetition,[31] and the significance of its various citations (from the 'Dies Irae', Tartini's 'Devil's Trill' sonata and Schubert's 'Death and the Maiden' Quartet, D. 810).

Poetry and voice

The addition of the voice to the string quartet brought to the genre an extra programmatic dimension in the form of the sung text. With it came an additional responsibility for the performers to familiarise themselves with the text and assist in the true musical expression of its meaning. The most celebrated example of this enlarged ensemble is Schoenberg's Second Quartet Op. 10, its last two movements featuring settings for soprano of poems by Stefan George. The verses embody the longing for elsewhere and the psychic and physical pain of existence pervasive throughout nineteenth-century European Romanticism. The soprano reaches an emotional nadir in the supplication of the 'Litanei' and her prayer is answered in the final movement's mystical rapture, the reunion (or the recognition of unity) with the Holy Fire and the Holy Voice.

Among those composers who have emulated Schoenberg by adding a soprano voice to the medium were Milhaud, whose Third Quartet is based on verses of the poet Léo Latil and is dedicated to his memory, Sculthorpe (No. 13), Rochberg (No. 2) and Ferneyhough (No. 4). Betsy Jolas even substitutes a soprano for the first violinist in her Second Quartet.

Music theatre

Theatre music has been a logical offshoot from the new-found freedom of open-form music and graphic scores of the 1960s. As early as 1959, Carter's Second Quartet set out to achieve an 'auditory scenario for the players to act out with their instruments', each instrument being assigned a different 'vocabulary' of characteristic intervals (melodic and harmonic), rhythms and expressive gestures, and the parts evolving not in terms of constant themes against varied backgrounds, but rather in terms of constant fields of possibilities realised in continually varied foreground shapes – as it were the same tones of voice uttering ever new sentences.[32]

Performers have been increasingly required to act, move, sing, narrate or make other vocal sounds. The score of Kagel's Quartet looks more like a script for a play than a piece of musical notation, particularly its first movement, in which much is made of the players' normal seating arrangements and of various eccentric alternatives. Near the beginning, for example, the cellist plays in his usual seat while the violist walks across the hall playing, then sits in a corner, and the two violins are heard from offstage. All is scrupulously notated. Similarly, Sylvano Bussotti's *I semi di Gramsci* (string quartet and orchestra, 1962–71, revised for string quartet as *Quartetto Gramsci*) includes the instruction (Adagio) 'While performing this piece, walk round'.

Some works require the performers to produce vocal sounds in addition to instrumental ones, including humming, singing, whistling (Penderecki No. 2), whispering, speaking, shouting, tongue clicking. popping sounds (with lips), grunting, hissing and blowing. The violin body is used as an amplifier for whispers and tongue-clicks in Crumb's *Black Angels*, offering a dual aural and visual effect. The players are also required to speak, in specified rhythms, as if in invocation or religious ceremony, the numbers from one to seven, or seven and thirteen, in French, German, Russian, Hungarian, Japanese, and Swahili. Among other examples of quartets with significant vocal effects are Kagel's work and Ferneyhough's Fourth.

Electronics and computers

One of the most radical innovations in quartet scoring has been the incorporation of electronics, generally involving the amplification of traditional instruments which are then manipulated by an engineer, as in Crumb's *Black Angels* for 'electric string quartet'. The instruments may have contact microphones attached, but Crumb's preference is for real electronic string instruments, with built-in pickup microphones. He prescribes an array of special violin effects such as harmonics and *sul ponticello*, which are transformed through amplification, as well as whispering or other vocal effects mentioned earlier. On other occasions composers such as Ferneyhough, Souster, Kevin Volans (Nos. 5 and 6) and Steve Reich (in his twelve-part Triple Quartet) have prepared electronically generated tapes to accompany live musicians in performance.

Lejaren A. Hiller, in collaboration with Leonard M. Isaacson, is said to have composed the first work to make use of computer technology – his

ILLIAC Suite (1957, later retitled String Quartet No. 4), so called because it was composed using the digital computer at the University of Illinois. Chance dictates the process of composition, using the 'so-called Monte-Carlo method of multiple probabilities' to control 'the selection of notes, rests, durations and dynamic intensities'.[33] Xenakis also used computers as compositional tools in his *ST/4-1,080262*, the numerical part of this title signalling the piece as one for four instruments computed on 8 February 1962. This work incorporates very detailed technical markings and effects in constant and rapid flux, causing complex performance problems and giving the intentional impression of 'hectic activity over the widest possible spectra of pitch and sonority'.[34]

The British music critic Hans Keller wrote in 1984 of the 'degeneration' of the string quartet in the late nineteenth and early twentieth centuries, blaming this on the medium's 'transfer to large concert halls'. He suggested that 'it was not until Schoenberg that true quartet sound was creatively recaptured; otherwise, the quartet had lost much of its *raison d'être* – its communication to the players rather than to an audience'.[35] The French composer, conductor and theorist Pierre Boulez had clearly thought similarly when, in the 1960s, he declared that the string quartet was dead. Indeed, it cannot be denied that the twentieth century has witnessed much sterile experimentation in the medium that has yielded little expressive fruit. Nevertheless, the pioneering work of quartets such as the Juilliard, Composers, New Music, LaSalle, Parrenin, Lydian, Arditti and Kronos, and their laudable objectives of encouraging and commissioning composers to write new music, working with them and formulating interpretations according to their intentions, have given renewed life to the medium; indeed, their work and achievements in the field were probably the prime cause of Boulez rescinding his controversial comment in the 1980s.

The volatile union of composer and performer in creating new work has always sparked innovation of some kind or other; but Stockhausen's *Helikopter* (1993) for four helicopters, four television cameras and four members of a string quartet was beyond the realms of expectation even of the Arditti Quartet, for whom it was written. It requires each player to perform to a click-track in a separate flying helicopter;[36] sound and vision are transmitted to the concert hall, where the audience watches the performers on stacked television monitors (three or four for each player), placed roughly where the players would normally sit if playing in the hall.

The twentieth century has witnessed a metamorphosis of compositional language coupled with the transformation of instrumental techniques and sound ideals. The string quartet has remained a relatively economic and intimate medium for thorough exploitation of such changes and has thereby won new territories in expression. Whatever direction its future takes, it will probably be the result of a creative symbiosis between composers and instrumentalists and will incorporate innovations in scoring, content, style and form. Many believe that non-Western or ethnic chamber musics will play a significant role in challenging 'accepted' conventions of what constitutes serious art music, just as an unmade bed and a sophisticated arrangement of vehicle tyres have done in exhibitions of contemporary art. If Stockhausen's most recent contribution to the genre is anything to go by, the term 'spatial effects' may assume a very different meaning during the course of the current millennium.

PART 4

The string quartet repertory

8 The origins of the quartet

DAVID WYN JONES

In the months that followed the death of Joseph Haydn in May 1809 the Leipzig journal *Allgemeine musikalische Zeitung* published a biography of the composer in eight instalments. Written by Georg August Griesinger and subsequently published as a single volume, it had been prepared in Vienna over a period of some ten years during which Griesinger had won the confidence of the composer. Its factual content and its tone were to play a significant part in determining the posthumous image of the composer. Both Griesinger and Haydn were conscious of the international esteem in which the composer was held and the biography sought to explore, through an attractive mixture of direct quotation, anecdote and reverential comment, how he had achieved this pre-eminence. Since the genre of the quartet was central to this fame Griesinger attempted to shed light on how Haydn had first come to compose such works:

> the following purely chance circumstance had led him to try his luck at the
> composition of quartets. A Baron Fürnberg had a place in Weinzierl,
> several stages from Vienna [about fifty miles], and he invited from time to
> time his pastor, his manager, Haydn, and Albrechtsberger (a brother of the
> celebrated contrapuntist, who played the violoncello) in order to have a
> little music. Fürnberg requested Haydn to compose something that could
> be performed by these four amateurs. Haydn, then eighteen years old, took
> up this proposal, and so originated his first quartet [quotation of opening
> of Op. 1 no. 1], which, immediately it appeared, received such general
> approval that Haydn took courage to work further in this form.[1]

Between them Griesinger and Haydn managed to emphasise the chance nature of these early quartets, encouraging the view that this acknowledged master of the genre had stumbled, in the emerging tradition of the questing creative genius, on a new medium; this interpretation was cleverly supported by the quotation of the opening of the work published as the first quartet in the notable complete edition of Haydn's quartets issued by Pleyel in 1801. In fact it is not known which was Haydn's 'first' quartet; it could be any one of ten. Even the aside about Haydn's age at the time, 'then eighteen years old', conveniently, if innocently, exaggerates the composer's youthful originality; the quartets were not amongst his first works after being dismissed from the choir school of St Stephen's Cathedral but were composed several years later when the composer was in his late twenties, between *c.* 1757 and 1762. Clearly, historical accuracy was not a prime concern of Griesinger and Haydn, as both willingly played their part in the evolving mythology of the composer and his music. Aside from querying the details, modern scholarship would dearly like to have asked the composer whether he felt he was doing something new in these works. Were they as epochal as the author and the composer imply?

Music for four solo string instruments can be traced back to Italian composers of the Renaissance and early Baroque such as Gregorio Allegri (1582–1652), Adriano Banchieri (1568–1634), Andrea Gabrieli (1533–85) and Florentio Maschera (*c.* 1540 – *c.* 1584), all of whom wrote such music; and although two twentieth-century ensembles, the Allegri Quartet (founded in 1953) and the Gabrieli Quartet (founded in 1966), were named after two of these composers, it is a mistaken act of homage for there is no continuity of tradition between this period and that of Haydn. Works in four parts composed in England for consorts of viols by John Jenkins (1592–1678), Henry Purcell (1659–95) and Christopher Simpson (*c.* 1605–69) can also claim to be quartets but this repertoire is even more circumscribed in period and influence.

From the late seventeenth century through to the middle decades of the eighteenth, the most commonly encountered instrumental ensemble was the trio sonata, two melodic instruments supported by continuo (normally, but not always, a keyboard and an appropriate bass instrument). Although a theoretical outlook that seeks to transform the Baroque trio sonata into the Classical quartet through the addition of a viola and the omission of a keyboard has some historical justification, it is the least important aspect of the pre-history of the quartet. More fundamentally, the familiar (and psychologically comforting) historical quest for one composer who made a decisive discovery breakthrough is misguided, owing more to nineteenth-century notions of creativity than to those prevalent in the eighteenth century. Varying aspects of performance practice in a range of instrumental and orchestral music in the first half of the century provide a more compelling and pervasive background from which the quartet emerged.

Alongside the trio sonata, works for three melodic instruments and continuo are numerous in the first part of the century. The received view of performance practice is that the continuo would consist of a keyboard and a bass instrument, but there is plenty of evidence to suggest that the continuo line could be played with or without a keyboard instrument.[2] Thus when Alessandro Scarlatti (1660–1725) wrote a set of six works with the title 'Sonata à Quattro per Due Violini, Violetta [viola] e Violoncello senza Cembalo',[3] effectively six quartets, he was merely making explicit a practice that was reasonably common.

Another widespread practice that could yield a work for two violins, viola and cello was performing four-part orchestral music with one player per part rather than multiple players. In the middle of the eighteenth century, for instance, the English musician Charles Avison (1709–70) offered advice on how to ensure that the distinction between ritornello and solo sections in concertos was maintained in performances with minimum forces:

> When Concertos are performed with three or four Instruments only it may not be amiss to play the solo parts *Mezzo Piano*; and to know more accurately where to find them, the first and last note of every Chorus [ritornello] should be distinguished thus (♪) and to prevent all Mistakes of pointing the *Forte* at a wrong Place that also ought to have the same Mark: By this Means the performer will be directed to give the *first* Note of every Chorus and Forte its proper Emphasis and not suffer the *latter* to hang upon the Ear, which is extremely disagreeable.[4]

In Avison's own musical heritage, therefore, works by Handel and Geminiani as well as his own that were normally heard orchestrally could emerge as quartets. In France Louis-Gabriel Guillemain (1705–70) published his instrumental music in eighteen collections in Paris between 1734 and 1762. His Op. 7, which appeared in 1740, was specifically written for minimum forces, reflected in the title: 'Six concertinos à quatre parties'. As in the case of Scarlatti sonatas without keyboard in Italy, Guillemain's concertos for two violins, viola and continuo were not followed by further similar works that might have established a beginning of a quartet tradition in France.

Producing *de facto* quartets from works that were normally performed with multiple performers was a natural part also of the rich Italian tradition of concerto writing from Arcangelo Corelli (1653–1713) and Giuseppe Torelli (1658–1709) to Antonio Vivaldi (1678–1741) and Giovanni Sammartini (1700/01–75). This repertoire is often divided into two types, concerto grosso and solo concerto, but a third type, orchestral concertos (or *ripieno* concertos) – that is works for three- or four-part strings with no soloists – is important in the process that made the composition of true quartets inevitable.[5] Vivaldi alone composed over thirty such works. This notable tradition merged imperceptibly with that of the early symphony, and works, whether concertos or symphonies, by Sammartini from the 1730s through to the 1760s that were scored for four-part string orchestras could easily become quartets in performance. When Griesinger suggested to Haydn that Sammartini was the true instigator of the quartet, Haydn was very dismissive, calling the Italian a 'Schmierer' ('a scribbler'); almost certainly the real reason for Haydn's comment was that he recognised that performance tradition was more important than one single composer, particularly one he did not admire.

Probably the first set of works in this rich Italian tradition of string music that was conceived as quartet music was that by Luigi Boccherini (1743–1805), composed in 1761 and subsequently published in 1767 in Paris as his Op. 1 (G. 159–164). These quartets were widely distributed throughout Europe and instigated a continuing commitment to the genre by the composer that was to produce over ninety quartets over the next five decades. There is nothing in them that shows that Boccherini was familiar with Haydn's earliest quartets or with others from the Austrian tradition discussed below. Like most of Sammartini's concertos and symphonies, they are in three movements (fast–slow–fast); the slow movements of nos. 1 and 2 feature extended cello solos, and the finale of no. 2 is a spirited fugue.

While extant sources and inventories in Austrian libraries show that Italian repertoire did feature in musical life in the Austrian territories in the middle decades of the eighteenth century, primacy of influence over locally produced music cannot be claimed. In particular, Austria had its own tradition in the early symphony, principally works by Georg Mathias Monn (1717–50) and Georg Christoph Wagenseil (1715–77). Both composers wrote symphonies for four-part strings alone and it may well be the case that some of these were first conceived as works for four solo players rather than for an orchestral ensemble, particularly when it is remembered that so-called orchestras might in certain circumstances, such as the smaller palaces and churches, consist of one player per part. Significantly there was no prevailing tradition in contemporary libraries of dividing instrumental music into orchestral and chamber music. It was all *Kammermusik*. Monn, for instance, is credited with fifteen works for four-part string orchestra, called 'sinfonia a quattro' and 'quartetto' in extant Viennese sources and probably composed in the 1740s in the years immediately before his death.[6] While they reveal stylistic features that are conservative alongside progressive ones familiar from the early music of Haydn (and others), at the same time they have an attractive coherence as individual works. Six of them were gathered together at the beginning of the nineteenth century by the Viennese publisher Bureau des Arts et d'Industrie, who issued them unequivocally as a set of quartets, to be performed alongside the works of Haydn, Mozart, Beethoven and others. There is a preference for cycles of three movements rather than four, and a clear distinction between substantial first movements in sonata form and much shorter finale movements in 2/4 or 3/8. The sonata forms often contain a deflection to the dominant minor in the second subject area; slow movements are harmonically open-ended, moving into the following fast movements; and there are some fugal movements. The one in a symphony in A is built on two rhythmically distinct themes. The polyphonic texture is maintained throughout and when played by a quartet invites comparison with another fugal movement in A major, the finale of Haydn's Op. 20 no. 6 (1772).

A uniquely distinguishing feature of instrumental music in Austrian territories in the middle decades of the eighteenth century was the use of the word divertimento to cover a range of instrumental genres. In essence, the term signalled a piece of instrumental music for one or more solo players, covering genres that were later to acquire more differentiated names such as sonata, violin sonata, string trio, piano trio, wind sextets and so on. As well as signalling solo performance per designated part, the divertimento was notable for the absence of a continuo instrument.[7] Thus the sixty or more divertimentos that Franz Asplmayr (1728–86) wrote in the 1740s and 1750s for two violins and bass constitute a clearly delineated genre, and are not trio sonatas without keyboard or solo versions of three-part orchestral music. Within this tradition works for solo keyboard and for string trio are the most numerous, but it was inevitable that divertimentos for two violins, viola and cello, the solo equivalent of a standard four-part orchestral disposition, would be composed; indeed, Asplmayr himself composed a set of quartets towards the end of the 1760s, his Op. 2.

Apart from Haydn, two other composers reared in the Austrian divertimento tradition wrote quartets early in the independent history of the genre: Ignaz Holzbauer (1711–83) and Franz Xaver Richter (1709–89). Their works may pre-date Haydn's Opp. 1 and 2, but specific evidence is not forthcoming. What, however, is true is that neither of these composers proceeded to compose further works in the medium.

Holzbauer was born in Vienna in 1711 and lived there for the first part of his life; in 1751 he moved first to Stuttgart and then Mannheim, where he remained until his death. Four extant quartets are attributed to him.[8] Apart from an appealing melodic style they have very little in common, which suggests that they were composed separately over a number of years. A quartet in B♭ has four movements – Allegro, Andante, Minuet and Presto – and has a good deal of unison writing for the first and second violin, which might indicate an orchestral origin. More individual in its scoring and its movement layout is a work in E♭. The opening Andantino con moto leads into an Allegro, whose fifty bars make a decisive move to C minor rather than the expected dominant of B♭, before gradually re-focusing on the tonic. By finishing on the fifth of a rising tonic triad the Allegro, in turn, leads into the next movement. Although it carries only the tempo heading of Andante grazioso this is clearly a minuet with two trios, the first composed for two violins and cello, the second for two violins and viola.

Born in Moravia in 1709, Richter received his early music education in Vienna before moving in 1736 to Stuttgart, then successively Kempten, Mannheim and Strasbourg, where he died in 1789. Richter's music enjoyed something of a vogue in London in the 1760s and in November 1768 a set of six quartets was published by Longman and Co. as his Op. 5. Extant manuscript parts for five of these works, originally owned by the Cistercian monastery of Osek in Bohemia, suggest that they were composed several years before this.[9] Even more tantalising is the following passage in Dittersdorf's autobiography: 'We set to work at the six new quartets by Richter, which Schweitzer had got hold of. He played the cello, I the first violin, my elder brother the second and my younger brother the viola. In between, we drank rare good coffee, and smoked the finest tobacco. How jolly it was!'[10] This account can be dated to 1757, when Dittersdorf was living in Hildburghausen, but whether these 'six new quartets' are the same as the ones subsequently published as Op. 5 or works that have not survived cannot be established.

All the quartets from Op. 5 are in three movements – fast, slow and fast – though some reverse the position of the slow movement and first fast movement. Most of the fast movements begin with a double announcement of the main theme, by each violinist in turn, a technique particularly associated with the old trio sonata but which is found in Haydn's early quartets and symphonies too. In all six works there is a determined attempt to give solo passages in fast and slow music to the viola and cello. Although Richter's differentiated textures, dynamics and articulation markings make the music constantly appealing to players and listeners, it is not supported by that fragmentation and reformulation of musical thought that is characteristic of Haydn's writing for the medium, even in his earliest quartets. The presto fugue that concludes the C major quartet has the heading *Rincontro* (that is a musical 'encounter') and although it readily reveals its indebtedness to species counterpoint in its two- and three-part lines it manages to transcend pedagogy, particularly when it discovers new rhythmic patterns later in the movement. The concluding fugue of the quartet in Bb is based on a lengthy single subject; as the music moves towards the dominant in the first half of the binary structure it becomes more homophonic in an attempt to create a stronger sense of polarity between tonic and dominant. The finale of the A major quartet is a minuet and trio; in the minuet itself the theme is played in octaves by the first and second violin, a scoring particularly associated with Haydn's minuets.

Like those of Richter and Holzbauer, Haydn's first quartets were the natural product of a broad performance practice that yielded music for two violins, viola and cello, particularly stimulated by the extensive Austrian tradition of divertimento writing. The opus numbers 1 and 2 originated in the 1760s when they were applied by two publishers, La Chevardière (Paris) and Hummel (Amsterdam and Berlin), anxious to issue works in the standard set of six; the numbers were perpetuated by Pleyel in his complete edition of the quartets published in 1801. The work familiarly known as Op. 1 no. 5 was not an original quartet but another example of converting a symphony into a quartet, in this case by simply omitting the parts for oboes and horns; likewise Op. 2 no. 3 and Op. 2 no. 5 were originally composed by Haydn as divertimentos for quartet plus two horns. In the 1930s a lost quartet by Haydn was discovered, a work in E♭ that was subsequently dubbed 'Opus 0'. In total, therefore, there are ten early genuine quartets by Haydn.

Written across a number of years, five or more, these ten early quartets are all in five movements, mainly a symmetrical formation of two presto movements enclosing two minuets that, in turn, surround a central slow movement. Haydn never used this neat pattern again, preferring the strongly differentiated sequence of movements that emerge in the standard four-movement patterns of fast, minuet, slow and fast or fast, slow, minuet and fast. Determining the character of the genre with a particular movement order is a feature of Haydn's music in general in the 1750s and 1760s and if this suggests an attitude that already sought to probe the particular potential of the medium then it is certainly borne out when the quartets are compared with works in other genres in the period. Following Asplmayr, Wagenseil and others, Haydn was a prolific composer of divertimentos for two violins and bass, at least twenty-one works, perhaps as many as thirty-six, composed from the early 1750s through to the mid 1760s. But it is a surprising fact that almost nowhere in the string trios does the scoring show the variety and, more particularly, variety as an active proponent of syntactical invention that is such a striking feature of fast movements and minuets in the early quartets. Haydn's divertimentos for larger forces, such as the two divertimentos for flute, oboe, two violins, cello and double bass (Hob.I:1 and 11), more frequently demonstrate these qualities and provide a more revealing background to the quartets than do the string trios.

Along with thematic economy and a very brisk tempo, unpredictability of phrase rhythms is a particular source of invention in the outer movements. In the opening Presto of Op. 2 no. 4 in F, standard four-bar phrases intermingle with three-bar phrases and six-bar phrases in a constantly vacillating relationship; also apparent is the supporting role of virtuosity, unexpected pauses and switches of tonal direction. Between them the two minuets in Op. 2 no. 4 reveal a heightened degree of linguistic craftsmanship: variety of phrase rhythms, contradiction of obvious patterns through imitation and a range of sonority, including, in the second minuet, octave scoring.

It is in the fast movements and minuets of the early quartets that Haydn's later supreme mastery of the medium is most consistently foreshadowed. Most of the central slow movements, on the other hand, have a concertante texture familiar from slow movements of Baroque concertos: a lyrical solo line for first violin spun out over a repetitive accompaniment. The Adagio of Op. 2 no. 4 is unusual in that it is the only movement in the minor key in the ten early quartets, though several trio sections turn, momentarily, to the minor. While for Haydn's players and listeners such slow movements provided a ready, and attractive, point of contact with the tradition of playing orchestral music with one player per part, for Haydn the inquisitive composer they came to be regarded as unsatisfactory as he sought to apply the kind of symphonic thinking shown in fast movement and minuets to slow music too.

Griesinger's comments on Haydn's earliest quartets contain one other misleading remark. He conveniently implies that once the early quartets had been written – by which the readers would have understood Opp. 1 and 2 – Haydn embarked without interruption on a continuing career of quartet writing. In fact, at least seven years were to elapse before the composer returned to the medium, with the completion of the Op. 9 quartets in 1769. In this period a number of other Austrian composers had written divertimentos for two violins, viola and cello, including Johann Albrechtsberger (1736–1809), Franz Asplmayr (1728–86), F. X. Dussek (1731–99), Florian Leopold Gassmann (1729–74), Leopold Hofmann (1738–93) and Johann Baptist Vanhal (1739–1813). Once again precise dates and circumstances of composition are not known, but it is clear that by *c.* 1770 the quartet had established itself as a favoured instrumental medium in the Austrian territories. Within a few years it acquired the same status elsewhere in Europe.

9 Haydn, Mozart and their contemporaries

W. DEAN SUTCLIFFE

The exclusive image of the string quartet, established relatively early in its history and lasting up to the present day, has determined that only a narrow range of works from the eighteenth century remains in general circulation. There is a comparative lack of editions, recordings and above all live performances of quartets by any composers other than Haydn and Mozart. This might seem to mirror the current representation of later eighteenth-century music altogether, confined like that of no other period to a tiny number of 'Classical' figures. Nevertheless, one senses a greater openness to unfamiliar repertory with other genres. It seems to have been assumed that it is the quartet that most readily finds out the lesser figures, that sorts the great from the good. The collective image of these lesser figures tends not to accord them much dignity: they are lightweights, and any attempted revival of their music may well prompt a bemused reaction.

This reflects an attitude towards the whole musical language of the time: that it is inherently undemanding, that only the best can transcend its expressive and technical blandness. This reflects (and misinterprets) the marked preoccupation with medium and low styles in this language, the aesthetic preference for accessibility, to the relative exclusion of a high style that was by definition associated with a less accessible past. The heart of the matter concerns technical rather more than expressive tone: just what constitutes good technique, how does it relate to genre and how conspicuously ought it to be displayed for the listener? Once more the question arises of how distinct a role the quartet plays in such a larger reception history. Such a consciousness of style and technique seems in fact to have been established almost with the birth of the genre, so that it colours not just later readings but also contemporary perceptions. In other words, it is not just a function of subsequent reception but inheres in the circumstances of the time. Technique was bound to become an issue when, for the first time in history, composers began to mix their styles in unpredictable ways within single movements, possibly going against the sense of what was appropriate for a particular medium.

On the other hand, one might want to withdraw from any reading which implies that the string quartet was particularly privileged within such debates. This is partly a tactical reservation, given the quartet's emergence as the most potent symbol of the traditional approach to later eighteenth-century music, one which has been strongly hierarchical in its treatment of genres, composers and geographical centres and is summed up by the very existence of the concept of a 'Viennese Classical style'. Indeed, a real mystique has grown up around the genre. Key aspects of string quartet lore include its purity, its privacy or intimacy, so bound up with the exclusive image mentioned at the start, its conversational properties and the equality of the four parts. Yet the implied distinctions from other genres are at least partly fictional. Almost all later eighteenth-century instrumental music can be understood as having conversational aspects; a heightened awareness of texture, as implied by the imperative of 'equality', surely marks all chamber music of the time; and all instrumental genres can be understood as metaphors for social relations.[1]

Whether such terms of reference are particularly applicable to the quartet – to the extent that they are valid in the first place – remains an open question through the following survey. The quartet can on the one hand be readily understood as representing a distinctive mode of musical thought. Historically, the genre did not really emerge gradually. At no point in its later history was it cultivated so extensively, by so many composers, as in its first few decades of existence. It was not just highly popular in many important European centres, it was commercially lucrative. And it went from being a fresh new form to a venerable one in not much more than a generation, establishing a mythology so deeply entrenched that it has survived more or less up to the present. On the other hand, in many important respects it is simply representative of broader contemporary concerns. My procedure will to an extent collude with the tradition of 'strong reading' of the genre, without assuming that this must entail clear distinctions from or superiority over other forms of the time.

The main evaluative categories will be texture and topic, in an attempt to observe social traces in the form. Counterpoint and conversation, as two of the most commonly evoked critical gambits, demand particular attention. It is important that counterpoint is not understood monolithically;[2] there are many types that do not revolve around set subjects and stylistic uniformity. Particularly relevant is what Hans Keller described as an 'intrinsic' texture of 'homophonic polyphony',[3] covering the endless means by which the notion of leading melodic and subordinate accompanimental parts can be inflected. Indeed, the ways in which composers deal with that vast grey area between absolute polyphony and absolute homophony is more significant, stylistically and statistically, than the handling of (strict) counterpoint altogether.

Conversation is often associated with one of the articles of faith about the string quartet, that there should be four equal parts. This is almost always defined in terms of distribution of melodic lines.[4] Yet any literal equality of melodic material is barely possible in later eighteenth-century instrumental style, premised as it is on accessible and 'natural' homophonic textures. The most common disposition will feature the melodic line at the top. Gravity pulls upwards in the string quartet, meaning that the first violin is bound to be the main melodic protagonist, and this 'law of nature' ultimately holds for at least all tonal music of the common-practice era. The melodic lead will of course alternate, but this rarely approaches statistical equality; and where it does, the results risk sounding contrived and mechanical, just the opposite of the imagined democratic ideal. A more fundamental principle is to establish separate identities for the four players, to lend them a sense of autonomy or individuality or agency, and this can be more consistently and subtly served by the 'intrinsic' compositional thinking outlined above.

A melody-centred view also accounts for some of the difficulties of the conversational metaphor. In a fine example of how the string quartet has tended to swallow up terms of reference that may be more widely applicable, the idea of musical conversation began as a means of describing various types of ensemble chamber music before it became more exclusively applied.[5] Given the logical difficulty that such conversations would literally imply the near-continual talking of all the protagonists, the tendency has been to equate speech with melody, or more broadly thematic material, and listening with accompaniment. Yet this understanding breaks down for the same reason as does the notion of melodically based equality – that it does not allow for the flexible boundaries between different constituents of a quartet texture.[6]

A focus on topic helps us to deal with the image of the genre: how does the 'exclusive' quartet square with the generally popularising and accessible 'Classical' style within which it is situated? Three topical types are of special interest: learned, popular-exotic and 'foreign' (denoting evocations of genres or mediums such as concerto, symphony, aria and even keyboard music). There are several more specific points of enquiry, some of which represent what I take to be generic fingerprints:

1. The use of unisons. While unison writing may seem in principle to negate the ideal of an individualised texture, in practice it can often heighten the sense of social awareness in quartet discourse.
2. The realization of cadence points. Heavily elaborated cadence points, often featuring a distinctive contribution from an inner part, are a real signature texture. They are perhaps a way of reaffirming, at a point of potential mechanical uniformity (where the demands of harmonic articulation overwhelm the ideal of a differentiated texture), that there are four individuals involved; the emergence of one stands for the integrity of all four. Such individualised parts will normally

fit graciously enough with the whole, though: they enact the balance between individual consciousness and social obligation that is part of any conversational ethos.

3. What I call a 'chorale' texture arises when all parts proceed in relatively homogeneous, even note values, generally in a fairly low tessitura and at a subdued dynamic level. The lack of rhythmic differentiation and the strong tendency towards stepwise voice-leading emphasise the way in which full harmony is created from parts with pronounced linear 'integrity'.[7]

4. Often overlapping with chorale texture is harmonic mystification, achieved through remote harmonies or unexpected progressions. This might be regarded as the embodiment of a harmonic 'high style' and was often a matter of comment in contemporary reception.[8] While a notable feature of much instrumental music of the time, it does appear to have been more intensively cultivated in the quartet.

5. The rhetoric of closure. Soft, often witty, endings become something of a trademark in the quartet, perhaps because they offer a way for the medium to advertise its private nature. As we shall see, though, privacy in the later eighteenth century could be quite a public affair.

6. Textural mobility. Quartet textures tend to involve a rapid turnover of different configurations; too much stability would suggest an 'anti-social' type of chamber behaviour. When this does happen, it is often a special effect. But then the same holds for almost all types of instrumental texture at the time. Here the social awareness – not droning on with one idea or topic for too long, the injection of a variety of musical image that will retain the attention of both player and listener – is more generally built in. Again the difference in the case of the quartet could only be one of degree.

One of the peculiarities of the Viennese environment that witnessed the birth of Haydn's early quartets was that a predominantly popular manner coexisted with a distinctly more elevated approach to chamber music. The latter was maintained above all by Joseph II, who held regular quartet performances in his apartments until his death in 1790. He had a strong preference for the traditional textural ways, and so many of the works associated with him feature complete fugal movements and other older touches. While statistically such works were to be overwhelmed by those written in a more accessible manner, the conservative tradition was never to be entirely lost, even when direct emulation of the style was not involved. Indeed, it is arguable that part of the particular prestige that was to accrue to the genre in Vienna derives from the imperial favour shown towards its more learned specimens.

The composers most closely associated with Joseph II, such as Florian Gassmann (1729–74) and Carlos d'Ordoñez (1734–86), seem to have differentiated between works destined for the Emperor and for a wider circle. Nevertheless, many of their quartets demonstrate that the gap between formal and informal counterpoint is not a clear one. The first movement of

Op. 1 no. 1 in A major by Ordoñez is based on a rhythmic motto, but flexibly treated so as to yield a clear sense of the motto being reinflected by differing personalities. It shows how an essentially learned idiom can be the basis of a conversational style.

While a composer such as Johann Albrechtsberger (1736–1809) continued the learned tradition into later decades, writing predominantly two-movement *sonate* for string quartet (effectively a homophonic prelude followed by a fugue), Franz Asplmayr (1728–86) cultivated a more consistently modern style. His Op. 2 set, written in the late 1760s and published by Huberty in Paris, appeared with the designation *quatuors concertants*. This common term did not, as we might imagine, have to denote extensive 'soloistic' passages; it was simply a way of advertising to potential purchasers that all four parts played a full and varied role in the texture. Our category of textural mobility is amply illustrated by Asplmayr's typical manner in these four-movement works, even when the individual dispositions sometimes suggest the trio sonata or orchestral writing.

When Joseph Haydn (1732–1809) returned to the quartet towards the end of the 1760s, he adopted a more systematic approach, with each set being carefully planned to yield a variety of keys (as Asplmayr had done with his Op. 2) and expressive typologies. Op. 9 was completed in 1769, Op. 17 in 1771 and Op. 20 in 1772. Haydn's obsession with the formal and affective properties of closure seems to date from the quartets of this vintage. Particularly common is the habit found in the minuets of making a beginning phrase into an ending one. The quartet is perhaps a particularly suitable locale for such game-playing. As a notionally non-public genre, there can be no sense, as there may be in a symphony, of a 'realistic' minuet for a social occasion. The effect also suggests a conversational mode, with the wit of discovering that a point made at the start has been returned to, 'proved' through subsequent discussion. It also flirts with the awareness of redundancy that must be central to a thoughtfully conducted conversation. Here of course the conversational ethos lies not so much in the interaction of individual parts as in a whole mode of utterance.

The sort of abrupt changes of tack characteristic of Asplmayr are also found in Haydn, especially in opening movements. The first movement of Op. 17 no. 1, for example, shows a remarkable range of textures and colours. The best way to brand a quartet as a quartet is to feature such versatility, as if to show beyond any doubt the autonomy of the four players. This creates a sense of informal, spontaneous discourse. The opening of Op. 17 no. 5 combines a highly asymmetrical sense of construction with a distinct lack of harmonic ambition – the music sits very comfortably on a root-position tonic. In bar 7 the second violin plays a B♭ in this very diatonic environment, like a sign of impatience. The same might be said of the *fortissimo* unison figure in bar 13. This also has a real sense of agency, like a corporate decision to move on by taking drastic action.

A sense of social comedy can also be obtained by the opposite means, by isolating the individual. The more or less literal equality so often held out as the ideal for a quartet texture would not allow the playing with established textural roles that Haydn in particular loves to exploit. In the current movement, near the end of the development, there is great fun at the expense of the leader as its phrase lead-ins turn into aimless wanderings. It effectively gets lost, as do its companions, as we can hear from the irregularly spaced accompaniment, which has a few stabs at following the leader before giving up. The players seem to wink theatrically at the listener, as if in a conspiracy of misbehaviour.

How do we square this theatricality with 'conversation' and intimacy? By bearing in mind that chamber-musical qualities are as much enacted as innate, that they form part of a consciously applied poetics of the genre. As Mary Hunter has recently reminded us, the line of demarcation between public and private spheres in the later eighteenth century was by no means secure.[9] If a medium like the quartet might seem to suggest a cultivation of the private or intimate, like the epistolary novel, it was a privacy that interested large numbers, one that was marketable, in short, one that was for public consumption.

Similarly, conversations – even if we understand them under an umbrella concept such as 'role play' or simply social interaction – are not 'real' but enacted, giving us the illusion of insight into the minds of several individuals. Their artificiality in fact obtains on two levels – not just in the fact that they represent 'public privacy', but also in the relatively formalised nature of the speech acts that they represent. This may be readily understood when we consider the modes of salon conversation practised at the time, and of course on a larger scale the status of high art music and the representation of the string quartet within that. But this should not alienate us too much from the type of communication they represent. Only a little linguistic knowledge is required to become aware of the formalised, even ritualistic nature of even the more relaxed conversations that we conduct amongst ourselves today, and of the interpersonal considerations that guide the rules of conduct. Thus the conversational metaphor has lost relatively little of its specific social force to the present day.

All of these terms – privacy, intimacy, conversation – trade in the 'supreme fiction of the listener's non-existence', to adapt Michael Fried.[10] They all imply a suspension of disbelief on the part of that listener, and so any flavour of theatricality that arises need not rub against such notions. In fact the theatricality suggested of the first movement of Op. 17 no. 5 becomes explicit in the third. The first violin's soliloquy has turned into a literal recitative, a borrowing from a clearly public and theatrical genre, yet this does not have to be understood as so topically far-fetched, given the social reading of texture suggested above.

Such concerns are also relevant to many of the finales of Opp. 9 and 17. In that of Op. 17 no. 6 the basic rising-third cell of the movement is inverted in the short coda and now played legato. Before the original answering two-bar unit can follow, the viola and cello have echoed this newly articulated third, and the movement then disappears in a brief flurry of this shape, played *pianissimo*. This is a *locus classicus* for the soft quartet ending. It is in fact more thrilling than a loud conclusion could be. Haydn has it both ways with this technique – his players assume a soft tone of voice that is proper to the chamber, but this also creates a sensational effect that will work with an audience, of whatever size.

A companion to the public–private duality that must inform any interpretation of quartets of this time is that between indoor and outdoor. Given all the terms of reference above, one might imagine the quartet to be an exclusively indoor medium, yet it seems to retain, from the celebrated early examples in Haydn, a hankering for the outdoors. In the Op. 17 set this is apparent once more in many of the finales, which offer not just earthy folk tones but also in some instances outright gypsy material, so there can be no doubt of the low style being evoked.

Compared with the consistent approach taken to movement-types in the two previous sets, in Op. 20 Haydn favours extravagant contrasts of typology, both formal and expressive. Indeed, of his future sets only Op. 76 is comparably diverse. This even applies to the three fugal finales, which have often been problematised, partly out of ignorance of their place in the Viennese tradition described earlier. The tendency to treat counterpoint monolithically has exacerbated this, blinding writers to the great variety found both between these three finales and within them (they are all based on several subjects). In one respect, indeed, Haydn provides a negative image of the monolith, instructing the players to perform each fugue 'sempre sotto voce', and it is only towards the end of each movement that the dynamic containment is overturned. Such softness of execution is incompatible with learned style, which demanded 'strength and emphasis',[11] nor is it what one would expect of a finale altogether.

Such containment may also be read as an attempt to draw both player and listener in, not so much simply to create a 'genuine chamber style' as to enact or dramatise a sense of genre. This also applies to the famous Affettuoso e sostenuto of Op. 20 no. 1. Proceeding almost uninterruptedly in even quavers in all parts, in a middle register and dynamic ('mezza voce'), this movement, more than any other, seems to have defined that part of quartet imagery that concerns communion, 'innerness' and privacy. It is not only a strong example of 'intrinsic' writing but also of chorale texture, and testifying to its impact is that at least three composers – Abel, Kozeluch and Mozart – seem to have used the movement as a model. The marking of harmony that naturally occurs in such a context, with so many other parameters being 'evened out', is even more apparent in the coda to the first movement of Op. 20 no. 5 in F minor, which contains a definitive example of a harmonic purple patch, marked 'piano assai'. Here the dynamic emphasises the mysterious and unfamiliar nature of the process, as if it were a 'secret science', yet it also draws the listener in. While the elevation suggests the connoisseurship of the few, the self-contained nature of such passages, and their clear signposting as special effects, invites a more broadly based listenership.

While in such examples the quartet seems to develop its own form of discourse, it remains open to impersonating or drawing from other media – a group of rustic musicians, the orchestra, vocal forms whether solo (aria) or even choral ('chorale' texture?), even, as William Drabkin has shown, the piano.[12] In Op. 20 no. 2 sections of both the slow movement and the Trio suggest a Baroque ritornello for orchestra (which was, after all, very often just a string orchestra), while in between the Minuet hints at a musette, like a memory of folk music. A different kind of versatility is evident in the slow movement of Op. 20 no. 3. Here the composer uses the technique of bariolage, the playing of a repeated note in alternating stopped and open-string versions. The first violin introduces the bariolage material near the end of the exposition; after the second violin's sustained use of it as a bridge back to the tonic, it passes to the viola at the end. Thus three of the protagonists play it, in a form of large-scale dialogue. Note, however, that it is not played by all four. On a shorter time-scale, such treatment of material *a quattro* is an obvious type of quartet syntax, one that is often used to define the boundaries of a thematic or modulatory area. But Haydn is not often arithmetical in this way; this avoids any sense of an imposed conversational structure.

Although Luigi Boccherini (1743–1805) was based in Madrid from 1769, he had spent some time in Vienna a decade earlier before returning to Italy. Most of his quartets were in fact published in Paris, the centre that saw the first clear explosion of interest in the genre. His Op. 2, published in Paris in 1767, had in fact been written in 1761, and it is immediately marked by a highly flexible conception of texture. Often this involves a nuanced form of antiphony, as in the opening of no. 2, which consists of three distinct elements that appear in three dispositions over the course of the movement. If this suggests the sort of *ars combinatoria* that was to occupy Mozart in his quartets, there are also many moments where the texture has soft edges, where a part rises to prominence in the most undemonstrative of ways. Witness the slow movement of no. 1, where the viola gently guides the closing phrases of each half to a close. The two violins have worked up to the apex of intensity, and the transference of role at this point of the line, the completion of the thought by the viola, exemplifies our category of 'worked' cadence points.

Several textural types found in Op. 2 become signatures of the composer. One is the centre-centred texture which arises when all voices play literally within an octave or less of each other.[13] This not only creates a particular warmth but represents a very distinct chamber-musical idiom, a type of writing that would not occur to a composer in an orchestral context. The cello often leads in such situations, but not conspicuously. This is also one way of avoiding what can be an uncomfortably exposed sound when the cello has the melody, since it has plenty of cushioning immediately below. The second type represents a form of obbligato homophony that I dub the 'music-box' effect – four clearly independent parts with air in the texture so that their simultaneous differences can be appreciated. It suggests a conception of music as object, with spatial emphasis, rather than as process, something which is also apparent in Boccherini's tendency to repeat sections with varied scoring. It is as if the performers are on a revolving stage. This gives listeners the chance to attend to different parts of the texture, building this into the 'performed time' of the work. It also means, of course, that players certainly get to know all the parts, a necessity that was already being stressed by commentators later in the century.

For all the textural versatility of these works, any analogy with conversation seems weak. The different 'speech rhythms' of Boccherini's syntax, especially the melodic material, play a part in this, but also the level of social tension seems low. More characteristic than a Haydnesque contest of wits is a premise of mutual acceptance, what Giorgio Pestelli happily calls 'a fundamental friendship of ideas'.[14] A more relevant conceit might be to understand the textural dynamic as pastoral. This is partly a function of the composer's preferred textural imagery, given the prevalence of the two strongest markers of a pastoral style, pedal points and the presentation of melodic figures in parallel intervals. It also agrees with the wider understanding of the pastoral style and with the particular reception accorded to Boccherini. In 1809, for example, Johann Baptist Schaul wrote: 'And what melody does one find in even the simplest accompanying voices! Everything sings. No single note fails to speak . . . Every voice portrays, so to speak, a member of a family, who share mutually their secrets, their sorrow with such . . . warmth, that every listener must think himself transported into a time of innocence and honesty.'[15] In this twist on the metaphor of quartet as conversation the type of social interaction suggested is idyllic and Arcadian.

The timelessness of this pastoral sphere also accords with the suggested emphasis on spatial properties in Boccherini, and Op. 8 (published in 1769) contains many examples of 'loop' structures. Often, as in the finale of Op. 8 no. 4 in G minor, these involve the sort of canonic writing also encountered in Gassmann.[16] More broadly, they suggest motion *around* rather than motion *towards*, in which everything seems to hover around or decorate a fixed central point. The frequency of voice exchange and swapping of parts also contributes to this flavour.

Meanwhile, in England Carl Friedrich Abel (1723–87) produced three sets of quartets. The first two, Opp. 8 (1769) and 12 (1775), suggest an older textural dynamic in which hierarchies are inviolable for the given unit. Thus there is plenty of imitation and sharing-around of melodic lines, but this is a formalised interaction. The accompaniments tend to be mechanical both in shape and syntax. This shows how melodic sharing alone does not generate the modern quartet idiom – it's the quality, indeed the very conception of 'accompaniment' that is decisive for chamber music in a later eighteenth-century sense. If we wished to apply a model of discourse to Abel's procedure, it would have to be in the nature of a formal debate; there is little chance of a conversational interruption, rude or otherwise. Although this reflects the trio sonata, one should not exaggerate the retrospective nature of such dispositions; the more literal forms of the *quatuor concertant* continue this relatively formalised approach to dialogue in the chamber.

Abel's Op. 15 (1780) was dedicated to Friedrich Wilhelm, Crown Prince of Prussia, who was to receive many more dedications and commission many sets of quartets.[17] As he was a cellist, this generally led composers into a more concertante style prompted by the need to let the cello shine, and this is certainly the case in Abel's set. Another kind of influence seems to obtain with the slow movement of no. 3, an Adagio in 3/8 and A♭ major, written in chorale texture. This seems to emulate the similarly constituted slow movement of Haydn's Op. 20 no. 1.

It was in the later 1760s that the string quartet began its spectacular progress in Paris. After earliest publications of Haydn's first quartets and Boccherini's first sets, and the appearance of the first set by a Frenchman, Antoine Baudron, in 1768, others entered the fray in the early 1770s, including François-Joseph Gossec (1734–1829), Jean-Baptiste Davaux (1742–1822) and Pierre Vachon (1731–1803). Vachon's first set, Op. 5, was published in about 1773 in London. Although the *quatuor concertant* is taken to be associated with the growth of the *symphonie concertante* in France at the same time, this need not imply an especially public face to the chamber form, least of all with Vachon. There are certainly no overheated textures in his quartets, and indeed he often writes for only two or three parts at any one point. Such reticence suggests there is a fair amount of 'listening' going on as well as 'talking', and an often 'tactful' relationship between the parts.

At the same time, Vachon does frequently follow the *concertante* precept whereby a 'solo' comprises one melodic unit. This is the case, for example, with the viola solo in the first-movement development of Op. 5 no. 1 in A major. (This was also to be a common location for an expressive viola solo in Cambini.) Like most of those one comes across, it is fairly high in pitch, and the same is true of the typical cello solo. It is much rarer to hear these instruments achieve melodic prominence in their lower registers. In other words, the terms of what constitutes a solo are set by the style, and range, of the traditional melodic instrument, the (first) violin. However, the viola passage here does prompt a turn to minor, and its timbre might seem to be especially well suited to the less stable processes of a central section.

Giuseppe Cambini (1746–1825) settled in Paris in about 1770 and wrote the first of his 149 quartets several years later. Nearly three-quarters of these works are in two movements (like most *symphonies concertantes* of the time), and most of the rest are in three. It was only towards the end of the century that four movements became the norm; prior to that, two- and three-movement schemes were just as likely and some composers, such as Boccherini and Pleyel, were notably versatile in their choices.

The *concertante* blocking-out of sections of melodic leadership is naturally one of the defining features of Cambini's quartets. Frequently individual contributions are concluded by the concerto-like cadential formula consisting of rapid figuration (most commonly an ascending scale) leading to a lengthy trill. It would not do to imagine that such devices somehow corrupt the pure discourse of the quartet. Such borrowings from other genres are after all a staple of almost all later eighteenth-century music, and this specific borrowing from the concerto (which itself derives from the aria) is found in all instrumental genres of the time. It does of course tend to have a public flavour, which the composer may choose to exploit as such. In a related example, the third and final movement of the Quartet Tr. 116 in G minor begins with orchestral flurries, involving tutti chords and endless repeated notes, suggesting a generic transfer from the symphony. The development, however, brilliantly fragments into a 'real' quartet style, with more reflective thematic work. The repeated notes, previously heard in two or more parts, are now isolated in single voices and played in dialogue.

It is also notable that the passages that follow explicit solos are often written in 'homophonic polyphony', where all four parts are clearly differentiated, as if in acknowledgement of the tension between a group and soloistic dynamic. It should be noted that, as with virtually all the eighteenth-century quartet repertoire, we have very little documentation about performances of Cambini's works in Paris. Public performances, in a straightforward modern sense, were almost unknown, except in London.[18]

Another highly prolific and successful composer of quartets was Ignace Pleyel (1757–1831). He dedicated his Op. 1 to his teacher Haydn, the first of some sixteen composers to do so.[19] Such dedications to fellow composers were becoming part of the ethos of the genre, as was the sort of more or less explicit modelling we also find in Pleyel. Thus the two fugues in his Op. 5 and the recitative in Op. 3 no. 6 show an engagement with particular earlier Haydn works. Such creative gestures of course reaffirm the weighty image of the genre, yet we must remind ourselves of the enormous popularity it was achieving at just this time. In 1786, for example, over 2,000 quartets were advertised as being available from Parisian publishers.[20] The real push in Vienna came with the establishment of music printing in 1778 by Huberty and Artaria, supplanting the previous practice of scribal copying.

If Pleyel was quick to take advantage of this new environment, rather too much has been made of the accessibility of his quartets, as if this were somehow at odds with the prevailing instrumental aesthetic of the time. Haydn's Op. 33 (1781) had shown that a popular manner and technical strength were perfectly compatible. Pleyel is notably inventive in his culti- vation of the soft, wry, comic ending, which seems to have been a Viennese speciality. A fine example is found in the finale of Op. 1 no. 2; after a big perfect cadence, the final two bars are a soft low horn fifth for first violin alone.

Topically similar is the finale of Op. 2 no. 2 in C major, framed by rustic material featuring sustained open fifths in the cello and an arpeggiated osti- nato in violin 2. Its return leads to another soft close, marked 'Perden[dosi]', with the second-violin figuration finishing two bars after the tune; the other parts have already come to rest on pedal notes. The final sustained chord is then held for over two bars, so that the work drains away rather than finishing as such (connoting the 'eternal rhythms' of nature and country living). This beautiful effect is not only an inventive variant on the soft close for the chamber, it once more takes the ensemble outdoors.

The soft ending is also cultivated by Johann Baptist Vanhal (1739–1813), another prolific writer in the medium. The final movement of his Op. 13 no. 2 already features an understated finish to the exposition, but its extension at the end of the movement creates a pronounced asymmetry. Such lop- sidedness would be inappropriate to a more public form such as the sym- phony or concerto. Nevertheless, as has been argued already, such private effects seem to demand some sort of public, even if this means only the players themselves. If the 'Classical' style dramatises the listening experi- ence (for the first time), part of this comes from the performers being heard to listen to each other (hence conversation rather than say declama- tion as a metaphor), and the concentrated sonority of the string quartet makes this particularly apparent. Vanhal often sets up a 'listening' texture through various techniques of reciprocal part-writing. Sequential movement may take the form of a dialogue between upper and lower pairs, slow movements sometimes feature cadenzas for the whole ensemble and there is frequent use of voice exchange, in which two voices swap a specific set of pitches.

Wolfgang Amadeus Mozart (1756–91) was, famously, another of the composers to dedicate a set of quartets to Haydn, the six works published as Op. 10 in 1785. Their most characteristic tone, one of sweet seriousness, and the technical intensity they display (which the composer virtually advertised in his dedication) were to be highly influential for the image of the genre. Such a high style is often marked by 'contrivance', by material that is clearly manufactured rather than 'natural'. This is the case with the Minuets of K. 387 and K. 464, which flaunt their contrived quality through both texture and dynamic markings, the opening theme of K. 428, the slow movement of K. 458 and of course the slow introduction to K. 465, 'The Dissonance'.

In the Minuet of K. 387 the celebrated *pf* markings on alternating notes of a chromatic scale really call attention to the artificiality of the enterprise. When these scales are played in canon, this has the disconcerting result that the dynamic alternations are opposed in the two parts: as one plays softly, the other is loud, and on the next beat the dynamic relationship is reversed. The players agree to disagree. In an example of connoisseur's economy, the insistent foregrounded presentation of this module justifies the later frequency of chromatic shapes, but they are now absorbed into a normal melodic style and relatively formulaic in their context. Above all what is being played with in this game of stylistic registers is a formula that originates in the learned past – the chromatic fourth.

Even more startling is the first movement of K. 428. The opening offers a strange line in octaves, like a sort of learned conundrum, and the harmonised version heard subsequently is hardly a solution, since it is out of scale with the surrounding harmonic rhythm. Later workings of the problem are also rather gaunt, a canonic presentation at the start of the development and a version in the reprise which is fitted with a Baroque walking bass. All of these presentations are aphoristically isolated within the whole, giving an uncomfortable sense of continuity. The following Andante con moto invokes again the slow movement of Haydn's Op. 20 no. 1. The ostentatious dissonances of its opening almost have an antique flavour, caused by a collision of semitonal ascents and descents, and this strongly suggests the opening subject of the first movement, so surprisingly isolated there.

A further example of this strain is the Adagio of K. 458. The opening, in Eb major, is awkward in terms of scansion; the first gesturally and texturally stable material does not occur until bar 7, but this is in C minor and turns out to be the start of a transition. That Mozart is in fact working along

Haydnesque lines of presenting misplaced material becomes clear in the coda, as he corrects the original 'errors'. In retrospect it becomes apparent that we started with a series of isolated closing gestures, and these are now reconfigured, more or less in reverse, to create a satisfying close. All of these conspicuously worked passages are calculated to appeal to connoisseurs (among whom must be reckoned the dedicatee). Also signalling a high style are such typical devices as harmonic mystification (the opening of 'The Dissonance' in fact did much to cement this procedure) and richly worked cadence points.

On the other hand, all such close reasoning is always ready to be countered by lower styles, creating a type of topical play that can seem particularly pointed in a quartet context. Thus in the Minuet of K. 428 a delightful musette texture is transformed into a canon, while in the slow movement of K. 464 the fifth variation, full of close imitations and chains of dotted rhythms, is succeeded by a sixth that suggests more popular strains, with its drum-like cello ostinato. The group changes from being a learned body into a band.

Something similar operates if we consider Mozart's basic mode of tex-tural thought. As elsewhere in his output, this turns on permutation as a fundamental principle: the re-allocation and -combination of composed entities, creating what Kofi Agawu calls 'a succession of variation states'.[21] It means a much more direct approach to thematic manipulation, indeed to the whole conception of what 'thematic' material is, than we find with Haydn, and also that the interaction of the parts can be more clearly grasped. On the other hand, some of the most brilliant effects in Op. 10 come not from such permutation but from more broadly conceived sonorities. Many involve octave doubling. The last four bars of the Trio of K. 428 feature the violins playing the same line two octaves apart. The fact that the viola and cello are low and close together adds to the extraordinary colour of the passage. The finale of K. 421 shows another expressive use of octaves between the violins. In Variation 3 these have a spectral character, then in the *maggiore* of Variation 4 they become popular and relaxing due to the change of mode. A strategic use of octaves and unisons is a very important part of the genre's textural palette, and Mozart offers some of the most striking examples.

The outright antiphonal treatment of melodic units does not in fact create a particularly persuasive sense of 'conversation', if we imagine this to imply a relative informality of exchange. This is most apparent in the first two of Mozart's 'Prussian' Quartets, which, in an attempt to please the intended dedicatee, offer a fairly literal 'equality' of melodic expression. The result has been described as resembling 'a committee in which all must have their say'.[22] More apt equivalents for the textural metaphor of conversation tend to be found in more indirect contexts. In the slow movement of K. 421 the frequent passing-around of an arpeggiated fragment gives a new perspective to the subsequent ensemble continuations of the theme. It makes us hear them as a combination of individual voices, implying a music presented by consensus rather than to order. This is particularly striking in the lead-up to the reprise, in bars 48–51. The clearest instance of syntax being determined by the medium occurs in the final few bars. This consists of four divisions, made up of successive high-to-low entries of the arpeggio. Only then can closure arrive, in a textural and performative sense.

In the first movement of the Quartet in D major, K. 499, the second violin is occupied with providing broken-chord figuration for several lengthy passages in the exposition, but a cadence formation in between these keeps all parts of the texture alive and meaningful. From bar 52 a cadence is built up to through four-part imitation, the same device just observed in K. 421, and here it is violin 2 that enters last, appropriately enough. It had in fact begun the previous long textural unit by itself, providing a submissive or supportive accompanimental gesture around which its colleagues can indulge in their antiphonal play. But its entrance for the cadence provides a more individualised version of the imitative point; instead of the long second note, it plays a poignant chromatic turn figure. The cadence achieved, it immediately returns to its broken chords, again beginning these by itself. This simple detail demonstrates that the surrounding homophony is consensual, that even the most apparently subordinate part is charged with agency.

Comparing the six works Mozart dedicated to Haydn and Haydn's previous set, Op. 33, is an established critical litany. This seems to have been invited by the dedication itself, and given that Mozart's six are longer and seem to be more ambitious and more varied, it is not surprising that one school of thought has 'found for' Mozart. This may be traced back to the theorist Heinrich Koch, and Mozart has continued to satisfy theorists more up to the present day. This derives partly from the greater directness of his technique, as we have seen, whereas the art of Op. 33, too often not understood, was to absorb technique into a flagrantly popular manner. If one wants to compare 'great men' in this way, Haydn's Op. 20 seems a closer point of departure for Mozart: it shares an almost programmatic emphasis on technical and expressive range. Another school of thought has been more diffident in assessing Mozart's contribution to the medium. Julian Rushton, for example, believes the composer was 'more confident in other genres, including those he invented' and, to return to our initial concern of the image of the quartet, suggests that Mozart's 'inhibitions, as well as his achievements, have coloured the medium ever since'.[23]

There were other composers of the time who, like Mozart, contributed sparingly but significantly to the genre. Leopold Kozeluch (1747–1818) wrote six quartets that, as was becoming common practice, were issued as two sets of three, Op. 32 in 1790 and Op. 33 in 1791. That modelling was becoming virtually part of the generic code may be seen in the slow movement of Op. 32 no. 1, based, once more, on that of Haydn's Op. 20 no. 1, while the equivalent movement of Op. 33 no. 1 seems to be inspired by the Capriccio of Op. 20 no. 2. Elsewhere there are hints of Mozart's K. 428 and K. 464, while the second movement of Op. 33 no. 2 combines the functions of a slow movement and finale, which could be indebted to similar structures by Pleyel, Haydn or possibly even Franz Anton Hoffmeister (1754–1812). The first movement of the latter's Op. 7 no. 1 also alternates Adagio and Allegro sections.[24]

If we wanted to construct a pattern of social interaction for Kozeluch's quartets, it would be that of a model society, where everything is sweet harmony. Ernst Ludwig Gerber in 1791 praised 'the noblest melody with the cleanest harmony and the most pleasing order',[25] and these attributes can be seen in the characteristically full textures and smooth contours. One type of writing that combines both attributes, much favoured by Kozeluch, is the 'chorale'. In the first movement of Op. 33 no. 2, for example, it creates a four-part harmonic style of noble simplicity. This texture was becoming increasingly favoured as an alternative to the more usual differentiated homophony; another example is the opening of the Quartet Op. 5 no. 2, dedicated to Haydn, by Peter Hänsel (1770–1831).

The six quartets of Carl Ditters von Dittersdorf (1739–99), published in Vienna in 1789, also show this foregrounding of harmony as a virtual string-quartet topic, but otherwise there could hardly be a stronger contrast to the civilised values represented by Kozeluch. No one flaunts incongruous topics, keys and textures with more relish than Dittersdorf. In his picaresque way, he seems to pursue a single issue: what is a suitable language for a string quartet? Among the 'foreign' topics explored are the overture, comic opera, gypsy fiddle-playing, the archaic and the great outdoors. The finale of Quartet no. 5, for instance, features a large-scale comic-operatic crescendo that could have inspired Rossini. This is as far from a nuanced quartet style as one could imagine, as is the section it leads to, where the lower three sustain a *fortissimo* C minor chord for thirty-eight bars while violin 1 plays a gypsy lament. The second movement of no. 4 is mainly a dazzling study in horn calls.

Most striking of all, though, are the composer's many references to archaic topics. 'Learned' would often be too soft a description, and there is generally no question of their being absorbed into a more modern type of quartet discourse. The middle section of no. 4's 'Minuetto', called 'Alternativo', begins with a strange phrase featuring a Phrygian cadence, while the

Alternativo to the Minuet of no. 3, built on a romanesca bass progression, also sounds archaic. One might imagine that such antique strains serve to flatter players and listeners, given the frequently aspirational nature of the genre, but the way in which Dittersdorf contextualises them means that they often carry startling expressive force.

Many of the composer's most memorable effects come from a blocking-out not just of topics but also simply of textures. Another type of texture that inheres naturally in the medium, unmentioned so far, involves generally the upper three parts playing parallel 6/3 chords while the cello either holds a pedal point or is silent. While almost all composers make frequent use of such progressions, in Dittersdorf they are often presented in the most unadorned form. One example comes in the exquisite Minuet of Quartet no. 3, where the parallel chords in violins and viola are answered by an extraordinary, wide-ranging cello arpeggio. Such a basic juxtaposition is far from the more worked style of quartet that was being increasingly cultivated; it can produce the most subtle of effects as well as the stylistic shocks described above. The particular fascination of Dittersdorf's contribution to the genre lies in the way he often deconstructs or exaggerates the most common generic moves. His quartets offer an instructive anthology of textural and topical possibilities that few other composers dared to present so boldly.

Another figure of exceptional interest is Joseph Martin Kraus (1756–92), six of whose quartets were published by Hummel in Berlin in 1784.[26] Kraus is greatly given to cultivating enigmatic formal structures, and the flavour of his work is hard to capture: his material is generally accessible, marked by both ardent lyricism and deadpan wit, yet there is something quite inaccessible about its bearing. For example, no one is more given to the device of the understated ending, yet its effect can be as much coolly diffident as comic.

A work that is elusive throughout is Op. 1 no. 3 in G minor. It opens with a most unusually placed fugal movement. Also remarkable is that the fugato texture is framed at the beginning and in the middle, by an exordium and a brief sighing Adagio passage. While this might owe something to the 'framed fugue', as practised by Christoph Sonnleithner (1734–1786) in his quartets written for Joseph II, the expressive sense is harder to gauge. At the least, such a structure seems to tell us that counterpoint can no longer be conceived as a self-evident stylistic quantity. The following 'Romanze' is clearly up-to-date, its serenade flavour strengthened by the use of another textural device not mentioned so far – the doubling of a first-violin melodic line not only an octave below but also at the lower sixth or tenth by violin 2 and viola. This disposition, particularly favoured by Kraus, generally conveys a popular, often outdoor flavour. The final Tempo di minuetto is an extraordinarily original movement, the outer sections of which contain a perfect cancrizans, not signalled by the composer. Such a 'learned' device clearly relates to the stylistic world of the first movement. Yet the music is also fascinating because of its elusive expressive make-up – gloomy, resigned yet also strangely decorous. The last two movements in fact show how textural interest may be maintained with almost no recourse to imitation or explicit turn-taking.

Not much less remarkable is the D major Quartet, Op. 1 no. 4, a potent example of how unison texture may be exploited, notably in the central Larghetto. After the model four-part scoring of the eloquent theme, followed by a central trio for the upper three instruments, the unison is used as a pivot back to the full texture, but it has a stark effect, particularly because we hear a rare literal unison: all four players deliver a three-note figure g♯–g♯–a.

Amidst the explosion of quartet writing in the 1770s and 1780s, Luigi Boccherini was continuing to contribute significantly. In his Op. 32 (unusually appearing first in Vienna, in 1781) instrumental role-play takes on a harder edge, although there remain many unforgettable Arcadian moments, often brought about by the composer's musing (over-)repetitions. The first movement of no. 4 is quickly taken over by the cello: busy arpeggios, interleaved with melodic writing, lead to a freakishly high dominant seventh arpeggio in long notes. A stunned silence follows, then the whole ensemble re-emerges *pianissimo* at a low tessitura. The dynamic level gradually grows towards a normal closing theme, as confidence is restored. Great social comedy is made of a virtuoso impulse, as if the cello has broken the decorum of the genre.

Topical contrasts have also become more pronounced, with some abandoned folk passages and strong archaic features, especially notable in no. 2 in E minor. The fifth quartet of Boccherini's final set, Op. 58 (1799), features one of the most explicit renditions of a rustic band in the literature – two passages in musette style, complete with flattened leading notes, marked 'pifferi di montagna'. Against the surrounding modern finale manner, these seem to represent an ancestral memory, of another kind of music-making.

Contemporary opinion seems not to have felt any great divide between Boccherini and his illustrious colleagues. For instance, the Englishman William Jones compared the grand old style of Corelli, Purcell, Geminiani and Handel with the modern ways of Haydn and Boccherini in 1784: 'they are sometimes so desultory and unaccountable in their way of treating a subject, that they must be reckoned among the wild warblers of the wood: and they seem to differ from some pieces of Handel as the talk and laughter of the Tea-table (where, perhaps, neither Wit or Invention are wanting) differs from the Oratory of the Bar and the Pulpit'.[27]

This allusion to a modern conversational mode, witty yet trivial, offers a nice contemporary take on Haydn's Op. 33. Has such consistently flippant music ever been hailed as historically so important? The seminal importance of Op. 33 has been virtually an article of faith for generations of writers, reinforced by the composer's famous letter in which he wrote of 'a brand new way' of writing string quartets and by the decision to drop Minuets in favour of movements entitled Scherzo. Of late, however, there have been strenuous attempts to demythologise the set.[28] Yet the music can be understood as demythologising itself, given the way it advertises its simplicity, its popular lightness of manner. This co-exists with a humour that ranges from the burlesque to the satirical. Thus the set is both popular and natural as well as polished and discursive; it has attributes of both the country and the city, of the outdoor and the indoor.

Op. 33 is celebrated for its integration of different strands in the texture, achieved above all by blurring the distinction between melody and accompaniment. This was in fact frequently evident in Haydn's previous quartets from the late 1760s and early 1770s, but it stands out more now due to the simplicity of means. The manipulation of a repeated-note shape in the opening paragraph of no. 1 in B minor shows how fine the margin can be between leading and subordinate part. Another kind of textural game is found in the Scherzo of Quartet no. 6. The constant imitation becomes so fascinating for all concerned that one member of the group, the viola, is caught in the act of playing a further entry when the other three have already reached the final cadence. We could compare it to a game of musical chairs, in which the viola is left standing when the music stops.

The Largo e sostenuto of Op. 33 no. 2 shows a quite different means of enhancing the social plotting of texture. It moves from the initial duo for viola and cello to a half-accompanied duo (via a highly original cello pedal expressed as a trill) to a fully accompanied trio (the trill-pedal still more autonomous) to a quartet presentation of the material near the end. In a wonderful contradiction of textural expectation, the first time all four instruments play, it is highly disruptive – a double presentation of a two-note figure that is loud, chordal, staccato (all has been legato to this point), topically dissonant (akin to an orchestral call to attention, as opposed to the previous singing style), in an unprepared G minor. A few bars later we hear another 'tutti' that is also disruptive and inappropriate to slow-movement style. It is actually a variant on the previous tutti's pitch structure, but it feels rather different, with obsessive syncopations and an odd dynamic structure: again it is clear that all four cannot be trusted together in the same room!

After the climactic four-part version of the opening, we hear the same original continuation, but now it is *piano* and legato. A bar later this sweet group behaviour is all for nothing; it is answered by a further disruptive version of the material. In the final bars there is another attempt to resolve this. With wonderful irony, this is now done by a duo, the two violins, suggesting that roles have swapped – the original duo has been amplified to a full texture and the original full texture has been reduced to a duo. There is also a social dimension to this, as if the violins decide that they had better confine this subject to themselves alone, given the destructive impact it always had before. Capping this, the final gesture is a solitary version of the two-note figure for all four, *pianissimo*, without a companion bar. This suggests first that the violins have shown the way to the others and now a proper form of the material may once more be tried, and second that it would be better not to aim for the full two-bar version. Of course we only know this in the unnotated bar of listening that follows the end of the movement. This witty asymmetry, this open effect, provides a precedent for the spectacular events at the end of the famous 'joke' finale, one of the most influential realisations of the soft-ending gambit.

It was only in fact in the later 1780s that Haydn began the sort of regular production of string quartets that had already been undertaken by the likes of Pleyel, Boccherini and Vanhal. After the single quartet, Op. 42, Op. 50 particularly continues the concern with power relations within the group.[29] This is associated partly with a heightening of thematic relationships between the voices. The set was dedicated to the cello-playing King of Prussia, but, unlike the many other composers who did the same, Haydn did not move towards a more overt *concertante* mode. The next twelve works, Opp. 54–55 and 64, however, were associated with or dedicated to the violinist Johann Tost, a member of the Esterházy orchestra. They do indeed feature much brilliance for the first violin, but this stops short of suggesting the genre of the *quatuor brillant* that was evolving in Paris (which could become a virtual concerto realised with chamber forces). The pure image of the quartet means that some may be uncomfortable with any thoughts of the medium being corrupted in this way; but virtuosity can be just as creatively inspiring as any other compositional factor.

This is evident in the wider dramatic range of Opp. 54 and 55 in particular, but it also sharpens certain textural possibilities. For a start, these works are full of manoeuvres to topple the leader. Op. 54 no. 2 in C major is in fact quite specifically premised on the notion of a brilliant first violin. Indeed, the instrument begins with figuration, as if it wants to dominate through sheer physical presence. Over the course of the movement there is a process of levelling-out, as the lower parts gradually gain ground. In the Adagio the first violin stands apart from the ensemble in the most obvious way – through the stylistic disparity between the quasi-passacaglia opening topic (also another example of chorale texture) and the gypsy layer the leader adds over the top of this from bar 9. There are also some obvious harmonic disparities, with the harsh dissonances brought about by the first violin's wild rhythmic abandon, the least group-minded display one could imagine.

The strong uniformity of texture and rhythmic disposition in the Minuet forms an obvious counter to the Adagio, as though the four are determined to be unanimous. The first sign of any autonomy comes just when we might expect the final cadence. The first violin (of course) adds two short scalic figures. The third, extended, version, though, is *forte* and for all, resulting in an extraordinary sonority of a line being played in four separate octaves, with a crescendo through to a big final cadence. The finale (mostly an Adagio!) soon presents a big first-violin tune, with purely accompanimental pulsings in the inner parts. However, the leader is somewhat upstaged by arpeggio figures in the cello that start off with a clear bass function, but rise and rise until they reach up to and sometimes beyond the violin's melodic register.

The Tost Quartets are notably vivid in their realisations of various signature textures. Harmonic mystification, in conjunction with chorale texture, takes especially dramatic forms in the finale of Op. 64 no. 3 and in the first movement of Op. 64 no. 5, 'The Lark', while the pronounced purple patches in the Allegretto of Op. 54 no. 1 are probably modelled on Mozart's 'Dissonance' Quartet.[30] The finale of this work features one of the most inspired realisations of the soft-ending gambit. The anacrusis that has been toyed with throughout turns into an *objet sonore*, a magical soft high chord.

What contributes much to the conversational quality in Haydn's quartets is the sheer rapidity of thought-process represented by the music; 'conversation' need not inhere only in how the parts interact. The finale of Op. 55 no. 3 offers a good example of this – its rhythmic brilliance gives a vivid sense of cut-and-thrust. The counterpoint is used to set the pulse racing, with little sense of the display of a learned style. This holds too, though, for the work of many of Haydn's colleagues.

The following six works of Opp. 71 and 74 (1793) are also not readily squared with the pure image of the genre. They were written for London, where there was an established tradition of quartet performances before large audiences. The first movement of Op. 71 no. 1 in Bb major is built on an antithesis of two brands of material, the melodic and the figurative, one which is modified as the movement progresses.[31] Such an antithesis could also be read in terms of private and public gesture (although we must of course be careful not to understand these terms as absolutes), in which Haydn ends up with a blend between the two. In other words, the changed circumstances are not simply a given which the composer reflects in his writing, but a subject for discussion and investigation. He in fact does something very similar in the first movement of his next Bb quartet, Op. 76 no. 4. Altogether Opp. 71–74 are marked by a profusion of arresting textures, not all in brilliant style, that can only be seen as a positive result of the London circumstances.

Haydn's final efforts in the genre comprise the six works of Op. 76, two more in Op. 77 and the unfinished Op. 103. Before the last three appeared, Pleyel, who had founded a publishing house in Paris in 1795, had embarked upon a ten-volume edition of all Haydn's quartets (1798–1802), a clear sign of both the marketability and prestige of the form. A common critical gambit of the time also recommended careful study of all parts by the players, while at the same time it had become standard practice for composers to put quartets into score for study purposes. Such needs were answered by Pleyel's invention of the miniature score, and he also issued all Haydn's quartets in this format. The string quartet had gained the greatest pedagogical and artistic standing in just a few decades.

One possible reflection of this is that archaic elements seem to become more insistent towards the end of the century. Within Haydn's last quartets we may count the slow movements of Op. 76 nos. 4 and 6 (a 'Fantasia' whose first half has no key signature) and the 'Witches' Minuet' of Op. 76 no. 2. In general, shifts of style and register become more brazen in these works, as in the unexpected setting of the finales of Op. 76 nos. 1 and 3 in the minor mode. In particular, the rustic element becomes more urgent. The public circumstances of Opp. 71 and 74 seem to have tapped this again; perhaps most surprising of all is the eruption of a peasant dance in E major towards the end of the development of the first movement of Op. 76 no. 3, which is mostly in a brilliant style. Perhaps, like the increasingly signposted archaic elements, they form part of more extrovert orientation apparent in quartets of the last years of the eighteenth century. But the rustic elements may also represent something of a safety valve. In the case of Haydn, they are often juxtaposed with a distinctly elevated type of utterance, nowhere more effectively than in Op. 77 no. 2, and they thus help to restore a common touch.

A similar case may be made for other composers writing quartets in the 1790s and 1800s. With a sense of weighty tradition springing up so quickly – a review in the *Allgemeine Musikalische Zeitung* in 1811 wrote that Haydn had brought the quartet to a 'position of honour' and 'his imitators to such despair'[32] – many, no doubt somewhat daunted, were cultivating a highly wrought style, one that advertised its technical accomplishment. (At this stage we should remind ourselves of Rushton's words on Mozart.) The danger was that this would turn into the overwrought and overrefined, and an increasingly picturesque approach to lower styles was a way of retaining some creative equilibrium.

If emulation was already a common part of quartet culture, the modelling seems to become more overt at this time. Two quartets, Op. 5 no. 3 by Franz Krommer (1759–1831) and Op. 13 no. 1 by Adalbert Gyrowetz (1763–1850), both published in 1796, have first movements based on that of Haydn's 'Lark' Quartet. The slow introduction to the Quartet Op. 2 no. 1 by Hyacinthe Jadin (1776–1800) clearly takes its cue from that of Mozart's 'Dissonance' Quartet, while the second movements of the Quartets Opp. 1 no. 3 and 2 no. 2 by Andreas Romberg (1767–1821) are modelled on the first movement of Haydn's Op. 55 no. 2 and third movement of his Op. 76 no. 2 (the 'Witches' Minuet') respectively. In the case of the Frenchman Jadin, who wrote twelve quartets at a time (1795–8) when the form had understandably suffered something of a setback in his country, the Mozart model suits his penchant for harmonic intensification and dark expression. This goes with a preference for full four-part textures, generally kept in middle registers – the 'chorale' influence.

Jadin's most remarkable quartet movement is the Minuet of his Op. 1 no. 3 in F minor. It is played entirely in *pianissimo* unison. Adding to the mysterious effect is the rhythmic elusiveness (each main phrase begins with an upbeat tied over to the following downbeat), legato articulation and absence of rests. The whole is brilliantly conceived as a negative image of typical quartet writing: an extreme in lack of differentiation of parts. It is intensely dramatic in generic terms for precisely this reason.

When used in more measured doses, unison may also have an absolute textural value in stopping textures from becoming too elaborate. This can be seen in the second quartet from the final set published by Gyrowetz, Op. 44 (1804), where unisons recur throughout as witty punctuation. Gyrowetz is also a great exponent of the understated ending. In all three finales, for instance, he sets up a big public close, usually with echoes of *opera buffa*, which is then undercut by a soft dynamic and different material. In each case there is a sudden ironic return to first principles, a reminder of a 'true chamber identity' – the medium should after all have no need of elaborate or forceful 'proofs' in order to achieve a rhetorically convincing close – but this too has become mediated through the contrast. The intimate and well-wrought is a mask too.

The Hamburg-based Andreas Romberg is representative of those composers who strengthened the associations of the quartet with learned or high style. This may shade into the antique, often in minuets, countered by trios with the sort of pronounced rustic writing alluded to earlier. Although Romberg's players often express themselves with that gentle seriousness that seems to have become a common tone of voice, they remain socially alert. The Minuet of Op. 1 no. 1 begins with a leaping upbeat motive from the first violin. The initial rising interval increases and has exhausted itself by early in the second section. There is a pause, the viola takes the motive over briefly, but then it is ditched; from that point all we hear are downbeats (including insistent syncopation). This creates a most unusual progressive thematic construction. It is of course another joke at the expense of violin 1, which clearly over-reaches itself; it also bears a conversational interpretation in that the subject has been exhausted, prematurely compared with the expectation of the participants, and so something new must be introduced. The nicest touch is that the viola tries to adapt it, as if to save the blushes of the first violin, but soon runs dry.

The three quartets Op. 30 by Johann Nepomuk Hummel (1778–1837), written around 1804, are quite specifically inhabited by ghosts from the past. The slow movement of no. 3 shades not just into archaism but actual quotation, from Handel's 'Comfort ye'. The significance of such features is not exhausted by noting their likely appeal to a certain high constituency of quartet lovers. The archaic seems to be a means to heighten expressive intensity, renewing a lyrical language through contemplation of the past. The finale of no. 2 contains two quotations from Bach's 'Goldberg' Variations,[33] while the Trio of no. 1 hints at a chorale-prelude texture. Hummel also shows a relish for counterpoint, but, as had become quite standard, it seems to be used primarily in order to achieve comic energy and textural brilliance. There is much brilliance too that does not derive from imitation, but it is significant that climaxes are often strangled as if to preserve generic integrity (based on the 'no need to shout' principle of the chamber). The most unusual movement is perhaps the creepy Allemande of no. 3, with archaic techniques again to the fore. This movement might sum up as well as any the riches of the quartet repertoire of this time that await general discovery.

The end of the Trio in Quartet no. 1 features a rising arpeggio spread across the four instruments. Both viola and violin 2 'imitations' of the cello's initial arpeggio are marked by a kink, in the viola one of articulation (a slur) and in violin 2 of dynamics (*sforzando* on the first note). This mediates wittily between two understandings of quartet texture: the unfolding of a single compositional process (here an unbroken arpeggiated line acting as harmonic preparation for the return of the Minuet) and the interaction of four musicians (hence the individual touches given to this group effort). After all, reading a string quartet texture is a game of attribution of agency. When we personify the conduct of the individual parts, this is based on an 'as if' assumption that must often allow the players to have telepathic or psychic powers. This is one of the reasons why the quartet must be understood theatrically as much as simply conversationally: the participants know their lines in advance, their dialogue is staged. On the other hand, when we witness a performance, the physical and social reality of four individuals attending to each other as they make music can readily persuade us that four voices – not one – are involved. Such a sense of multiple agency inheres in any performance from a score, of course, but the particular textural attributes of the string quartet of this time lend the process a more pronounced ambiguity.

10 Beethoven and the Viennese legacy

DAVID WYN JONES

The composition and publication of Beethoven's first six quartets, Op. 18, are intertwined with those of Haydn's Op. 76 and Op. 77. Haydn had completed the six quartets of Op. 76 in 1797 but they were not published until the July and December of 1799, dedicated to Prince Joseph Erdödy who had commissioned them. Meanwhile Haydn had embarked on a new set commissioned by Prince Lobkowitz, completing two works in 1799; progress on a third work was painfully slow and eventually the two completed quartets only were issued, as Op. 77 in September 1802. The dedicatee, Prince Franz Joseph Maximilian Lobkowitz, was one of Vienna's leading patrons of music, devoting large amounts of money to the commissioning, purchasing and performing of all kinds of music, from songs to oratorios, and sonatas to symphonies. Over the next decade he was to become one of Beethoven's most ardent supporters, a process that began in 1798 in a deliberately significant manner with the commissioning of six quartets. Beethoven began work on them in the summer of 1798, and handed over copies of the first three in autumn 1799 and the final three in autumn 1800. They were not published, however, until 1801. In the case of both Haydn and Beethoven these contemporaneous quartets – Op. 76, Op. 77 and Op. 18 – initially remained in the private possession of the two aristocrats who had commissioned them, Erdödy and Lobkowitz, until their publication when they were released to the public with formal dedications. While it is possible that Beethoven may have seen manuscript copies of Haydn's Op. 76 and Op. 77 (particularly the latter because they were commissioned by Lobkowitz) before completing his set, it is likely that only with the publication of Op. 76 in the period July–December 1799 was Beethoven able to study any of Haydn's latest quartets. Having already completed three of the quartets of Op. 18 (nos. 1, 2 and 3), Beethoven revised them in the summer of 1800, and it is tempting to speculate that the revision was in part prompted by the publication of Op. 76.

While there is no biographical evidence to support this appealing hypothesis, the musical evidence suggests that Beethoven's first quartets were written independently of Haydn's Op. 76 and Op. 77. Indeed, in many ways Haydn's Op. 76, in particular, is more free-thinking than Beethoven's Op. 18, with two quartets, Op. 76 nos. 5 and 6, beginning with a movement not in sonata form and two finales (Op. 76 nos. 1 and 3) setting off unexpectedly in the minor key before returning to the home major tonic; more generally there is a variety, sometimes an idiosyncratic variety of scoring and textural density, in Haydn's quartets not apparent in Beethoven's first essays in the medium. Unlike Mozart in his 'Haydn' quartets, Beethoven's Op. 18 cannot, therefore, be viewed as a response to Haydn's latest works. Instead the stance is a broader one. Beethoven's understanding of the genre had taken several years to develop and reflected a general knowledge of the quartet repertoire from the 1780s and early 1790s rather than an exclusive knowledge of one striking set. In addition, as several commentators have pointed out, there is a particular debt to Beethoven's string trios, five works composed between 1794 and 1798 (two single works, Op. 3 and Op. 8, and a set of three, Op. 9), in which the challenges of writing for a medium in which every note counts were first encountered head on.

The most obviously Haydnesque work in Op. 18 is the first quartet, in F major. The first movement is an intense sonata form that exhaustively explores the potential of a motivic cliché, a turn figure. The opening movement of Haydn's quartet in D minor, Op. 76 no. 2, was a very recent example of this kind of concentrated writing for the medium (in this case featuring the interval of a fifth), but a more likely stimulus for Beethoven was another first movement by Haydn, Op. 50 no. 3 in E♭, which is similarly governed by a turn figure. But a telling difference emerges in any comparison. Whereas monothematicism in Haydn's case leads to a blurring of the internal paragraphs of sonata form, these divisions are clearly articulated in Beethoven's movement; the moment of recapitulation, for instance, in the Haydn quartet is quite undemonstrative while in Beethoven it is heralded by a lengthy dominant preparation and a crescendo towards the *fortissimo* of the recapitulation.

The format of the slow movement, *concertante* melodic line over a repetitive accompaniment (in this case repeated quavers in the 9/8 metre), is as old as the genre itself, especially favoured by Haydn but also found in Mozart. Since Beethoven's movement evokes a duet rather than an aria (first violin and cello in the first subject, second violin and first violin in dialogue in the second subject, and so on), comparison with the slow movements of Haydn's Op. 20 no. 2 and Mozart's 'Hunt' quartet (K. 458) are appropriate. More generally relevant are the large numbers of string quartets issued in Vienna in the 1780s and 1790s that were arrangements of vocal numbers from popular operas and oratorios. For instance, Johann Traeg, the leading music dealer in Vienna in the last two decades of the eighteenth century, advertised arrangements for quartet of movements from operas by Dittersdorf, Gluck, Grétry, Mozart, Paisiello, Salieri and others.[1] Given the prevalence of this market, now completely forgotten, it is not surprising that a friend of Beethoven, Karl Amenda, should have remarked that the movement seemed to him to portray the parting of two lovers. Beethoven apparently vouchsafed that the particular impulse was the tomb scene from Shakespeare's *Romeo and Juliet*, a confidence supported by some annotations he made on sketches for the movement. Quartet arrangements of theatre music are especially invoked in the coda, where the cello and a highly charged 'orchestral' accompaniment apparently depict the suicide of Romeo beside his beloved Juliet. Originally Beethoven intended the F major quartet to be the third in the set of six, with the D major quartet (Op. 18 no. 3) appearing first. Given the very strong and contrasting character of the two opening movements of the F major in comparison with the less demonstrative quality of the D major work as a whole, it is not surprising that Beethoven should have changed the order.

Op. 18 no. 1 continues with a movement headed Scherzo, one of four such movements in the set; Op. 18 no. 5 has a *Menuetto*, while Op. 18 no. 3 has a 3/4 movement with only a tempo marking, Allegro. Beethoven's piano sonatas and string trios from the 1790s have a number of one-in-a-bar scherzos which, in turn, might have prompted three similar movements in Haydn's Op. 76 and Op. 77 (though the older composer retains the title of minuet). While the low centre of gravity that marks the scoring at the beginning of the scherzo in Op. 18 no. 1 and the abrupt changes of harmonic direction that feature later in the movement can be traced to the influence of Haydn rather than Mozart, they are, like the overcoming of similar influences in the first and second movements, wholly individualised.

When he embarked on the composition of Op. 18 Beethoven copied out (in whole or in part) two quartets by Mozart, K. 387 in G and K. 464 in A. The latter has long been regarded as exerting an influence on the Op. 18 no. 5, also in A:[2] the *Menuetto* is placed second in the cycle, the third movement is a set of variations on a theme in D major – mature Haydn is much more likely to use alternating variations or hybrid constructions of rondo and variations – and the finale, too, is modelled on that of K. 464. Mozart rather than Haydn may be sensed, too, in the background to the standard one work in the minor key in the set, no. 4 in C minor. That key was already Beethoven's favoured minor tonality, prompted by his admiration for C minor movements by Mozart such as the piano sonata (K. 457) and the piano concerto (K. 491). While Beethoven was to produce several piano sonatas of character in C minor (including the *Sonate pathétique*, composed shortly before Op. 18) and a piano concerto too, his one quartet in C minor disappoints. The opening of the first movement is artificially bolstered by energising turn figures, *sforzando* markings and triple stopped chords. There is no eloquent, deeply felt slow movement such as is found in the *Sonate pathétique*, and the finale is a very four-square sonata rondo. The only movement in C major is the second, a Scherzo in full sonata form in which the constituent paragraphs all begin with points of imitation; at the recapitulation the first subject is presented as a constituent line in three-part invertible counterpoint. While the effect is certainly whimsical and engaging, the craftsmanship shows the pedagogic training that Beethoven had undergone a few years earlier with Haydn and Albrechtsberger.

As well as beginning the standard set of six quartets with the most impressive work Beethoven followed the common eighteenth-century practice of concluding his set with the most lighthearted work. For much of the nineteenth and twentieth centuries the B♭ quartet, Op. 18 no. 6, endured a mixed reception, regarded as inferior to the other five and almost certainly, it was often conjectured, drawing on much older material. In fact there is no evidence to suggest that the work was the equivalent in the quartet genre to the B♭ piano concerto, reworked several times over ten or more years; it was almost certainly entirely composed alongside its companions in 1799–1800. Commentators now also are more willing to appreciate its distinctive qualities, for wit and irony are as much a part of Beethoven's musical make-up as are the seriousness and pathos that appealed consistently to posterity.

The first movement of Op. 18 no. 6 has a lightness and transparency of texture that is absent in the other quartets in the set. The deliberately comic dialogue between first violin and cello over a simplistic accompaniment recalls the opening of Haydn's Op. 77 no. 1, which suggests that Beethoven did catch sight of the work before it was published; however, as in most of the sonata forms in Op. 18, Beethoven prefers the Mozartian approach, with contrast of themes rather than a monothematic approach. No fewer than thirty-five bars of the development, approaching half the section, are given over to dominant preparation, ending with an open fifth.

Dialogue also features in the slow movement, though in a less rigidly formal manner. The main theme is announced by the first violin; on its repeat, played by the second violin, it acquires a commentary from the first violin. Later interjections are more pointed: staccato figuration in dotted rhythms, creating a complex rhythmic web that is entirely conceived in terms of the medium. The Scherzo offers yet another kind of dialogue, an ever-present conflict between music in 3/4 (the notated time signature) and 6/8. The Trio highlights the contrast by making all its metrical and phrase rhythms entirely regular.

There is no precedent in the quartets of Haydn and Mozart for the finale of Op. 18 no. 6. Headed 'La Malinconia', the opening Adagio is initially built on the standard pattern of a descending chromatic bass line beginning on the tonic, but when the cello reaches F♯ 'La Malinconia' collapses into something much more distraught as the movement loses its harmonic direction. From E minor (a tritone away from the tonic) the music makes its way back to the dominant of B♭ using a rising chromatic bass. What follows is an uncomplicated Allegretto quasi Allegro in B♭, a German dance of the kind featured in the drinking chorus in Autumn from Haydn's *The Seasons*. Set as a rondo, the Allegretto is clearly meant to disperse the melancholy until, wholly unexpectedly, the darker mood twice interrupts the flow of the music in a kind of mental flashback, before the fast music prevails. A third would-be interruption turns out to be only a hesitant version of the main theme before a Prestissimo coda ends the movement. Interrupting one kind of music with another, often with programmatic overtones, was to fascinate Beethoven throughout his life (from the contemporary *Sonate pathétique* to the 'Dona nobis pacem' of the *Missa Solemnis*), and in the genre of the quartet he was to return to it in his very last quartet, Op. 135.

Although the Allegretto does not carry a descriptive heading the finale as a whole is clearly a dialogue between two opposites. Beethoven might have well have known a trio sonata in C minor (H. 579) by C. P. E. Bach that has the title 'Conversation between a Sanguineus and a Melancholicus'. Although Bach's dialogue is spread across the two movements of his trio sonata, his comment on the second, 'Melancholicus gives up the battle and assumes the manner of the other', is an apt description, too, of the final stages of Beethoven's movement.

The completion of the Op. 18 quartets and of the First Symphony in 1800 has always been celebrated as the point when Beethoven demonstrated that he had absorbed the legacy of Haydn and Mozart and that he had his own views on how both genres might be developed. In the case of the symphony Beethoven went on, almost immediately, to the composition of the Second Symphony and by 1803 he had completed the *Eroica* Symphony, too. In the medium of the quartet, on the other hand, for which there was a much more eager market in Vienna, Beethoven did not return to the genre for six years, composing the three quartets of Op. 59 in 1806, probably between February and November.

This narrative is slightly misleading in that in the winter of 1801–2 Beethoven made an arrangement of his keyboard sonata in E, Op. 14 no. 1, for quartet, the only instance of an authentic arrangement for the medium by Beethoven, though many of his other works – sonatas, piano trios, symphonies, even *Fidelio* – were issued in arrangements for quartet prepared by other musicians. He transposed the work up a semitone, to F, presumably to make maximum use of the lowest, C string of the cello. But what is most striking in this transcription is the lightness of the quartet texture, especially in the first movement, in comparison with Op. 18.

One of the leading patrons of chamber music in Vienna was the Russian ambassador, Count Andreas Razumovsky, himself a competent violinist. Commissioning three works rather than six is part of a broader trend at the turn of the century; indeed Beethoven's own Op. 18, as well as Haydn's

Op. 76, had been published in two instalments, labelled 'books'. There is no denying the unprecedented ambition and scale of the three works, the product of Beethoven's artistic imagination and of a musical society in Vienna that increasingly valued the connoisseurship associated with the medium. Although the scale of each of the three works has always invited comparison with the *Eroica* Symphony, this is, in many ways, an inade-quate juxtaposition, for Beethoven draws on a range of musical resources not evident in the symphony; in particular none of the three quartets evokes the characteristic heroic quality evident in that work and others from the period such as the *Coriolan* overture, the Fifth Symphony and *Leonore*.

The expansiveness (as well as the key) of the opening movement of the F major quartet owes more to the *Pastoral* Symphony than to the *Eroica*, with its leisurely paragraphs that prefer lyricism to forceful drama and its many passages of slow harmonic movement. The first subject is remarkable, nine-teen bars of melody built on an elongated version of the standard cadential progression Ic–V–I. From this simple harmonic base the quartet moves to embrace a much wider harmonic and tonal vocabulary than is used in the equivalent movement of the *Pastoral* Symphony. Midway through the de-velopment section the music reaches a very distant E♭ minor and embarks on a *pianissimo* fugato that eventually pushes the music on to a prolonged G major chord that enables the following paragraphs to move by fifths to the tonic and the recapitulation.

The variety of sonority and texture that is suggested by the first subject and the fugato passage in the development section is a major advance on the more circumspect textures of Op. 18. In the following movement this new-found confidence and freedom is allied to an unprecedented manipulation of phrase rhythm and tonal direction, together with an allusion to a formal structure rather than an obvious statement of one.[3] In temperament it is clearly a scherzo, but it does not have that title and does not use the familiar pattern of scherzo and trio, at least not obviously so. A simple antecedent phrase in the cello on the tonic B♭ prompts a standard consequent from the second violin that modulates politely to the dominant; thereafter the two opening figures appear regularly but their relationship is wholly unpredictable in harmonic direction and phrase length. Equally perversely, the structural tonal goal of the music is not the dominant, F major, but F minor. Bars 155 onward may be viewed as a development section but the return to the tonic at b. 259 is fantastically confused in its messages, as fantastic in its way as the early entry of the horn at the recapitulation in the first movement of the *Eroica* Symphony: the first violin with its trill on f^1 and subsequent ascent up to bb^2 suggests a dominant preparation but the second violin, viola and cello are simultaneously playing one of the main themes in the tonic. As in the celebrated moment in the symphony the subsequent *ff* marks the real beginning of the recapitulation.

The following slow movement in F minor is again in sonata form, the constituent paragraphs this time clearly marking its progress. It draws on the expressiveness of the slow movement of Op. 18 no. 1 and the finale of Op. 18 no. 6. In sketches for the movement Beethoven wrote 'A weeping willow or acacia tree onto the grave of my brother' which commentators have always been willing to interpret biographically while simultaneously noting that both of the composer's brothers, Carl and Johann, were, in fact, very much alive. Perhaps the title was that of an engraving that had caught Beethoven's attention rather than being a rather perverse remark on a family member. Whatever its particular stimulus or its indebtedness to previous slow movements in the composer's quartets, the intense melancholy and lyricism of the movement are unparalleled. The careful 'drifting in' of members of the ensemble across three beats at the beginning rather than a formal tutti first chord was to become a favourite ploy of the composer, and the ready eloquence of the movement naturally embraces a new theme in the development, in Db major. The subsequent move to the dominant of F minor for the recapitulation is a routine one in the Classical style, but the three-note pattern, Db, C and F, that governs it, is one that features elsewhere in the quartet.

The theme of the finale itself is a Russian folksong, included in obvious deference to Count Razumovsky. As the slow movement merges into the finale, a modal quality hinting at D minor is combined with lengthy trills on the dominant of F, an insecurity of tonality that recalls the scherzo. Thereafter the movement, the fourth in full sonata form, is more securely diatonic.

Op. 59 no. 2 in E minor is a shorter work, with more variety of formal patterns (two sonata forms, followed by a scherzo and trio, and a sonata rondo) and with cross references between movements that rely on harmonic gestures rather than motivic links. While E minor and E major are not especially common tonic keys in Mozart's instrumental music, the more common occurrences in Haydn's output share a predisposition to be monotonic works, a characteristic of Beethoven's quartet, too. All the movements are in E: minor in the first movement, third movement and finale, major in the slow movement and in the trio section of the scherzo, a balance of opposites rather than a dramatic move from minor to major. One consequence of this emphasis on E minor and major is that the finale can broaden its harmonic horizons by always beginning the rondo theme off-key in C major. The semitonal relationship of C to B is heard locally within the rondo theme and in the second subject in B minor when it shifts, quite undemonstratively, to the Neapolitan. When this theme is repeated in the tonic in the recapitulation there is an exaggerated emphasis on the Neapolitan (bb. 232–44). The highest note in the entire quartet (c³) occurs as part of a *fortissimo* Neapolitan chord in the coda. Such relationships play a determining role in the finale but they had been glimpsed in earlier movements too, for instance the sideways shift at the beginning of the first movement and the *forte* and *fortissimo* outbursts of the scherzo.

The Russian folksong quoted in the trio section stands apart from this network of harmonic gestures, though Razumovsky the connoisseur would no doubt have taken delight in the union of folksong and learned fugue that constitutes that movement.

Fugue had featured incidentally in Op. 59 no. 1, in the development section of the first movement, and centrally in Op. 59 no. 2, in the folksong section in E major. In the C major quartet Op. 59 no. 3, fugue features in a climactic position, in combination with sonata form in the finale. As such, it is an obvious statement of pedagogical mastery to be placed alongside the finales of Mozart's 'Jupiter' symphony, his Quartet in G major (K. 387) and Haydn's Symphony No. 95. Together with the use of a *Menuetto*, labelled 'Grazioso', for the third movement (rather than scherzo) it suggests a more conscious awareness of eighteenth-century inheritance than is evident in the two other quartets, though the way the coda of the minuet allows the fugue to emerge as the logical way forward, rather than beginning as a set piece, is a very Beethovenian thought-process.

While the previous quartets in the Razumovsky set had drawn attention to a Russian folk melody with a heading ('Thème russe'), none is to be found in the C major quartet. As many commentators have noted, however, the rather bleak slow movement, a sonata form in A minor, especially the tendency for the first subject to use the harmonic minor scale (with augmented seconds) rather than the melodic minor scale, was probably intended as an evocation of Russian folk music, even if it does not actually quote a folk theme. More perplexing in its harmonic colouring is the slow 'Introduzione' that begins the quartet. Comparison is often made with the slow introduction that opens Mozart's 'Dissonance' quartet (K. 465) but whereas the harmonic asperity of Mozart's opening is immediately clarified by the first subject of the ensuing allegro Beethoven steadfastly avoids such a resolution. From the first diminished seventh chord of the 'Introduzione' the music has an aimlessness that is exaggerated rather than resolved by the beginning of the Allegro. In particular, instead of resolving into F major at b. 30 (which might have provided Beethoven with an opportunity for a first subject tinged with the subdominant), it resolves on to the dominant seventh of G, followed by a harmonically unsupported line for first violin that leads to a *forte* imperfect cadence in D minor. It requires a ruthlessly diatonic theme in C major, with repeated quavers in the cello and octave scoring between first and second violins, to establish the tonic.

Beethoven's next quartet, Op. 74 in E♭, is probably his most neglected work in the genre, despite its appealing nickname 'Harp', prompted – not very convincingly – by the unusual pizzicato figuration in the first move-ment. It was composed in the summer of 1809 alongside two other works in E♭, the Fifth Piano Concerto and the 'Les Adieux' sonata. It is not known what occasioned the composition but its dedicatee was once again Prince Lobkowitz; during the winter his palace in Vienna was the venue for private quartet parties every Thursday evening and the work may well have been composed for one of these concerts. A major reason for its comparative neglect is that it does not seem to embrace the progressive agenda evident in Op. 59 and, even more obviously, his next quartet, also a single work, Op. 95 in F minor. Also, had it belonged to a set of three or six it might have commanded more attention; as a single work it has tended to be forgotten.

If Op. 59 no. 3 in C looks over its shoulder to some notable works by Haydn and Mozart from the 1780s and 1790s, this retrospective air, even more apparent in Op. 74, seems to focus on Haydn and Beethoven's own music from the 1790s. As often in Beethoven's output, retrospection does not produce a dated, characterless work, but promotes a new coherence. At the end of May 1809, Haydn had died and it is possible that this quartet was begun as a private tribute to the pioneering master of the genre. The finale is a set of variations that, as James Webster and others have pointed out, clearly invokes the first movement of Haydn's Op. 76 no. 6, in that both themes are in 2/4 with a series of short, repeated motifs over a strong bass line, rather than a broader theme.[4] Rather than emulating Haydn by moving to a fugal conclusion, Beethoven is quite content, in a deferential way, to write six variations, all in the major, plus a coda. The previous movement, too, is reminiscent of Op. 76 no. 6. In both trio sections a contrapuntal texture is woven out of a rising and falling scale, mainly *piano* and presto in Haydn, *fortissimo* and 'Più presto quasi prestissimo' in Beethoven. In anticipation of the finale being grounded in E♭ because of its variation form, the scherzo is placed not in the customary tonic but in C minor with the alternating trio (heard twice) in C major. Not only does the movement lead into the finale, but the structural modulation midway through the binary variation theme cleverly embraces the tonality of the scherzo by moving to the dominant of C minor rather than the routine destination of B♭.

The slow movement has none of the emotional power of the equivalent movements in Op. 59 nos. 1 and 2 but returns to the restrained eloquence and rich sonorities of a movement like the Adagio of the *Sonate pathétique*. The form is a straightforward ABACA but, as in many such movements by Haydn, the A section is varied on both returns; also section B is in the tonic minor rather than the dominant. More conventionally section C is in the subdominant, D♭.

While the choice of Ab, the subdominant, for the slow movement is a routine one, for which there are several precedents in Beethoven's instrumental music from the 1790s in particular, this fall down to the comforting subdominant is prefigured in the Poco Adagio introduction to the first movement; the very first progression tilts the music towards Ab, later made more obvious by two *forte* chords. Both main subjects in the following sonata form are coloured momentarily by the subdominant, but the lengthy coda to the movement, where one might conventionally expect a subdominant bias, cleverly avoids one so as not to detract from the effect of the following slow movement, a harmonic plan of avoidance cleverly supported by the most rhythmically energetic music in the movement. Thus the first movement and the slow movement are bound together in a harmonic relationship, as are the scherzo and the finale. But the first movement highlights the second harmonic relationship too. At the beginning of the development the music begins on the dominant of C minor (a G major chord that follows on from the Bb that concludes the exposition), a gently startling opening for which there are ample precedents in the Classical style; here, however, it leads into a lengthy, agitated section in C major, an anticipation of the tonic note of the third movement.

Following the customary etiquette, for about a year, Beethoven's Op. 59 quartets had been played from the manuscript parts effectively owned by Count Razumovsky before the works were published, on general release as it were, by the Bureau des Arts et d'Industrie. This element of a discriminating connoisseur formulating taste amongst a privileged elite was becoming increasingly associated with the genre in Vienna, as composer, patron, four players and invited guests probed the potential of the genre. A brief report in the Leipzig journal the *Allgemeine musikalische Zeitung* in May 1807, eight months before the publication of Op. 59, hints at this process: 'In Vienna Beethoven's newest, difficult but substantial quartets are giving ever more pleasure; the amateurs hope to see them soon in print.'[5] Pleasure in difficulty was to become a recurring characteristic of contemporary comment on Beethoven's music. The composer's next quartet, Op. 95 in F minor, is probably the most extreme example, not forgetting the late quartets, of that intellectual satisfaction that was increasingly associated with the composer's output.

Op. 95 was composed in 1810–11 and the autograph manuscript carries a dedication to one of Beethoven's most faithful patrons, Count Nikolaus Zmeskall von Domanovecz. An official in the Hungarian Chancellery in Vienna who owned wine estates in Hungary, he was a competent cellist who regularly held quartet parties; he also composed fourteen quartets himself. When Haydn sanctioned a new edition, by Artaria, of his Op. 20 quartets in 1800 it was dedicated to Zmeskall and Beethoven's teasing nickname for him, 'Conte di Musica', was a friendly acknowledgement of his understanding patronage. Five years, however, were to elapse before the quartet was published, by Steiner and Co. in Vienna in 1816, and when Sir George Smart enquired whether Beethoven had any recent quartets he could forward to London the composer replied, 'The Quartett is written for a small circle of connoisseurs and is never to be performed in public. Should you wish for some Quartetts for public performance I would compose them to [*sic*] this purpose occasionally [i.e. specifically].'[6]

The original manuscript has the title 'Quartett[o] serioso'. 'Serioso' rather than the correct Italian 'serio' was, at one level, a self-deprecating remark that would have appealed to Zmeskall but it hid, as connoisseur and composer fully knew and appreciated, a quartet of unprecedented seriousness. It is possible to view the title in the same light as others such as *Sonate pathétique*, *Sinfonia Eroica* and *Sinfonia pastorella*, indicating an exploration of 'seriousness' in the same way as the piano sonata had explored the world of the 'pathétique' and the two symphonies heroism and the pastoral respectively. However, unlike the others, the title does not appear on the printed edition, which suggests that the reference was a private one and not a public indication of expressive content.

To date Beethoven's quartets had invariably shown their ambition by becoming progressively longer. In Op. 95 Beethoven does the reverse, compressing each of the four movements to form what is his shortest quartet. The resulting intensity of argument is especially evident in the first movement which takes fewer than five minutes in performance, compared with the ten minutes or so taken by the 'Harp' quartet. Nothing is made easy for the listener. There is no double bar in the sonata form and the music alternates aggressive gestures with wisps of melody to form what Joseph Kerman memorably termed 'excruciating discontinuity'.[7] Its driving force is the same motif of a turn that Beethoven had used in an earlier 'serioso' movement, the opening Allegro of Op. 18 no. 1, but whereas in the earlier quartet it had very consciously figured throughout here it has two clearly delineated functions: as the headmotif of the brutal first subject and the legato accompaniment pattern to other thematic material. The tonal goal of the exposition is not the conventional relative major of Ab, but Db major. Beethoven supplies a cantabile second subject, but it is only two bars long and is concealed in the lower part of the texture (bb. 24–6). In the same way as the turn motif figures in the second subject area, the first unexpected harmonic shift of the movement, from F minor to Gb major (b. 6) recurs in the second subject area, as the music is twice dragged off-course from Db to D major. This compelling network of aggression and allusion is clothed in a profusion of forceful performance markings, in particular exaggerated contrast of dynamics and accentuation and the demand that semiquavers be played 'non ligato'.

The longest movement in the quartet is the following Allegretto ma non troppo, an up-dating of the kind of slow movement often found in Haydn (as in Op. 76 no. 2) where expressive reserve is complemented by counterpoint. The key is a very distant D major (a continuation of the semitonal dislocation of Db found in the first movement) and the movement is introduced by the dedicatee, Zmeskall the cellist. In formal outline and temperament the following scherzo is more comfortable, but the last movement, with its short slow introduction leading into an Allegro agitato in sonata rondo form, again almost defies comprehension; in particular, the final move in the coda to an exhilarating F major – except that it is mostly in a *piano* dynamic – has puzzled commentators. The self-avowed difficulty of the quartet as a whole invites comparison with the late quartets, but the later works find a cohesion that is more satisfying than that evident in Op. 95. Rather than looking forward, perhaps it is more profitable to look back and view the work as a disintegration of middle-period Beethoven, not into empty gestures but into a fiercely channelled, deliberately provocative expression. It may not convince but it is utterly absorbing.

Op. 95 was published in Vienna in 1816. Nearly six years were to elapse before Beethoven began thinking seriously once more about composing quartets. In 1822, another Russian aristocrat, Prince Nikolas Borisowitsch Galitzin, wrote from St Petersburg requesting 'one, two or three quartets'. Three quartets were eventually written for Galitzin, Op. 127 in Eb (completed in March 1825), Op. 130 in Bb (completed in January 1826) and Op. 132 in A minor (completed in November 1825). As Galitzin's 'one, two or three quartets' implies, these three works are single ones rather than the traditional set of three and they were subsequently published as such by three different firms (respectively Schott, Artaria and Schlesinger). A few months after the initial enquiry from Galitzin, Beethoven's favourite violinist, Ignaz Schuppanzigh, returned to Vienna after a seven-year absence in St Petersburg. He immediately set about organising several subscription concerts of chamber music by Haydn, Mozart and Beethoven, including quartets from Op. 18, Op. 59 and Op. 74. These performances, expertly led by Schuppanzigh, no doubt encouraged Beethoven to fulfil the commission from Galitzin. He maintained this interest beyond the commission, completing two further quartets in 1826, Op. 131 in C♯ minor and Op. 135 in F; these, too, were published as single works, by Schott and Schlesinger respectively.

Their identity as five single works is a clear one, further borne out by the fact that each has a different overall movement pattern and, though extant sketches for the works reveal that certain characteristics – a novel structural approach or a thematic pattern, for instance – were at one stage intended for a different quartet, nothing should be allowed to detract from the formidable integrity of each of the five. The critical approach that seeks to establish some kind of cyclic unity based on recurring motifs not only undermines this integrity but is fundamentally at odds with what Beethoven intended and his audience clearly expected.

While Schuppanzigh was a career violinist, the second violinist in his quartet, Karl Holz, was a minor official in local government and only a part-time musician. Appropriately it was to this representative of a musically receptive elite in contemporary Vienna that Beethoven made the following comment about the late quartets: 'Art demands of us that we should not stand still.' The use of the first person plural ('us' not 'me') is significant. This was not a lonely creative figure striding into the unknown but a composer very conscious of a particular quartet audience in Vienna that had emerged over the previous quarter of a century, one that treasured exclusivity and nurtured the composer's individuality.

Op. 127 is the most traditional and, for that reason, approachable of the late quartets. It has the conventional four movements, a sonata-form allegro, a slow movement cast as a set of variations, a scherzo and trio, and a finale in sonata form. The work opens with a short introduction of six bars which, like those in Haydn's Op. 71 and Op. 74 quartets, are used to launch the movement rather than to provide a formally complete section. It reappears twice in the movement as a clear aural landmark, before the development section and at the climactic point in that section. Elsewhere constituent paragraphs are less clearly articulated. The first subject, for instance, begins on the subdominant chord and though it has a series of four-bar phrases there is very little cadential emphasis. What might nominally be called a second subject (b. 41) is in G minor rather than B♭ and has the same legato character, four-bar phrases and underpowered cadences as the first subject.

The slow movement is in the very traditional subdominant, A♭ major, and has its own introduction, two-and-half bars that build up a dominant seventh chord, note by note, to settle the music in the slow tempo and to prepare for the main theme. The compound time (12/8) in which there is little discernible emphasis on the pulse of the music, the instruction 'molto cantabile', the unconventional use of chords in second inversion (e.g. the first chord of the melody, b. 3) rather than emphatic root position or first inversion, and a liberal attitude to the harmonic role of the cello (which is as likely to change within a phrase as between phrases, e.g. bb. 38–9) are all recurring features in the late quartets.[8] As in other similar movements in the late quartets, Beethoven does not label the constituent sections of the movement, theme, six variations and coda, but the sentence structure is clearly articulated and each variation has a highly distinctive rhythmic configuration. The third variation is placed in the key of the flattened sixth (F♭ major = E major), but Beethoven is careful to avoid the kind of rhetoric that often follows when such a paragraph moves back to the tonic; in b. 77 the music simply slides down from an octave unison E to an octave unison E♭; it is left to the wide-ranging arpeggios of the cello at the beginning of the next variation to re-establish the tonic. The fifth variation is even more remote, D♭ major, then D♭ minor (= C♯ minor), allowing the final variation to sit firmly in A♭. The coda includes another decisive move to the flattened sixth before the music is once more undemonstratively channelled back to the tonic.

The introduction to the scherzo has four pizzicato chords to set up one of those gently jesting movements by Beethoven that consist of short phrases that move in one direction followed by similar phrases in the opposite direction. The incessant dotted figuration recalls the scherzo of Op. 95 and anticipates that found in the *Grosse Fuge*, but more peculiar are the short interruptions in 2/4, as if the music was about to embark on a Rhenish dance before being hauled back to the main business of the movement. The trio section is in the tonic minor, E♭ minor, but idiosyncratically makes its first structural cadence in D♭ major.

A different kind of function is given to the introductory passage in the finale. Beginning off-key in C minor, it provides a distinctive harmonic colouring at the beginning of the exposition and, later, the development, but in the coda it is transformed into C major in order to initiate a new harmonic journey towards E♭ in a new tempo (Allegro commodo), a new time signature (6/8) and a new texture (fast-moving triplet semiquavers).

One of the consequences of the largely undemonstrative nature of the opening and closing movements of Op. 127 is that attention is focused on the emotional core of the work, the Adagio. In Op. 132, the next quartet to be completed, the slow movement is even more central, the third movement in a sequence of five. Prompted by Beethoven's own illness in the summer of 1825, the movement alternates two kinds of music, both given titles that reflect the composer's temporary circumstances: 'Heiliger Dankgesang eines Genesenen an die Gottheit, in der lydischen Tonart' ('Sacred Song of Thanksgiving to the Deity from a Convalescent, in the Lydian mode') and, much shorter, 'Neue Kraft fühlend' ('Renewed Strength'). The Lydian mode of the first section is a very deliberate choice, prompted by Beethoven's reading of Zarlino's treatise *Istitutioni harmoniche* (1558) where the mode is described as 'a remedy for fatigue of the mind and likewise for that of the body'.[9] While this might be construed as a vain display of erudition on Beethoven's part, reflecting his general interest in older music and music theory, it did tap

well into musically educated taste in Vienna, a reference which connoisseurs such as Archduke Rudolph (who owned a copy of Zarlino's treatise)
and Raphael Georg Kiesewetter (who organised regular private concerts
of old music in his home) would have appreciated. Moreover, the points
of imitation and block chord homophony that characterise the 'Heiliger
Dankgesang' would have been generally familiar to Viennese audiences from
church services, which still regularly featured the music of Palestrina alongside new music written in an up-dated *a cappella* style. If the opening music
has sacred associations readily perceived by Beethoven's public, then the
music associated with 'Neue Kraft fühlend' has strong secular associations;
it has many of the standard ingredients of a German dance – 3/8 pulse,
heavy accents in the bass, simple diatonic harmony, even the trill in the first
violin – but the slow tempo (Andante), contradictory emphases on third
beats and the irregular phrase structure mask that association. From these
two contrasting sections of music Beethoven builds a structure of alternate
variations, ABABA, finishing in the Lydian mode with a tonic F major chord.

The arch structure of the slow movement is placed within an overall
five-movement structure that reveals a strong sense of symmetry; one layer
out are two dance movements in A major, a scherzo and trio (movement 2)
and a march (movement 4); the outer layers consist of allegro movements
in A, a sonata-form first movement and a sonata-rondo finale.[10] Such a neat
symmetry had last been used in the genre in Haydn's earliest quartets and is
unique in Beethoven's output. The first movement is another exploration
of how a short introduction can be related to the following Allegro. In addition it casts a shadow over the remainder of the work in that the motivic
texture and the white-note notation of the opening bars are an anticipation
of the 'Heiliger Dankgesang', while the key of the second subject, F major,
is a foretaste of its tonic. Linking penultimate movements into finales had
long been a characteristic strategy in Beethoven's instrumental music. Here,
through careful thematic anticipation in an overtly theatrical texture, the
transition from the fourth to the fifth movements makes the latter sound
inevitable but it also prevents the preceding march from sounding danger-
ously brief. Exploring movement structures larger than the conventional
four along with the new possibilities of balance and progression that result
are compelling features of the next two quartets, Op. 130 and Op. 131, also.

Op. 130 in B♭ major has six movements. In its original form the finale
was a vast, intimidating fugue of 741 bars. Beethoven was persuaded by his
publisher (Artaria) to provide a new finale, a rondo movement of 493 bars;
the original fugue was then issued separately with the rather matter-of-fact
title *Grosse Fuge* and its own opus number, 133. Whether the quartet is performed with the original *Grosse Fuge* or with the substitute finale it is possible
to read the cycle as a compendiun of contrasting movement types, sonata

form, scherzo and trio, slow movement as variations, a German dance, a slow movement in ternary form, and a fugue or rondo; instead of choosing four from these movement types Beethoven provides them all. But once the key structure is taken account of, a distinct sense of two halves to the work emerges. First the quartet moves forward in a conventional way from B♭, to B♭ minor for the scherzo and to D♭ major for a slow movement; at this point the work could have returned to a finale in B♭ but, instead, makes a leap to the furthest possible point away from D♭ – G major – for a movement of stunning simplicity, the 'Alla danza tedesca'. This is then followed by the Cavatina in E♭ and the finale in B♭; the opening of the *Grosse Fuge* and the rondo both emphasise G, a sustained octave unison in the former and part of a dominant seventh of C minor in the latter, to provide a second fall of a third between consecutive movements in the second part of the quartet. Beethoven's willingness to provide a new finale, the much less demanding rondo, allowed the composer to follow the new directness of appeal apparent in the second half of the work. The original finale, the *Grosse Fuge*, gives a new sense of heightened contrast and climax, in part the natural legacy of fugal movements in the Classical period (in Beethoven's own Op. 59 no. 3, the 'Hammerklavier' sonata, Mozart's Quartet in G major (K. 387), Haydn's Op. 50 no. 4 and several symphonies, and any number of masses), more particularly the product of a movement of often obscure erudition and calculated reference back to thematic and tonal concerns from earlier movements.[11]

It would be difficult to imagine Beethoven contemplating an alternative conclusion to his next quartet, Op. 131 in C♯ minor, since the broad progression is from a contemplative fugue in C♯ minor to an active sonata form in C♯ minor which becomes C♯ major in the last few bars. Though evident in the last few bars, minor to major is not the main tonal concern of the work; rather it is the more intriguing semitonal relationship of C♯ and D, as in Op. 59 no. 2 and Op. 95. Typically the very first event in the work, the *sforzando* a[1] in the second bar of the fugal subject, prefigures the Neapolitan D major chord that is often going to clothe it in the remainder of the movement; the subsequent six movements of the work are heavily influenced by this initial inflection. Other broad characteristics of the quartet are the familiar ones of making a slow movement in variation form the core of the work (movement 4) and providing a mix of movement types that promote continuity. Thus, the third movement is a recitative that moves the music from B minor to A major for the central Andante ma non troppo e molto cantabile; unlike the variation movement in Op. 127 this one remains in the tonic, which in the broader scheme functions both as the dominant of D and the flattened sixth to C♯ minor. The fifth movement is a regularly constructed scherzo and trio in a presto tempo; the home key is E, a stage further along the sharp route from D, but, crucially, the trio section (heard twice and then once, allusively) veers decisively, with a tell-tale change of key signature, to the pivotal A major. The sixth movement, marked Adagio quasi un poco andante, begins its twenty-eight bars in G♯ minor, ending on the dominant of C♯ minor in readiness for the finale. Although the thematic material at bb. 21–3 of the finale alludes very pointedly to the head motif of the fugal theme from the first movement, it stops short of the point when one might hear a D major chord; that tonal feature is featured instead in the recapitulation when it is fittingly heard as substitute tonic, instead of the real tonic, C♯ major, for the presentation of the second subject. The coda includes one deflection to D major before it is finally incorporated within the orbit of C♯.

Having gradually expanded from four movements in Op. 127 to seven in Op. 131, Beethoven's final quartet returns to the traditional four – sonata form, scherzo, slow movement and sonata-form finale. Lasting some fifteen minutes fewer in performance than Op. 127, it is sometimes seen as a retreat by Beethoven from the discoveries of previous works, the equivalent in the quartet genre to another F major work, the Eighth Symphony. But in the same way as the apparently conservative features of the symphony do not preclude newer characteristics, Op. 135 similarly creates its own individuality. Once more a variations movement in a slow tempo (Lento assai, cantante e tranquillo) forms the still centre of the work; as in the fifth variation in the slow movement of Op. 131, rather than adding decoration for the first variation, Beethoven reduces the texture to its harmonic skeleton, here with the additional bleakness consequent on turning the music from the major (D♭) to the minor (C♯) and requiring an even slower tempo (Più lento). The thematic material of the first movement is quite eccentric: the merest suggestion of a motif for the first subject and a second subject (b. 38 onwards) that could be taken from a *quatuor concertant* by any number of composers from the 1780s and 1790s. Even more eccentric is the finale, which makes use of a vocal canon by Beethoven, 'Es muss sein' (WoO 196), the composition of which was prompted by the unwillingness of an acquaintance, Ignaz Dembscher, to pay for a private performance of Op. 130: 'It must be! Yes, yes, yes, yes! Out with your purse' runs the insistent text. Beethoven turned the demand of the opening motif of the canon into a question by inverting it and placing it in the minor. The two motifs then feature in the finale, with a portentous title 'Der schwer gefasste Entschluss' (The Difficult Decision). One consequence of this extra-musical stimulus is that Beethoven for the first time in his quartets used a device featured by Haydn in Op. 76 nos. 1 and 3 of introducing the tonic minor as a point of contrast in the finale rather than earlier in the cycle. Beethoven's slow introduction is in the minor and returns before the recapitulation. Meanwhile the exposition had presented the first subject in F major and by placing the second subject in A major had referred back to the trio section of the scherzo. But the more carefree, or rather apparently carefree, side of Beethoven's musical nature, another clear inheritance from Haydn, emerges increasingly in the course of the movement. So certain is the composer of his craft that he allows the players to decide whether they want to repeat the development and recapitulation ('Se repete la seconda parte al suo piacere') and a flippant pizzicato (as in the finale of Haydn's Op. 76 no. 1) initiates a cheerful coda.

11 The Austro-Germanic quartet tradition in the nineteenth century

STEPHEN E. HEFLING

With the publication of Haydn's Op. 33 (1782) and Mozart's ensuing 'Haydn' Quartets (1785), the influence of the Austro-Germanic string quartet spread throughout Europe concurrently with the gradual emergence of professional quartet ensembles. Like nineteenth-century symphonists, quartet composers faced a formidable heritage, especially after Beethoven. Brahms summed it up famously: 'You have no idea how it feels to the likes of us always to hear such a giant (Beethoven) marching behind one.'[1] In the context of current musical discourse, it might seem naive to accept Brahms' observation as the starting point for an historical overview of quartet literature. Yet careful study of works by both famous and lesser-known composers points one repeatedly to the problem of the Viennese inheritance, and not only in German-speaking lands.[2] Accordingly, this chapter focuses on the quartets of four acknowledged nineteenth-century masters of the genre and one whose works, although all but forgotten today, were widely acclaimed during his lifetime.

Schubert

Among the first to sense the giant marching behind him was Franz Schubert (1797–1828), who was born in Vienna just as the twenty-six-year-old Beethoven was becoming securely established in the Austrian capital; he would survive Beethoven by only twenty months. Although he is best known today for his *Lieder*, chamber music occupied Schubert more consistently than any other type throughout his regrettably short career: string quartets dating from 1810 or early 1811 (D. 18–19a) are among his earliest known pieces, and his last completed instrumental work is the extraordinary C major String Quintet with two cellos (D. 956) composed just weeks before he died.

Schubert's quartets as a whole fall conveniently into two groups: (1) eleven early works from the years 1810/11 to 1816, which are rarely heard today, and (2) three quartets from 1824–26 – the 'Rosamunde' in A minor (D. 804), 'Death and the Maiden' in D minor (D. 810), and the vast G major quartet (D. 887) – which are performed and recorded by nearly every prominent professional quartet. Between these two clusters is the *Quartettsatz* of 1820 (D. 703),[3] the head-movement of an unfinished quartet, which in its bold design and expressive intensity stands apart from all Schubert's previous instrumental works.

The early quartets can be further subdivided into: (a) seven compositions of a talented but not-yet-mature student (D. 18, 94, 32, 36, 46, 68, and 74, 1810/11 – August 1813), plus (b) five works written between November 1813 and 1816 that are, on the whole, more imposing and better focused (D. 87 in E♭, Op. 125 no. 1; D. 103, in C minor, now incomplete; D. 112 in B♭, Op. 168; D. 173 in G minor, and D. 353 in E, Op. 125 no. 2); in these the young composer has begun to find his own musical personality.

As a boy Schubert was violist of the family string quartet, and his studies at the Stadtkonvikt (City Seminary) provided additional opportunities for chamber music. The fruits of his early practical experience are twofold: from the outset Schubert handles the ensemble assuredly, yet most of the early works contain frequent echoes of Mozart, Haydn, and (less often) Beethoven. The first seven are experimental in nature, sometimes rather awkwardly so. Nevertheless, they provide ample evidence of young Schubert's prodigious talent, and they reveal notable growth in technique from the time he began studying with Antonio Salieri (D. 32 and 36, 1812–13). To listen through them in chronological order is to retrace a wonderful journey of discovery.[4]

In 1814 Schubert composed both his earliest consummate Lied, 'Gretchen am Spinnrade', and his first enduring piece of chamber music. In the B♭ major Quartet, D. 112 (posthumously published as Op. 168) he successfully manages his own style of first-movement sonata form comprising a three-key-area exposition and a development based on plateaux and repetition, both of which become characteristics of several later works. And he produces a finale fitting for the work as a whole.[5]

As far as is known, Schubert wrote no more quartets for four years. Then in December 1820 he penned the C minor *Quartettsatz*, D. 703, which heralds his full maturity as an instrumental composer. It is a brilliant projection of drama through form. The entire movement is dominated by its opening, a traditional symbol of lament: the descending tetrachord (c^1–b♭–a♭–g),[6] embellished by trembling neighbour notes. Like the onset of a sudden squall, the music sweeps within seconds from a single hushed middle c to a shrieking Neapolitan chord, *ffz* through four octaves, then collapses into a weary cadence. (Brahms clearly recalls this gesture in the opening of his own C minor Quartet, Op. 51 no. 1.) Hitherto the development section had generally not been Schubert's strongest suit (nor would it be in future by comparison with Mozart or Beethoven). But the *Quartettsatz* transforms limitation into virtue. The ceaselessly regular, repetitive two-bar units characteristic of its exposition are not highly malleable; yet as regards affect and drama, what is there to develop, or to resolve through reprise, in a piece so fixated on its beginnings? Abandoning the premise of conflict resolution, Schubert elides the development into the recapitulation of the second theme. The agitated opening bars, which have never really left our awareness, are withheld until the movement's bitter, inevitable close – an extraordinary instance of the tragic reversed recapitulation.[7] Why Schubert left unfinished a quartet that begins so impressively remains a mystery.

Once again, four years passed yielding no new quartets. Meanwhile Schubert had contracted syphilis, which would make him intermittently miserable during his remaining years. Yet in February 1824 as his health declined, his productivity soared: by the end of March he had completed the Octet, D. 803, as well as two string quartets in a projected set of three: the A minor and 'Death and the Maiden'. Nevertheless, he characterised himself at this time as 'the most unhappy and wretched creature in the world', and the poignant pathos often apparent in the two quartets strongly suggests that they reflect his inner world.[8]

The A minor Quartet D. 804 is a fundamentally lyrical work cast in a satisfying succession of movements. Like the 'Unfinished' Symphony, it opens with a broad sonata form based on two Lied-like themes. The sombre opening already reflects in memory, as it were, the development's dissonant denouement (bb. 140f.): the trembling vamp of the first two bars is the shockwave of the crisis yet to be revealed.[9] Overall, the first movement and the third, a touching treatment of the age-old minuet, sing of longing, disappointment, and occasionally horror, with no resolution of affective discord. Between them the Andante, based on an entr'acte from *Rosamunde*, is a bucolic interlude (like the scene it introduced in the play),[10] yet is also disrupted by agitation. Neither in this quartet nor in later chamber works does Schubert attempt a heroic conclusion. The A minor closes in a freewheeling sonata-rondo based entirely on gypsy idioms – drone harmonies, accented second beats, a variety of dotted rhythms, and quasi-improvised ritardandos. Such *style hongrois* is apparently Schubert's symbolic identification with the gypsies, those passionate, melancholy bohemians rejected by bourgeoisie and aristocrats alike, whose wretched circumstances probably seemed similar to his own.[11]

The end-dance without consolation shapes Schubert's last two quartets as well. Each ends in a long tarantella, the legendary ritual dance to prevent madness and death, which also carried ironic overtones of the carnivalesque.[12] The subtitle 'Death and the Maiden' is not Schubert's, but comes from his famous song that furnishes the theme of the quartet's slow-movement variations. There Schubert ignores the maiden's terrified outbursts in the song and incorporates only Death's solemn, oracular phrases;

the last portion of the theme (bb. 17ff.) originally bore his words, 'Be of good courage! I am not savage, / You shall rest peacefully in my arms.' Thus, in contrast to the first movement, the reaper with the scythe (for so he is depicted in the volume from which Schubert got the poem) initially seems benevolent rather than punitive. But as the variations unfold the conflict re-emerges, and it is not difficult to associate the roles of Death and the Maiden with the voices of cello and first violin respectively. The ensuing buildup reaches a point of crisis and disintegration. Then all energy and resistance subside, and there follows a celestial coda almost devoid of material substance. If Death has won, he seems at last a comforter, as promised in the song.

Reportedly Ignaz Schuppanzigh, the Viennese quartet leader and friend of Beethoven to whom Schubert dedicated his A minor Quartet, did not like 'Death and the Maiden'. And not until June 1826 did Schubert return to the genre, dashing off in approximately ten days his last and most extraordinary string quartet. As Gülke suggests, the G major seems in certain respects like an expansion and intensification of the D minor (although they lack thematic connections).[13] By this time Schubert had probably heard some of the late Beethoven quartets, which Schuppanzigh premiered in 1825 and 1826. Yet the scope and originality – epic strangeness, one may even say – of the G major Quartet are without precedent. The vast opening movement quakes feverishly in tremolos and triplets almost throughout, and is fraught with the ambivalence of seemingly endless oscillations between major and minor modes. As Dahlhaus notes, this is music that unfolds through remembrance, turning from later events back to earlier ones, rather than through goal-consciousness (i.e. by pressing onward from earlier to later). Therein lies one of its chief differences from Beethoven.[14] Moreover, Schubert treats the exposition's materials episodically, much as he might in a development section. The result resembles a double variation set almost as much as a sonata form, and seems to proceed *sans but précis*.

The Andante begins *fz* in all four voices, rather like the momentary interruption of an ongoing dream. A wafting cello melody ensues – yet what, we wonder, could have come before? The answer emerges retrospectively when the unison *fz* returns (b. 109) after the shocking secondary section (bb. 40ff.). Here somnolent quiescence yields to nightmarish horror in merely four bars, a contrast more violent than any other in Schubert's chamber *œuvre*. As in sleep and dreaming, the kaleidoscopic shifts of feeling proceed in a rondo-like format, eventually arriving at a temporarily peaceful conclusion that in no sense resolves the movement's conflicts. Following a scurrying nocturnal scherzo, Schubert again strikes up the tarantella, more riotously and relentlessly than in 'Death and the Maiden'. As there, the vast structure is logical: a sonata-rondo with displaced reprise of the primary material. But

its perpetually rushing rhythm, endless two-bar phrases, dizzying modal
shifts, lurching modulations (frequently by half-step), and wild dynamic
changes yield forth a driving delirium that sweeps beyond all boundaries –
an infinite Dionysian dance whose purportedly curative powers seem
irrelevant.

Spohr

Among the most prolific and respected German musicians in the first half
of the century was the violinist, composer, and conductor Ludwig (Louis)
Spohr (1784–1859). At the age of twenty Spohr was already an outstanding
soloist and quartet player. He was deeply impressed by both the playing
and the compositions of Pierre Rode, leading exponent of the French violin
school, whom he sought to emulate. Although Spohr was prolific in nearly
all genres, chamber works comprise about half of his 152 opus numbers; the
34 string quartets, largely unknown today, span most of his fifty-one-year
career.[15] They are of two types: eight that he regularly termed *quatuor brillant*
or *Solo-Quartett*, which, in the French manner, are chiefly three-movement
violin solos with string-trio accompaniment (Opp. 11, 27, 30, 43, 61, 68,
83 and 93), while the remainder are of the type a contemporary chronicler
termed the 'true quartet', in which all four voices are prominent.[16]

Spohr recognised that the 'true' string quartet was 'possibly the most
difficult type of composition'.[17] His first venture in the genre was a pair
of works in C major and G minor written during 1803–5 and published
as Op. 4 in 1806. Promising though they are, Spohr was soon dissatisfied,
and understandably so.[18] Much of the music is clearly indebted to Mozart,
whom Spohr admired deeply, as well as to Haydn and, occasionally, early
Beethoven,[19] whose quartets he performed regularly. To be sure, Spohr's
Op. 4 rarely approaches their assured mastery. But certain features of his
own style found frequently in his later quartets are already emerging: (1) a
generally lyrical rather than dramatic approach to the first movement, with
a good deal of symmetrical phrasing, and an outburst of passagework after
the second theme followed by more lyrical 'simmering down' just before
the double bar; (2) the tendency to build periods through repetition of two-
or four-bar units; (3) a predilection for the dotted rhythms (particularly in
catchy finales), trills, passagework, up-bow staccatos, and 'Viotti' bowings
of the French violin school (especially for the dominant first violin, but also
sparingly for the other instruments); (4) the sharing of motivic kernels across
the various sections of a movement; (5) a fair amount of neighbour- and
passing-note chromaticism, both in the melody and the lower voices (a trait
that would increase in later works); (6) an apparent delight in establishing

the dominant of an unusual key area and then side-stepping to another tonal centre (predictably via an augmented sixth chord); (7) relatively short development sections based largely on harmonic movement rather than motivic working-out; and (8) the tendency to turn the trio of a minuet or scherzo movement into a little character piece for the first violin. As Brown notes, the slow movements of Op. 4 are the most interesting:[20] here Spohr's capacity to write singing melodic lines with rich harmonic and textural support is most clearly in evidence.

Spohr's next pair of quartets, Op. 15, was composed in 1807–8 and published in 1809. Here he adopts the elegant triple-time opening movements of Mozart (K. 464 and 589) as models for his first movements, as he would in several later works as well. Overall, Op. 15 no. 1 in Eb is Spohr's closest imitation of classical style.[21] No. 2 in C, however, is a much gawkier piece in which classical techniques of motivic concentration are pedantically overworked. During the same period Spohr wrote his first *quatuor brillant*, Op. 11 in D minor (1807, published in 1808). Based on the Rode model, Op. 11 also establishes patterns found in Spohr's later works of this sort. All of the principal material is given to the solo violin, and the other parts merely accompany. In essence, the first-movement exposition is a sandwich of two lyrical themes interspersed with bravura transitional passages, while the development comprises just under a minute of non-stop virtuosity over a simple harmonic plan. The slow movement, in classical binary format, opens with a warm hymn-like symmetrical melody for the violin. Trills and fioriture gradually emerge and predominate, and in the reprise Spohr maintains the eighteenth-century custom of further embellishing the principal theme. Predictably, however, the rondo finale is his *tour de force*: a jaunty, dotted march tune in French style gradually gives way not only to the usual runs, arpeggiations, and trills, but parallel thirds in the second theme, broken tenths, and, just before the final appearance of the rondo tune, parallel tenths alternating with a dominant pedal. Yet for all their showiness, this and the later *quatuors brillants* contain pleasant, characteristically Spohrian music of greater substance than much of the vapid virtuoso repertoire that remains perennially popular, and enterprising ensembles should consider including them in recitals.

Spohr spent the years 1813–15 in Vienna, where interactions with many prominent musicians, including Beethoven, were a powerful stimulus to his creativity. In addition, the merchant and music patron Johann Tost, who had commissioned several Haydn quartets, now sought chamber music from Spohr, who did not disappoint him. In the latter two of the three quartets he wrote for Tost – Op. 29 nos. 1 (Eb) and 2 (C) – Spohr's quartet style crystallised: they are among his finest, and the critic Fröhlich, having heard Spohr play them in 1815, later declared no. 2 'one of the most

significant works which this branch of music possesses'.[22] There is greater
assuredness and variety, more momentum and integration, yet also greater
craftsmanship and charm than in the earlier works, and certain passages
are quite memorable. Overall, the Eb seems slightly bolder, particularly in
the wide-ranging harmonic tour of its first-movement development. The
C minor slow movement is a variation set on a treading theme that vacil-
lates intriguingly among tonic, submediant, and tonic major; subsequently
Spohr varies the harmonic scheme further. If the variation spotlighting the
first violin seems a bit trivially cheery, one can forgive him. The scherzo is
successfully canonic in its first half, and interestingly imitative throughout.
Characteristically Spohrian, as Brown notes, is the theme of the finale, in
which the harmony and texture transform a potentially banal idea into one
of pervasive good spirits.[23] Here and elsewhere, one hears harbingers of
Mendelssohn.

Some thirty-five years later, when Spohr's thirty-second string quartet,
Op. 141 in C major, had appeared in print, an anonymous critic in the *Neue
Zeitschrift für Musik* would observe: 'Spohr's 31st quartet [*recte*: 32nd], 141st
opus! This really says all that is necessary for our review. Whoever has become acquainted with the 141st opus of this composer has got what he
expected!'[24] If exaggerated, this viewpoint conveys a kernel of truth: despite
various attractive works one might point out – e.g. Op. 45 nos. 1 and 2,
and especially Op. 84 no. 1, with its unusually intense first movement – the
fundamental aspects of Spohr's quartet style did not greatly change after
he left Vienna in 1815. Overall, this is music of *Gemütlichkeit* – always well
crafted, yet avoiding high drama, and somewhat prone to lulling repetitions,
predictable patterns, chromaticism that can seem cloying, and occasional
echoes of Mozart, Haydn and early Beethoven. But although Spohr had
been on good terms with Beethoven and would frequently perform the first
four symphonies and the piano concertos, he never took up the challenge of
Beethoven's middle-period style, and was openly critical of his late works.[25]
Indeed, Beethoven's Op. 18, published in 1801, arguably presents greater variety, drama and dynamism than any six contiguous Spohr quartets written
from fifteen to fifty years later. It can be tempting to bracket these works as a
manifestation of the convivial, complacent Biedermeier *Zeitgeist*, although
Carl Dahlhaus has underscored the difficulties of successfully distinguishing
a Biedermeier musical style from that of the 'genuine romantics'.[26]

In any case, at the time of his death Spohr was widely regarded in
Germany, Austria and England as one of the most important composers
in the history of music, 'the last representative of that noble line . . . that
had its roots fixed in Classical ground,' according to the *Neue Berliner
Musikzeitung*.[27] But his popularity soon plummeted, and by the 1920s
his chamber music was almost entirely neglected. As Brown notes, the

self-contained distinctiveness of the style he had brought to ripeness by the age of thirty provides the key both to his influence in his own day and to his long-term decline;[28] ultimately he was overshadowed by both older and younger contemporaries.

Mendelssohn

Undoubtedly among the best educated musicians of the nineteenth century, Felix Mendelssohn Bartholdy (1809–47) was ideally situated to enhance the legacy of the Austro-Germanic string quartet. Tutored in the Bach tradition by Carl Friedrich Zelter, young Mendelssohn was a master of counterpoint at the age of twelve. A capable violinist and violist, Mendelssohn played chamber music gladly, and was thoroughly steeped in the Viennese Classical repertoire. His writing for strings, while challenging, reveals the insider's knack for obtaining the best effect with the least technical awkwardness.

Mendelssohn's musical style was formed in the conservative cultural milieu of Restoration Berlin; clarity, polish and symmetry are the heritage of his methodical training.[29] And perhaps owing to his extraordinary talent and precocity, he appears to have been relatively unintimidated by the weight of the past and the imperative of novelty; in the best case, he declared, the artist 'did things imperceptibly better than his immediate predecessors'.[30] Schumann famously dubbed him 'the Mozart of the nineteenth century'.[31] Yet he was deeply affected both by Beethoven's powerful innovations and by the swelling currents of Romanticism.

All of these influences are apparent in the seven string quartets spanning Mendelssohn's career from his student days to his last months. The most adventurous and impassioned of them are the first he published (A minor, Op. 13, 1827) and the last he completed, just before his death (F minor, 1847, published posthumously as Op. 80). Between these extremes lie the trilogy of Op. 44, rich in variety and craftsmanship yet tamer overall, and an early counterpart to the A minor, Op. 12 in E♭ (1829).

Mendelssohn left unpublished a student quartet in E♭ written in 1823.[32] The first quartet of his maturity, the A minor, Op. 13, was composed in 1827, very much under the spell of Beethoven's late A minor Quartet, Op. 132 (1825).[33] Motivic connections between the two works have often been noted, especially in their first movements, and both employ an impassioned violin recitative to introduce their finales.[34] The bleak, chromatic fugal section of Mendelssohn's Adagio non lento (bb. 20ff.) recalls that in the Allegretto of Beethoven's Op. 95, and at various points Mendelssohn evokes the late Beethovenian sound world, particularly in its individualised and often fragmentary part writing. Mendelssohn is thus the first composer to come partially to grips with a musical style widely considered unfathomable during the next half-century. In correspondence with the Swedish composer Adolf Lindblad, Mendelssohn reveals he was especially impressed by Beethoven's organically relating 'movements of a sonata to each other and their respective parts, so that from the bare beginning throughout the entire existence of such a piece one already knows the mystery . . . that must be in the music'.[35] Yet in many if not more respects, Mendelssohn does not emulate late Beethoven:[36] the intensity of Op. 13's outer movements notwithstanding, they lack the elemental, sometimes bizarre, disruptiveness and formal daring of Op. 132, as well as its macrocosmic sense of irresolution. (To be sure, Mendelssohn becomes re-engaged with such matters in his final quartet, as noted below.) Overall, in Op. 13 he is much more inclined than Beethoven to write balanced antecedent–consequent phrases with internal repetitions, and his suave stylistic control is everywhere apparent beneath the anguished surface. Indeed, this quartet grows directly from the lyrical, symmetrical impulse of Mendelssohn's song 'Frage' ('Question'), Op. 9 no. 1, a simple setting of love poetry (possibly his own) that he appended to the quartet as its 'theme'. 'You will hear its notes resound in the first and last movements', he wrote to Lindblad, 'and sense its feeling in all four.'[37] Through this unifying device, and also by explicit cross-references in the finale to both the first and second movements, Mendelssohn achieves a degree of taut integration approaching that of late Beethoven while maintaining his own musical identity throughout, 'bridging the realms of chamber music and the art song and testing the ability of instrumental music to imitate a vocal model', as Todd aptly observes.[38]

Just as E♭ stands far removed from A minor, so the warm affective world of Op. 12 contrasts with the agitation of Op. 13 – at least for the first three movements. Nevertheless, in this quartet of 1829 Mendelssohn pursues even further his goal of developing the 'entire existence' of the work from its 'bare beginning': the introduction presents kernels significant throughout, and the first movement generates a gentle, yet far-reaching tension resolved only on the last page of the finale.[39] Quite possibly the compact, yet passionate slow movement was inspired by Mendelssohn's covert crush on his childhood neighbour, Betty Pistor, the private dedicatee of Op. 12.[40] Most striking is the finale, launched not in E♭ but in C minor. Its racing triplets, relentlessly driving compound metre, block-like hybrid form, and extensive quotations of previous movements suggest possible acquaintance with late Schubert.[41] Ultimately the serenity of the E♭ first movement prevails, far more convincingly than in its own coda, yet still through cyclic persuasion rather than heroic force. Only Mozart could manage the minor-to-major finale conclusion with equal sophistication and effectiveness.

Not until 1837 (during his honeymoon) did Mendelssohn resume quartet composition: his first effort was the E minor work subsequently published as Op. 44 no. 2. Traditional wisdom has long maintained that compared to his earlier quartets, Op. 44 represents a reactionary retreat to classicism.[42] Mendelssohn's sister, Fanny Hensel, reveals a partial reason for this in a letter to Felix of 1835: 'we were young precisely during the last years of Beethoven, whose manner we readily and extensively assimilated. It is, however, entirely too agitating and forcible. You lived and composed your way through this . . .'[43] Whatever the reason, a sea change is unmistakable – yet so, too, is the masterly beauty of Op. 44 no. 2. Like much Mozart, the excellence of this music may be missed owing to its exquisite polish.

Although eschewing Beethovenian extremes – Op. 59 no. 2 in E minor (1806) is more radical – Mendelssohn's E minor is a richly dramatic work based on the Classical conflict of minor mode *versus* major: the tension between them is sustained until the very end. As so often throughout these quartets, the impetus for the first movement is song. Yet beneath the poised, often symmetrical surface is a current of impassioned restlessness (first manifest in the agitated syncopations and rushing semiquavers) that remains unresolved at the movement's end. And the agitation is simply shunted aside during the two ensuing intermezzos, both quintessentially Mendelssohnian: a puckish four-minute scherzo and an elegant song without words shaped like a Classical binary slow movement.

The work's overarching drama resumes in the finale. The driving metre and tempo of the scherzo return, but now in the minor, as though the scherzo's symmetrically phrased exhilaration had turned demonic. Although lasting only seven minutes, this quasi-Schubertian sonata-rondo can seem long, repetitive, and discursive,[44] and its waltzing second subject (bb. 75ff.) somewhat Biedermeier. But these features also contribute to the ongoing tension: when, for example, headlong quavers combine with sentimental waltz in the Animato section (bb. 155ff.), a positive major-mode conclusion seems plausible. Ironically, however, just this passage (bb. 405ff.) at length yields without resistance to the minor mode at the onset of the coda (b. 425). Yet only the last thirty bars – the most intense of the entire quartet – seal the minor outcome irrevocably.

It must be admitted, however, that Mendelssohn does not consistently maintain such dramatic continuity within a classicising context throughout Op. 44. In the E♭ no. 3 (chronologically second, February 1838), no unifying thread binds either the cycle overall or the outer movements within themselves, which are the longest and most discursive in all of Mendelssohn's quartets. Their brilliant moments nostalgically evoke his Octet, Op. 20 in the same key, yet never quite achieve the fusion of panache plus coherence central to that youthful triumph. The C minor scherzo, by contrast, is

vintage Mendelssohn, skilfully seasoned with contrapuntal zest.[45] And the
A♭ major Adagio non troppo, thematically inspired by Mozart, is exquisite
in its emotional depth and formal novelty – a rich blend of sonata and
ternary structures that Brahms cannot have overlooked.[46] In Op. 44 no. 1
(July 1838), the contrasts between outer and inner movements are similar
but less pronounced. Both the first and the final movements sound more virtuosic than they are, and the traditional brilliance of D major string writing
in Op. 44 no. 1 is perhaps its strongest unifying feature.

Nine years after completing Op. 44 Mendelssohn drafted his final quartet,
the F minor, in the wake of his beloved sister Fanny's death (May 1847):
this highly discordant work seems permeated with his shock, outrage and
grief. From the first tremblings of the opening movement everything sounds
amiss; symmetrical phrasing, so central to Mendelssohn's earlier style, here
becomes a foil for agitation that swamps formal boundaries right through
to the last raging bars of the finale. Nevertheless, the cycle is subtly unified
by a recurring motivic cell first heard in the opening five pitches of the first
violin, and there are numerous other links between movements.

The swell of the first nine bars is the first of three false starts. The resigned
effort at transition (bb. 28ff.) turns straight back towards the tonic, yielding
a surge of storming triplets recalled in the coda of the finale. At length this
outburst gives way to the lyrically lamenting second theme, but the underlying agitation remains. There is no double bar: the development's sudden
onset (b. 96), quaking like the movement's opening, only underscores how
fundamentally unstable the entire exposition has been. What follows becomes more so, culminating in a rising wail that soars to bb^3 for the first
violin (bb. 161–5). Only retrospectively do we realise that, meanwhile, the
development has collapsed into the reprise. In the coda this agonising chromatic ascent clatters diatonically downward in a demonic mockery of the
movement's previous high point.

The fury continues in the F minor Scherzo, resembling a Czech *furiant*
in its rampant hemiolas;[47] the trio approaches late Beethoven in its oddness.
Even the binary Adagio (possibly an elegy for Fanny) is unsettled in several
respects. Its second half (bb. 50ff.) expands into a climactic passage that recalls swelling chromaticism from previous movements and fragments into
dejection before the course of the reprise resumes, 'cantabile', as though
nothing were amiss (b. 83). The finale is filled with the syncopations, diminished sevenths, distorted symmetry, and interrupted periodicity of musical
Zerrissenheit. Wistful reminiscences of earlier Mendelssohn in the transition
(bb. 49ff.) and Schubert in the development (bb. 213ff.) are of no avail. The
reprise (b. 269) brings back the storming triplets of the first movement, and
in the coda (b. 375) they combine contrapuntally with the main theme,

dramatically highlighting its cyclic derivation from the first movement (bb. 41ff.) in a manner anticipating Brahms.[48]

Op. 80 is a work of gripping intensity and strong contrasts, which Mendelssohn heightened in his polishing of the score.[49] It ventures into new expressive regions within the standard four-movement format; save for Schubert's last quartet (G major, D. 887, then still unpublished), nothing this unusual had been written since late Beethoven. Yet like Beethoven and Schubert, Mendelssohn ended his career with chamber music for strings: the F minor Quartet was his last completed composition.[50]

Schumann

Schumann's three string quartets, Op. 41, date from the summer of 1842, his 'chamber music year', during which he also composed three works for piano and strings (Opp. 44, 47, and 88). Mendelssohn, to whom Op. 41 is dedicated, considered these quartets the best works of Schumann's earlier period, and Schumann agreed.[51] Long a chamber-music enthusiast, Schumann in 1836 began attending rehearsals of the quartet led by Ferdinand David (Mendelssohn's friend and concertmaster); there he learnt a wide variety of music, including late Beethoven. As editor of the *Neue Zeitschrift für Musik,* he declared in 1838 that Beethoven's Quartets in E♭, Op. 127, and C♯ minor, Op. 131, were works 'for whose greatness no words can be found'; together with the best of Bach, they 'represent the outermost limits that human art and imagination have yet reached'.[52] Thus inspired, Schumann attempted a first quartet of his own, of which nothing survives. The following summer (1839), he was determined to conquer the genre, and sketched openings of two quartets while assiduously studying late Beethoven 'right down to the love and hate in them'– all to no avail.[53]

Two more years elapsed before Schumann completed a quartet. Meanwhile, as Daverio has shown, Schumann the journalist was shaping his own aesthetic of the genre while reviewing the efforts of others.[54] Two main points emerge. First, in 'a true quartet . . . everyone has something to say'; it should be 'a conversation, often truly beautiful, often oddly and turbidly woven, among four people'.[55] This echoes Goethe's famous pronouncement (to Mendelssohn's teacher Zelter) that in a quartet 'one hears four rational people talk among themselves, one believes that one gains something from their discourse . . .'[56] Accordingly, 'operatic, overladen' music as well as 'symphonic furor' must be avoided.[57] Second, the composer must be steeped in the heritage of the genre without slavishly imitating older models.[58] Late Beethoven should be the benchmark, and for Schumann, only Mendelssohn and Onslow among his contemporaries approached that standard.[59] Nevertheless, he believes there is much to be gleaned from further study of Haydn and Mozart as well.[60]

Schumann's First Quartet Op. 41 no. 1 begins with a rather bleak A minor introduction perhaps influenced by that of Beethoven's Op. 132, and also by the haunting C♯ minor fugue of Op. 131.[61] But if so, Schumann clearly avoids slavish imitation: only the first six bars are strictly imitative, and the music lacks the premonitory power inaugurating Op. 132. Indeed, it almost constitutes a short movement unto itself. The ensuing sonata form, a lilting 6/8 Allegro, is surprisingly in F major: whether F or A is the true tonic will be settled only in the finale. Metre, rhythms, and texture here all recall the quirky D major Allegro molto vivace that follows the fugue in Beethoven's Op. 131; and a quick comparison spotlights a problematic aspect of Schumann's thematic style throughout Op. 41. Even over static pedals, Beethoven generates phrase overlaps and ambiguities that propel the piece forward, whereas Schumann proceeds in repetitive two-bar segments always adding up to eight (or ten).[62] Such self-contained symmetry smacks more of songs and character pieces than of traditional Viennese sonata forms; nevertheless, this is an aspect of Schumann's effort to revitalise the genre.

Just when a transition is expected a fugato arrives, its subject derived from the close of the first group (bb. 76–9 = melody of 72–5). Yet this dissolves after the fourth entry (bb. 92ff.). For the second theme proper an idea from the exposition's third phrase (bb. 50–1) combines with a jagged countersubject (bb. 101ff.) recalling the rushing triplet passages in Beethoven's *Grosse Fuge* (albeit without their ferocity). This is, however, sequential material, treated as one might expect in a Mendelssohn development section. And Schumann indeed recycles both this idea and the next (bb. 117ff.) twice in his own development section – one of several in his works composed in 'sequential block' manner.[63] Such a procedure derives from Schubert, whose music Schumann loved. Yet this quartet's development proceeds consistently in restless four-bar segments lacking apparent overriding purpose. Then with no preparation and little sense of resolution, the recapitulation (bb. 231ff.) precisely retraces the course of the exposition, adjusting only the modulatory scheme – a more 'classical' treatment of form than one often finds in Haydn and Mozart.[64]

A minor returns in the scherzo, whose clipped phrases and scurrying parallel motion are clearly indebted to Mendelssohn (Op. 44 no. 3). But Schumann's formal scheme (ABA′) is less complex than Mendelssohn's: the scherzo proper is ternary whilst the trio is a delightful 'Intermezzo' in C major and duple metre that flows gracefully over drone basses. The Adagio, an extraordinary mixture of strophic variation and ternary form, is undoubtedly the highpoint of this quartet. Following three bars of rhythmic and harmonic ambiguity, a hymn-like melody initially recalling the slow movement of Beethoven's Ninth settles into F major as the ostinato accompaniment evokes the song-without-words style of Mendelssohn. By the fourth phrase, however (bb. 16ff.), Schumann's harmonic and melodic intensity portend greater complexity that emerges fully in the middle section, launched by an abrupt plunge into A♭ (b. 29). Such brusque contrast plus fragmented texture and the ensuing slow-motion intensification of the theme's fourth phrase all invoke the world of late Beethoven. In the reprise these tensions recede, yet without resolution, and the music sinks slowly back into its dream-like introduction.

His earlier objections notwithstanding, Schumann unleashes considerable symphonic furor in the A minor finale, a swashbuckling sonata form that is essentially monothematic. The cascading quavers of the opening are inverted (in C, b. 22), then re-inverted (sequential, bb. 43–62), and at length augmented and combined with the inverted quaver form (in C, bb. 63ff.). F major makes a strong appearance in both exposition (bb. 31ff.) and development (bb. 152ff.), signalling that the question of overall tonality still remains undecided. A restless affair, the development continues to rehearse the bustling combined scale contours, often moving sequentially in four- or eight-bar clumps. Then suddenly, F major from nowhere (b. 152): Schumann makes an audacious false reprise by splicing in the entire 52-bar block, transposed, from the exposition's arrival in the relative (bb. 23ff.) until just before the double bar. It now seems that the movement must surely end in F. Yet in three bars' time the course shifts back towards A minor, and by bar 214 it is clear there will be an A minor reprise as well. In the manner of Mozart and Mendelssohn, a last effort to escape the minor tonic fails (bb. 234–42), and just when closure seems inevitable, the whimsical musette variant, Moderato and major, appears as though by magic (bb. 254ff.) – shades of Op. 132, but also a moment of arabesque probably inspired by early Romantic literature.[65] This sets the stage for the concluding minor-to-major transformation, which, if less elegant than that of Mendelssohn's Op. 12, is convincing nonetheless.

The opening movement of Op. 41 no. 2 in F major swings with the exuberance of a waltz, in sweeping eight-bar units. In other respects, however, it proceeds along the lines of the First Quartet's F major Allegro. Like that movement it is essentially monothematic; the entire exposition through the first ending is a perfectly symmetrical 96 bars (8 × 12). And the development is of the sequential block variety, containing a direct splice of material from the exposition.

Perhaps the most unusual movement in all of Op. 41 is the ensuing 12/8 Andante, quasi Variazioni in A♭. Not, however, the initial music but rather the second, more complex sixteen-bar segment (bb. 16–32) actually becomes the basis for four ensuing variations (all delineated by double bars). The first and third of these reveal the influence of Beethoven's variations in Op. 131; the second begins like a *Ländler*, but subsequently becomes rather bravura. Variation 4 could be an ironically cheery song from Schumann's *Dichterliebe* cycle, and ends flippantly in its thirteenth bar. The introductory section returns, followed by a coda in the style of the *Ländler* variation.

The C minor scherzo in ABB′ form is an arpeggiating syncopated tongue twister. Beneath the frolicsome surface, however, are the same regular phrase units (here eight bars) standard in this quartet. The finale has the madcap gait of a *Galopp*, the German dance popular for the rousing conclusion of a ball,[66] combined with *moto perpetuo* figuration chiefly for the first violin – all within the structure of a full-blown sonata form (including repeated second half).

Schumann's Third Quartet Op. 41 no. 3, long his most popular, is also the longest and in many respects most idiosyncratic. Shadows of late Beethoven have largely receded here, yet each movement contains innovative variants upon standard procedures, the best of which are richly satisfying. A brief introduction highlights the first movement's motto gesture – a falling fifth (initially $f\sharp^2$–b^1) over a ii^6_5 chord.[67] The motto's non-tonic ictus generates momentum within the main theme of the Allegro and at each of the movement's structural divisions. The early onset of transitional material (b. 17) leads to a song-like second theme cleverly derived from the first and driven by sequencing plus a restless off-beat accompaniment. Such simple yet effective procedures give new life to Schumann's penchant for symmetrical phrasing. A moment of characteristically capricious arabesque briefly interrupts the momentum (*un poco ritenuto*, bb. 77ff.) shortly before the exposition's close. And the development, the most concise in Op. 41, dissolves similarly. It is based entirely on sequential treatment of the motto; accordingly, the recapitulation is reversed (beginning with the second theme at b. 154), and a brief coda brings this bright movement to a close.

Variations are common in string quartets, but not in the place of a scherzo. The F♯ minor Assai agitato begins as though it were a nervous, fleeting post-Beethovenian 3/8 (constant syncopations recall the Vivace of Op. 135). Then follows the loosely imitative first variation, in which the syncopated anacruses have expanded to two detached quavers. The second variation presents tight stretto imitation in duple time with a flavour of archaic severity. Variation 3, Un poco Adagio, reduces the theme to classical simplicity, revealing that it is derived from Mendelssohn's scherzo in Op. 44 no. 2 (bb. 141ff.). The fourth variation evokes *style hongrois*, the passionate, exotic idiom of the Gypsies. This stomping energy is suddenly defused by the magical stroke of the coda – tonic major over drones. A memorable drop by third relation (F♯ to E♭, bb. 233, 241) brings a reminiscence of the capricious arabesque from the first movement, and the piece fades dreamily in major–minor undulation.

The ensuing Adagio molto is a poignant rondo form alternating lyrical tenderness and intense, unresolved anguish in a manner distinctly Schumann's own.[68] The crowning achievement of Op. 41, it comes closest to his ideal of 'a conversation, often truly beautiful, often oddly and turbidly woven, among four people'. The viola is the voice of angst here (bb. 8ff.). Its dialogues with the first violin in the B sections reveal the menacing undercurrent of the main theme (bb. 26, 66f.), and two-thirds through these episodes the viola breaks into low-register sobbing (bb. 35, 74ff.). By the coda this tenor voice can no longer respond to the soprano, having become fixated upon the ominous dotted motive from the accompaniment of the B material. At movement's end only the viola part is marked *morendo* (dying).

In the rondo finale, a 'mosaic-like succession of miniature character portraits',[69] the morose dotted rhythms of the Adagio transmigrate into the energetic skipping of the refrain, while the 'Quasi-trio' features the characteristic rhythm of a gavotte.[70] Although the tiles of a mosaic traditionally create the illusion of a larger picture, here the disjunctiveness of the fragments seems to obscure the broader line as Schumann stands the rondo paradigm on its head: atypically, the episodes are harmonically and metrically more stable than the refrain.[71] Only in the coda does the music really take flight, in a Dionysian dithyramb of dotted quavers enlivened by unusual harmonic twists. And therewith Schumann took his leave of the string quartet, never to return.

Brahms

Johannes Brahms (1833–97) was already writing string quartets when, in 1853, Schumann famously declared him the composer 'called to utter in ideal manner the highest expressions of the times', who had sprung forth 'fully armed like Minerva from the head of Jupiter'.[72] But Brahms destroyed those juvenilia as he would some twenty quartets before finally releasing Op. 51 no. 1 in C minor in 1873, twenty years after his first visit to the Schumanns.[73] Having also met Liszt in 1853, Brahms already realised his aversion to ' "symphonic poems" and all that stuff',[74] an opposition he and Joseph Joachim made public in 1860. Thus, it was natural that Brahms should champion chamber music, which the New German School regarded as *passé*, and within his lifetime he became recognised as the pre-eminent chamber composer. His friends in Vienna's Hellmesberger Quartet would perform his music there frequently, as would Joachim in Berlin and elsewhere. Publication of several important Schubert chamber works as well as Mendelssohn's last quartet during the 1850s placed Brahms among the first to experience the full weight of the Austro-Germanic tradition.

By the mid-1860s Brahms had published an impressive amount of chamber music (including Opp. 8, 18, 34, 36, 38, and 40). But Beethoven overshadowed the string quartet as much as the symphony, and Brahms lacked Mendelssohn's equanimity towards the 'giant marching behind'. He entered both genres with C minor works long in the making and of decidedly Beethovenian stamp.

Brahms' First Quartet Op. 51 no. 1 is a milestone, markedly different from anything the forty-year-old composer had previously written.[75] Terse, inexorably logical in its local and long-range motivic concentration, and obdurately agitated in three out of four movements, it is a tragic work – determinedly so, as MacDonald observes.[76] By comparison, Brahms' earlier chamber music, strongly influenced by Schubert, seems capaciously luxuriant.[77] Initially the first movement's main theme echoes that of Beethoven's C minor 'Pathétique' Sonata, Op. 13. But the quaking accompaniment and rapid swell from c^1 to a shrieking ab^3 (b. 7) followed by immediate collapse point to Schubert's C minor *Quartettsatz*, D. 703.[78] Brahms also adopts Schubert's *lamento* bass (c–bb–ab–g) in his first seven bars, doubled in thirds.[79] Between the Ab (b. 5) and G (b. 7) of the cello part, however, Brahms interpolates the pitches Eb and C: this articulates an augmented inversion of the violins' Ab arpeggiations in bars 5–6, which grew from the tonic arpeggiation motive of bar 1. Derived from Beethoven, such 'developing variation' (Schoenberg's term) is impressive throughout this quartet; unfortunately very few instances can be discussed here.[80]

From the outset this music projects nervous instability. Already in the first phrase chromaticism destabilises the tonic; the second phrase drifts past V to an unharmonised f♯ (bb. 20–1: lower neighbour to V, or V of B minor?). Then, almost diffidently, cello and viola assume the arpeggiating main motive as the violins execute a furious diminution of it. Now the *lamento* tetrachord arrives on top via invertible counterpoint (bb. 24–31), and bars 24–5 invoke the grim 'omnibus' harmonic progression that Mozart and Schubert had linked to fear of death.[81] Like the opening antecedent phrase (bb. 1–22), this consequent is also open-ended. As in the 'Pathétique', the mediant minor is the unstable harmonic goal of the exposition, but it is fully confirmed only some forty-three bars later (with substantial modal mixture). Motivically, everything is developed from the first group: there is neither the time nor the poise for a distinctive second subject. Even the Schumannian arabesque closing the exposition (bb. 63ff.) is motivically derived.

The relatively brief development focuses on familiar material while dramatic harmonic action renders it more volatile than the exposition. Block-like episodes (bb. 92–9, 100–7) and further sequencing precipitate a fierce struggle over the tonicization of C♯ minor (bb. 112ff.), which is then inconclusively displaced. The ensuing Brahmsian recapitulatory overlap liquidates the developmental process and launches a large-scale anacrusis to resumption of the exposition's agitation.[82] The tonic, however, will not recur in root position until the coda, which glimmers with a fury fully released only in the finale.

Entitled 'Romanze', the ternary Poco adagio transforms the anxiety of the first movement's opening. Its charmingly asymmetrical main theme is cast in a simple aaba' *Lied* form, yet does not quite achieve closure. The ensuing 'B' section reveals uncertainties that will affect the quartet's finale as well: minor mode, hushed quaking, cross-rhythms, and fragmentary phrasing characterise this music (which partially recalls the *beklemmt* mid-section of Beethoven's Cavatina in Op. 130). Its triplets proliferate into the reprise of the main material that, formerly veiled in intimacy, becomes overtly ardent. Yet the 'B' music returns as coda, almost tipping the movement's form to binary (ABAB), and unsettling its idyllic closure.

The *lamento* tetrachord (c^2–g^1) plus wailing chromaticism over a relentless 4/8 tread mark the 'scherzo', whose motto progression is Neapolitan to dominant in C minor. That tonality predominates until the closing section of the second half (bb. 66ff.), where F minor (equally grim) at length prevails. In contrast, the F major trio is this quartet's sole invocation of Brahms' earlier chamber music style; here the rustic bariolage accompaniment and cheerful Schubertian themes recall the Sextets, Opp. 18 and 36.

If the F minor Scherzo provides tonal impetus for the finale's raging off-tonic onset, the 'Romanze', ironically, furnishes both rhythm and initial contour of its unison motto motive (the high ab^3 and falling diminished seventh stem from the quartet's beginning).[83] A transformation of the Scherzo's repetitive slurred duples (bb. 3ff.) animates much of the principal material, and the bass expands the ubiquitous descending fourth down to the open C string. Two-bar phrase units, inaugurated by the motto, are the most regular feature of the exposition overall, yet their combination into larger configurations is often unpredictable. These basic kernels are spun out further in the second and third tonic-minor ideas (bb. 21, 33ff.).

Like the first movement, this music is too agitated and obsessively developmental to entertain seriously the possibility of tonal and thematic contrast. At length the motto returns and collapses (bb. 68ff.), yielding to the 'second subject' – the main idea of the 'Romanze', *piano* and *poco tranquillo* over a dominant pedal of E♭, which blossoms into a rhapsodic reminiscence of the slow movement's ardour. But E♭ is never fully confirmed, and gradually the initial anxiousness resumes. The motto launches the brief 'sequential block' development in bar 94. Here Brahms' masterly tactics are apparently derived from the tragic reversed recapitulation of Schubert's *Quartettsatz*: the development is elided into the recapitulation of the exposition's third idea (bb. 124ff.; cf. b. 33), now in A minor. Yet escape from the tonic is illusory. The exposition's stepwise descent (c → B♭ (=V/E♭)) must here bring on the dominant of C. And therewith arrives the 'Romanze' second subject, imploringly extended – to no avail. As though a horrid force were suddenly released in all its fury, the primary material returns, surging forth into a coda bound relentlessly to the tonic pedal of the cello's open C string (bb. 231ff.). The final cry from this musical maelstrom is the very opening of the first movement (bb. 244–6), quaking now in the paired duplets common to all four movements. Three clipped cadential chords, and all is done.

Joachim had urged his friend to compose quartets, and Brahms evidently responded by spelling their bachelorhood mottos in the primary theme of his Second Quartet, Op. 51 no. 2: a^1–f^2–a^2 is the inversion of Brahms' 'frei aber froh' (free but happy), and f^2–a^2–e^2 represents Joachim's 'frei aber einsam'.[84] In the event this proved ironic: the friends quarrelled seriously in 1873, and the dedication of Op. 51 went to Dr Theodor Billroth; subsequently Brahms supported Joachim's wife in his divorce suit. That notwithstanding, the Second Quartet is generally less frenetic and determinedly tragic than the First, even though it ultimately yields to just those two attributes. A certain melancholy lyricism prevails in the A minor, yet its contrasting theme groups and key areas function with greater autonomy than those of the C minor.

From the outset the pace is more regular and contemplative (Allegro non troppo), and Brahms' penchant for endless development is somewhat less daunting. It swells up (as in Beethoven) during the transition (bb. 20ff.), then simmers at the approach of the generously lyrical second theme (bb. 40ff.) – which nevertheless recycles pitches prominent in the first six bars of the main subject (e^2, g^2, f^2, d^2, a^2). Characteristically Brahmsian are its cross-rhythms and violin fioriture as well as its subsequent brusque transformation (bb. 84ff.); the whimsical halt of this onslaught, however, is indebted to Schumann. The development proper is shorter than that of the C minor Quartet, yet more volatile because driven by a seemingly impotent rage unable to achieve anything other than an unwanted reprise. At its crisis point the entire quartet becomes mired in obsessive repetition emphasising e^3–f^3 in the treble and E in the bass (bb. 159–60). Then follows a four-bar collapse from f^3 to E, grimly invoking Joachim's motto as the recapitulatory overlap begins. None of this tension is resolved, and the movement ends much as it begins, only more vehemently.

Even more than the 'Romanze' of the First Quartet, the modified ternary A major Andante moderato of the Second is a study in lyrical ambivalence. Pellucid in its overall bar format (aab), the tightly woven principal material nevertheless seeks digression, most notably as its segments approach closure.[85] The source of uneasiness is starkly revealed in the B section – a two-fold outpouring of anguished alienation in gypsy style, almost surely influenced by Schubert.[86] Although only seventeen bars long (including a recall of A at b. 48), this disruption is far-reaching: through three varied false reprises the music searches for centrality, wistfully regaining it only thirty-odd bars later, and ending in fragility. What follows is among Brahms' most original intermezzos, anticipating that of his Second Symphony. The archaic-sounding 'Quasi Minuetto' (A minor) proceeds haltingly in three- and six-bar units, largely over rustic musette drones. This alternates with a chipper 2/4 Allegretto vivace in the major; the two segments are subtly related,[87] yet neither seems to hold sway until, as though reluctantly, a full reprise of the minuet brings ambivalent closure.

Although related to the finale of the First Quartet, the Second's concluding movement differs in significant respects.[88] In honour of Joachim, who was Hungarian, its main theme converts both contour and three-bar units of the A minor minuet into a gypsy dance laced with hemiolas;[89] this is further transformed into a carefree waltz for the second group (bb. 45ff.). Such topoi would seem unthinkable in the C minor. Formally, the A minor finale is closer to a sonata-rondo, with the added twist that both dance themes return at pitch before the onset of the developmental passage (bb. 162ff.). Such a 'blocky' structure not only reflects the nature of the principal idea, but also masks the movement's eventual outcome (whereas the mounting agitation of the C minor's second theme telegraphs the nature of the ending well in advance). Yet the second appearance of the waltz (bb. 144ff.) seems illusory, and the third (in the tonic major, b. 238) truly *passé*. The coda resorts to Schumannesque rêverie to forestall the inevitable, but ultimately the furies have their way.

Conventional wisdom has it that in 1875, having successfully challenged Beethoven in the genres of both quartet and symphony, Brahms indulged in 'unbuttoned style' and 'naive eccentricity' in the Bb major Quartet[90] – a work 'full of cheerful unorthodoxies' and 'as carefree and capriciously inventive as the Op. 51 Quartets had been severely logical and serious-minded', as MacDonald puts it.[91] Its opening 6/8 Vivace combines gigue and hunting topics in a manner dear to Mozart ('Hunt' Quartet in Bb, K. 458, String Quintet in Eb, K. 614), and its outer movements are 'Classical', even Haydnesque.[92] All true up to a point, and yet – the sophistication beneath the surface is uncanny. Whereas Op. 51 responds chiefly to middle-period Beethoven, the 'classicism' of Op. 67 is refracted through the lens of

Beethoven's late quartets; the opening movements of Opp. 130 and 135 are the ancestors of Brahms' 'cheerful unorthodoxies'.

Moreover, Brahms here produces his first overtly cyclical work in conjunction with his first variation-set finale (likely a nod to Mozart): the seventh variation suddenly conjures forth the quartet's opening, revealing a carefully wrought linkage between the two movements that is pursued to the end of the work. Thus 'Classical' variation and 'New German' cyclicism are united in distinctly Brahmsian manner. And because all of the first movement's material is derived from the first group, its connection to the finale becomes retrospectively tighter. Yet despite such motivic coherence, the opening sonata form is unusually disjunctive. Its dancing first group proceeds by call-and-response, while the second is bipartite – first dominant major and florid (b. 31), then minor and condensed (b. 50), yet ever derived from the first. What seems to be closing material in 2/4 – a 'prim little polka'[93] – expands inordinately to forty-odd bars, reaching the double bar with a shrug. The four-part development is framed by an undevelopmental version of the first group's arch contour, weirdly *sotto voce* in parallel octaves and thirds; its inner segments (bb. 127, 149ff.) rehearse the first and closing ideas inconclusively.

Brahms' D minor Agitato 'scherzo' is, once again, no joke, but rather a curiously transformed waltz chiefly for solo viola. Perhaps somewhat ironically, he once characterised it as 'the most amorous, affectionate thing' that he had written.[94] That description better fits the *cantabile* main theme of the Andante, which is related to the slow movement of Op. 51 no. 2 in its overall ternary shape and two-fold outburst of gypsy anguish in the B section. Here in Op. 67, however, the disruption results in lyrical, seemingly improvisatory musings leading to a muted crisis (bb. 51ff.). Then follows a single off-tonic reprise in which the first eight bars of the initial melody are coolly liquidated, somewhat in the manner that Brahms will treat the finale's theme in its sixth variation.

Although he would write an additional thirteen works of chamber music, Brahms, like Schumann, ceased quartet composition after completing three. (Nor did he compose more than three pieces in any other form of chamber music.) Possibly his recognition of Dvořák's success in the genre influenced him to leave it in younger hands,[95] although it is difficult to imagine Brahms' abandoning the quartet only for that reason; one senses the need to move beyond preoccupation with the past. In any case, so great was his influence that by 1922 Leichtentritt could justifiably claim 'from about 1880 all chamber music in Germany is in some way indebted to Brahms'.[96] Zemlinsky, Reger, and Schoenberg were all among his devotees, and the latter two became leading quartet composers in the early years of the twentieth century. Nevertheless by 1889, well before Brahms' death, a current of modernism far-reaching in its impact is apparent in the first enduring works of two post-Wagnerians, Strauss and Mahler (neither of whom wrote chamber music beyond their student years).[97]

Deploying the Brahmsian techniques Schoenberg later coined 'Grundgestalt' and 'developing variation', Schoenberg and Reger pursued the tendency to make every voice thematically significant at all times,[98] while simultaneously stretching and weakening the central organising force of tonality. In the opening Allegro agitato of Reger's G minor Quartet, Op. 54 no. 1 (1900), for example, 'one has the impression of a man gesticulating wildly, trying to make his intentions plain in a language over which even he has lost control', as Griffiths observes.[99] If the inner movements are somewhat more conventional, the fugal procedures of the finale only just manage to contain its digressive forces. Reger's Third Quartet in D minor, Op. 74, expands the form to the dimensions of the late-century symphony: it lasts over fifty minutes. Dahlhaus would have it that in the first movement, 'categories such as first and second theme, thematic contrast and manipulation, and exposition and development can still be viable even when the tonality is weak'.[100] Yet whereas the modern orchestra provides Strauss and Mahler a vast arsenal of sonic techniques with which to project such categories in their gigantic movements – which only occasionally approach Reger's tonal ambivalence – the palette of the string quartet is notably more limited.

Schoenberg would achieve a better balance of monumentality and miniaturism in his First Quartet in D minor, Op. 7, a four-movements-in-one work (like Schubert's 'Wanderer' Fantasy, D. 760) completed in 1905. Yet as Daverio argues, Schoenberg's Op. 7 may be understood to embody both a guiding aesthetic claim of late-century modernism and, simultaneously, a critique of it.[101] In his Second Quartet, Op. 10 of 1908, Schoenberg would take fewer cues from modernist symphonic and operatic music. Believing the time had come for 'air from another planet', he took the bold steps of making chamber music the carrier genre for a new style that moves beyond the limitations of tonality. Thus, in one sense, Reger, Schoenberg, and a host of others were undoubtedly Brahms' heirs. Yet the mutually reinforcing interaction of tonality, form, and motivic work that had been central to quartet writing since Haydn was becoming *passé*. In that respect, the tradition of the Austro-Germanic string quartet was already drawing to a close with Brahms.

12 Traditional and progressive nineteenth-century trends: France, Italy, Great Britain and America

ROBIN STOWELL

Introduction

As has clearly been demonstrated in the previous chapters, the art of the string quartet was taken to its heights by the Austro-German composers of the late eighteenth and the nineteenth centuries. It was not until the second half of the nineteenth century that equally fertile traditions began to emerge elsewhere. These trends, discussed in this and the subsequent chapter, signal the development of the genre into a medium adopted by composers worldwide, who gradually exploited it as a vehicle for the most concentrated, the most experimental, the most radical as well as the most intimate compositional thought.

Austro-German influence nevertheless remained predominant; in Britain, for example, even the major string quartet ensemble of the second half of the nineteenth century, the (English) Joachim Quartet, was led by a German, Joseph Joachim. American composers had still to find their own voice; and whatever Italian ensembles there were continued to perform the works of the Austro-Germans to the exclusion of almost everything else, so immersed were their fellow countrymen in vocal music, and particularly in opera and in the instrumental traditions fostered by the Viennese Classical composers. Despite the relatively large number of string quartets composed in France during the nineteenth century, no distinctively French string quartet tradition developed until the late 1880s, when César Franck (1822–90) and his circle of composers contributed to a native quartet tradition in France, albeit with a strong German seasoning.

France

String quartet composition in France had passed through the phase of the lyrical, elegant *quatuor concertant* and the *quatuor concertant et dialogué*, in which the material was fairly evenly distributed amongst the parts, often as a conversational sequence of solos.[1] Established in Paris by Giuseppe Cambini's (1746–1825) *c.* 150 works in the genre, as well as those of his numerous successors, it was superseded by the *quatuor brillant* – essentially a concertante violin solo accompanied by the three other instruments.[2] This type of quartet was introduced by Giovanni Battista Viotti (1755–1824) and cultivated largely by violinist-composers such as Rodolphe Kreutzer (1766–1831), Pierre Baillot (1771–1842) and Pierre Rode (1774–1830).

In mid nineteenth-century Paris, serious chamber music was performed regularly in major concert series such as the Société Alard et Franchomme (also known as Société de Musique de Chambre), the Société des Derniers Quatuors de Beethoven, the Société des Quatuors de Mendelssohn, the Séances Populaires and, to a much lesser extent, the Société Sainte-Cécile.[3] Matinée and soirée concerts were also held in Parisian private homes. The works of the Austro-German composers predominated, as Momigny confirms, and Baillot, having been introduced to Haydn in 1805 by the Bohemian composer Antoine Reicha, established a quartet in 1814 expressly to introduce the works of Haydn, Mozart and Boccherini as well as Beethoven's Op. 18 quartets to a wider Parisian public.[4]

Baillot's former composition teacher, Luigi Cherubini (1760–1842), who was director of the Paris Conservatoire from 1822, wrote six string quartets (the first three dedicated to Baillot), each in four movements. The early works display some influence of the Viennese Classical composers – the symphonic introduction and first movement of the First Quartet (1814) and the scherzo and finale of the Second Quartet in C (1829; adapted from an earlier Symphony in D), for example, smack of Beethoven; but they also demonstrate operatic influences – note the dramatic recitative in the third movement of the Second Quartet, the treatment of the opening recitative of the Third Quartet and its cantabile, aria-like Larghetto scherzando. From his Third Quartet onwards, the influence of the legacy of Haydn, Mozart and Beethoven becomes increasingly evident, notably in the finales of the Third and Fourth Quartets and much of No. 6. Cyclical elements are fundamental to all six of Cherubini's works – for example, the scherzo of No. 4 is related to the main themes of the first two movements, and midway through the finale of No. 6 themes from the first three movements are recalled. However, despite Schumann's esteem for his quartet style, Cherubini's works did not receive lasting recognition, based as they were on a blend of French, Italian and Viennese traditions.

A mix of Viennese and French influences is demonstrated in the works of Pamphite Aimon (1779–1866), Napoléon-Henri Reber (1807–80), Alexandre Boëly (1785–1858), Auguste Morel (1809–81) and J. B. Charles Dancla (1817–1907). Reber was a belated classicist, remembered almost entirely for his *Traité d'harmonie* (Paris, 1862). According to Saint-Saëns, 'he seemed like a forgotten man from the eighteenth century, wandering through the nineteenth as a contemporary of Mozart might have done, surprised and somewhat shocked by our music and our ways'.[5] Boëly was

arguably more progressive, looking towards Schumann in his four quartets
Opp. 27–30, composed in the late 1820s, while Morel, self-taught in composition, was praised for the 'clarity, expressiveness, and . . . strong melodic
sense' of his five quartets, two of which were awarded the Prix Chartier.[6]
Dancla established his own quartet in 1838. This group's concerts at Hessel-
bein's home were a regular feature of the Paris season from the 1840s, and
doubtless inspired Dancla to compose many of his fourteen string quartets
between 1839 and 1900.

Several composers who achieved greater notoriety in operatic circles
followed in the wake of torchbearers such as Cherubini. Prominent among
them were Félicien David (1810–76), Ambroise Thomas (1811–96) and
Charles-François Gounod (1818–93). Thomas' String Quartet in E minor
Op. 1 (1833) confirms his admiration for Beethoven and incorporates 'passages of skilful contrapuntal writing'.[7] David published a Quartet in F minor (1868) and left at least three further string quartets in manuscript. His
music, according to Hugh MacDonald, 'falls into the French tradition of being agreeable diversion, strongly coloured but emotionally naive'.[8] Gounod
composed at least five string quartets, but allowed only one, a work in A
minor (1895), to be published. A String Quartet Op. 17a (1887–8) by one of
his (and Franck's) pupils, Sylvio Lazzari (1857–1944), also lay dormant for
some years before it reached the Société Nationale de Musique (1888) and
the public domain in 1904.

The Anglo-French composer George Onslow (1784–1853) was arguably
the predominant quartet writer in France during the first half of the nineteenth century, contributing some thirty-seven quartets, most of which were
printed between 1810 and 1840. The early ones Opp. 8, 9, and 10 seem imma-
ture but clearly demonstrate Viennese Classical influence, especially that of
Haydn. The introduction of Beethoven's late quartets to Parisian audiences
from 1828 caused Onslow first to denounce them yet later to gain inspiration
from them, particularly in the works from his Op. 46 onwards, which display a wealth of harmonic, rhythmic and structural invention.[9] Vestiges of
Schubert and Mendelssohn are also evident in Onslow's later, more progressive works, which demonstrate a clear sense of architecture and an
harmonic language that was among the most interesting of the period.[10]

In 1855 Edouard Lalo (1823–92) became a founder-member and violist (later second violinist) of the quartet established by Jules Armingaud to
make better known the quartets of Haydn, Mozart, Beethoven, Mendelssohn
and Schumann. His own String Quartet Op. 19 (1859) was firmly based on
such models. Its opening Allegro is characterised by violent contrasts, yet is
Classical in mould, while the Andante, in the relative minor, features three
themes which undergo effective developmental treatment. The G minor
scherzo (Vivace) also treats, and with striking chromatic interest, three ideas,

the last of which is a rhythmic ostinato, while the ensuing trio (E♭ major) offers more lyrical fare. The finale, more pathetic than violent, pursues its Beethovenian objectives, its development incorporating some skilful contrapuntal writing. Not well received on its premiere in 1859, the work was revised in 1880 as Op. 45 but has never been fully recognised for its pioneering role in the development of the genre in France.

The establishment of the Société Nationale de Musique in 1871 to promote 'Ars Gallica' symbolically heralded the further development of French chamber music. Meanwhile, Alexis de Castillon (1838–73) had published a Quartet in A minor (1867) and a movement ('Cavatine') from an unfinished Quartet in F minor (1869). Some quartets/quartet movements by another Franck disciple, Guillaume Lekeu (1870–94), date from 1887, notably an unpublished *Commentaire sur les paroles du Christ* and a Quartet in D minor; but it was not until nearly twenty years after the Société's foundation that Franck's String Quartet in D (1889–90) marked the beginning of a golden age for the genre in France, even though a good proportion of those composers whose string quartets were premiered under the auspices of the Société (notably Franck and his pupils Ernest Chausson and Vincent d'Indy) were greatly influenced by Wagner.

Franck's Quartet is his last completed work. Composed between 20 October 1889 and 15 January 1890, it is ambitious in scale and makes complex use of cyclical form; its quasi-orchestral textures sometimes appear to be on the verge of bursting the seams of such an intimate chamber music genre. D'Indy tells us of the pains Franck took with the lengthy first movement and the beautiful slow movement and the work certainly incorporates some of its composer's most profound and compelling thought.[11] The unusual structure of the first movement has been likened to a gigantic Lied, the central section of which, including a fugal development, is itself a complete sonata-movement. As in the finale of Beethoven's Ninth Symphony, the introduction to the finale recalls themes from the scherzo and trio and the Larghetto, while the principal theme of its sonata-form structure is derived from that of the first movement and subjected to augmentation and much contrapuntal development. Towards the end there are also reminiscences of the second movement – a Mendelssohnian scherzo whose trio makes fleeting reference to the principal cyclic idea – and the ternary, contemplative Larghetto, which has its own sharply contrasting ideas and reminiscences. While at times looking back to Beethoven, Schubert and Schumann, Franck invents new and individual solutions, even quoting himself, taking up a few motifs or phrases from his Violin Sonata, the last section of his *Prélude, Aria et Finale* and his Piano Quintet.

Foremost among Franck's pupils who perpetuated his ideals were D'Indy and Chausson. D'Indy (1851–1931), together with Charles Bordes and

Alexandre Guilmant, founded the Schola Cantorum in 1894, broadening its narrow initial remit for sacred music performance into a general music school founded on Franckist principles by the turn of the twentieth century, which eventually rivalled the Paris Conservatoire as France's pre-eminent musical centre. His musical objectives, though fervently nationalistic, embraced Wagnerian principles for French music, favouring the Teutonic fondness for continuity, thematic links and cellular development. He attached special importance to the string quartet, composing his first essay in the genre at the age of forty, completing two others and leaving a fourth incomplete at his death.

Each of D'Indy's first two quartets is based on a motto theme and their employment of short phrases, pregnant with dramatic possibilities, recalls Beethoven's legacy, particularly his 'late' quartets. D'Indy was not totally satisfied with his First Quartet in D Op. 35, premiered in 1891, because it does not derive all of its melodic elements from a single motivic idea. Nevertheless, the four-note motif (reminiscent of the 'Bell motif' from Wagner's *Parsifal*) of the sustained slow introduction plays a significant unifying role in the ensuing sonata-form movement as well as in the second movement (*Lent et calme*) and finale (*Assez lent*). The third movement is an interesting combination of Lied and rondo forms in which the motif plays no part.

D'Indy realised more closely his ideal in his much acclaimed Second Quartet in E major Op. 45 (1897), based on a four-note germ that generates practically the whole work. Not until 1928–9 did he venture into the medium again, when he composed his Third Quartet in D♭ Op. 96 in a markedly different, more refined Classical style. The initial impression is one of austerity, conveyed by the widely spaced intervals of the cyclical motif announced in the introduction and relentlessly pursued in the remarkably cohesive sonata-form movement that ensues. The *Intermède* contrasts a stately dance with a more lyrical 'trio' section, while the slow movement comprises a theme based on the germ motif and seven variations unified by two harmonic and rhythmic ideas. The germ motif appears in inverted form at the opening of the finale, initiating a rhapsodic rondo with five refrains and culminating in the reappearance of the theme of the slow movement, triumphantly resounded by the first violinist.

D'Indy also completed, at the request of Ernest Chausson's (1855–99) family, the concluding seventy-three bars of the third movement (*Gaiement et pas trop vite*) of his compatriot's Quartet in C minor Op. 35, left unfinished in sketch form at Chausson's premature death. This movement has similarities with the Scherzando vivace of Beethoven's Op. 127. D'Indy decided to end the movement, begun in the subdominant key of F, with a return to the key of C major. The first movement (Grave) also looks to the past, incorporating echoes of Franck in the way in which the cello's noble introductory theme is treated as the subject for the movement's whole development – somewhat surprising when one considers Chausson's works of the period. Also surprising, and somewhat bemusing, is his citation, at pitch and with the same harmonies, of the opening phrase of Debussy's String Quartet. That Chausson was also an enthusiastic Wagnerite is nowhere more evident than in the central slow movement (*Très calme*) as well as in the skilful employment of thematic transformation, even though use of such a technique has resulted in a tendency towards wearisome repetition.

Chausson was for a time an important influence on Claude Debussy's (1862–1918) life and career. Being rich and well-known in the *beau monde*, he had been able to introduce Debussy to a wide variety both of socially 'smart' artists such as Proust and also many of the more bohemian set of painters, writers and musicians. Debussy's solitary Quartet in G minor (1893) caused a sensation with the Parisian audience on its premiere by the Quatuor Ysaÿe at the Société Nationale (29 December 1893). Some were bewildered; others recognised Debussy's attempt to make himself at home in the world of Franckian rhetoric; still others showed particular enthusiasm for the work's new syntax, inspired partly by Borodin, whose quartets Debussy had heard at the concerts of Russian music organised by Belaiev during the Paris Exhibition of 1889. Particularly striking is its thematic treatment of brief ideas, freedom of rhythm and tempo, textural variety and striking fluidity of line, form, harmony and modality.

The opening germ idea of the work, with its descending second and third, is modally harmonised. It is reshaped for cyclic occurrence in both the second and fourth movements. The first movement's contrasting Massenet-like material makes its effect without ever undermining the forward motion of the music, and such a combination of energy and lightness is maintained in the Scherzo, which is adventurous in its percussive writing and use of ostinati. Debussy's mastery of the medium is clear, as is his absorption of gypsy and Javanese sounds. The gentle, muted ternary Andantino has often been linked with Borodin's influence, but its chromaticism, tending to whole-tone emphasis at times, is already personal to Debussy himself. The finale begins hesitantly before settling into a mood that drives forward to a brilliant and spirited conclusion. Sometimes criticised as looking backward to Franck, notably from a formal aspect, Debussy's Quartet nevertheless proved to be a beacon that was to guide many future efforts in the genre.

Maurice Ravel (1875–1937) dedicated his Quartet (1903) to his teacher Gabriel Fauré, who was not so flattered as to conceal his opinion that the finale was a failure. Debussy, whose influence is also clearly evident, was more enthusiastic, and his advice (which Ravel followed) was not to alter a single note. Alteration could have meant improvement: the contrasts within the finale seem exaggerated, and the third movement verges on the self-indulgently rhapsodic form. Yet Ravel was already too experienced a composer to intend the sort of half-hearted *obéissance* in the direction of the Franckists made, for example, by Debussy in his Quartet. The traditional forms are used as pegs on which to hang an impressive display of cyclic thematic derivation, but the themes and harmonic processes are so characteristic of Ravel himself that any awkwardness in their structuring is of minor account.

The two principal themes of Ravel's sonata-form first movement were clearly designed with the potential for developmental combination in mind. They also generate most of the significant material for the rest of the work; the second has particularly close connections with the scherzo and the first with both slow movement and finale. Throughout Ravel's melodies have a characteristic modal cut and are integrated with striking mastery of instrumental colour, yet the lyrical outbursts are held firmly within the Classical form. The scherzo comes second, characterised by its juxtaposition of pizzicato, bowed and tremolo phrases and percussive rhythmic effects that are reminiscent of Ravel's Spanish-inspired works; its alternation of 6/8 and 3/4 metre heightens this Hispanic flavour. It is interrupted by a muted slow section in which its two dominant themes appear. The rhapsodic, ternary slow movement illustrates Ravel's tonal freedom, commencing in A minor-D minor and concluding in a G♭ major that has been intermittently present throughout the movement. The evocative finale, a loosely-knit rondo with its principal idea in 5/8 metre, was probably inspired by Russian folk models. Its second idea, based on the work's first four notes, leads one to expect a cyclic roll-call of the work's main themes in the coda; however, Ravel was probably too proud to indulge in such an obvious unifying ploy, preferring to allude rather than to assert.

In the same year as Chausson composed most of his unfinished quartet, Camille Saint-Saëns (1835–1921), one of the principal personalities involved in the establishment of the Société Nationale, penned his First String Quartet Op. 112 (1899), his first chamber work without piano. This was retrospective in its revival of what is to some extent a *quatuor brillant*, dedicated to the Belgian violinist Eugène Ysaÿe. Counterpoint is characteristically well to the fore with fugato episodes in three of its four movements, while the development section of the finale incorporates a notable recall of the work's elegiac opening. This opening and the freely lyrical slow movement, founded on two contrasting themes, clearly provided Ysaÿe with an excellent vehicle for his noble and expressive style, while the first movement's più allegro, the rhythmic, energetic scherzo and the finale show off the first violinist's virtuoso capability. Saint-Saëns's Second Quartet Op. 153 (1919) also looks backward – to the eighteenth century and beyond. Emile Baumann has described it as 'very simple – even Mozartian',[12] and the Classical refinement of its outer movements certainly supports such an observation. Its various modal cadences perhaps suggest even earlier influences, but its abrupt key changes and its adventurous, wide-ranging tonal scheme (notably in the Molto adagio) confirm its twentieth-century origins.

Fauré's (1845–1924) String Quartet in E minor Op. 121 (1924), his only chamber work without piano, is also retrospective and proved to be his last work. Fauré admitted to his wife that he was 'terrified' at the thought of following Beethoven in the quartet genre and he kept his indulgence in the medium very quiet until it was near completion.[13] The extent to which his confidence was at a low ebb is demonstrated in a letter shortly before his death requesting that the quartet be 'given a trial in the presence of a small group of friends who have always been the first audience of my works: Dukas, Poujaud, Lalo etc. I have confidence in their judgement, and so I leave the decision to them whether this quartet should be published or destroyed.'[14] He never heard the work performed, but his advisers were adamant that his doubts were ill-founded. The opening Allegro moderato, in sonata form, is firmly based on two principal themes extracted from Fauré's unfinished Violin Concerto Op. 14, composed over forty years earlier. Its argument, involving notable dialogue between the first violin and viola, demonstrates a remarkable economy of expression, as does the content of the jovial finale, a quasi-rondo structure. However, the core of the work is the profoundly expressive central Andante, with its intricate polyphony and elegiac viola melody, which many have interpreted as the composer's melancholy prefiguration of death.

The masterpieces by Franck, Debussy, Ravel and Fauré were to stimulate numerous talented French successors to take an interest in the string quartet. Albert Roussel, Maurice Emmanuel, Jean Roger-Ducasse, Charles Koechlin, Florent Schmitt, Darius Milhaud, Louis Durey, Arthur Honegger, Henri Sauguet, Pierre Menu, Henri Dutilleux and many others wrote significant works in the genre, but few of these have gained a permanent niche in the repertory.

Italy

An Italian taste for chamber music was perpetuated in the first half of the nineteenth century in four principal centres, but it largely failed to encourage a truly native quartet tradition. In Milan, Alessandro Rolla's (1757–1841) three quartets Op. 5 (published in 1807), like most Italian instrumental works of the period, followed Viennese Classical models. They comprise the customary four movements, but two of the three place the minuet second, rather than third, a pattern adopted later by Nicolò Paganini (1782–1840) in his string quartets.[15] Rolla's sonata-form first movements include some dramatic inflections but little true thematic development, while the slow movements are often intensely lyrical (though Op. 5 no. 2 is a theme and variations) and the finales are rondos, often incorporating technical challenges particularly for the first violinist. Such virtuoso demands are even more prevalent in his three *Quartetti Concertanti* Op. 2, published in 1823.

In Bologna, Felice Alessandro Radicati (1775–1820) was an influential champion of the cause, composing nine string quartets and numerous other chamber works which were disseminated by some of the most prestigious publishers of his time. After various tours and sojourns abroad, Giovanni Battista Polledro (1781–1853) settled in Turin from 1824 and, as *maestro di cappella* at the court, did much to foster chamber music in the city. Following the foundation in Florence (1830) of the Società Filarmonica (the first in Italy) to disseminate Classical (and especially instrumental) music, the initiative of the Italian music critic Abramo Basevi (1818–85) in establishing in that city a series of concerts called 'Mattinate Beethoveniane' (from 1859) with the objective of awakening Italians further to the German instrumental tradition led to the formation of the Società del Quartetto di Firenze (1861). The violinist/composer Ferdinando Giorgetti (1796–1867) was among this society's prime movers, modelling the instrumental style of his three string quartets (1851–6) on that of Haydn, Mozart and Beethoven and earning for himself the nickname 'Tedescone'. The Società's success led to the rapid establishment of a network of such quartet societies over Italy, notably in Milan and Turin in the 1860s, Palermo in 1871, and Bologna in 1879.

By the time he was twenty-five years old, Antonio Bazzini (1818–97) had already forged a successful career as an itinerant virtuoso, performing in the most important musical centres of Italy, Germany, France, Belgium, Denmark, Spain and the Netherlands. Following his return to Italy in 1864, he became active in promoting and composing for quartet societies in Italy, eventually settling in Milan. He released five quartets into the public domain between 1864 and 1893; an early work (Op. 7) in the genre remained unpublished. The celebrated double bass player and conductor Giovanni Bottesini (1821–89) also wrote chamber music in the intervals between concert tours abroad. From 1862 to 1865 he subscribed to the Società del Quartetto di Firenze and his output includes eleven string quartets. The three string quartets published by Girard as Opp. 2 in Bb, 3 in F♯ minor and 4 in D confirm his development of a more personal language, especially Op. 4, which won the second Concorso Basevi in Florence (1862).

Two of the most important non-operatic composers who contributed to the renascence of Italian instrumental music and Italian concert life in general were Giovanni Sgambati (1841–1914), who was based largely in Rome, and Giuseppe Martucci (1856–1909) who worked principally in Bologna and Naples. Martucci composed little of significance for string quartet, but Sgambati's rhapsodic String Quartet in C♯ minor gained some measure of international popularity in the 1880s.

Several composers who are better known for their ventures in opera also contributed to the quartet repertoire. Giovanni Pacini (1796–1867) was a principal player in the Italian operatic scene from *c.* 1820 to 1850; his instrumental music, however, dates from his final years and includes six quartets (1858–65), which reveal a mixture of Viennese classical influence and that of Italian predecessors such as Rossini. Gaetano Donizetti (1797–1848) composed most of his eighteen or so string quartets for musical gatherings at the house of one Bertoli in Bergamo, where the German composer Simon Mayr often played the viola. Following Viennese structural models, including numerous monothematic finales in the manner of Haydn, they demonstrate remarkable assurance in the medium, even if their *Gebrauchsmusik* intentions have prevented them from taking hold in the repertory.

The efforts of most Italian composers in the genre were eclipsed by Giuseppe Verdi's (1813–1901) sole instrumental work, his String Quartet in E minor, written in March 1873 during a month of enforced leisure in Naples. Verdi himself attached so little importance to the work that for some time he would not allow it either to be heard in public or to be published – it was eventually premiered by Camillo Sivori's French ensemble (Sivori, Marsick, Viardot and Delsart) in 1876. A unique work in his output, it especially demonstrates Verdi's easy and informal mastery of the resources of counterpoint. Recapitulation and development are condensed into one in the opening, sonata-form Allegro (i.e. such development as there is finds its way into the transitional part of the recapitulation), with its expansive first theme and chromatically harmonised second theme (G major). The charming Andantino might almost represent a *scena* of some opera, while the brilliant scherzo (E minor) incorporates a startling modulation to A♭ (really G♯) major in its middle section. The finale, as Verdi indicates in his movement heading, is a joke-fugue (Scherzo Fuga). It may well be considered as a preliminary study for the celebrated choral fugue which crowns his last opera, *Falstaff*, to the words, 'Tutto il mondo e burla' ('All the world's a joke'). Its mood is similar, though its theme is different; but the lively result is a fully worked-out and quite 'learned' fugue on a skittish, six-bar (*leggierissimo*) subject.

Verdi's quartet had few Italian successors in the nineteenth century. Ferruccio Busoni's (1866–1924) flirtations with the genre are early products from the late 1870s and 1880s composed under the influence of Brahms. They include two full-scale quartets (in C minor and F minor; both 1876) without opus numbers, some individual minuets and other movements for the medium, a Quartet in C Op. 19 (*c.* 1883) and the best of the bunch, the

Quartet in D minor Op. 26 (*c.* 1887). In his correspondence Busoni considered Op. 26 his 'most significant work so far'. He described to Melanie Mayer (the daughter of his composition teacher in Graz, Wilhelm Mayer-Rémy), the grand, almost symphonic scale of the first movement, the 'deeply felt and extremely carefully worked out' Adagio, the 'wild and demonic Scherzo' and the humorous theme of the boisterous finale, which 'finally combines the theme with that of the first movement, after which a spirited coda makes for a great and effective climax'.[16] Busoni later admitted (1909) having plans to write a quartet in one movement, 'which should be *my* masterwork and really stir up emotions'.[17] Regrettably, such plans were never brought to fruition.

Giacomo Puccini's (1858–1924) string quartet music, with the exception of some student exercises, dates, like Busoni's, mostly from the early 1880s (before the operas for which he is best remembered) and remained mostly unpublished. His best-known work for the medium, *Crisantemi*, was written on the death of a friend, Prince Amadeo, Duke of Savoy, in 1890. The restrained, rhapsodic grieving of the music reflects the strong melancholic vein in the composer himself. Puccini connoisseurs may recognise the work's two principal themes, which reappear in *Manon Lescaut* – in Des Grieux's address to Manon in prison ('Ah! Manon disperato') and at the opening of the final act.

Finally, Ottorino Respighi's (1879–1936) four completed quartets deserve passing mention, particularly No. 4, 'Quartetto Dorico' (1924), a through-composed, thoroughly unified work in which modal material is skilfully utilised. 'Dorico' refers to the Dorian scale on which the principal theme of the work is founded. This theme pervades the quartet in various guises and transformations, ensuring its unity and cohesion. It plays a particularly important role in the finale, a complex passacaglia in 7/4 metre, either in *quasi recitativo* or in the final climactic section, in which its very last appearance is punctuated by rapid ascending scales.

Great Britain

British contributions to the quartet repertory were somewhat spasmodic during the nineteenth century; however, the chamber music output of John Lodge Ellerton (1801–73)[18] was unusually large for his time. Closely modelled on the work of the Viennese Classical masters but written in a style tinged with Romanticism, Ellerton's fifty string quartets composed between the 1840s and 1860s represent a significant (if not especially original) corpus of works in the genre. The contributions of others were less substantial. Arguably the most distinguished English composer of the Romantic period, Sir William Sterndale Bennett (1816–75), managed only one work in the genre, while the only string quartet (in C minor) of Sir Frederic Cowen (1852–1935), who studied in Leipzig from 1865, was premiered at the Conservatoire there in 1866. Between *c.* 1834 and 1878 Sir George Macfarren (1813–87) composed five string quartets whose popularity was also short-lived.

Later in the century other British 'knights' Sir Hubert Parry (1848–1918), Sir John McEwen (1868–1948), Sir Alexander Mackenzie (1847–1935) and Sir Charles Villiers Stanford (1852–1924) dominated British composition, although their contributions to the chamber sphere were variable. Parry composed two Mendelssohnian quartets (1867, 1868) as a student at Oxford University and he added Brahms and Wagner to his list of influences in No. 3, completed a decade later; however, he became celebrated more for his choral works than his chamber music. McEwen, on the other hand, was a prolific composer of string quartets, contributing nineteen finely wrought works. Some of them synthesize Romantic elements with Scottish folk idioms (as in No. 15 'A Little Quartet "in modo scotico"') and sometimes even French folk influences (as in No. 6 'Biscay' and No. 16 'Provencale'); but perhaps the best known are No. 9 ('Threnody'), a highly emotional, through-composed work written during the strife of war, and No. 10 ('The Jocund Dance'), which is essentially a suite of dance tunes.

The hallmarks of Mendelssohn and Brahms are also especially strong in Mackenzie's only string quartet and Stanford's eight quartets, these latter tinged also with his Irish folklore heritage; however, Stanford's influence as a teacher is probably more noteworthy than his works in the genre, since so many of his pupils contributed significantly to the revival of a native chamber music in Britain, among them Samuel Coleridge-Taylor (1875–1912), Ralph Vaughan Williams (1872–1958), Thomas Dunhill (1877–1946),[19] Frank Bridge (1879–1941), Herbert Howells (1892–1983), John Ireland (1879–1962),[20] Eugene Goossens (1893–1962) and, briefly, Sir Arthur Bliss (1891–1975).[21] Coleridge-Taylor's *Five Fantasiestücke* (1895) and his unpublished String Quartet in D minor Op. 13 date from his student days at the Royal College of Music under Stanford, where he gained an assured technique and added Stanford's Brahmsian influence to his own enthusiasm for Dvořak's work.

Irish-born Charles Wood (1866–1926) was brought up in the same London 'stable' but went on to Cambridge University, became known primarily as a composer of Anglican church music and received many prestigious awards for his contribution to British musical life. His six completed string quartets, edited by Edward J. Dent and published posthumously in 1929, rarely escape the influence of Parry and Stanford. But many of their themes are derived from, or inspired by, Irish folk music – the A minor Quartet (1911) is a notable case in point. Wood also wrote some *Variations on an Irish Folk Song* (?1917) and numerous other movements for the medium.

In Wales, the music of another Parry – the Merthyr-born disciple of Sterndale Bennett, Joseph Parry (1841–1903) – enjoyed great popularity.[22] The three movements of his String Quartet demonstrate his rather cosy operatic manner imbued with an earnest academicism. Its opening sonata-form Allegro is preceded by a severe slow introduction in 'the old style'. The slow movement displays Parry's Italianate lyricism to the full and the work ends with a fugue whose material is resourcefully manipulated, the main idea itself being subjected to stretto, inversion, augmentation and diminution.

At the beginning of the twentieth century, string quartet composition was further encouraged in Britain by the prize competitions instituted in 1905 by Walter Willson Cobbett, a successful businessman and enthusiastic amateur musician.[23] Cobbett favoured the 'Phantasy' – a through-composed, single-movement piece generally comprising sections varying in tempo and character – and a large number of Phantasie Quartets and Quintets for various instrumental combinations were written as a result of this stimulus. Phantasie String Quartets by Bridge (in F minor, 1905), William Hurlestone (1876–1906; 1906) and Howells (Op. 25; 1916–17) are notable examples of the genre.

Sir Edward Elgar (1857–1934) came to the string quartet late in life; earlier attempts to contribute to the genre never bore fruit. His diary records him writing 'E minor stuff' in April 1918 and it is significant that of the four works dating from this period, three are in that key, including his String Quartet Op. 83. The Quartet is a much less grandiose affair than its immediate successor, the Piano Quintet Op. 84: in mood it foreshadows some of those uneasily elegiac qualities which make the Cello Concerto so memorable. The restless, sonata-form first movement adopts the compound (12/8) metre which had proved so successful a channel for the vigorous flow and nobility of thought of the first movement of his Second Symphony. The contrasting, tranquil slow movement (Piacevole) has an almost *Wand of Youth*-like charm. It is light music, though serious thoughts are not excluded, and the design has a breadth for which the very simple song-like material proves surprisingly apt. The finale has a rhetorical, even extrovert air in its early stages, though some of its more chromatic episodes may seem too dependent upon well-tried Elgarian mannerisms. It is a passionate movement with many other satisfying features, nevertheless, and the spirit of Falstaff conquers that of Gerontius to ensure a lively close.

America

The seeds for the growth of chamber music in the Americas were scattered towards the end of the eighteenth century in Pennsylvania and the Carolinas, where the German-speaking communities of Moravians and other central Europeans began to develop an active chamber music culture. But the symphony was the predominant instrumental genre, and it was only after the establishment of societies such as the Harvard Musical Association (1844), the Mason–Thomas concerts in New York (1855) and the Briggs House Concerts in Chicago (1860) and the formation of professional groups such as the Mendelssohn Quintette Club in Boston (1849) that the chamber music repertory was disseminated to a wider audience.

European Classical fare dominated the programmes, but string quartets by native Americans were gradually introduced, fired by a number of short-lived groups with varying degrees of nationalistic purpose.[24] Prominent among these groups were William H. Fry (1813–64) and George Frederick Bristow (1825–98), each of whom contributed to the cause two quartets (1849) of essentially Classical proportions and style.[25] Two quartets by Charles C. Perkins are also significant landmarks in that they were among the first American music published by the Leipzig firm Breitkopf & Härtel (1854 and 1855).

Musical studies in Germany became the vogue for budding American composers; perhaps not surprisingly, the works of Mendelssohn, Schumann and Brahms provided the models for the likes of John Knowles Paine's (1839–1906) String Quartet in D Op. 5, written as a student exercise in Berlin in the late 1850s and published posthumously in 1940, and Horatio Parker's (1863–1919) Quartet in F Op. 11 (1885), composed while he was a student in Munich. George Chadwick (1854–1931), who undertook a somewhat belated systematic musical education at the Leipzig Conservatoire from 1878, benefited from the concert opportunities there which spawned the first two (in G minor and C) of his five string quartets. His return to Boston (1880) and his association with the first renowned American string quartet, the Kneisel Quartet (formed in 1885), led to the composition of his Third (c. 1885) and Fourth Quartets (1896). The latter was directly inspired by Dvořák's F major Quartet Op. 96 ('American'), which had received its first performance by the Kneisel Quartet in Boston early in 1894 and provided a major stimulus for native American interest in the genre. It demonstrates Chadwick's attempts to liberate his musical expression from German influences and incorporate, as in the second and third movements, 'a free imitation of and a refinement upon the idiom of negro music'.[26] Such trends are further evident in his Fifth Quartet in D minor (1898), written for the Adamowski Quartet, and in later American works such as Daniel Gregory Mason's (1873–1953) *String Quartet on Negro Themes* Op. 19 (1918–19), with its use of spirituals and some occasional Debussian impressionism. Chadwick's fellow Bostonian Arthur Foote (1853–1937) also wrote quartets after Dvořák's American sojourn, following his Op. 4 in G minor (1883) with Op. 32 in E (1893) and a Third

Quartet in D (1907–11); but these were essentially American works written in a predominantly Austro-German language.

The early twentieth century brought with it a wider variety of styles for American music. French currents, detectable in some of the quartets of, for example, Frédéric Ritter (1824–91), are also evident in the work of Charles Martin Loeffler (1861–1935; 1889), John Alden Carpenter (1876–1951; 1927) and Edward Burlingame Hill (1872–1960; 1935). Furthermore, composers such as Frederick Converse (1871–1940; three quartets, 1896–1935), Henry Gilbert (1868–1928; Quartet, 1920) and Arthur Farwell (1872–1952; String Quartet 'The Hako', 1922) introduced elements of American folk music in an effort to cultivate an independent American style.

With similar aims, Charles Ives (1874–1954), while studying with Parker at Yale, based his First Quartet (1896) on American hymn tunes. His unorthodox approach, which also involved a fugal first movement later re-used in his Fourth Symphony, heralded a corpus of works in the medium by American composers as diverse as Walter Piston (1894–1976), Henry Cowell (1897–1965), Quincy Porter (1897–1966), Roy Harris (1898–1979), Virgil Thomson (1896–1989) and Ruth Crawford Seeger (1901–53). The most significant of these are discussed further in Chapter 14.

Other countries

Few other pockets of quartet activity not covered elsewhere in this volume are worthy of note. The long-standing traditions of *Hausmusik* in Switzerland yielded little home-grown compositional talent of significance in the nineteenth century, while the influence of German composers was predominant in most other European countries. The Netherlander Johannes Verhulst (1816–91), for example, trod a fairly lonely path as a composer of three string quartets, but these works date from his sojourn in Leipzig. Schumann, his close friend during that period, particularly praised the Adagio of Verhulst's Quartet in A♭ major Op. 6 no. 2 (1840); Verhulst's Third Quartet Op. 21 (1845), however, received a mixed reception, its ideas 'being traceable not only to Mendelssohn and Schumann, but also, in the adagio, to Beethoven (Septet)'.[27]

The conservatoire in Madrid was the focal point for string quartet concerts in nineteenth-century Spain. But one of the most significant Spanish composers in the genre was Juan Crisóstomo de Arriaga (1806–26), who studied at the Paris Conservatoire under Baillot and Fétis. His three quartets (in D minor, A major and E♭ major), composed at the age of sixteen, make one wonder what his stature might have been in the medium had he lived longer. Fétis commended them for their originality and elegance.[28]

Based firmly on the Classical style, they incorporate splashes of native Spanish colour, especially the D minor Quartet, which has a Spanish *jota* as its trio. Among other nineteenth-century Spanish composers who contributed to the repertory were Federico Olmeda (1865–1909), Felipe Pedrell (1841–1922), Ruperto Chapí (1851–1909) and Tomás Bretón (1850–1923).

With the cultivation and development of the genre throughout Europe and America during the nineteenth century, string quartet composition, though still focused on Austro-German traditions, was ready to enter a new era, one in which the scope, tastes, expectations and popularity of the medium would undergo much more radical and dramatic transformation.

13 Nineteenth-century national traditions and the string quartet

JAN SMACZNY

In the developing national musical traditions of the nineteenth century, certain genres, inevitably, were privileged. Given its explicit, decorative, often political nature, opera became the major mode of projecting nation and national character, followed at some distance by the symphonic poem and programme symphony. In such an environment the string quartet, which of all the major genres of the eighteenth century that continued to flourish in the nineteenth tended to retain its abstract credentials, was hardly a priority as a means of expression for the more nationally inclined composer. The landmarks of nationalism, such as Musorgsky's *Boris Godunov*, Moniuszko's *Halka* and Smetana's *The Bartered Bride* and *My Country* represented the public face of the composer both serving and dramatising the nation, courting and exploiting the aspirations of contemporary fashion in their nations' passage towards the construction of an identity.

For the reflective composer working within national traditions, the string quartet offered the chance to explore a hard-won compositional technique, but also, notably in the case of Smetana, to project a more personal mode of expression once the requirements of the nation had been served. Thus, paradoxically, given its abstract origins, the quartet, reimaged by nineteenth-century aspirations, not only could embody the rigour of orthodoxy, but for the programmatically orientated Smetana proved also to be the means of explicitly dramatising his life;[1] and in the hands of the Russians Tchaikovsky and Arensky the quartet could in the manner of Renaissance and Baroque *tombeaux* commemorate a life.[2] If the programmatic quartet was very much an exception, very few composers among the Slavs in the latter part of the nineteenth century could resist playing the national card: among the Russians this amounted to the frequent use of folksong, while the Czechs, in general resistant to the quotation of folk material, made extensive use of native dance rhythms, in particular the polka and *furiant*. If not as 'in the face' of the public as the monuments of national opera, the quartet could reinforce constructions of nationalism while still affording composers, notably in the Czech tradition, a means of realigning with the Classical canon.

Where the quartet did flourish, a crucial feature was an institutional infrastructure that supported the performance and composition of chamber music; of equal significance was the rise of the professional quartet (see Chapters 3 and 4). Among the Czechs, for example, there was a burgeoning musical life in which the salons and concert-giving bodies of Prague developed favourable conditions for chamber music, assisted by the increase in the number of professional ensembles. In this environment the string quartet flourished and in the fourteen quartets of Dvořák provided Romanticism with its most substantial contribution in the second half of the nineteenth century.

Russia

As with most other cultural developments in Russia, the rise of the string quartet was very much a tale of two cities: St Petersburg and Moscow. One of the significant musical figures of St Petersburg in the early nineteenth century, Alexander Alyabyev (1787–1851), who from 1836 lived and worked with success in Moscow, produced the earliest Russian string quartets of note. His first quartet in E♭ (1815), though expert in its handling of textures (including giving much independence to viola and cello in the first movement) and pleasingly melodic (particularly in the trio of the third movement), has a rather formulaic cut; his second in G major (1825) has more individuality and essays the national accent in the slow movement based on his song, hugely popular in St Petersburg,[3] *The Nightingale* (Solovey). Mikhail Glinka (1804–57), another composer nurtured by St Petersburg, and decisive in founding what became known as the Russian style, was not greatly exercised by the quartet medium: his first, in D major (1824), was left unfinished; his second, in F major (1830), is more fluent and shows a clear appreciation of Classical procedures, but it marked the end of his interest in the genre. In fact, his quartets impinged so little on his consciousness that towards the end of his life Glinka failed to recognise one of them when performed for him.[4]

The musical institutions of St Petersburg and Moscow developed vigorously throughout the nineteenth century. In St Petersburg concert life was much enhanced by the Philharmonic Society, founded in 1802, which attracted visiting artists of the calibre of Berlioz, Schumann and Liszt. Chamber music was served by a number of musical salons; from 1871 the Russian Quartet gave frequent performances in St Petersburg and the following year a chamber music society was established which flourished until the revolution. A key figure in promoting opportunities for quartet performance and composition in St Petersburg was Mitrofan Belyayev. His fortune derived from the timber trade, but his passion, as a keen amateur viola player, was chamber music. Apart from setting up the Russian Symphonic Concerts in

1885, an important nexus for string quartet composition was the chamber music session he held regularly on Friday nights. Rimsky-Korsakov painted a lively picture of these events during which new quartets would be 'baptised' with bottles of champagne, a prelude to further bibulous celebrations.[5] The practical results of these gatherings, entirely typical of the collaborative tendency among St Petersburg composers, were collective compositions, including a string quartet whose main motif was based on Belyayev's name (B–la–F) written by Rimsky, Lyadov, Borodin and Glazunov.[6] In Moscow opera and ballet were central to musical life, but increasing concert activity through the nineteenth century saw the steady tread of distinguished European artists to the city. As in St Petersburg, a number of salons grew up, and from the middle of the century the opportunities for performing chamber music developed strongly. If not exactly an equivalent to Belyayev, Nikolay Rubinstein became a major player in the city's musical life, instigating the Moscow wing of the Russian Musical Society and founding the Moscow Conservatoire.

Given a prevailing ideological mistrust of abstract music – Vladimir Stasov, the high priest of this tendency, had an attack of the vapours on hearing that Borodin had sketched a string quartet[7] – it is perhaps surprising that the string quartet flourished so extensively in Russia in the nineteenth century. A consistent, if not particularly distinctive, thread was provided by Anton Rubinstein (1829–94), who composed ten string quartets, six of which were published, and Nikolay Afanas'yev (1821–98). Afanas'yev's twelve string quartets include 'The Volga' in A major (1866), in part based on the songs of the boatmen of the great Russian river. Quartets of greater substance and character are to be found in the work of an estimable handful of the more familiar names of Russian nationalism.

Among the St Petersburg *kuchka*, Borodin (1833–87), apart from his single-movement contribution to Belyayev's Friday evenings, produced the most substantial quartets. His first, in A major, composed between 1873 and 1877, was described on its title page as being 'inspired by a theme of Beethoven'; in fact, as David Brown points out,[8] only the opening of the Allegro of the first movement owes anything to Beethoven, a passage from the finale of his Op. 130. This first movement shows genuine understanding of quartet texture with imaginative use of the two lower instruments; Borodin's technical agility is also evident in the fugal writing in the development and a general enrichment of texture with counterpoint. At the opening of the slow movement, Borodin defers to his St Petersburg colleagues by quoting a folksong in the viola part.[9] Borodin's textural and contrapuntal expertise are again apparent in the scherzo and finale; the latter also takes a lead from Glinka's *Kamarinskaya* in making use of a varied ostinato for much of its material.[10] Given the combination of compositional logic and colourful handling of instruments, it is little surprise that the first performers of the quartet, in St Petersburg in 1881, were delighted with the work.[11] Borodin's Second Quartet, in D major (1881), one of his best-known compositions, if not explicitly Russian in terms of the quotation of folk melody, evokes a tone that has come to be associated with Russian nationalism: reflexive melody in the first movement, repetition as a developmental device in the scherzo and, as in the last movement of the First Quartet, the cumulative power of ostinato and variation in the finale. But it is the Notturno slow movement that sticks in listeners' minds as something of a *locus classicus* of Russian Romantic music: ravishing, asymmetrical, frankly vocal melody unashamedly presented.

Of the remainder of the *kuchka*, only Musorgsky did not touch the string quartet; indeed, he joined Stasov in having a panic attack on hearing about Borodin sketching such a work.[12] In 1854 Balakirev (1827–1910) began, but did not complete, a 'Quatuor original russe'; Cui (1835–1918) completed three quartets (C minor, 1890; D major, 1907 and E♭ major, 1913), some of the most substantial instrumental works from a composer who tended to cultivate the miniature. Rimsky-Korsakov (1844–1908) wrote a number of works for string quartet, including three full-length works in F major (1875) and G major (1897); the third (1878–9) was a quartet in which each of the four movements is based on specified Russian folk songs. The remainder of Rimsky's contribution comprised four movements written as part of the collaborative quartets for Belyayev's entertainments.

Four classically influenced (though quirkily original) short movements for quartet from 1863 and 1864 preceded Tchaikovsky's first serious effort in the medium. In this work, a single movement in B♭ major from 1865 just before he took up teaching in Rubinstein's Moscow Conservatory, Tchaikovsky essayed the folk manner later favoured by his St Petersburg counterparts. Tchaikovsky shows more than competence in dealing with the quartet medium in this work, in which a distinctive, chorale-like Adagio misterioso frames an unsettled and slightly wayward sonata Allegro con moto based on a Ukrainian folksong. His first official quartet, in D major (1871), enjoyed a high-profile premiere at a benefit concert for its composer; predating the completion of Borodin's First Quartet by six years, the work was viewed by its contemporary audience as something of a milestone for the genre in Russia. David Brown, quite rightly, points out the similarity to Schubert in its delicately syncopated opening,[13] but much of the success of this first movement derives from Tchaikovsky's bold use of harmony and creative disposition of counterpoint through the texture. The slow movement, based on another Ukrainian folksong, has charm and elegance. Both scherzo and finale benefit from rhythmic unpredictability, the latter developing exhilarating impetus.

The contemporary success of the First Quartet was well deserved and Tchaikovsky built fruitfully on the experience in his second. Written three years later in 1874, the quartet's process of composition was, by Tchaikovsky's own account,[14] remarkably fluent. All of the movements mark an advance on the First Quartet: the slow movement is unquestionably more profound, the scherzo and finale both more ear-catching as well as demanding; even more remarkable is the first movement, whose introductory Adagio provides one of Tchaikovsky's most searching explorations of chromaticism. His Third Quartet, written early in 1876, shows for much of its length an even greater emotional engagement than in the second. Although it was a public success at its first performances, Tchaikovsky harboured doubts about the work, fearing that he was repeating himself.[15] The first, third and final movements are richer in texture and affect than their counterparts in the earlier quartets. The slow movement was intended to commemorate the death of the Czech violinist Ferdinand Laub, who had settled in Moscow in 1866 and who had led the group which premiered Tchaikovsky's first two string quartets. While sincerely intentioned, the quasi-Baroque rhetoric of the opening, with its dotted rhythms and lack of melodic substance, leaves a slightly stilted impression.

The tradition of the commemorative quartet continued in the second (A minor, 1894) of Anton Arensky (1861–1906). St Petersburg trained, but a teacher of composition at the Moscow Conservatory from 1882, Arensky was much mentored by Tchaikovsky. On the older composer's death he wrote a distinctive quartet, scored originally for the sombre colouring of violin, viola and two cellos, though later arranged for the conventional combination, as an 'in memoriam'. Each movement is based on pre-existent material: Orthodox chant, a Russian folksong in the finale (familiar from Beethoven's 'Razumovsky' quartet Op. 59 no. 2) and a song by Tchaikovsky, from the Sixteen Children's Songs Op. 54, in the middle movement. Though occasionally inclined to the formulaic, particularly in the first movement, the writing is frequently striking in its volatility.

One of the most substantial bodies of Russian string quartets was left by Alexander Glazunov (1865–1936). The first of his seven quartets (D major, Op. 1, 1882) attracted the favourable attention of Belyayev, who took the young composer under his wing. For his part, Glazunov became an enthusiastic participant in Belyayev's Friday soirées for which he wrote a number of quartets, including Five Novelettes for String Quartet (Op. 15, 1886), whose cosmopolitan credentials are proclaimed in designations such as Alla Spagnuola, Orientale and All'Ungherese. A major player in the latter stages of Russian Romantic nationalism, Glazunov consistently adopted the Russian style: his Third String Quartet (G major, Op. 26, 1888), however, was published under the rather more generalised Slavonic title 'Quatuor

Slave'. This engaging work includes an ostinato-based Interludium by way of a slow movement, a Mazurka third movement and an extensive finale entitled 'A Slavonic Festival'. Glazunov continued to compose string quartets for much of the rest of his career – the last, 'Hommage au passé' (C major, Op. 107), was completed in 1930. Arguably his finest quartet is the fifth (D minor, Op. 70), composed in 1898 when Glazunov was approaching the height of his powers. Beethoven appears to be an influence in the first two movements: his late style in the fugal introduction to the opening Allegro, and the Razumovsky quartets in the Scherzo. Throughout there is abundant evidence of Glazunov's burgeoning originality, not least in the profound Adagio.

Taneyev (1856–1915), as his soubriquet 'the Russian Brahms'[16] might suggest, was the most abstractly inclined of Russian quartet composers. Scholarly and fastidious, Taneyev studied Renaissance counterpoint, Bach and, on a visit to Salzburg, the manuscripts of Mozart. His six 'official' quartets (two incomplete quartets were written respectively in the mid 1870s and in 1911; three more date from the 1880s) on the whole tread the path of orthodoxy, although the first (B♭ minor, Op. 4, 1890) is something of an exception. Cast in five movements, the work contains some arresting gestures in the first movement and at the start of the fourth. But much of the material cannot entirely escape the charge of blandness, even triviality in the finale. There is little sign of the influence of his teacher Tchaikovsky, to whom the quartet is dedicated, but Brahms at several junctures is a potent presence. The Second Quartet (C major, Op. 5, 1895), composed at the Yasnaya Polyana dacha of Tolstoy, with whom Taneyev played chess, retreats towards orthodoxy in both outward shaping and, with the exception of the darkly coloured scherzo, content. The sixth published quartet (B♭, Op. 19, 1906) is a slightly curious spectacle: the first movement is ultra-conventional, but there is an original, neo-classical cut to the Giga third movement, and the finale plays interestingly with varied tempi.

Scandinavia

The quartet among the Scandinavians had an estimable currency. If opera proved less of a preoccupation than in Russia and Central Europe, owing largely to a less developed infrastructure, the main medium for national expression tended to be incidental music, most famously Grieg's for Ibsen's *Peer Gynt*. The prevalent tendency in abstract music through much of the nineteenth century was to favour German models: in his single quartet in A minor (1831), the German-born Danish composer Kuhlau (1786–1832) pays homage to Beethoven's Op. 132 within the context of the more brilliant style favoured in the 1820s. Scandinavian affinities with early German Romanticism were reinforced in Norway by a steady procession of composers to Leipzig to study, including Johann Svendsen (1840–1911), Edvard Grieg (1843–1907) and Christian Sinding (1856–1941), all quartet composers. Among the Danes, Johan Hartmann (1805–1900) travelled extensively in Germany, where he met Mendelssohn, and Peter Heise (1830–79) also studied in Leipzig. For Hartmann, whose main contribution to the national cause resided in incidental music for the stage marked by his affinity for Scandinavian mythology, quartet composition was not a major priority and he completed only two works of relatively conventional cut. Heise, on the other hand, composed six quartets, the most distinctive of which, in C minor (1857), shows a clear personality extending beyond the influence of Beethoven and the early German Romantics.

The formative connection with Mendelssohn's Leipzig had been made by the Dane Niels Gade (1817–90), whose First Symphony, conducted by Mendelssohn, was given there to acclaim in 1843. Gade taught in Leipzig and, briefly, succeeded Mendelssohn as conductor of the Gewandhaus Orchestra before returning to Copenhagen in 1848. Gade was very much the overarching figure in Danish music and a major influence generally in Scandinavia. Central to the musical life of Copenhagen, this essentially conservative musician influenced at least three generations of composers, from Heise and Grieg to Nielsen (1865–1931), who mourned Gade's passing with due sincerity. Although Gade was an avid quartet player, leading an ensemble in Copenhagen whose preferred repertoire was Beethoven, he left only three string quartets complete. An early movement in A minor (1836) and an incomplete work in F major (1840) prelude his first completed quartet; dating from 1851, this F minor quartet was designated a 'practice piece' by the composer.[17] Though under-formed in some ways, the quartet shows far more than competence in the idiom; particularly engaging is the lilting passacaglia that introduces a finale with the character, almost, of a late eighteenth-century Central European Pastorella. A six-movement quartet in E minor from 1877 (usually heard in a much-edited five-movement version)[18] marks a considerable advance: the angularity and impetus of the scherzo is impressive and the succeeding Allegretto has an arrestingly original profile, though the finale retreats toward the manner of Mendelssohn.

Gade's D major String Quartet (completed 1889), his only one to be published (Breitkopf & Härtel, 1890), reveals his strengths and weaknesses as a quartet composer. The formal craft is excellent, as is the handling of texture; even at this late stage in his career, Gade's admiration for Beethoven and Mendelssohn is clear, though there is much in the work that shows him to be far more than a pale imitator, notably the brooding approach to the recapitulation in the first movement and the arresting central episode of the brilliant, though otherwise Mendelssohnian, scherzo. The main problem is that these moments of real originality expose the fundamentally conservative background. The case that these works should be heard more often is unanswerable; at no stage does their quality fall towards the routine, but they are not distinctive enough, in the manner of Smetana and Dvořák, to provide a lead for a national school, even if their sheer competence might well have supplied a technical basis for one.

Given his unease with larger abstract forms, it is perhaps not surprising that Grieg's extant works for string quartet[19] comprise only one completed work in G minor (1877–8) and two movements from 1891, though both quartet and torso have a far more national cut than any by Gade. The G minor Quartet is interesting from many points of view. While the work's national credentials are vested mainly in the use of folk style in parts of the finale, it is mainly remarkable for its originality. Despite Debussy's caustic critical views of Grieg, amounting in some cases to the near-abusive,[20] the French composer seems to have recognised the quartet's progressive qualities; a number of writers have noted the impact of Grieg's quartet on Debussy's in the same key, composed some fifteen years later.[21]

Original in form and content, both tonal and textural, the quartet is one of the most cyclic works Grieg wrote. The falling motif which unites the work is taken from *Spillemaend* (Minstrels), Op. 25 no. 1, one of the finest of Grieg's middle-period songs. Based on a Norwegian legend in which an artist gains enlightenment from a water-sprite at the cost of personal happiness, the song was written at a time of marital tension, a fact that has prompted autobiographical interpretation.[22] Given the extensive use of the opening theme of the song in the quartet and the stormy nature of, in particular, its first and last movements, the element of autobiography may have been carried over into the chamber work. The theme is heard at its broadest when used as the second subject of the first movement's main Allegro molto ed agitato, but is at its most dramatic in the doom-laden introduction to the work and in the impressively portentous approach to the conclusion of the finale (these final bars also make cyclic reference to the start of the first movement's main Allegro). Grieg's daring handling of texture and harmony is evident in the striking transitional material to the first movement's second subject which appears, at first, as an almost separate melodic unit (comparable to the presentation of the second subject of the finale of his Piano Concerto). When reduced to a more succinct three-note motto, the theme is a significant element in the lighter inner movements and both initiates and dominates the finale.

The national element pioneered by Grieg in Norway is only overtly apparent in the finale (again in common with the Piano Concerto and other works); what is most impressive about this quartet is its impassioned rhetoric and the arresting angularity of much of the material in the outer movements. This impressive, and underrated, work[23] unfortunately had no complete successors. It is easy to admire the craftsmanship of the two movements that exist from the F major Quartet of 1891, in particular the broad Allegro vivace, and to note Norwegian dance rhythms in the Allegro scherzando; but the energy and intensity that make the G minor Quartet such a compelling work, in which Grieg's particular difficulties with broader structures prompted impressively original solutions, are lacking.

As Grieg struggled to finish his F major Quartet, the Dane Carl Nielsen (1865–1931) had already completed four works and sundry other movements for the medium. A good violinist, Nielsen seems to have gravitated naturally to the string quartet as a means of learning his craft. His first completed quartet, in D minor (1883; unpublished), impressed Gade sufficiently to allow the teenage Nielsen into the Royal Conservatory in Copenhagen. Another tiro work followed (in F major, 1887; unpublished) before the sequence of four quartets that make up his published contribution to the genre: no. 1 in F minor (Op. 5, 1890); no. 2 in G minor (Op. 13, 1887–8, revised 1897–8); no. 3 in E♭ major (1897–8, new version 1899–1900) and the Quartet 'Piacevolezza' Op. 19 (1906, revised as the String Quartet in F major, Op. 44, c. 1919).[24] All four published works have strong parallels with the central symphonic thread of Nielsen's output, and it is the subject of regret among commentators that he did not pursue the genre in his deeper maturity.[25]

The F minor Quartet has much in common with Nielsen's First Symphony, also from 1890; both first movements have a bracing, headlong impetus, their thematic design is reflexive and harmonies incline at times to an almost 'bluesy' approach. Brahms is present in the tightness of the motivic design, the swaying secondary material and, as Charles M. Joseph observes,[26] the string writing. In both quartet and symphony, what impresses most is not the trail of influences on a still young composer, but the assured handling of the idiom, the unaffected sincerity of the slow movement and many aspects of thematic and harmonic design, even if, as David Fanning points out, there is a self-confessed tendency in the work to stick too closely to the tonic.[27] This quartet was played to none other than Joseph Joachim; despite the evident audacity of some of its harmonies it evidently secured the approval of the venerable violinist.

The G minor Quartet, originally composed two years before the F minor, also has much in common with the First Symphony, once again mainly in the first movement; the melodic and motivic writing in the first two movements seems to nod in the direction of Dvořák rather than Brahms; while the episodic, bitter-sweet third movement comes close to Dvořák's *dumka* style. Perhaps inevitably, the C minor scherzo brings to mind the determined Beethoven manner often prompted even late in the nineteenth century by the key, though the artful simplicity of the trio, with its drone bass, clearly evokes the national manner. Despite some astringent harmonies, the finale is the most conventional in cut of the four movements.

Nielsen's first two quartets, despite sporadic originality, were still very much products of the nineteenth century. Written just before the turn of the century, the Third String Quartet is very much a work for a new age. Each movement is couched in a relatively conventional formal frame, but the musical language at every stage is identifiable with the composer's early maturity. The first movement mingles intensity with a quizzical quality that has much in common with the Allegro collerico of the Second Symphony ('The Four Temperaments'), written at much the same time. The opening of the slow movement, with its probing, unresolved dissonances, introduces one of Nielsen's most profound statements to date. Throughout this comprehensively impressive quartet, the handling of texture is confident and far less derivative than in earlier works; if some of the counterpoint in the finale begins conventionally, it soon veers off into unexpected directions. The Fourth Quartet is built on the advances of the third and with greater textural refinement. Unquestionably fascinating, with almost Mahlerian ironic gestures in the first and third movements, this work has many rewards. Nevertheless, it is perhaps the Third Quartet that prompts the most regret that Nielsen did not pursue the genre further with a series of works to parallel his later symphonic development.

In common with the Danes in the nineteenth century, there was also something of a 'Leipzig tendency' among the Swedes: Lindblad (1801–78) studied with Zelter and knew Mendelssohn; although he is remembered mainly for his songs, he composed seven string quartets; over a generation later, Ludvig Norman (1831–85) was also educated in Leipzig and, perhaps predictably, his six string quartets display the influence of Mendelssohn and Schumann as well as of Gade. But by far the most distinctive Swedish nineteenth-century quartets were by a figure whose affinities were largely oblique to the Leipzig aesthetic. Franz Berwald (1796–1868) was born into a distinguished family of Swedish musicians of German origin; a distinguished professional violinist, he appears to have been self-taught as a composer. Against this background, his three string quartets are doubly remarkable; if they do not fit the narrow definitions of nationalism in the use of the popular or folk manner, they possess a sheer originality that gives them a unique profile in Scandinavian music of the period. Although Berwald worked extensively in Germany and Austria, his style defies canonic definition. While the musical language of his early First String Quartet (G minor; 1818) is founded on German late classicism, expectation is constantly defeated, notably in the first movement where the agenda is set by an opening that casts its net broadly both tonally and stylistically; abrupt changes of direction become virtually a formal feature in this sizeable movement. The Poco adagio is of a more conventional cut, but the scherzo, which frames a hauntingly attractive trio, and finale return to the audacity of the first movement, although the latter courts the dangers of collapse from the sheer disparity of its material.

Berwald's remaining two quartets, both from 1849, were completed after his final return to Sweden. Though more succinct than the first, the Second Quartet, in A minor, retains the ability to surprise; its greater economy imparts coherence, and Berwald's use of the instruments is far more resourceful than in the First Quartet. In general, the formal outline of each movement follows convention, but the quartet as a whole is played without a break. The most successful inter-movement transition is from the slow movement into the elusive scherzo; less convincing is the bridge from the first movement, in which a long wind-down concludes with a brusque chord leading straight into the slow movement.

From nearly every point of view Berwald's Third Quartet, in Eb major, transcends both his earlier efforts. Formally, the work is startlingly experimental: after an introduction, the main material of the Allegro di molto frames an Adagio which in turn has at its heart a brief scherzo movement. Each section is played without a break, and in direct anticipation of later nineteenth-century cyclic works, the Adagio, with its built-in scherzo, is sandwiched between the conclusion of the first movement's development and its recapitulation; rather more impressively, this arch-form arrangement of the five sections also looks forward to Bartók's Fourth String Quartet. For all its formal innovation, the musical language of the Eb major quartet is both more controlled and settled than that in its predecessor, offering the listener a clearer route through its novel structure. This synthesis of formal experiment with a more approachable musical language results in one of Berwald's most impressive instrumental compositions.

Given the dominant, at times decidedly oppressive role played by Tsarist Russia in Finland through most of the nineteenth and in the early twentieth centuries, it is hardly surprising that nationalism was the major force in the 'grand duchy's' music of the period. The prevalent means of musical-national expression was the choral song, with instrumental and eventually orchestral music employed largely as a means to evoke the beauties of Finland's lakes and forests. In this context the string quartet had little part to play, although Fredrik Pacius (1809–91), a pupil of Spohr and perhaps the greatest champion of Finnish music of the mid-nineteenth century, left a single German-influenced quartet (1826). The connection of an even greater champion of Finnish music, Sibelius (1865–1957), with quartet writing has interesting parallels with Nielsen's. Like Nielsen, he was a violinist from his youth and during the 1880s did much quartet playing which continued into his days in the Helsinki Music Institute, where in 1887 he became the second violinist of that establishment's main string quartet.

Sibelius' earliest attempts at quartet writing reflect the domestic setting in which he enjoyed playing quartets in his youth: an Eb quartet from 1885 leans heavily on his experience of Haydn.[28] Sibelius returned to the medium as a means of learning his craft, notably in a Fugue for string quartet composed in 1888 during his studies with Wegelius, which, as Tawaststjerna observes, anticipates the composer's only canonic quartet, *Voces Intimae* (1909).[29] An Adagio for string quartet and a Theme and Variations in C♯ minor date from the same period; when the latter was given in a concert at the Helsinki Conservatoire, it attracted the attention of Karl Flodin, the premier Finnish critic of the time. Flodin's approval of the work was capped by his enthusiasm for Sibelius' A minor Quartet, which he praised for its originality and technical mastery, adding the prophetic encomium: 'Mr Sibelius has with one stroke placed himself foremost amongst those who have been entrusted with bearing the banner of Finnish music.'[30] The following year, Sibelius began a quartet in Bb (1890, Op. 4). Wegelius admired the work in its early stages and some indication of its advance on the A minor Quartet can be gauged from the reaction of Albert Becker, Sibelius' teacher in Berlin, who was, apparently, so alarmed by it that 'he nearly had a heart attack'.[31] The Bb major Quartet's broader lyrical paragraphs and distinctive melodic accent, notably in the main melodies of the Andante and rondo finale, give clear indications of the mature composer.

There is an irony in the fact that Flodin's praise of Sibelius as one suitable to become the banner-bearer for Finnish music was prompted by a string quartet. Sibelius, as he embarked on the 1890s, the decade in which he established his mature style, turned his back on the string quartet entirely. In his maturity, Sibelius completed only a single quartet, though he may have worked on more.[32] The D minor Quartet (1909, Op. 56) takes its title, *Voces intimae*, from a comment Sibelius pencilled in over a passage in the central Adagio di molto:[33] this moment of ear-catching poetry occurs as the strings play three chords of E major, *ppp*, in breathtaking contradiction to the Eb major in which the music had settled in the previous bar. As a whole, the musical language of the quartet looks back to the Second and Third Symphonies, the Violin Concerto, and, particularly in the finale, the symphonic poems of the early 1900s rather than on to the Fourth Symphony. Cast in five movements, the work shows a succinct approach to thematic development; Sibelius also made a number of subtle links between the first and second movements, and the central Adagio and succeeding Allegretto. For all the quartet's affinities with the style of his great orchestral works of the late 1890s and early 1900s, Sibelius' writing for the four instruments is entirely idiomatic, if at times strenuous.

Central Europe

The considerable variety of musical provision in Central Europe in the nineteenth century resulted in a mixed fate for the string quartet. Musical organisations were, inevitably, affected by local political circumstances. Opera was, of course, the genre of choice, but where circumstances were favourable, the string quartet flourished. The rise of concert opportunities in Prague in the 1850s and 1860s, for example, had a marked effect on chamber-music performance which paid off handsomely in the 1870s, perhaps the crucial decade for the development of what we now see as the Czech string quartet tradition. Elsewhere, matters were more fragmented.

Despite Poland's divided status throughout the nineteenth century – it was partitioned between Prussia, Russia and Austria in 1795 – its nominal capital, Warsaw, saw the development of a lively musical life impelled by the presence of educational institutions, including the Warsaw Lyceum. Given that it was centred on the National Theatre, opened in 1779, and later the Wielki Theatre, it is not surprising that the major musical investment was on opera, with vocal and piano music bringing up the rear. Despite increased political control from Russia after the 'November Uprising' of 1831 and the loss of potential leaders such as Chopin, musical life managed to prosper. Although string instrument manufacturing enjoyed demand, a sure reflection of contemporary taste was a major growth in piano-making in the first half of the century. Concert life certainly flourished, but tended to favour, as elsewhere on the concert trails of Europe, the local or international soloist.

If the string quartet did not exactly prosper in this environment, it did not wither on the vine. As in most areas, Elsner (1769–1854) took something of a lead in importing a Polish flavour, via the use of national material, into the string quartet, notably in his three quartets, Op. 1, published in Vienna in 1798, with the subtitle 'meilleur goût polonois'. But given the more explicit national advocacy that opera afforded, it is perhaps unsurprising that his greatest successor after Chopin, Moniuszko (1819–72), only left two string quartets and those were confined to his apprentice years in Berlin (1837–9). While there is little evidence that any composer was prepared to cultivate the quartet at the expense of other genres, or to bring to the style a distinctive nature, a handful of works, mainly of a conservative cut, exists from the likes of Dobrzynski (1807–67; 3), Orlowski (1811–61; 2), Noskowski (1846–1909; 4), and the tragically short-lived Stolpe (1851–72; 2); Paderewski's

(1860–1941) only contributions to the string quartet are a set of variations and a fugue from 1882 which remain unpublished.

In another part of Austrian-dominated Europe, Hungary, matters were surprisingly similar. The *verbunkos* style, endemic in central Europe from the late eighteenth century, and a manner that attracted Romantic composers as various as Brahms and Liszt, thrived throughout the nineteenth century. Although Budapest boasted a successful chamber music series in the 'National Casino' in the 1830s and 1840s, and two excellent string quartet groups, a national style of quartet writing is not a prominent strand in Hungarian music in the nineteenth century. Neither of the two Hungarian musicians who dominated their country's musical life, Liszt and Ferenc Erkel, wrote string quartets. As in Poland, the major effort of composers was directed towards opera and the symphonic poem.

This is not to say that quartet writing was wholly unknown in Hungary; the seven string quartets of Mihály Mosonyi (1815–70) are effective, classically conceived works which show the influence of Beethoven, and the quartets of Odon Farkas (1851–1912) and Emil Ábrányi's (1882–1970) quartet of 1898 are touched by a clear national accent. The political constriction which affected all aspects of life in Hungary for much of the nineteenth century and the lack of opportunity for aspiring composers drove many away: Karl Goldmark (1830–1915), whose musical language was frequently coloured by native material and who played a role in Hungary in the uprisings of 1848, spent most of his career in Vienna, where the Hellmesberger Quartet's performance (1860) of his single string quartet in B♭ major, Op. 8, did much to help establish his reputation. Balancing the loss of the émigrés, there was an immigrant element in the fate of the string quartet in Hungary, notably from Robert Volkmann (1815–83), who settled in Budapest in 1841. A distinguished figure in the life of the Hungarian capital – he taught at the National Hungarian Academy of Music, founded in 1875 with Liszt as its principal ornament – in his six string quartets he maintained Classical credentials rather than exploring the native accent of his adoptive region. An indication of the polyglot nature of the Hungarian lands is the contribution of Ján Levoslav Bella (1843–1936). A Slovak who was educated in Vienna and whose affinities were Slavonic rather than Hungarian – an acquaintance of Smetana and Dvořák, he aimed to establish a specifically Slovak style – he nevertheless produced among his four string quartets music that reflects both a Hungarian accent and a more broadly central European culture. His 'Christmas Sonata' quartet in F major of 1866 appears to be lost, but was likely a recrudescence of the Pastorella style of Christmas music, built on Christmas carols and much beloved throughout central Europe. His Second Quartet in E minor of 1871, however, is frankly titled 'Hungarian' and duly makes allusion to the native manner.

If there was little about the Romantic Hungarian string quartet that even began to approach the contribution made by Bartók in the twentieth century, there were intimations of an improving situation towards the end of the nineteenth century. Ernő Dohnányi's (1877–1960) three string quartets (A major, 1899; Db major, 1906 and A minor, 1926) are powerful testimony to a major musical personality. Understandably, the First String Quartet, composed when Dohnányi was in his early twenties, inclines toward Brahms in the first movement. The second, a work of far greater substance, is one of the finest quartets of the early twentieth century. The handling of texture is entirely assured and there is a Straussian virtuosity in the blending of tempi in the first movement. The passionate tone of the musical language is set by the striking opening melody which, throughout the quartet, acquires an almost autobiographical role: it supplies fibre for the initial Allegro, but also underpins many an adventurous harmonic move and rises like a question mark over the movement's conclusion, the answer to which is delivered only at the end of the work. The Scherzo middle movement, as Tovey pointed out,[34] has evident affinities with the opening of *Die Walküre*; its pounding forward motion is, however, halted for a moment of stillness out of which emerges an exquisite chant-like melody. The extended concluding Molto adagio reveals the breadth of Dohnányi's vision: themes from both earlier movements make up a large part of the material; after an impassioned climax it becomes clear that the opening theme of the quartet is destined to dominate. Dohnányi's Third Quartet, composed some twenty years later, is more brittle and ironic than the second; the harmonic language is also more challenging, with occasional moments of bitonality, although it rarely approaches the astringency of Bartók's nearly contemporary Third String Quartet. If Dohnányi's quartets set no agendas in Hungarian national music, they represent the peak of excellence before Bartók.

If the string quartet flourished only sporadically in certain of the national traditions, it had more promising currency among the Czechs. In the last seven of Dvořák's fourteen quartets, the genre acquired its most distinctive and sustained profile in the nineteenth century after Beethoven and Schubert, and in Smetana's autobiographical First Quartet, a tradition was established for programme and experiment, the culmination of which, arguably, is to be found in the two quartets of Janáček.

Quartet writing was as avidly cultivated by the Czechs as by any musical population in the eighteenth century. In the nineteenth century the pattern begins to change: the three quartets of Tomášek, a dominant figure in the musical life of Prague in the first half of the nineteenth century, belong to the eighteenth. For all its role as one of the stop-off points on the trail of the itinerant virtuoso, where music was concerned, Prague did not begin to approach the specific gravity of Vienna until the middle of the century. While the Estates Theatre, the Cecilia Society and the Sophie Academy (the two last founded in 1840) ensured a continuity of musical life, new musical energies did not materialise until the national revival of the 1860s. The opening of the Prague Provisional Theatre (the precursor of the National Theatre) did much to impel the development of a national style, as did the Artists' Society, founded in 1863, which opened a music publishing house in 1871. Institutions favouring chamber repertoire were slightly longer in coming: in 1876 the German-speaking community of Prague set up a Kammermusikverein which was eventually joined by the hugely productive Czech Society for Chamber Music in 1894, set up three years after the establishment of the Czech Quartet.

That the quartet developed strongly in Prague after the Mozartian twilight that descended on the city in the first two decades of the nineteenth century was in no small part due to Václav Veit (1806–64). All his four quartets (D minor, 1836; E major, 1837; E♭ major, 1839; G minor, 1840) were published in Leipzig and were well known at home and abroad. Veit introduced into Czech chamber music the early German Romanticism of Leipzig, also apparent in the three quartets of the opera composer František Škroup (1801–62) and the single quartets of František Skuherský (1830–92) and Karel Bendl (1838–97); the influence of Mendelssohn and Schumann also resonates strongly in the earliest chamber works of both Dvořák (1841–1904) and Zdeněk Fibich (1850–1900).

Dvořák's first quartet (A major Op. 2, B 8, 1862) is both confident and original, although the imprint of Mendelssohn, as Dvořák was happy to admit,[35] is clear. Many features of Dvořák's mature style are present, including a sense of forward motion and a penchant, in the first movement in both melody and figuration, for pentatonics. The main problem is an overly high tessitura for the first violin. Dvořák did not return to the string quartet until the end of the 1860s, by which time his style had undergone a considerable, almost ideological, change. Three quartets (D major, B 18; B♭ major Op. 4, B 17; E minor, B 19) composed towards the end of the 1860s show a marked tendency to experiment; Wagner and Liszt are both exemplars, but the sheer audacity of the E minor Quartet goes well beyond the musical language of neo-Romanticism. Both the first movements of the D major and B♭ quartets are gigantic. That of the B♭ lacks points of structural coherence, a situation improved in the D major by greater adherence to Classical models. The remainder of the B♭ Quartet is more expert, with a slow movement whose exploration of textures anticipates later works, such as the E♭ Quintet Op. 97 (B 180) and the G major Quartet Op. 106 (B 192). One unusual feature of the D major quartet is that the main theme of the scherzo is a popular song of Polish origin, 'Hej, Slované!', possibly a salute to the oppressed Poles who had been in revolt as recently as 1863 and virtually the only such use of frank quotation in Dvořák's output.[36]

The improvisatory handling of material and the use of continuous variation in these two quartets reaches an apotheosis in the E minor. Cast in a single movement lasting nearly forty minutes (quite possibly Romanticism's longest abstract structure up to that point), it is replete with harmonic and tonal experiment. Dvořák did not supply a key designation and E minor is barely accurate in conventional terms, since it is abandoned soon after the opening and the entire work comes to an end in B major. Two outer sections, in which the motivic development is enormously assured, frame an Andante religioso[37] whose symmetrical melody offers a certain repose after the storm and stress of the opening, although being based on a pedal F$\sharp$ lasting the entirety of the section's ten minutes leads to some surprising harmonic tensions.

The 1870s was the decisive decade for fixing Czech style in the string quartet. Dvořák moved away from acute experiment in his two quartets in F minor (Op. 9, B 37) and A minor (Op. 12, B 40), both composed in the autumn of 1873. The first movement of the F minor Quartet shows another tendency that would become common in Dvořák's chamber music: the following of an understated opening idea with a brisk call before moving onto the main business of the exposition.[38] However, at 630 bars, the movement suffers from the rampant gigantism of his earlier quartets. The Tempo di valse third movement and the finale are both more orthodox in form and successful in their roles, even if the latter tends towards orchestral effects. The gem of the quartet is the slow movement: the main melody, one of the most vocal Dvořák had employed in an instrumental work hitherto, artfully straddles F minor and A♭ major; it being too good to waste, Dvořák made a well-known arrangement of the movement for violin and orchestra, entitled Romanze Op. 11 (B 39).

Dvořák's first version of his A minor Quartet seems to return to the formal experiment of the E minor; arranged in five movements with interlinking motivic features, two slow sections, placed second and fourth, frame a scherzo. A thorough revision transformed the quartet into a more conventional four-movement work; while some transitions are awkward, the general shaping is convincing and it is a pity that Dvořák left the finale incomplete.[39] Composed a year later in September 1874, Dvořák's next quartet (again in A minor) Op. 16 (B 45), marks, as far as his chamber music is concerned, his arrival at orthodoxy. Adopting a Classical frame which looks back beyond the early German Romantics to Haydn and early Beethoven, the first movement has a success deriving from formal clarity articulated by clearly apprehended melody. If the pastiche world of the slightly stilted slow movement disappoints, the scherzo, originally a Menuetto, is effective and looks forward to Dvořák's maturity. Unfortunately, his new-found confidence deserts him in the finale, where the orchestral style and (potentially innovative) decision to begin in a foreign key are distractions.

While Smetana and Dvořák provided the signal works of the repertoire in the 1870s, a decisive move towards the Czech manner came from an unlikely quarter. The Leipzig-educated Zdeněk Fibich wrote three works for string quartet (A major, 1874; G major, Op. 8, 1878; Variations in B♭ major, 1883). The A major is also the first avowedly national Czech string quartet: the main theme of the slow movement includes the folksong 'Ah, not here, not here' ('Ach není tu, není') and the third movement is a polka,[40] anticipating Smetana's use of the dance form in his First Quartet by two years. Elsewhere Mendelssohn is an influence, though there are many strikingly individual moments, not least the approach to the recapitulation in the first movement and the lively contrapuntal opening of the finale. Folk elements also occur in Fibich's Second Quartet, composed four years later: the trio of the scherzo is an upbeat polka and the finale, with its drone effects and abundant hints of national dance, is dominated by folk tone. Despite expertise in the quartet writing, as a whole the G major Quartet lacks the purposeful expressive depth of the first. The Theme and Variations from 1883 have a slight air of pastiche, although, as ever, they are expertly written.

For Smetana, who spent most of his creative energies on such public works as opera and programmatic symphonic poems, chamber music was used for more personal statements. When his first daughter, Bedřiška, died in 1855, he commemorated the event in his Piano Trio in G minor. When personal disaster, in the shape of deafness, struck in 1874, Smetana eventually turned to the string quartet to express his reaction to this life-changing tragedy. Though quite capable of writing in abstract forms, Smetana was, through and through, a composer of programme music. Thus, as he admitted in a letter to his friend Josef Srb-Debrnov, the quartet is entirely programmatic: 'I did not want to write a quartet according to a recipe and to the standard usage of form . . . For me the form of every composition depends on its subject.'[41] This statement was followed by a description of the first movement as 'My yearning towards art in my youth, my romantic frame of mind, the inexpressible longing for something I could neither put into words nor truly define . . .'[42] Smetana then went on to define the dramatic falling fifth heard first on the viola as a premonition of fate and the long held E, introduced near the end of the finale, as 'the fateful whistling of the highest tones in my ear which in 1874 announced to me my deafness'.[43]

For all Smetana's programmatic intentions, there is a formal neatness evident in each movement of the quartet that sets off admirably the near-operatic drama of its opening and tragic conclusion. The Polka second movement, evocative of his youth as a 'passionate dancer', is rollickingly infectious with its trumpet imitations in viola and second violin. In the slow movement, with its poignant cello solo opening and deeply felt climax articulated by a double and triple stopped chordal outburst, Smetana commemorated his love for his first wife. The finale is the most operatically conceived of the four movements. At first it seems a triumphant conclusion: the composer revelling in his discovery of national musical elements, with Kecal, the marriage broker of *The Bartered Bride*, brought to mind in the bustling material heard just after the opening. When all appears set fair for a joyous close, the strings plunge into a tense tremolando, over which the first violin plays that fierce high E; a quotation of the fate motif which began the work ushers in a subdued coda. The first public performers of the quartet[44] claimed that the trio of the Polka, with its double-stopped chords, was unplayable; but the work became a classic of the Czech tradition. The use of national elements and an autobiographical programme are not in themselves features that guarantee immortality; it is Smetana's original handling of the medium and the quartet's dramatic force that secured its audience and, in a very real sense, paved the way for Janáček's similarly programmatic quartets.

Smetana's Second String Quartet, composed in the winter of 1882–3, a year before his death, is more challenging. Written while Smetana was in the last stages of syphilis, the quartet gave the composer considerable difficulties: organising material was problematic with even simple cadence patterns proving evasive. Although the work lacks the programmatic detail of the First Quartet, its bold juxtaposing of ideas was undoubtedly expressive of Smetana's state of mind. Smetana was aware that the first movement might cause problems for the listener. The sporadic nature illness imposed on Smetana's work patterns is reflected in the wealth of tempo markings to be found in the first and last movements, but Smetana's operatic sense of timing means that volatility rarely undermines coherence. The second movement, a haunting polka with frequent cross-accents, is the most accessible. The third movement, returning to the stark conflict of ideas found in the opening movement, is perhaps the most problematic for both players and listeners: contrapuntal ideas jostle with material which is almost vocal in rhetoric, looking forward to the expressive passion of Janáček.

In the second half of the 1870s, Dvořák moved steadily towards what might be viewed as his archetypical contribution to the Czech national quartet, the E♭ Quartet Op. 50 (B 92). In 1876, the same year in which Smetana wrote his First Quartet, Dvořák composed his eighth, the E major Op. 80 (B 57). Dvořák's handling of texture is now entirely consistent and reaches heights of poetry in the slow movement. His handling of formal outline, well exercised in the Fifth Symphony of the previous year, is expert. Into this frame, elements associated with Dvořák's Czech style settle comfortably: a tendency to melancholy in the first movement, a *dumka*-like accent in the main theme of the slow movement and *furiant* cross rhythms energising the third movement. Dvořák dedicated to Brahms his next quartet, in D minor, Op. 34 (B 75), composed in the following year. Written in only twelve days, the quartet is remarkable for its fluency and the unforced confidence with which Dvořák, for example, links the accompaniment of the first movement's opening idea with the second subject, a feature doubtless appreciated by the work's dedicatee. The national imperative is served in the 'Alla polka' second movement; though attractive, it lacks the character of Smetana's string quartet polkas and, in common with the finale, there is a tendency to favour compositional process above natural and unforced lyrical development.

No such criticism shadows Dvořák's last quartet of the 1870s, the E♭ major Op. 51 (B 92), completed at the end of March 1879. In this work, Dvořák draws on the populist qualities of the first set of Slavonic Dances, composed the previous year; he also displays quartet writing far superior to anything he had done to date. National dance rhythms underpin several parts of the quartet: Polka in the transitions of the first movement and Furiant in the lively sections of the Andante con moto. This same movement is explicitly entitled 'Dumka', a form, perhaps adapted from Russian and Ukrainian literary models,[45] alternating slow and fast sections, which has come to be read as synonymous with Dvořák's national manner. Dvořák also projects a pastoral air, particularly in the first movement, where its pulsing opening pedal confirms its Slavonic credentials. Perhaps the most impressive aspect of the quartet is the way motif and texture, best illustrated by the magical opening of the work, are often united. Dvořák rounded off 1879 by arranging for string quartet the two most engaging waltzes (B 105) from his Op. 54 piano waltzes (B 101).

Witness to Dvořák's growing reputation as a composer is that both the E♭ quartet and his next, in C major, Op. 61 (B 121), were commissioned by professional quartets, respectively the Florentine and the Hellmesberger. Dvořák's first attempt at a quartet for Hellmesberger was abandoned with only a single, unquestionably proper, but rather disappointing, movement in F major (B 120). The C major Quartet, completed on 10 November 1881, is far more satisfactory. Its first movement is both powerful in development and subtle in accompanimental detail. As in Op. 51, melody and texture intermingle fruitfully in the slow movement. The scherzo is one of Dvořák's most thoughtful and richly textured in his chamber music up to that time. In the finale, Dvořák adopts the national tone, though, with an eye to the scrutiny of his Viennese audience, he balances it with rigorous contrapuntal development.

Although Dvořák continued to compose chamber music throughout
the 1880s, he did not return to the string quartet (apart from arrangements
for quartet in 1887 of twelve of the songs from his early cycle *Cypresses*)[46]
until 1893, during the first summer of his sojourn in America. In many
ways the 'American' Quartet Op. 96 (B 179) epitomises what has come to
be seen as Dvořák's 'American' style: open-hearted, symmetrically phrased
melody, a penchant for pentatonic writing and dynamic ostinati. In fact,
all of these qualities were evident in earlier works,[47] but they are most
apparent in the works Dvořák composed in his first two years in America.
The sketch for the 'American' was made in a few hours spread across three
mornings in June 1893, and is one of his most fluent. Another aspect of the
work reflecting Dvořák's preoccupations in America is the clarity, not to
say simplicity, of form, a characteristic prompted by the need not only
to address a less critical audience, but also to produce a model for his
composition pupils in New York. As a whole the quartet is a work of vivid
moods and delicate instrumental effects, not least the opening of the first
movement (possibly prompted by the start of Smetana's First Quartet). The
slow movement is one of Dvořák's most lyrically intense statements. The
two remaining movements may well reflect a programmatic response to
Dvořák's surroundings in the rural Czech community of Spillville, where
he wrote the quartet: birdsong in the scherzo and a reference to the village's
church organ in the finale.

Dvořák's last string quartets, in A♭ major, Op. 105 (B 192), and G major,
Op. 106 (B 193), are farewells to abstract music – he devoted the rest of his
life to symphonic poems and opera. Although it bears the lower opus number, the A♭ major Quartet was completed after the G major. Both quartets
show Dvořák returning to the structural subtlety of his pre-American works.
The G major Quartet is the more substantial. Despite the almost throwaway
character of its pentatonically inflected first theme, the first movement is
very closely argued; indeed, the contrast between joyous exultation and high
seriousness are marked features of the first movement, scherzo and finale.
The Adagio ma non troppo, one of Dvořák's greatest slow movements in
any genre, is built on a strongly elegiac melody; the air of nostalgia evoked in
parts of this slow movement returns in the finale, where twice its impressive
sweep is interrupted by the leisurely second theme of the first movement.

The A♭ major Quartet is slighter than the G major. Although it does not
attempt the depths of the earlier work, it is one of his most perfect compositions. The cross-rhythms of the scherzo could be read as a reference to
national tone, but the style adopted has an abstract quality that transcends
the local. Of biographical interest is the work's emotional volatility; moments of apparent neurosis, perhaps reflective of Dvořák's own psyche in
his later years, emerge in the tense slow introduction to the first movement,

the searching, dissonant harmonies heard at the end of the slow movement and the nervy start to the finale.

Towards the end of the nineteenth century the younger generation fielded a number of quartet composers. Josef Bohuslav Foerster (1859–1951) composed five string quartets in his long career (E major, Op. 15, 1888; D major, Op. 39, 1893; C major, Op. 61, 1907/1913; F major, Op. 182, 1944; F major entitled *Vestec*, 1951, the place where the composer died; there also exists a 'Prayer' for string quartet from 1940). While they are all effectively written, more distinctive contributions came from two of Dvořák's pupils, Vítězslav Novák (1870–1949) and Josef Suk (1874–1935). A tribute to Dvořák's teaching is that he did not impose his own personality on the work of pupils; both Novák and Suk rapidly developed distinctive musical personalities of their own.

While Suk's first quartet, a student work in D minor (1888), shows only sporadically the composer to come, his second, in B♭ major (1896; revised 1915), offers ample evidence of the future artist. Dvořák is a presence in the opening Allegro moderato, but a tendency to veer towards minor keys and hints of Impressionist colouring look forward to the composer's maturity. The remaining movements also leave little doubt as to Suk's individuality: a robust Intermezzo, a passionate and volatile Adagio, rich in expressive dissonance, and an exuberant finale. Given that he was a talented violinist (he was second violinist of the Czech Quartet), it is hardly surprising that his handling of texture is assured. The same virtues are apparent in his one-movement quartet, Op. 31 (1911), and the 'Meditation on the old Czech choral, St Wenceslas', the latter a fine example of Suk's expressive, inward-looking manner.

Novák wrote three quartets. The first, in G major, Op. 22 (1899), reflects the composer's penchant for folksong from the Valašsko and Slovácko regions. His Third Quartet Op. 66 (1938), from close to the end of his career, was arranged for string orchestra. But his most interesting contribution to the genre is the Second Quartet in D major Op. 35 (1905). This remarkable two-movement work illustrates Novák's fascination with cyclic procedures. The title of the second movement, Fantasia, gave the composer licence to amalgamate three thematically linked movements: an Allegro, a scherzo and a brief Largo. The serene opening of the first movement, entitled Fuga, furnishes the material for the entire quartet. Here Novák treats his theme in the fugal manner suggested by the subtitle for some twenty bars before abandoning strict counterpoint for more leisurely exchanges between the players; the use of the strings is particularly inventive in the latter part of the movement, where the textures are both rich and novel.

14 The string quartet in the twentieth century

KENNETH GLOAG

Although the string quartet did not regain the privileged position it enjoyed during the Classical period, many twentieth-century composers from many different cultural backgrounds and stylistic positions looked to the genre as a context suitable for their most intimate thoughts. Throughout the century the string quartet was often viewed not only as a medium conducive to experimentation and formal innovation, but also for its positive re-engagement with tradition; this double focus was symptomatic of the multifarious nature of modernism, an 'ism' which encapsulated the defining aesthetic trends of the early decades of the century. This sense of experimentation and innovation often led to an expansion of playing techniques, an increase in the expressive parameters of the music and departures from the standard four-movement pattern of the Classical quartet. However, despite its use as a vehicle for change, the string quartet continued to provide a generic framework which reflected the inherited traditions and conventions as accumulated through the history and stylistic developments of the genre, even if in some cases it was only to construct a point for new departure. This relationship between tradition and innovation, a relationship which was at times oppositional, at others interactive, will come to be seen as a defining reference point for a generalised understanding of the string quartet repertory of the twentieth century. It will become pertinent through regional/national surveys of some of the main composers and works in the medium. Such surveys are not necessarily intended always to suggest national style groupings; rather they are used merely as a convenient and accessible format through which the principal works can be presented.[1]

Austria/Germany

The struggle to come to terms with the accumulated weight of the inherited traditions and conventions of the string quartet genre is rendered most explicit in the Austro-Germanic context, which can be seen as partly formed through this encounter with the past. The figure of Arnold Schoenberg (1874–1951) assumes a central position within this particular historical narrative, both as a composer of string quartets and as a focal personality in the often turbulent and challenging nature of the modernist culture of the period.

Schoenberg's engagement with the string quartet provides a logical continuity with the inherited legacy of the Austro-Germanic tradition as mediated through Brahms. Although often regarded as a conservative counter-balance to the progressive identity of Wagner, Brahms was claimed by Schoenberg, in a seminal essay titled 'Brahms the Progressive', as a prototype for his own stylistic innovations.[2] It is also significant that in this essay Schoenberg takes the string quartet writing of Brahms as one of his models. The harmonic context of a significant extract from the first movement of Brahms' C minor quartet Op. 51 No. 1 (bb 11–23) 'competes successfully with that of many a Wagnerian passage'.[3] Schoenberg's first practical translation of this Brahmsian legacy is the String Quartet in D major. Composed in 1897, but not published until 1966 and not seen as forming part of Schoenberg's acknowledged output, this is clearly an apprentice work. However, it also demonstrates a high degree of confidence and technical fluidity. Like the string quartets of Brahms, it exhibits the classic four-movement pattern of the traditional quartet. The conventional nature of this formal outline provides a parallel to the key scheme of the work: D major, F♯ minor, B♭ minor and D minor. This key scheme, while emphasising the traditional aspects of tonality, also includes the possibilities of expansion of tonality, an approach which Schoenberg will increasingly exploit. According to Arnold Whittall, the third-based key relationships suggest 'a manner reminiscent of the later Beethoven (for example, the "Hammerklavier" Sonata)',[4] a suggestion which emphasises Schoenberg's initial debt to his predecessors.

During this early formative stage of his career Schoenberg benefited from the general artistic climate of Vienna and the support of several other young composers. The most notable was his close friend Alexander von Zemlinsky (1871–1942), a composer who also explored the possibilities of the string quartet, often in ways which could be seen to provide a certain parallel to Schoenberg's stylistic development. Schoenberg's first acknowledged string quartet is his Op. 7 in D minor. In contrast to the conventional four-movement pattern of the earlier unpublished quartet, this work continues Schoenberg's emergent experimentation with form and the linking of ideas and movements to provide a single movement of concentrated thematic material and development. And yet, like its Romantic predecessors (Liszt's B minor sonata), it conveys an evident sense of division and change, with the presentation of thematic material corresponding to a formal design of initial allegro movement, scherzo, slow movement and a rondo finale. Although in no sense monothematic, the work shows a strong sense of thematic development throughout, a process which Schoenberg came to understand as 'developing variation', and one which, in the immediate context of this quartet, he saw as being derived from his understanding of Beethoven's *Eroica* symphony. However, although the work is defined through this thematic dimension in association with the compressed formal model, the harmonic language of this quartet is still largely that of the late nineteenth century.

Schoenberg's Quartet No. 2, Op. 10 (1907–8), reverts to the standard four-movement model, yet it is clearly a radical advance on his previous quartet in that it provides a marked departure from the tonal stability of his earlier works to something which at crucial moments evidences greater fluidity and less certainty in terms of its tonal identity. The first movement utilises a sonata-form design based upon the F♯ minor tonality. However, although this tonality is clearly in operation, there is little sense of functional harmonic progression. The most notable aspect of this work is its introduction of the human voice (soprano) in the third and fourth movements, perhaps reflecting Schoenberg's awareness of Mahler's use of the voice within the symphonic context. The third movement, which contains a setting of Stefan George's intensely expressive poem 'Litanei' (prayer), takes the form of variations, producing a texture that is saturated by thematic material derived from the first two movements. The natural restraint of the variation process also provides a controlled contrast to the intensity of the text and its vocal realisation. The final movement, which like the first corresponds to sonata form, again sets the poetry of Stefan George. This movement is often referred to as forming part of Schoenberg's departure from tonality to atonality. While this is certainly a seminal moment for Schoenberg and there is a real sense of difference to the music, it would be wrong automatically to define it through any simplistic struggle or separation between tonality and atonality. Rather it is better to hear the music as a gradual drift into a condition of difference or 'otherness' ('I feel the air of another planet') through a heightened sense of ambiguity, an ambiguity which is constructed through an ever-increasing expansion of the possibilities of tonality towards an indefinable point where tonality no longer seems to be meaningful.

Anton Webern (1883–1945) and Alban Berg (1885–1935), Schoenberg's two best-known students, continued to explore the possibilities of the string quartet but essentially achieved quite different results. Webern's writing for the medium marks a shift of emphasis from the quartet as a genre to the quartet as a texture/instrumental ensemble. In other words, he does not explore the formal conventions and expectations of the genre but does remain interested in the actual sound produced by the ensemble. Webern's first exploration of this texture is the early string quartet of 1905 (without opus number and not performed until 1962), a work which he seems to have consciously modelled on Schoenberg's *Verklärte Nacht* (1899), but which also

demonstrates an awareness of his mentor's Op. 7 quartet. The resemblance
to these works is based upon Webern's attempt to blend contrasted sections and textures into a single-movement form. The drive towards unity
and coherence in this early work seems in sharp contrast to Webern's *Five
Movements for String Quartet* Op. 5 (1909), which inhabits the familiar
Webernesque sound-world of short gestures and fragmentary textures. But,
as always with Webern, there is an underlying coherence. This apparent
paradox between fragmentation and coherence is explored at a higher level
in the *Six Bagatelles for String Quartet* Op. 9 (1911–13). Alban Berg's First
String Quartet Op. 3 (1909–10) is a two-movement work which seems more
indebted to the sound world of late Romanticism than the contemporary
works of Webern. The last work of Berg to be completed under Schoenberg's
tutelage, it marks his emergence as a distinctive and original composer,
demonstrating his fascination with and mastery of complex motivic and
thematic detail while maintaining an intense and directly expressionistic
mode of communication.

Schoenberg's development of serialism in the early 1920s also coincided
with a rediscovery of Classical forms, the radical ordering of the pitch material being seen to require a traditional order and context within the formal
dimension. This is reflected in both Schoenberg's Third (Op. 30, 1927)
and his Fourth (Op. 37, 1936) string quartets, both of which revert to the
Classical four-movement pattern most typical of the genre. In contrast to
this return to the archetypal features of the quartet, both Berg and Webern in
their quartet writing after their adoption of serialism continued to explore
diffuse textures and differentiated contexts. For example, Berg's second and
final work in the medium, his *Lyric Suite* (1926), consists of six movements
which juxtapose fast and slow tempi. It also features a juxtaposition of serial
and non-serial pitch materials. However, this juxtaposition assumes the appearance of an integrated musical language, one which continues to reflect
the expressive and dramatic nature of Berg's music in general. Webern's
String Quartet Op. 28 (1936–8) is also representative of his own manifestation of serialism; its use of palindromes and canonic and variation textures
is typical of Webern's music of this period. The first of its three movements
makes this clear through the use of a theme and six variations which also
have a larger sense of form. However, although this is clearly a rigorous
and at times formidable musical language, it is also an engaging one, which
generates its own unique sense of musical drama and tension.

The development of Schoenbergian serialism coincided with the rise of
neo-classicism, which, in the German context, was most readily identifiable
with the music of Paul Hindemith (1895–1963). Although serialism and
neo-classicism were commonly perceived as opposites, there is a certain
sense of convergence between the two in that both reflected, although in

very different ways, a 'return to order' after the seemingly anarchic period prior to the First World War. Hindemith's string quartet writing generally follows his main compositional concerns and reflects the prevailing orthodoxies of his neo-classicism: traditional formal models, contrapuntal textures, and repeated rhythmic patterns. It is also notable that Hindemith's quartet writing generally makes fewer demands on playing techniques than the contemporary works of Schoenberg, Berg and Webern, and its accommodation within standard technical limitations as well as formal conventions is a further reflection of the reconstructed notion of tradition evident within this particular stylistic category. The claimed accessibility of aspects of Hindemith's neo-classicism emphasises the functional aspects of this music (*Gebrauchsmusik*) and in some instances took the form of a concern for amateur music making, a concern which was in keeping with the original, private conception of chamber music to which the string quartet once belonged.

After the conclusion of the Second World War, an emerging generation of composers mainly associated with the Darmstadt summer school avoided traditional genres as part of their compositional aesthetic, although their fascination with the music of Webern provided a certain point of continuity with the more immediate past. However, during the post-war period several significant composers continued to explore the possibilities of the historicised genres of music, including the string quartet. One of the most notable is Hans Werner Henze (b. 1926). Following an early essay in neo-classicism (1947), Henze's Second Quartet (1952) absorbs the prevailing influences of the period. He remarked: 'Four or five years [after the first quartet] I made a new attempt in this difficult genre. Meanwhile the encounter (in Darmstadt) with René Leibowitz had taken place, and the music of the Second Viennese School had begun to exercise its overpowering influence on us, the younger generation. There was practically no-one who didn't consider it a matter of great urgency to get to grips with its potential inheritance. My Second String Quartet should be seen as an eloquent witness to this tendency.'[5] While this influence is less marked in the later works, it is clearly an active presence in this, Henze's first mature quartet. However, although this work can be considered a success, Henze did not return to the genre until the mid 1970s, at which point he produced a remarkable trilogy of quartets (1975–6). The final work of this trilogy, the Fifth String Quartet, is dedicated to the memory of Benjamin Britten, and the six movements of this work reflect the symbiotic relationship between drama and lyricism which is definitive of Henze's music of this period. The composer claims that this work seems to 'remember the historical concept of the string quartet as a place of inward intensification, of maximum concentration, of contemplation'.[6] This is a good description of this specific work, but it is equally an effective reminder of the unique and often personal nature of the string quartet as a historical genre.

Henze's positive re-engagement with the tradition of the quartet has been continued by Wolfgang Rihm (b. 1952). Rihm was part of a generation of German composers who rejected the perceived austerity of the Darmstadt avant garde, and his mature music reflects a concern with communication and comprehension. However, as with Henze, this does not result in a necessarily simplified or compromised musical language. In his Fourth String Quartet (1981), Rihm produces a work which is overflowing with expressive gestures, a quality which brings to mind the music of Berg, within a texture which is often fragmentary and resistant to formal categorisation, thus highlighting the individuality and intensity of the music. Through this expressive framework Rihm produces a glance backwards towards the expressionism of the early works of Schoenberg but in a fundamentally contemporary way. He thus situates himself within the compositional mainstream of twentieth-century German music, a mainstream which has returned in many different ways and contexts to the string quartet as both a genre and a texture.

Italy

Clearly the traditional genres of music, with the obvious exception of opera, were not as embedded in the history of Italian music as in that of Austro-Germany. However, certain Italian composers of the twentieth century have produced string quartets of note. For example, Alfredo Casella (1883–1947) marked the onset of his neo-classicism in the early 1920s with two string quartets (1920 and 1923–4), and Gian Francesco Malipiero (1882–1973) produced eight published quartets, the first in 1920 and the last in 1964.

The generation of composers which emerged after the Second World War was in the main more interested in an avant-garde experimentalism (often involving the voice) rather than exploring the continuing potential of a now historicised genre such as the string quartet. For example, the leading Italian composer of this period, Luciano Berio (1925–2003), has made only occasional forays into string quartet writing (Study for string quartet, 1952; String Quartet, 1955–6; *Sincronie* for String Quartet, 1963–4; *Notturno*, 1993). However, there are some notable contributions, perhaps the most dramatic being that of Luigi Nono (1924–91). His *Fragmente – Stille, an Diotima* (Fragments – Silence to Diotima) (1979–80) has an extra-musical dimension, based around the poetry of Hölderlin (a love poem to Diotima).[7] The work consists of a number of fragments, often bordering on silence. Its careful dynamic gradations put great demands on both the player and listener, yet this suppression of sound becomes in itself a musical gesture, one which is hauntingly dramatic, the sense of dramatic tension providing a reflection of both Nono's own musical language and the wider landscape of contemporary Italian music.

Great Britain

The resurgence of musical life often referred to as the 'English Musical Renaissance' featured a new found interest in generic composition, with the progenitors of this 'renaissance', Hubert Parry (1848–1918) and Charles Villiers Stanford (1852–1924), demonstrating a certain interest in the string quartet. This interest reflected the influence of the sublimated Romanticism of Brahms, an influence which also became evident in the string quartet writing of Edward Elgar (1857–1934).

Although many English composers of the early decades of the century produced string quartets – Smyth, Moeran, Bax, Delius, Vaughan Williams – it was Frank Bridge (1879–1941) who produced the most sustained contribution to the genre in the first half of the century. Bridge was himself a professional violinist and he had an intimate familiarity with the general context of chamber music, which is reflected in his own wide-ranging output for chamber ensemble. The first of Bridge's four numbered quartets was premiered in 1906 and, following its initial success in a competition in Bologna, takes the name of that city as its informal title.[8] The work is in four movements and is in the key of E minor. Its musical language is largely that of Romanticism as contained within essentially Classical formal models. This is evident in the first movement, which echoes the string quartet writing of Brahms through the deployment of a traditional sonata form design in conjunction with lyrical thematic material. This echo is most evident in the extended second subject, which, though expansive and lyrical, perhaps lacks formal direction. His Second String Quartet (1915) defines itself as the first major chamber music of his compositional maturity and has been described as marking 'a new level of technical accomplishment in British quartet writing . . . not to be surpassed till Bridge returned to the medium 11 years later'.[9] In this work, Bridge's musical language becomes more chromatic and, consequently, experiences an increase in its intensity, yet the effect is still largely traditional. For all their formal and thematic intricacy, each of the work's three movements is accommodated within an accessible and recognisable framework. However, Bridge's Third (1926) and Fourth (1937) Quartets move towards a more radical sound-world, one in which this unique composer found his true voice, articulating his English musical background in conjunction with his modernist aspirations.

Bridge also assumes a position of importance as the teacher of Benjamin Britten (1913–76). Although Britten achieved most in the context of opera and vocal works, his Second and Third String Quartets represent major achievements in their own right, as well as providing valuable signposts to his wider compositional concerns. Britten's first work in the genre, the early quartet in D major, was composed rapidly in 1931. It is still clearly a student work, but it is one which indicates the veracity of his precocious development. Nevertheless, the attempted connection and unification of ideas and materials do not seem to sit easily in relation to Britten's general musical instincts. Britten did not return to the string quartet until 1941 (String Quartet No. 1). The Second Quartet (1945) was to be his last instrumental sonata-related work for some time. It represents an ambitious and imaginative response to the demands of quartet writing. Its outline consists of two outer slow movements with a shorter, fast movement as its centre. This central movement seems much like an interruption to the large-scale, slow-moving textures of the outer movements. The first movement, defined by its initial thematic material and its C major tonality, suffers from structural and formal flaws. According to Arnold Whittall, the extended exposition in conjunction with a highly compressed recapitulation 'produces a movement of peculiar proportions and uncertain direction', and he goes on to conclude that 'The first movement of the second quartet attempts three things at once; to be more economical in material, more expansive in design, and more explicitly unified in spirit.'[10]

In contrast to the formal complexity of the first movement, the second is relatively straightforward, comprising a concise ternary structure, which encapsulates the increased sense of movement and mobility. The third movement carries the title of Chacony, which conveys Britten's ongoing fascination with the music of Purcell (the work was first performed on the 250th anniversary of Purcell's death). It begins with a Purcellian ground bass theme which is repeated as a sequence of variations. These variations are presented in groups which are linked by solo cadenzas. The different formal identities of each of the three movements could seem to suggest that this is a diffuse, eclectic work. However, while it is clearly an individual work which is specific to this stage of Britten's career, it is also a quartet of great power and effect.

In contrast to Britten's general avoidance of historical genres (such as the symphony and string quartet), his contemporary Michael Tippett (1905–98) saw the presence of these genres as something which demanded a positive and sympathetic response. Tippett's First String Quartet can be described as 'the fruit of a very long apprenticeship'[11] and was certainly not Tippett's first attempt in the genre. However, it is a work which marks Tippett's early maturity as a composer. Originally composed in 1935, the first version consisted of four movements, but in 1943 the composer significantly revised the work and replaced the first two movements with a new single movement. The third and final movement is nevertheless the most remarkable. It is a rapidly moving fugue which reflects both Tippett's general feel for contrapuntal textures and, more specifically, his understanding of Beethoven's late style.

Tippett's Second Quartet was composed between 1941 and 1942 and therefore predates the 1943 revision of the first quartet. It may be that it was the process of working on the Second Quartet that led to his dissatisfaction with the first. This quartet seems traditional, comprising four movements and with a stated key signature (F♯ minor). As in the First Quartet, use is made of a fugal texture. Now it is the second movement (Andante) which is presented in this way.[12] This interest in fugue forms part of the prevailing neo-classicism of the period, an aesthetic which was directly fashioned on the reinterpretation of the past. However, rather than producing something which is merely typical of its time, Tippett now presents something which is distinctly his own. His Third String Quartet, composed between 1945 and 1946, confirms the sound-world of the first two quartets while also engendering its own unique sense of identity. In contrast to the four-movement pattern of the Second Quartet, this work is symmetrical in form, consisting of five movements: three fast fugues (movements 1, 3 and 5) and two slow movements (2 and 4). While this seems to be a highly individual outline, Arnold Whittall suggests that it 'perhaps reflect[s] Tippett's awareness of the fourth and fifth quartets of Bartók'.[13] As well as this suggestion of Bartók, the continuing focus on fugal textures again draws attention to the importance of Beethoven's use of fugue in his late works as a historical model for Tippett.

Following these early explorations of the string quartet, Tippett did not return to the genre until the later 1970s with a Fourth String Quartet (1977–8) which, given his wide-ranging stylistic development since the earlier quartets, is very different. However, although his sound-world has changed dramatically, there is a certain continuity in terms of Tippett's response to the Beethovenian legacy. Tippett here builds a single overall structure out of four linked movements (slow, fast, moderately slow, very slow), an approach which has precedents in the late quartets of Beethoven (Opp. 130, 131 and 132) and is also echoed in other major works of this period of Tippett's career (notably the Fourth Symphony (1976–7) and the Triple Concerto for violin, viola, cello and orchestra (1978–9)). This Beethovenian reference is confirmed through Tippett's deliberate adoption of the theme from Beethoven's *Grosse Fuge*, although fugue, in contrast to the earlier quartets, is notably absent. Tippett's fifth and last quartet (1990) comes from the remarkable final stages of his compositional career. While it would be only too convenient to interpret this work as a culmination or summation of Tippett's quartet writing, there is a sense of revisiting past concerns. For example, the play with the drama of a sonata-style form in the first of two movements, and the moments of expansive lyricism, have always been reinvented as consistent features of Tippett's musical language. However, these concerns are effectively contained within what is by definition Tippett's late style.

Tippett's five quartets give a remarkable insight into the development of his compositional maturity and play a significant part in the concluding part of his career. While it is perhaps cause for regret that he did not turn his attention towards the quartet in the middle stages of his career, the focus on the historical archetype of the genre and the restatement of Tippett's engagement with the Beethovenian legacy situate the five quartets in the centre of his *œuvre*, making him a figure who seems to personify the dialectic between innovation and tradition which defines so much of twentieth-century music.

Elizabeth Maconchy (1907–94), a contemporary of Tippett, produced her most distinctive work in the string quartet medium. Her thirteen quartets, composed between 1933 and 1983, constitute one of the most sustained and significant bodies of string quartets by a British composer. Maconchy explains the perpetual challenge of writing string quartets as 'The pursuit of the argument, its shaping into a satisfying musical form, the cut and thrust of the counterpoint – these all stimulate and stretch the intellect . . .'[14] Her initial response to this challenge was the First String Quartet, composed between 1932 and 1933. This is a four-movement work, with each movement presenting its own character. The first movement (Allegro feroce) is defined by its rhythmic energy, with the repetition of a syncopated figure being the defining element of the movement. The subsequent movements (Scherzo, Andante sostenuto and Presto) relate quite directly to the inherited models of the string quartet. The first departure from this pattern comes in the Third Quartet of 1938. This work takes the form of a single movement with distinctive sections. The composer describes it as being 'in a cyclic form, one continuously unfolding movement';[15] the opening Lento section articulates an initial sequence of ideas which are subsequently developed. Maconchy's musical language in her quartets is an increasingly modern one, but one which is enclosed within a positive response to the traditions and expectations of the genre.

This positive re-engagement with tradition in the form of a historicised genre is vividly present in the music of Robert Simpson (1921–97). His eleven symphonies and sixteen string quartets (the first composed in 1952 and the last in 1996) effectively define his career, with the symphonic concern with unity of form and content conditioning his response to the string quartet. His music is permeated with compositional precedents (notably Haydn, Beethoven, Sibelius and Nielsen) which are defined through this preoccupation with musical unity. In terms of his string quartets, the influence of Beethoven is most notable. For example, his Fourth, Fifth and Sixth Quartets are a compositional response to Beethoven's Razumovsky quartets. His use of preformed material is most evident in the Ninth Quartet (1982), Variations and a Fugue on a Theme of Haydn (based on a theme from Haydn's symphony No. 47 in G). This is a massive display of compositional virtuosity in the spirit of Bach's Goldberg Variations and Beethoven's Diabelli Variations. However, this emphasis on compositional precedents should not be seen to undermine Simpson's own musical identity or originality, which lies in his effective treatment of these precedents, shaping them into his own unique musical identity.

The string quartet writing of Brian Ferneyhough (b. 1943) has been in sharp contrast to composers such as Britten, Tippett and Simpson. Ferneyhough adopted as his starting point the post-war avant garde of Boulez and Stockhausen, producing a sound-world which has often been described as 'complex'. His *Sonatas for String Quartet* from 1967 is one of his first major works and one which immediately provides an outline of his compositional concerns. As is evident from the title, this work is not concerned with the string quartet as a genre. Ferneyhough claimed Purcell's Fantasias for viols as a starting point, but the general fragmentary nature of the textures and the highly sectionalised format of the score bring to mind Webern. The work consists of twenty short movements with silence forming an important part of the texture. The fragmentary nature of its material places certain demands on both listener and player, but there is an underlying sense of continuity and expansion which gives a greater feeling of purpose to the seemingly fragmentary moments. Ferneyhough's Second (1979–80) and Third String Quartets (1987) belong to a stage of his career by which he had already established the central aspects of a consistent style and musical language. The Second Quartet constitutes one relatively brief movement which is conditioned by a dense interactive sense of polyphony; this again can appear fragmentary, but there is an underlying notion of structural coherence which gives direction to the music. The quartet writing of Ferneyhough seems far removed from the traditional expectations of the genre. It places great demands on the players (particularly in terms of its rhythmic and temporal complexity) and may appear as forbiddingly complex to some listeners. However, there is a dramatic tension which manifests itself in sharp contrasts and fleeting textures, and it is Ferneyhough's great compositional achievement that he is able to give a real sense of structural logic and musical direction to these textures.

The wide differences of approach to the string quartet by composers such as Britten, Tippett, Maconchy, Simpson and Ferneyhough will no doubt intensify in our age of increasing stylistic and cultural pluralism and it is intriguing to wonder how our perception of the genre will be challenged by Peter Maxwell Davies' declared intention to turn his attention to the sustained production of string quartets over the next few years.

Russia/Soviet Union

One of the most notable Russian contributions to the quartet during the early part of the century is the *Three Pieces for String Quartet* of Igor Stravinsky (1882–1971). Composed in 1914, these pieces are a radical exploration of the string quartet texture and occupy a significant point in Stravinsky's career. Coming after *The Rite of Spring* (1913), the work through which Stravinsky most clearly articulated his own vision of modernism, they condense some of the essential features of that large-scale orchestral ballet into the quartet medium. The first piece consists of a short melodic phrase in the first violin part which is based on only four notes (G, A, B, C) and conveys a sense of folk-like simplicity through its repetitive nature. This melodic cell is supported by the sustained D and C♯ in the viola while the second violin has a four-note cell (F♯, E, D♯, C♯). This material acts as an intrusion into the repetitions of the four-note cell of the first violin and thus helps generate the sense of tension evident within the piece. The bass of the texture is provided by a three-note cell in the cello (C, D♭, E♭) which is repeated continually throughout the piece. The effect of these different coexisting cells is very much that of collision (or collage) with very little obvious sense of convergence between them. This almost Cubist effect seems to extrapolate the cell idea from *The Rite of Spring* and explore its possibilities on a condensed yet more consistent and systematic level. The second of the three pieces again explores possibilities of juxtaposition, but now those of textures and ideas rather than the coexistent cells of the first piece. The final piece again explores the repetition of a basic idea (C, D, E♭), but in a much more subdued and contemplative way than the first. Stravinsky was to return to the string quartet only in passing (*Concertino* for string quartet (1920), *Double Canon* for string quartet (1959)) and, while his relationship to his homeland was to become increasingly detached, the *Three Pieces for String Quartet* serve as a valuable reminder that he was a quintessentially Russian composer who constructed his own sense of modernism, quite distinct from that of the Austro-Germanic strand, as represented by Schoenberg.

The changing political and economic landscape which helped drive Stravinsky from Russia had the same effect on Sergey Prokofiev (1891–1953), who, for a period until his return to the Soviet Union in 1936, moved to the USA. Prokofiev's First String Quartet Op. 50 was composed in 1930, during his period of exile. He claimed that this work had emerged as a consequence of his study of Beethoven's string quartets. However, the three movements of this work reflect Prokofiev's general neo-classicism of the period rather than any direct Beethovenian influence. His Second Quartet, composed after his return and during the Second World War (Op. 92, 1941), reflects the folk music of the Northern Caucasus, to which Prokofiev was evacuated during the war, a factor which gives the work a unique identity and provides a certain contrast to the First Quartet.

Of the many significant composers who chose to stay and work within the Soviet system one of the most intriguing is Nikolay Myaskovsky (1881– 1950). Although most prolific as a composer of symphonies, he produced a total of thirteen string quartets throughout his career. This was a time of political oppression, during which the regime placed certain demands on composers, along with other artists and writers. Myaskovsky seemed outwardly reconciled to the political nature of his role as a composer and had a high profile and a number of official functions. However, many have suggested that his public persona was merely a mask which covered his true beliefs and concerns. In 1948 Myaskovsky was accused, along with Prokofiev and Dmitry Shostakovich, of 'formalism', a label which reflects the scrutiny to which these composers were subjected.

At times Shostakovich (1906–75) was undoubtedly torn between his role as a public figure in support of the regime and his personal vision as a composer. Whatever the political connotations, it is clear that he viewed the string quartet as a viable medium for the construction and articulation of his own personal sound-world. He composed fifteen quartets through- out his career. His First String Quartet, composed in 1938, is an outwardly simple work of which the composer later recalled: 'I visualised childhood scenes, somewhat naive and bright moods associated with spring.'[16] While some may wish to claim that this description of the music is a conscious denial of the dark reality of the political climate of the time, it is, however one chooses to interpret it, a realistic description of the music. The first of four movements is based on its C major tonality and works through a highly condensed formal outline. The unassuming nature of the material is reinforced by the moderato tempo which helps convey the deceptive sim- plicity of the movement. This mood is effectively continued in the second movement, also headed 'Moderato'. This movement begins with a single melodic line in the viola which is clearly folk-like in character; yet, as in the first movement, this simplicity is deceptive. As the movement pro- gresses it takes on different characteristics but not to the extent that it is rendered complex or inaccessible. This quartet's four-movement structure may lead to an association with the traditional nature of the string quartet. However, there is a remarkable sense of individuality to this music, for, by this stage in his career, Shostakovich had already outlined some of the main features of his mature style. The seemingly simple and direct melodic lines, the motor-type rhythmic effects in the accompaniment, and an elusive sense of irony are already evident in his music and will reappear in various contexts, including the string quartet.

If the First Quartet is defined through its seeming simplicity, then Shostakovich's later quartets take on a more substantial and often darker quality. This is certainly the case with the Eighth Quartet in C minor Op. 110, undoubtedly one of Shostakovich's finest achievements. He composed it in 1960 during a visit to Dresden, where he witnessed the destruction caused by the Allied bombing of the city during the Second World War, and he consequently dedicated it to the memory of victims of fascism and war. However, although this suggests a public, outward-looking musical statement, the work itself is intensely private. In fact, it could be described as autobiographical. This sense of musical autobiography is provided by Shostakovich's use of his DSCH (D, E♭, C and B) motive, which is Shostakovich's own musical signature, as well as references to some of his own works, including the opera *The Lady Macbeth of the Mtsensk District* (the work which had led to his problems with the authorities), the First Symphony, the First Cello Concerto and the Tenth Symphony. As well as these self-reflexive gestures there are also citations from other composers, including the funeral march from Wagner's *Götterdämmerung* and passages from Tchaikovsky's Sixth Symphony, a process which suggests that the work is preoccupied with memory. Nevertheless, Shostakovich shapes these elements into something which is uniquely his own and which suggests a unity born out of diversity and conflict.

The work consists of five movements. The first is a Largo which is built on an imitative, fugal texture. The initial idea is the D, E♭, C, B (DSCH) motive. This is introduced by the cello and is then taken up by the other instruments in ascending sequence. The effect is of a slow-moving but increasingly intense texture, which is dramatically heightened by the increased chromaticism of the movement's central section. The contrast between the Largo of the first movement and the Allegro molto of the second is extreme. However, Shostakovich achieves a simple but effective connection between the two, something he will explore in other quartets. The first movement ends with a cadence on C, with the second violin repeating G, but this is immediately replaced by the sustained G♯, which becomes the tonic of the second movement, with G now heard retrospectively as F𝄪, the leading note to G♯. Although this connection is technically effective, the impact of the sudden momentum of the second movement is one of surprise and forms one of this work's most notable features. The intensity of the first two movements is further contrasted by the scherzo-like Allegretto which again uses the DSCH motive as its basic idea. The fourth and fifth movements revert to the solemn Largo of the opening movement. The finale recalls the first movement not only in terms of its tempo, but also in the use of the DSCH motive as a fugue subject, thus reinscribing the importance of memory evident in both the musical and the extra-musical dimensions of the work.

Shostakovich's later quartets continue to expand the parameters of the genre. The four-movement pattern of the First Quartet is generally avoided and the linking of movements becomes increasingly common. This expansion is most evident in the Eleventh (Op. 122, 1966) and Fifteenth Quartets (Op. 144, 1974). Both are multi-movement works with the movements interlinked. Shostakovich's last quartet has a valedictory and contemplative character and combines with other of his late works, such as the Fifteenth Symphony, to provide a final realisation of the personal vision of this remarkable composer.

Of the Soviet/Russian composers who emerged during the later stages of Shostakovich's career, perhaps the most notable is Alfred Schnittke (1934–88). Schnittke's individuality is best exemplified in his Third Quartet of 1983. The first of three movements begins with three distinct quotations: a cadential gesture from Lassus' *Stabat Mater*, the main thematic material of Beethoven's *Grosse Fuge* Op. 133 and Shostakovich's DSCH motive. This process recalls Shostakovich, a suggestion which is reinforced by the DSCH motive, and the construction of a musically inscribed memory. Schnittke builds a perception of 'the past' out of these materials in a way which avoids any overt neo-classicism or reconstruction of tradition. The effect of the music is highly distinctive, providing at times a glimpse of the 'polystylism', the pluralisation of style, which was to become the defining quality of Schnittke's music in general and, for some, an appropriate reflection of contemporary cultural conditions.

Hungary

In Hungary, Ernő Dohnányi (1877–1960) composed three quartets (1899, 1906 and 1926 respectively), while Kodály's (1882–1967) two quartets (Op. 2, 1908–9 and Op. 10, 1916–18) reflect his early style; the inspiration of Hungarian folk music is evident in the thematic materials, textures and sonorities of both works. However, Bartók (1881–1945) dominates Hungarian music of the period, his six string quartets constituting one of the peaks of the twentieth-century string quartet repertory.

After several early quartets, which are now lost, Bartók composed his First String Quartet (Op. 7) in 1908–9. This remarkable work reflects a transition in his style at this stage in his career. The first movement of what is a highly individual three-movement design begins with a canonic texture between the two violins in a slow tempo (Largo) followed by the introduction of viola and cello. The sound-world of this movement is still that of late Romanticism. The slow-moving texture and the heightened chromaticism combine to suggest a Tristanesque sense of yearning and instability, an interpretation which is perhaps reinforced by the knowledge of the end of Bartók's affair with the violinist Stefi Geyer and the fact that the opening material was derived from a four-note figure which Bartók associated with her in this and other works. The central section of the movement involves a change of texture and mood before the opening canonic texture is briefly regained. The movement concludes with a somewhat abrupt gesture which leads directly to the waltz-like second movement. A short transitional passage (Introduzione) provides the connection to the finale, which is on a much larger scale than either of the first two movements. Its expanded dimensions are related to a more complex formal and thematic design, based on sonata form, the first subject being a transformation of one of the main thematic ideas of the second movement.

The generally introspective nature of the First Quartet is carried forward into the Second. Composed between 1914 and 1917, it also uses the three-movement shape of the First. The first movement is generally relaxed (Moderato) and well balanced. This feeling is sharply contrasted by the second movement, which is fast (Allegro molto capriccioso) and direct in manner. The main thematic ideas of the movement are based on the tritone (B–F, later transposed to C–F♯ and D–A♭) and are largely fragmentary and sharply articulated. It is the third and concluding movement which lends an air of introspection. The slow-moving tempo and texture (Lento) offer a real contrast to the intensity of the second movement and the relaxed feel of the first, while also providing a fitting conclusion to the work.

Bartók's Third and Fourth Quartets come from the 1920s (1927 and 1928). The Third Quartet is the most radical of the six. Its musical language is defined through harsh dissonances while its compressed formal model, a single continuous movement with sub-divisions, is in sharp contrast to the earlier quartets, the brevity of the whole presenting a concise and direct statement of Bartók's musical direction at this point in his career. While the string sonorities may be similar and the expressive gestures equally intense, the formal dimensions of Bartók's Fourth Quartet are very different from the Third. It was originally planned as a four-movement work, but Bartók added another movement to produce a symmetrical five-movement pattern, with this sense of symmetry articulated throughout the work. The central point of this outline is the slow third movement, characterised by homophonic textures which create the impression of harmonic stasis. This

central movement is enclosed by two shorter fast movements, while the
finale features loosely defined reworkings of thematic materials from the
first movement.

The symmetry evident in the Fourth Quartet is repeated in the Fifth
(1934), but with a scherzo as the central third movement. This scherzo
is flanked by two slow movements (the second is marked Adagio molto
and the fourth Andante). The fascination with symmetrical patterns is also
evident within movements. The first movement consists of a sonata-form
structure with three thematic ideas; these are stated in reverse order in
the recapitulation, placing the development section as the mid-point of an
arch structure. In contrast, the Sixth Quartet (1939) consists of the four-
movement shape that was once the norm of the genre, without necessarily
corresponding to the inherited forms and characteristics of the movements
of the traditional quartet. The work begins with a solo viola melody which
establishes a melancholic, nostalgic atmosphere, one which is perhaps a
reflection of the changing political circumstances and the impending war,
which would lead to Bartók leaving his Hungarian homeland for the USA.

Another significant composer who would leave Hungary for political
and economic reasons is György Ligeti (b. 1923). Following the suppression
of the uprising against the communist regime in 1956, Ligeti settled in
Vienna, where he was able to enjoy a wide-ranging cultural environment.
His First String Quartet, which is subtitled 'Metamorphoses nocturnes', was
composed in Hungary between 1953 and 1954 but not performed until 1958
in Vienna. It is clearly an apprentice work and one which reflects the direct
influence of Bartók, with the single-movement form reflecting an awareness
of Bartók's Third Quartet and the folk-like rhythmic patterns and thematic
shapes articulating an understanding of Bartók's more generalised interest
in folk materials. In contrast, Ligeti's Second Quartet (1968) comes from an
important and highly creative stage in his career and reflects a more mature
response to the challenge of the string quartet. It is also a work which places
great demands on the performers, utilising a wide range of ever-changing
performance indications and frequent harmonics.

Having decided to remain in Hungary after 1956, Ligeti's near contemporary György Kurtág (b. 1926) has, albeit somewhat belatedly, found a
wider reception in the West. Kurtág has not written consistently for string
quartet, but his Op. 1, like Ligeti's First Quartet, reflects the influence of
Bartók. This time it is the symmetrical shapes of Bartók's Fourth and Fifth
Quartets that provide the models. Kurtág's Quartet consists of six short,
fragmentary, rather Webernesque movements. The arch-like pairings of
movements (the first and last movements relate, while the second and fifth
provide a certain parallel) form an overall shape which gives some structural

logic to these fragmentary textures. After this initial work Kurtág has not returned to the quartet as a genre, although two of his works use the string quartet texture: *Hommage à Mihály András* (12 'microludes' for string quartet), Op. 13 (1977), and *Officium breve in Memoriam Andreae Szervánszky* Op. 28 (1988–9). Both works reflect the more generalised concerns of Kurtág's later career.

Poland

Polish music of the early twentieth century is dominated by the music of Karol Szymanowski (1882–1937), who strove to articulate a national identity in his music. He composed two quartets (1917, 1927). His First Quartet consists of three movements, opening with a substantial but concise sonata-form design in C major. Its introduction incorporates a broad lyrical theme which leads into the main Allegro moderato. This theme introduces some chromaticism which is further expanded as the movement progresses, generating an expressionist intensity which is reflective of Szymanowski's music of this period.

Although the generation of Polish composers who emerged after the Second World War demonstrated an awareness of the historical genres of music (such as Lutosławski's sequence of symphonies), it did not show extensive interest in the string quartet. Nevertheless, there are some notable contributions, including one (1964) by Witold Lutosławski (1913–94) and two by Krzysztof Penderecki (b. 1933; 1960, 1968). However, despite their title, Penderecki's works do not suggest any meaningful affiliation with the genre. His First String Quartet explores a challenging sound-world which demands new conceptions of playing techniques evident in Penderecki's better-known works for massed string orchestra. As Wolfram Schwinger explains: 'Everything hitherto demanded of a mass string orchestra in *Emanations*, *Threnody* and *Anaklasis* is demanded of the four soloists who constitute a string quartet. All the methods of sound production are now applied, the more clearly, to solo instruments: bowing, plucking, hitting one or more strings near or on the bridge or tailpiece, various kinds of tremolo or vibrato.'[17]

France

While our perception of the French string quartet of the early twentieth century may be largely conditioned by the quartets of Debussy and

Ravel, it is the prolific output of Darius Milhaud (1892–1974) which is sustained throughout the period. Milhaud composed eighteen string quartets, the first in 1912 and the last in 1950, all of which reflect in their own ways his own idiosyncratic sense of style. Of the composers who emerged in the years immediately following the Second World War, Pierre Boulez (b. 1925) has generally been received as the most significant. Like his contemporaries of the post-war avant garde, Boulez showed little interest in the traditional genres of music. In fact he set himself in direct opposition to any such notion of tradition. However, he has demonstrated an interest in the string quartet as an ensemble and texture in one early but important work, his *Livre pour Quatuor* of 1948–9. This work reflects Boulez's avant-gardist aspirations of the time. It was essentially conceived as a collection of movements from which the performers could determine their own selection, thus anticipating the interest in chance procedures. The actual musical details are also significant, as they suggest Boulez's progression towards the establishment of a total serialism, a concept through which all parameters of music, not just pitch, are subjected to the logic of serialism, and one which he would pursue in a number of major works.

The Czech lands

The two string quartets of Leoš Janáček (1854–1928) belong to that remarkable flowering of compositional activity which formed the final period of his life. The first, based on an interpretatation of Tolstoy's *The Kreutzer Sonata*, was composed in 1923, while the Second Quartet (*Intimate Letters*) was composed in the final year of Janáček's life and not performed until after his death. Both correspond to the outer expectations of the genre in that they both comprise four movements. However, their programmatic associations also create a certain distance from those expectations.

While Bohuslav Martinů (1890–1959) spent a large part of his life away from his native Czechoslovakia, he remained an essentially Czech composer. His large output featured a prolific sequence of chamber music, with his seven numbered string quartets (the first from 1918 and the final one completed in 1947) forming useful signposts to an understanding of his somewhat eclectic approach to composition. His Fifth Quartet (1938), for example, represents the stylistic position he adopted in the 1920s, with a focus on fast motor-like rhythmic patterns and a harsh dissonant quality which is still contained within an idiosyncratic understanding of tonality.

Scandinavia

The best known twentieth-century composer from the Scandinavian countries was undoubtedly Jean Sibelius (1865–1957), who strove to establish a national musical identity for his native Finland. After some early attempts in the genre, his only string quartet was composed in 1909 with the subtitle of *Voces Intimae* (see p. 277 above). In the key of D minor, this five-movement work has a wonderfully dark and sombre quality, generating a sense of introspection which is not dissimilar to aspects of Beethoven's late quartets.

Fartein Valen (1887–1952), Norwegian by birth and location, had a truly international perspective which sought to embrace some of the innovative features of modernism. His two quartets (1928 and 1930–1) reflect these wider concerns while also suggesting an awareness of the generic associations of the medium. The most prolific Scandinavian composer of string quartets was Vagn Holmboe (1909–96). This Danish composer produced ten unnumbered and twenty-one numbered quartets. The first three numbered quartets come from the 1940s, a time at which Holmboe achieved compositional maturity.

America

The recurrent historical narrative of twentieth-century American music features Charles Ives (1874–1954) as the focal point of an experimental, eclectic tradition, which is clearly evident in his two string quartets. The first consists of materials assembled between *c.* 1897 and *c.* 1909, *From the Salvation Army*; its content is often based on hymn tunes, a characteristic of Ives's music of this period. The Second Quartet (*c.* 1913–15) consists of three movements, each of which has a descriptive title – 'Discussions', 'Arguments' and 'The Call of the Mountains' – pointing to Ives' wider musical concerns.

In his own unique way John Cage (1912–92) sustained, in fact heightened, the experimental aspirations of American music. That he would show no interest in the traditional genres of music is a reflection of Cage's wider musical and cultural aesthetic, so it is little surprise that he did not produce a series of works titled string quartet. However, he did write a number of interesting works for the medium, among them his *String Quartet in Four Parts* (1949–50). This work tends to be overshadowed by the percussion and prepared piano works of the 1940s and by the exploration of chance procedures in the 1950s. However, it is a notable work in its own right. The

'Four Parts' in the title refer in effect to four movements, each of which carries a descriptive title: 'Quietly Flowing Along', 'Slowly Rocking', 'Nearly Stationary' and 'Quodlibet'. However, these four parts do not in any way correspond to the individual characteristics of the movements of the Classical string quartet; rather they are in a sense programmatic/descriptive, drawing upon the images and atmospheres invoked by the Hindu sequence of the seasons, in which spring, summer, autumn and winter correspond to creation, preservation, destruction and quiescence. Part 1, 'summer', is followed by an ongoing decrease in tempo to part 3, 'winter', which is effectively static. This is followed by the contrast of the concluding quodlibet which signifies spring. Although it is through such shifts in tempo and character that the work is essentially defined, there is a general evenness of sonority and flatness of texture, with no real sense of climax or contrast. Cage returned to the string quartet in works such as *Thirty Pieces for String Quartet* (1983) and *Four* (1989) without showing any sustained interest in the ensemble of two violins, viola and cello.[18]

In contrast to Cage, Elliott Carter (b. 1908) and Milton Babbitt (b. 1916) in quite different ways present a modernism which is complex and challenging while recognising the aesthetic parameters of music. Both have produced a significant body of string quartets. Babbitt's six quartets extend from the early style of his First Quartet (1948, now withdrawn) through to the consolidation of his own rigorous realisation of serialism in the Third (1969–70) and Fourth Quartets (1970). Carter has also evolved a formidable musical language of which his sequence of five string quartets form a major element. Carter's First Quartet (1950–1) consists of a four-movement pattern which, although it at times alludes to composers such as Bartók and Berg, establishes some of the essential features of Carter's music, including the concern with temporal mobility through careful gradations of tempo. Carter's Second Quartet (1959) marked his 'belated arrival in American musical life'.[19] This breakthrough work is concerned more with the individual characteristics of the four instruments rather than the combined effect. As David Schiff remarks: 'The first violin is "fantastic, ornate, mercurial", the second violin "has a laconic, orderly character which is sometimes humorous", the viola is "expressive", the cello "impetuous".'[20] Schiff goes on to suggest the possibility of this contrast of character having its origin in the Arguments movement of Ives's Second Quartet.[21] The work also has a distinctive formal model, consisting of nine sections which are played without any break, even though four of the sections assume the appearance of movements. The sense of contrast evident through these sections and the characterisation of the instruments is developed in Carter's Third Quartet (1971) into a sense of collage through the superimposition of ideas and textures. Carter's string quartets represent his own 'high' or 'ultra-' modernism, within which a complex, rigorous musical language is active. But this is a music which, through its conflicts and contrasts, enacts a real sense of musical drama and tension, qualities which make Carter one of the leading composers of his time. His string quartets articulate his vision of an 'ultra-modernism' while still retaining a residual grasp, at times a very distant one, on the inheritances and affiliations of the genre.

15 The string quartet as a foundation for larger ensembles

COLIN LAWSON

Introduction

Ensemble combinations based on the string quartet have inspired some of the most expressive and intense pieces of all chamber music. The various genres examined in this survey attracted a remarkable array of composers, so their vast field of work can only be given a brief overview here. There is no space for detailed musical analysis or even a listing of every work of notable significance. Such enduring masterpieces as Mozart's G minor Quintet and Schubert's C major Quintet are illustrations of the inspiration afforded by the addition to the quartet of just one stringed instrument. However, the necessity to integrate extra players within an established quartet means that such works have tended to find their way into the concert hall only on an occasional basis. Long before these pieces were familiar through recordings, Walter Cobbett in 1929 went so far as to advocate the formation of string quintets specifically for touring purposes, as a way of doing justice to both the quality and the quantity of the repertory. The age of recording has consolidated the reputation of many of the pieces discussed below, including larger-scale string pieces such as Brahms' sextets and Mendelssohn's Octet, whose live performance has continued to be inhibited by practical and economic considerations.

Since the middle of the nineteenth century the medium of the piano quintet has become established as an important element in the repertories of both pianists and string quartets, with masterly contributions from such front-rank composers as Borodin, Brahms, Dvořák, Elgar, Fauré, Schumann, Shostakovich and Schnittke. Their various solutions to the balance of form, content and texture illustrate the distinctive versatility of the medium. Many of these composers also wrote for the closely related piano quartet, representative of a large body of chamber music which dispenses with a second violin and thus strictly lies outside the scope of this chapter.

Among wind instruments, the clarinet has been the string quartet's most regular partner ever since Mozart created the clarinet quintet medium in 1789. A century later Brahms won the hearts and minds of players and audiences with his Clarinet Quintet, widely regarded as pre-eminent among his chamber music in terms of emotional intensity and beauty of tone-colour. Its success was immediate and from the beginning it was played much more often than Brahms' fine late String Quintet Op. 111 which preceded it. Other wind instruments have been less richly served, notwithstanding such fine music as Mozart's Horn Quintet, as well as oboe quintets by Bax, Bliss, Finzi and a number of others.

The twentieth century explored quartet-based ensembles in a variety of new and effective ways, such as Ravel's Introduction and Allegro (with harp, flute and clarinet), Elgar's Introduction and Allegro (with orchestra), as well as song cycles by Vaughan Williams, Warlock and others. The medium of the clarinet quintet has proved congenial to the avant-garde, while the combination of quartet and string orchestra has found its way into minimalist activity at the hands of John Luther Adams and others.

Music without keyboard

The eighteenth century

In the string quartet's infancy it was common for one of the violins to be replaced with a wind or keyboard instrument. The celebrated orchestra at Mannheim was at the forefront of the development of wind repertory, inspiring chamber music as well as concertos featuring its principal players. Mozart had already composed chamber music with flute and with oboe when he composed his Horn Quintet in 1782, a concertante work which employs the natural horn to ingenious effect. Mozart achieves an appropriately dark texture from the replacement of second violin by second viola. The Clarinet Quintet K. 581 of 1789 remains his only work with a wind instrument in which the usual quartet combination forms the basis for a larger ensemble. Mozart contrived to integrate the clarinet with the strings and yet incorporate many elements reflecting the virtuoso playing of his friend Anton Stadler. His vocal style of clarinet writing features wide leaps that no singer could ever produce, the thematic substance wholly idiomatic and seemingly unconfined by the character of the wind instrument. The work as a whole makes use of a wide range of textures and colours and was to have a seminal effect on later composers, radically enhancing the profile of the clarinet for years to come.

The string quintet with two violas was one of the many ensembles cultivated by Michael Haydn in Mozart's home city of Salzburg. He was probably the inspiration for Mozart's early Quintet K. 174 of 1773, a somewhat experimental work in a mixture of styles culminating in an elaborate, quasi-contrapuntal finale. It was much later, in 1787, that Mozart turned again to this relatively unfamiliar form, which was highly personal and more suited to his current mood than the symphony or concerto. In the spring and summer of 1788 he attempted to sell on subscription three quintets, in order to repay one of his many debts to Michael Puchberg. One of these was the arrangement K. 406 of his C minor Serenade K. 388, in which the pungency and varied colour of the wind octet is not quite compensated by the richness of the inner part-writing for the two violas. He entered the C major Quintet K. 515 in his catalogue on 19 April 1787 and the G minor K. 516 on 16 May, a contrasted pairing which finds a parallel in other genres, including the late symphonies. The addition of a second viola opened up for Mozart a new world of expression, offering tonal and contrapuntal enrichment and the opportunity to plan the music on a much enlarged scale. The five instruments could be grouped more flexibly than in the quartet. Both the cello and the inner parts could move with greater freedom, within outer parts that were spaced more widely. Mozart succeeded in preserving the proportion and balance of all five parts, while maintaining their full equality. He did not, like so many of his successors, rely upon mere brilliant and concertante effects. The C major Quintet K. 515 moves away from the taut melodic material of the 'Haydn' quartets towards divergent yet organised structures. Scholars have drawn attention to the quasi-symphonic nature of the material within its chamber environment. Whilst the sonata rondo finale of K. 515 is the longest of any of Mozart's instrumental movements, the G minor Quintet K. 516 is altogether more compact and motivic. The rich inner parts are used to sustain emotional tension, with melodic material often overlapping or in imitation. Chromatic language contributes to the music's violent intensity, which (as scholars from Abert to Hyatt-King have detected) inhabits the world of Tamino and Pamina in *Die Zauberflöte*.

Mozart's last string quintets date respectively from December 1790 and April 1791, thus written after the 'Prussian' quartets, many aspects of whose exploration of sonority and technique they share. K. 593 in D major balances lyricism and tension, inspiring Alfred Einstein to remark upon its wild, disconsolate, mirth. K. 614 in E♭ is even more original, the warm vitality of the first three movements finally giving way to the finale's sardonic humour and caprice.

One of the most prolific composers to take the string quartet as a basis for larger ensembles was Luigi Boccherini, who wrote quantities of flute quintets, piano quintets and string sextets, some of which post-date Mozart's career. Notwithstanding his *c.* 100 string quartets, it is the quintets that have attracted scholarly attention. The vast majority of these hundred or so works are scored with two cellos and remain little known. Boccherini's flexible and virtuosic compositional technique played an important part in the establishment of classical chamber style. Intensity of the moment rather than intricate development in his music meant that his reputation quickly went into decline with the rise of Haydn and Mozart. Although Gerber's

Lexicon (1791–2) called him the greatest of Italian instrumental composers, many nineteenth-century writers cited the *Allgemeine musikalische Zeitung* of 1779, which declared that Boccherini never achieved the 'complete fulfilment of a bold genius', but was 'superficial, monotonous and unimpressive'.[1] However, the brilliance of his string writing is reflected in his realisation of the potential of the cello within the ensemble.

The early nineteenth century

The early years of the nineteenth century were a glorious period in the promotion of wind instruments and their repertory. In an age devoted to virtuosity the clarinet achieved a natural pre-eminence, inspiring a large number of concertante quartets and quintets with strings. Contributors in Vienna included Leopold Kozeluch, Peter von Winter and Franz Krommer;[2] one of the most integrated works is Hummel's Clarinet Quartet of 1808, whose string parts carry much of the rhythmic and melodic interest. Of clarinettist-composers, Bernhard Crusell takes pride of place with his three imaginative quartets. The quintet by the Nuremberg virtuoso Heinrich Backofen is unusual in opting for a second viola rather than a second violin, a preference found also in the quintets by Krommer and Andreas Romberg. Weber's clarinettist Heinrich Baermann was a seminal influence on the genre, writing quintets with virtuoso solo parts, of which his Op. 23 includes an emotive Adagio long attributed to Wagner; he was also the inspiration for Meyerbeer's Quintet.

Weber's Clarinet Quintet was to find a place in the repertory alongside the Mozart and Brahms works, although it is essentially a miniature concerto, with a wide range of expressive devices that are overtly theatrical. The strings contribute occasional dramatic touches and are assigned an important imitative episode in the finale. Reicha's Clarinet Quintet is still occasionally heard, although its invention is less obviously dramatic than Weber's. Reicha contributed much else to the medium of solo wind plus string quartet, including works for flute, oboe, horn and bassoon. Beethoven's Sextet Op. 81b for two horns and string quartet is another important contribution to this virtuoso tradition, reflecting his early appreciation of the respective roles of high and low horn players. As the art of natural horn playing declined, the Sextet retained a formidable reputation, the first edition of *Grove's Dictionary* in 1879 stating baldly that it was so difficult as to be never played.

Beethoven's Septet Op. 20 established a model for many of his contemporaries, including Franz Berwald, Conradin Kreutzer and Friedrich Witt. The origins of the medium lie with the serenades and cassations of the eighteenth century, which had often combined winds and strings in a relatively free sequence of movements. Beethoven's lucid structure and distinctive themes contributed to the Septet's popularity and wide influence. His use of the double bass is an especially important feature borrowed from contemporary *Harmonie* bands. The octet medium (with the addition of second violin) had already been established by Reicha when Schubert turned to it in 1824. With consistent quality of invention Schubert's Octet contrives to invest an old-fashioned divertimento form with the new spirit of chamber music, delighting in instrumental colour in a quintessential Romantic manner.

During the second half of the nineteenth century wind instruments fell from favour within solo or chamber music. Hanslick may have spoken for a large element of the public when in 1870 he advised the Italian clarinet virtuoso Romeo Orsi to 'join an orchestra – that is the place where we know the value of clarinettists, flautists, oboists and bassoonists; the times are past when crowds of these wandering musicians came to give recitals on their boring little pipes'.[3] In *Grove's Dictionary* Philipp Spitta wrote in 1889: 'Wind-instruments are now out of fashion for concert playing, and one seldom hears anything on such occasions but the piano and the violin, instead of the pleasing variety which used to prevail with so much advantage to art.'[4]

In this context Brahms' encounter with the Meiningen clarinettist Richard Mühlfeld towards the end of his life is especially remarkable, because at the time he had already announced his retirement from composition. Brahms' Clarinet Quintet was immediately recognised as a wonderful achievement on its appearance in 1891. The sheer novelty of the reinstatement of the clarinet within chamber music is reflected in a letter of 1 December 1891 written from Hamburg to Hanslick in respect of the Joachim Quartet's Berlin concert series: 'Joachim has sacrificed the virginity of his Quartet for my newest things. Hitherto he has carefully protected the chaste sanctuary but now, in spite of all my protestations, he insists that I invade it with clarinet and piano, with trio and quintet.'[5]

Although Brahms' Clarinet Quintet is traditionally regarded as an autumnal and even nostalgic work, its formal architecture is in no sense reactionary. Furthermore, Brahms' integration of clarinet and strings is a substantial achievement in its own right, with fewer opportunities for bravura than for refined musicality. The clarinet's large effective range, tonal flexibility and dynamic variety enable it variously to merge with the strings and to stand out clearly as soloist. The Quintet's mood is markedly influenced by the degree to which the tonic key of B minor prevails. Thematic material is equally characteristic, with a falling motto theme permeating each of the four movements to produce a cyclic effect. In each of the movements there are some important structural and thematic parallels with Mozart's Clarinet Quintet. As Walter Frisch has recently observed, musical analysis and criticism too often fall short of communicating either a conscious intel-lectual admiration for Brahms' technical achievement or a less voluntary enchantment with the aesthetic experience.[6]

A rich century of string ensemble music began with Beethoven's String Quintet Op. 29 (1801), which forms a bridge between his Quartets Op. 18 and Op. 59. Its orchestral richness and weight have been reckoned to show the influence of Aloys Förster rather than Mozart, combining breadth with an economy of line even more marked than Op. 18 no. 1. It exhibits a formal expansiveness often associated with the middle-period quartets, characterised by a leisurely pacing and unfolding of ideas. Among early Romantic works for enlarged string ensemble were Mendelssohn's Octet and Schubert's String Quintet. Mendelssohn's youthful Octet was written in 1825, thus post-dating the first of Spohr's Double Quartets by a couple of years. The experience of his early string symphonies must have enabled Mendelssohn to produce the Octet's effortless fluency and exhilaration; he left careful instructions that all the instruments should play in symphonic style, with particular attention to dynamics. The Octet was dedicated to Mendelssohn's violin teacher Eduard Rietz, whose playing is reflected in the soaring violin phrases from the outset. The Scherzo evokes a world of spirits characteristic of the composer, while the finale is a compositional *tour-de-force*. A significant number of octets was to follow in the nineteenth and twentieth centuries, though none at quite the same level of inspiration.[7] Mendelssohn's amiable String Quintet Op. 18 (1826) is milder and less adventurous, charming and more diffuse, although its finely judged pro-portions and texture match those of the contemporary *Midsummer Night's Dream* Overture. The much later Quintet Op. 87 (1845) is stiffer and more pompous, its energy expended on more trivial material.

In his C major Quintet D. 916, Schubert followed Boccherini rather than Mozart in opting for a second cello. Its presence seems to have inspired the composer to his most intimately compelling utterance, with a richness of material handled with skill rather than academic learning. The two cellos enable reinforcement of the bass by occasional unison or octave passages and Schubert also takes the opportunity to use the first cello as a solo instrument in the upper part of its compass, sometimes doubling the first violin at the octave. In general, the textural contrasts which pervade Mozart's quintets are less significant than Schubert's attachment to a characteristic richness of texture. The particular sound-world of the five instruments is especially evident in the slow-moving Adagio and in its subsequent turbulence.

Surprisingly, Schubert's scoring inspired few successors, notwithstand-ing some little-known examples by such diverse figures as Glazunov, Taneiev and Milhaud, amongst others.[8] George Onslow (1784–1853) left a total of thirty-four quintets, mostly scored with two cellos though playable on a variety of instruments (for example, with second viola or double bass instead of one of the cellos). A French composer of English descent, Onslow was one of very few of his countrymen to produce a large quantity of chamber music; its elegance and grace belie thematic material which is commonplace rather than inspired, consigning his reputation to history books rather than the concert hall. In 1829 he was made partly deaf in one ear by a stray bullet during a boar-hunt; he recorded this incident in his String Quintet No. 15, Op. 38, which attempts to portray the various phases of his illness and recovery.

For thirty years after the death of Beethoven, Onslow's contemporary Louis Spohr (1784–1859) was regarded by many musicians as the greatest living composer. Yet within a quarter of a century of Spohr's death, the bulk of his music had disappeared from the repertory and the extent of his undoubted influence was largely forgotten. The history of music provides no parallel case of a composer upon whom posterity has so decisively reversed the judgement of his contemporaries. In the twentieth century, writers drew conclusions without a knowledge of his music or his nineteenth-century status. Yet for any student of the violin and its chamber music he remains an important figure, leaving in addition to his many quartets a number of ensemble pieces for larger string-based combinations. The Octet and the Nonet for mixed winds and strings have enjoyed a modest revival in recent times. A total of seven quintets (with two violas) reveal at their best a balance between brilliance and a true chamber-music idiom. Op. 33 no. 2 in G won immediate acclaim from the *Allgemeine musikalische Zeitung*, which praised the variation movement as 'a model for all time, so long at least as the taste for true art does not perish; Haydn, Mozart and Beethoven themselves have created nothing more magnificent of this kind'.[9] The outer movements respectively reveal Spohr's ability to make a movement grow almost entirely from a single idea, or to create a structure teeming with thematic material. Another successful work is the B minor Quintet Op. 69 of 1826, whose sense of the dramatic never gives way to the familiar formulae and lack of distinctive material which often afflict his later pieces.[10]

The qualities of the Sextet in C Op. 140 (1848) were immediately recognised in *The Musical World*, which described it as 'a work which, while showing all the experience of age, displays in an astonishing degree that freshness and spontaneity which are supposed only to belong to youth. One of the last chamber compositions of Dr Spohr, this sestet is equally one of the finest and most captivating of them all.'[11] Spohr's thematic expansiveness surely provided Brahms with an important influence.[12]

In 1823 Spohr wrote to Wilhelm Speyer, 'I have already completed three movements of a double quartet. This is a wholly new kind of instrumental work which, so far as I know, I am the first to attempt. It is most like a piece for double chorus, for the two quartets who co-operate here work against each other in about the same proportion as the two choirs do. I am very eager to hear the effect and am consequently hastening to finish.'[13] As Clive Brown observes, Albrechtsberger had published three sonatas for double quartet, each comprising an Adagio and Fugue, as early as 1804. But Spohr derived the idea from Andreas Romberg who at his death had completed two movements of a projected double quartet, which the two composers had discussed together. In Spohr's first Double Quartet Op. 65, the second quartet acts essentially as accompaniment and the work was even arranged by his pupil Hubert Ries as a concerto for string quartet and orchestra. This transcription must in turn have been the inspiration for Spohr's original concerto Op. 131 for the same medium. Op. 65 was well received and Spohr continued to develop the unusual combination, eventually producing in Op. 136 a more integrated work in which the quartets are treated more equally and more subtle use made of the antiphonal possibilities of the ensemble.

The first important nineteenth-century Dutch composer, Bernardus van Bree (1801–57), wrote an Allegro for four string quartets which illustrates his preference for the German tradition at a time when Amsterdam showed a strong predilection for French music.

Brahms revitalised instrumental genres whose profile had recently been overtaken by a Romantic emphasis on programme and text. His links with the past and developing compositional processes may be observed in the two string sextets of 1860 and 1864–5, a medium which he effectively inaugurated, naturally surpassing Spohr's mild and scholarly approach. As Michael Musgrave has observed, Brahms must have known Schubert's Quintet from the time of his first Viennese visits and a copy of the first edition of 1853 remained in his library.[14] In the B♭ Sextet Op. 18 Schubert's intense lyricism is an obvious influence, yet Brahms' first mature chamber work combines a Classical surface with new possibilities of instrumental sonority. Technical challenges arise from the pervasive role of counterpoint and use of high, exposed registers, especially for first viola and cello. At the same time, the variation slow movement betrays Brahms' preoccupation with Baroque style and language, especially the chaconne. The greater subtlety and personal Romanticism of the G major Sextet Op. 36 has led at least one writer to regard it as 'surely the greatest successor to the Schubert String Quintet in the nineteenth century'.[15] Brahms develops a rich variety of colouristic effects, including tremolando and the combination of arco and pizzicato, whilst utilising a more developed contrapuntal technique involving inversion, stretto and diminution. His Scherzo moves away from tradition to a new type of 2/4 movement in the minor mode.

In the 1880s Brahms turned to the string quintet, producing a pair of radically contrasted works. The F major Quintet Op. 88 is the more classically orientated, with a fugal finale recalling Beethoven's C major Razumovsky Quartet. The G major Quintet Op. 111, on the other hand, combines gypsy and dance music with a sophistication of melody and harmony. The cello solo with which it begins caused its first performers considerable strain, though Brahms retained his original dynamic markings against the advice of Joachim. Equality of voices even outside contrapuntal contexts is an important feature, as is the forward-looking economy of means, worked fluently and spontaneously. The slow movement shows a special harmonic individuality that was immediately noted by Joachim.

Bruckner's string quintet of 1879, premiered by the Hellmesberger Quartet, brings religious overtones into the sphere of chamber music. Bruckner's musical language recalls Schubert in its shifting harmonies, modulatory charm and broad sense of tonality. Schubert's promotion of semitonal relationships is evident in Bruckner's Adagio, couched in Gb within the overall main key of F. Its spiritual dimension gives way to an orchestrally conceived finale, whose structure is enhanced by ingenious contrapuntal workings.[16]

Pre-eminent among nationalist composers of chamber music was Dvořák, who brought a highly personal flavour to his harmonic language and rhythms, often literally adopted from popular music of the day. While seldom polyphonic in texture, his music abounds with imaginative accompaniment figures. His works for extended string ensemble are perhaps not his most characteristic. Dvořák's Op. 1 (1861) was a quintet, characterised by confident sonority rather than nationalist tendency. Of mature works, the Quintet in G Op. 77 (1875) pre-dates his real freedom of lyrical expression. Because of some operatic associations, its unusual textures for quartet and double bass and the casual arrangement of keys, it is nevertheless rather exceptional for a chamber work.[17] The Sextet Op. 48 is at once Slavonic, fully representative of his nationalist style and Schubertian. The themes are developed with delightful ease, with his practice of generating ideas from a phrase of his main theme most happily in evidence. The slow movement is marked 'dumka', incorporating gypsy music and also a lullaby. Local colour also appears in the *furiant* scherzo. The String Quintet Op. 97 has an exoticism that derives from Dvořák's interest in the Iroquois Indians. This includes transformed fragments of Indian song. The variations of the Larghetto follow Haydn's example in having a double theme. Some writers have suggested that Dvořák was beginning to exhaust his American sources of inspiration: 'the end of the Quintet with its ponderous descending bass – which cries out for the brass – and orgy of triplets and dotted quavers is perhaps the worst bit of chamber music writing Dvořák ever perpetrated'.[18]

At the end of the century, programme music found itself harnessed to the chamber tradition in Schoenberg's *Verklärte Nacht*; the scoring of string sextet for such a work is highly unusual. Schoenberg was particularly attracted by the poems of Richard Dehmel (1863–1920). The first three of the Four Songs Op. 2 (1899) are settings of his work, as is the third of the Six Songs Op. 3. *Verklärte Nacht*, Schoenberg's major work of 1899, composed in three weeks in September, is also based on a Dehmel text, but now used as a programme for a symphonic poem. The basic form of words and music is very simple. Three stanzas descriptive of the forest and of the lovers' progress frame the two more extended statements of the woman and the man. Yet simple descriptive means are turned to sophisticated musical ends. The large-scale musical edifice is built by transformation motifs that serve every conceivable expressive purpose. They graphically depict the initial, trudging depression, the woman's agitation, the man's calmness and the ultimate transfiguration of doubt into serenity. The score is a miracle of clarity, despite the often elaborate contrapuntal textures, and Wagnerian and Brahmsian modes of thought meet in harmonious accord. But Schoenberg's distinctive themes, instinct for polyphonic potential and harmonic vocabulary are masterly. The work shows Schoenberg's irresistible instinct to build on the essence of the musical past. A knowledge of this unlikely tale is of secondary importance to the listener because the lack of action enables the work to be understood as a single-movement abstract composition.

The string sextet has attracted other composers of varying significance, including Tchaikovsky, D'Indy, Kornauth, Bridge, Roy Harris, Martinů, Milhaud, Glière and Korngold. These works tend to shy away from radical elements, although they take advantage of the expanded medium in a variety of imaginative ways.

The twentieth century

At the beginning of the century the most enduring works were often associated with new instrumental combinations. Ravel's *Introduction and Allegro* for flute, clarinet, harp and string quartet moved far away from previous models, combining brilliant harp writing with sonorous yet delicate ensemble. In 1919 the harp literature was further enhanced by Arnold Bax's Harp Quintet, whose varied themes and conciseness may well have been connected to wartime events some three years earlier. Elgar's *Introduction and Allegro* Op. 47 (1905) finds a rich fund of beauty from within the string ensemble in a manner reminiscent of Bach's Brandenburg Concertos. Its variety and contrast belie its simple yet original design that is illuminated by a mastery of idiom and compositional technique. No other twentieth-century work for the medium of quartet and orchestra achieved remotely comparable status, despite representation by Conrad Beck (1929), Virgilio Mortari (1938), Benjamin Lees (1964), Alvin Etler (1968), and Lyell Cresswell (1996). The concerto (1930) by Erwin Schulhoff has the string quartet as soloists against a background of a fifteen-strong wind orchestra. This original if daring experiment in instrumentation may well have been inspired by the scoring of Kurt Weill's Concerto for Violin and Wind orchestra, written some five years earlier.

The string quartet has impinged on the world of song to considerable effect. In *On Wenlock Edge* (1909) Vaughan Williams makes atmospheric and elaborate use of a string quartet accompaniment in addition to the piano. The composer's poetic impulse and audible country imagery illuminates and transcends Housman's epigrammatic texts. Written just after his studies with Ravel, the work includes consecutive triads as well as old-fashioned chromaticism in its harmonic language. More than one commentator has judged that the cycle's total powerful effect is greater than the sum of its parts. The quartet made some further significant forays into the song repertory, for example Finzi's cycle of Hardy settings *By Footpath and Stile* published in 1925. Peter Warlock's *The Curlew* combined flute, cor anglais and string quartet to accompany the tenor voice with original textures and harmonic colours. The young Samuel Barber entertained the notion of pursuing a singing career, having studied at the Curtis Institute and in Vienna. He recorded his own *Dover Beach* (1931) for baritone or mezzo-soprano and string quartet. Though he was still a student when the work was composed, it is remarkably assured, with the long lyric lines and idiomatic text-setting that were to remain a feature of later compositions.

The success of these works, together with other examples by Arthur Bliss and Ivor Gurney in England and Chausson and Jongen in France, tend to disprove the celebrated assertion by Frank Howes that the string quartet, 'contrary to expectation, hardly ever makes a good accompaniment for the human voice'.[19] The very year that those words found their way into print, further contradictory evidence appeared in the backing arrangement for the Beatles' *Eleanor Rigby* (1966), where the idiomatic string writing is à 4, though for eight players. The arranger George Martin credited the influence upon him of Bernard Herrmann's score for the film *Fahrenheit 451*. Against a warp of mechanical and strident chords (played non-vibrato in short, choppy down-bows near the frog and close miked) is woven a series of continuously varied and syncopated melodic counter-figures in the cello or violin. The continued attraction of the medium within pop culture is illustrated by the collaboration between Elvis Costello and the Brodsky Quartet, which dates from 1992. Costello's *The Juliet Letters*, a song sequence for voice and string quartet, gave rise to a highly successful world tour; his current projects include a work for Anne Sophie von Otter and the Brodsky Quartet, entitled *Three Distracted Women*.

Traditional larger combinations of wind instruments and string quartet tended to discourage progressive styles of writing. For example, Schubert's octet medium did not survive changing musical tastes despite some occasional examples by Badings, Ferguson, Françaix, Hindemith and Wellesz. In the arena of the clarinet quintet Brahms' intoxicating cocktail of lyrical and dramatic elements within a closely argued structure eluded many of his successors. Reger's Clarinet Quintet is widely regarded as his crowning achievement, though the wind writing is less idiomatic than Brahms'. Motivic ideas form part of a densely integrated texture, without the overt lyricism of his predecessor. Another original though conservative quintet is by Robert Fuchs, friend of Brahms and teacher of Mahler, Schreker, Schmidt, Sibelius and Zemlinsky. This work inhabits a sound-world related to Brahms and Reger, but distinguished noticeably by his use of the B♭ rather than the more mellow A clarinet. It nicely illustrates Fuchs' lyrical gifts, allied to a strong grasp of harmonic and contrapuntal texture, enabling him to continue the tradition of Brahms without the stylistic innovations wrought by many of his contemporaries. The substantial list of Austro-German clarinet quintets written before 1945 (as well as examples from other parts of Europe and from America) contains few of lasting significance.[20]

Brahms' influence upon English composers was of special significance. After a performance of Brahms' Clarinet Quintet in 1895 at the Royal College of Music, Stanford challenged his composition class to write a similar work. The twenty-year-old Samuel Coleridge-Taylor rose to the occasion with his highly individual and rhythmically complex Quintet Op. 10, which won him wide recognition. Stanford became interested in the revival of the Elizabethan 'fancy' and this rhapsodic form inspired many of his pupils, notably Herbert Howells. Howells' *Rhapsodic Quintet* is one of his finest pieces, though (as Marion Scott observed) it remains difficult to interpret because the characteristic traits of several styles of writing are closely combined. The lyrical yet dramatic potential of the clarinet quintet medium manifestly suited the style of English music. Late in life Stanford was finally tempted to the genre in his two Fantasies of 1921 and 1922, which lay unpublished until relatively recently. Other British composers for clarinet quintet included Somervell, Holbrooke, Scott, Bowen, Wood, Reizenstein and Ruth Gipps. None reached the level of the Quintet by Bliss, a work of striking personality written at a time when he was rediscovering the forms and idioms of established tradition. The heart of the work is its third movement, whose central section has an intensity and idiomatic language comparable with Brahms.

The oboe also proved a particular attraction to the same generation of British composers, for whom Leon Goossens was a special inspiration. Arnold Bax introduced genuine Irish material into his Oboe Quintet of 1922, where, despite his declared dislike for Brahms and Stanford, he contrived to quote from Stanford's 1882 collection *Songs of Old Ireland*. Bliss wrote his Quintet for the 1927 Sprague-Coolidge festival in Venice, where he was pleased to receive the congratulations of Alban Berg. He later wrote, 'It is always a joy to write with a superlative artist in mind, and besides the sound of the oboe with strings is exquisite.'[21] In 1931 Gerald Finzi heard the first performance of Imogen Holst's Oboe Quintet and produced his own *Interlude* (1936), probably also inspired by Bliss. Its sinuous, Baroque sensibility – of chromaticism, agility and virtuosity – shows flexibility if a shortage of thematic material. Rubbra and Howard Ferguson immediately approved, Vaughan Williams observing that it was 'rather different from your style as I know it – but all you all the same'.[22]

The post-war years brought further clarinet quintets from Jacob, Wordsworth, Bush, Frankel, Cooke, Maconchy, Simpson, Hamilton and many others. The fluent French tradition is especially well represented by the Quintet by Jean Françaix. The 1980s alone saw significant contributions from Harrison Birtwistle, Morton Feldman and Isang Yun. Birtwistle's title Clarinet Quintet denotes a decidedly anti-Classical impulse, and a purposeful tension between the title and the music. The work involves short musical statements analogous to postcard messages or diary entries. Birtwistle added links that simultaneously join and separate the main modules. He also cross-related the links both to each other and to the original 'statements'. The outcome of these compositional stages is a work in which the modular and the continuous are indissoluble – a paradox in words, but not in Birtwistle's musical imagination. The clarinet quintet has continued to prove itself a vibrant medium at the hands of such significant figures as Magnus Lindberg (1992), who has written of attempting to imitate the tutti of a full orchestra through the five instruments. His Finnish compatriot Jouni Kaipainen introduced a doubling contrabass clarinet to the ensemble in his polished yet expansive four-movement quintet (2000). Elsewhere, the combination has moved in yet other directions at the hands of Milton Babbitt (1996).

Music with piano

By comparison with the string quartet, chamber music with piano was scarcely developed by the 1770s, lacking four-movement structures, closely-wrought sonata schemes and a great degree of instrumental parity. Whereas the string quartet offered the potential for perfect blend, keyboard ensemble music was altogether more diverse, often involving amateur string players in accompanying roles. From the 1760s larger ensembles might involve three or four accompanying strings in the music of Mannheimers such as Filtz, Holzbauer and Richter, Viennese such as Wagenseil, Vanhal and Monn and immigrants to Paris such as Cambini. Expatriate Germans in Paris included Johann Schobert, an important influence on Mozart and composer of four quartets for harpsichord, two violins and bass. In London around 1770 the Neapolitan Tommaso Giordani produced Six Quintets Op. 1 for the combination which would become the piano quintet; their sharing of material among keyboard and strings is a significant stylistic feature.

Mozart's Quartets in G minor K. 478 and E♭ K. 493 radically advanced the combination of piano and strings in their balance of style, structure and content. The initial resistance which the Hoffmeister edition of the G minor Quartet encountered has been variously attributed to the unfamiliarity of the genre, the depth of expression which greatly exceeded popular taste and the fact that the work proved too difficult technically for amateur purchasers.[23] Mozart's integration of texture had little effect on the next generation of virtuoso pianists, for whom the piano quartet (sometimes expanded to include double bass, as in Schubert's 'Trout' Quintet) was little more than a vehicle for virtuoso display.[24] Boccherini's six Quintets Opp. 56 (1797) and 57 (1799) for piano and string quartet have been cited as an exception to this general rule.[25] Other early Romantic composers for piano quintet included Dussek and Louis Ferdinand, whilst Onslow, Ries, Glinka and Sterndale Bennett all wrote sextets with piano, string quartet and double bass.

As the genre developed, blend and balance were explored in a variety of ways. Themes and accompaniments were often exchangeable between strings and piano, the latter frequently of motivic significance. More homophonic or theatrical styles could involve more extended solo writing and often a larger amount of doubling. The future history of the piano quintet would produce a variety of relationships of style to scoring, since the distribution of themes and their accompaniments and true integration of forces would present the greatest technical challenges to the composer. Among effective types of scoring are those in which themes and accompaniments can be exchanged, immediately or at long range between the different 'sides' of the ensemble, and those in which the accompaniments are of genuine motivic significance. Yet more homophonic, theatrical writing requires more extended solo writing, more antiphonal display and even a larger amount of straightforward doubling. Style, therefore, cannot be judged in isolation, but only in relation to the wider musical style that it serves. There are some important differences in the approaches of Schumann, Brahms and Dvořák, and also between those of Franck and Fauré.

In terms of sheer quality of invention, Schumann's Piano Quintet of 1842 represents a watershed in the history of piano and string quartet collaboration. The organic development of material allows for integration of all the voices, though the piano writing is sometimes athletic and allowed to dominate. Doubling of voices is a much more pervasive feature in Schumann's sonorous textures than short-scale exchanges, with accompaniments largely of a neutral character. Thematic transference between movements is a particular feature of the Quintet, which Smallman attributes to a widespread vogue among chamber composers of the period, for example Spohr in his Piano Quintet in D minor Op. 130 of 1845.[26] Schumann's Quintet enjoyed immediate success, his wife Clara taking part in many early performances.

Schumann established the quintet as a vehicle for Romantic expression, to which his successors brought their own national dialect. For example, Franz Berwald's two poetic and original piano quintets, written in the 1850s, received a mixed critical reception, doubtless partly because of their structural unorthodoxy. Significantly, he echoed eighteenth-century writers in wanting his pianist interpreters to play from the heart and not merely the fingers. Folk elements with modal colouring and note-patterns transferred from one movement to the next are features of Borodin's C minor Quintet of 1862.

Dvořák had already attempted a piano quintet in 1872 and had written a successful Piano Quartet Op. 23 in 1875 when he produced his Quintet Op. 81 of 1887, one of the most original yet accessible works for the medium. It is distinguished by melodic beauty and workmanship, with a new-found appreciation of the piano. Many generations of scholars have expressed admiration for the work, noting the way in which it epitomises the quintessential features of Dvořák's music: melody and countermelody, vital rhythm, varied and colourful scoring, a kaleidoscope of moods ranging from sorrow to gaiety. Among many instances of textural skill is the opening of the 'dumka', where the tune is for the high register of the piano while the strings' countermelody (viola/first violin) is placed low down. The approach to the recapitulation in the first movement gradually grows in intensity and power until the main theme bursts out tutti. As a viola player Dvořák was strongly drawn to the chamber music of his Classical precursors. By the time he reached the piano quintet, his keyboard writing was confident and effective, with a genuine appreciation of the vast range of mood and expression of which the piano is capable. His own viola playing was a considerable advantage in that it helped him to write idiomatically for the strings. It does not, however, explain fully why his chamber works possess an indefinable quality, more apparent to the players than to the listener, which is due largely to their strikingly individual textures.

Brahms' Piano Quintet Op. 34 is a highly important work from early in his life, combining motivic and lyrical impulse. Having begun life as a string quintet with two cellos, it was first recast for two pianos, at Joachim's suggestion. The final version combines elements from both, exploiting an especially resourceful and varied texture drawn from the piano and strings, while confining his keyboard part to the style and pitch-range of the strings, unlike the piano quintets of some of his contemporaries. The first movement has a clear formal outline, with many thematic links and fluid phrasing which mark it out as his most sophisticated sonata structure to date. Immediate and long-range thematic exchange within the ensemble reflects Brahms' motivic approach. Transformations of material are occasionally supplemented by barely disguised cross-references across movements.

In contrast to Brahms' Classical restraint comes César Franck's Romantic rhetoric, adopting freer formal procedures and a highly coloured harmonic palette. His Quintet of 1879 is more overtly theatrical, beginning with dialogue of strings and piano before the exposition proper and proceeding with cyclical and motto connections. Such instrumental contrasts have often been associated with his half-conscious leaning towards organ registration rather than a personal association with strings or piano. Soon there followed a flood of French symphonic chamber music with piano, including quartets and quintets by Chausson, Roger-Ducasse, Fauré, Schmitt, D'Indy, Pierné and Vierne, with emphasis on thematic unification and extreme richness of texture.[27] Chausson's Concerto Op. 21, published in 1892, is scored for the unusual combination of violin, piano and string quartet. Its cyclic form, ambitious modulatory patterns and intensely expressive lyricism betray the overwhelming influence of Franck, while at the same time signalling certain more innovative directions. On the other hand, Fauré's two piano quintets Opp. 89 and 115 pursue a more classically poised and delicate approach to the medium. He often has polyphonic strands in the strings and only occasional melodic input from the piano.

Brahms provided an inspiration to Dohnányi's C minor Quintet Op. 1 (1895) and to early works by Bartók, Berg and Webern. Reger and Pfitzner also brought their own characteristic musical personalities to bear on the medium. In 1914 Dohnányi returned to the piano quintet for his Op. 26, opting for lighter scoring and more restrained keyboard writing. The refinement of each of the three movements is illustrated by their quiet concluding bars. As with the clarinet quintet, piano chamber music in England came under Brahms' influence, for example, Stanford's Quintet Op. 25 of 1886, with its juxtaposition of Irish and German Romantic elements. British composers subsequently contributed substantially to the medium of the piano quartet and quintet, among them Bridge, Bax, Howells, Elgar and Walton. Bax's Quintet in G minor (1915) shows a luxurious Romantic warmth, a rich harmonic palette and a rhapsodical manner. Elgar's late Piano Quintet in A minor is also ambitious in scope, with a quasi-orchestral approach to the medium. By now, chamber music for strings and piano had acquired a somewhat conservative profile, far from major developments such as impressionism, jazz, atonality and serialism. Exceptionally, Koechlin's First Quintet Op. 80 uses a modern dissonant style within a controlled musical structure to portray the experience of war. Bloch's First Quintet

Op. 33 (1923) is eclectic, drawing on a variety of influences, including his own Jewish heritage, expressed partly in quarter-tone language. His sharp contrasts of mood and dynamics emerge from an especially evocative handling of the medium. Bloch returned to the medium in 1957, making use of twelve-note themes for purely melodic purposes, without adhering to any dodecaphonic conventions. During the intervening period, a number of composers with (like Bloch) links in Paris and the USA were attracted by the combination of piano and strings, among them the Americans Copland, Piston and Harris, the Czech Martinů and the Frenchman Milhaud. Martinů's two Quintets of 1933 and 1944 betray his native roots, as well as the influence of his teacher Roussel. His polytonality and leaning towards Baroque models owe something to his contacts with 'Les Six', as do the jazz and blues elements in his music.[28]

Lying outside the mainstream outlined above is the creative use of quartet-based ensembles by Charles Ives during the first dozen years of the twentieth century. These include *Fireman's Parade on Mainstreet* from Op. 70 (string quintet, piano), *Hallowe'en* Op. 71 (string quartet, piano, optional drum), as well as *In Re Con Moto et al* Op. 72, *Largo risoluto no. 1* Op. 74 and *Largo risoluto no. 2* Op. 75 (all piano and string quartet).

Of mixed wind and strings with piano, Prokofiev's *Overture on Hebrew Themes* has the clarinet (like the piano) fulfilling accompanying roles of some intricacy. The work shows a deep and keen sense of the specific beauty and originality of Jewish music. The combination of lyric and grotesque elements, the sparkling wit and the fine detail contribute to the originality of the piece. The same combination recurs in Sextets by Roy Harris and by Copland, the latter's an arrangement of his 'Short Symphony' for the Orquesta Sinfonica de Mexico. Latin America is an important influence throughout, the rhythms of the finale close to the Afro-Cuban danzón and (in the piano part) agitated jazz. The music is a highly sophisticated and yet authentic stylisation of primitive rhythmic and melodic patterns.

The Piano Quintet Op. 57 (1940) by Shostakovich was perhaps the most significant work of this period. At first it divided opinion, drawing sharp criticism from Prokofiev for its innate conservatism, though in fact marking the beginning of a clearer but highly individual musical language. The Quintet's variety of moods ranges from rhetoric to comedy, unified by thematic cross-reference and enriched by colouristic effect. The lightweight finale evokes Classical rather than Romantic influence, perhaps (as Smallman suggests) modelled on Mozart's G minor Quintet. Like the Fifth Symphony, the Quintet is predominantly lyrical, yet profound and philosophical, alternating poetry and zest. The fugue in the second movement has the piano entering quite late in the proceedings, and relates emotional content with intricate structure.[29]

Characteristic of more recent works is Shostakovich's inclusion of separate extended sections for each side of the ensemble and the adoption of lean piano writing. Textural simplicity of great imagination may be found in both the Shostakovich and Schnittke quintets. The latter also illustrates the use of microtones already found in Bloch's earlier Quintet, as well as keyboard effects such as silent touch and creative use of sustaining pedal. Indeed, Schnittke's Piano Quintet must be regarded as one of the most significant recent works in this survey. Begun in 1972, it marks a move away from the techniques and aesthetic of the post-war avant-garde, evolving a simpler musical language away from what Schnittke had come to see as the artificial nature of serial writing. This working through complexity towards musical essentials accounts for some similarities with late Shostakovich, an affinity reinforced by Schnittke's capacity for brooding meditation and anguished yet economically designed lament. His basic musical elements avoid technical virtuosity, although his Quintet needs intensive rehearsal and empathy between the players. Schnittke's third movement opens for strings alone with three short sections of canon in progressive augmentation, recalling the practice used by Ockeghem in his *Missa prolationum*. As Alexander Ivashkin has observed, 'The way in which the final movement sets what happened earlier into a new perspective, and resolves the accumulated intensity, is something audiences can't easily find in everyday life, so they respond to the way in which Schnittke is seeking to communicate with them.'[30] Gidon Kremer adds that the Quintet can be understood intuitively by listeners with no background or previous experience of Schnittke's music, its polystylistic aesthetic allied to deep emotion.

Like the clarinet quintet, the medium of the piano quintet shows every sign of continued good health, on more than one occasion having broken free of the conservatism that has often been its hallmark. The contribution by Elliott Carter (1997) for the occasion of his ninetieth birthday attracted immediate critical acclaim. At least one reviewer has already felt moved to nominate it as the greatest piano quintet of the century, drawing attention to the truly Beethovenian conflict between the percussion instrument that is the piano and the string parts, in which the composer outshines himself in melodic lyricism. Though part of Carter's Indian summer, the Quintet makes for challenging listening. Like Birtwistle, Carter makes concessions neither to his audience nor to his performers. We must be grateful that the quartet-based ensemble within a contemporary context is still capable of engendering such a level of inspiration.

Notes

Preface

1. Yehudi Menuhin, *The Violin* (Paris and New York, 1996), p. 248.
2. In George Stratton and Alan Frank, *The Playing of Chamber Music* (London, 1935), p. 5.

1 The string quartet and society

1. Norman Lebrecht, 'The Chamber Revolution', *Daily Telegraph* (2 May 2001), p. 21.
2. Curiously enough, the modern literature is thin. No broad-based, extended social-economic history of the string quartet has yet been written, arguably because the localised, in-depth histories of concert life, ensembles, recording and broadcasting on which it would have to be built have only recently started to emerge. Books that touch on some of these themes include: Joël-Marie Fauquet, *Les sociétés de musique de chambre à Paris de la Restauration à 1870* (Paris, 1986); Timothy Day, *A Century of Recorded Music: Listening to Musical History* (New Haven and London, 2000); and Jennifer Doctor, *The BBC and Ultra-Modern Music, 1922–1936: Shaping a Nation's Tastes* (Cambridge, 1999). There are also several monographs about particular ensembles, but as yet no over-arching history.
3. I am grateful to Cyril Ehrlich for reading an earlier draft, and for much stimulating discussion.
4. For a history of the quartet genre see Stanley Sadie (ed.), *The New Grove Dictionary of Music and Musicians*, 2nd edn (29 vols., London, 2001), vol. XXIV, pp. 585–95, s.v. 'String Quartet'. The changing social function of chamber music, broadly defined, from its beginning to the present day is traced in *ibid.*, vol. V, pp. 434–48, s.v. 'Chamber Music'.
5. The derivation of the term 'music of friends' is uncertain. The phrase was used by Richard H. Walthew to define the essence of chamber music in one of his published lectures for the South Place Institute, London, in 1909; see his *The Development of Chamber Music* (London and New York, [1909]), p. 42.
6. In a letter to C. F. Zelter, 9 November 1829, reproduced in *Goethes Werke*, Abteilung IV: *Briefe*, vol. XLVI (Weimar, 1908), pp. 139–41.
7. Not all instruments were deemed socially acceptable for domestic use in gentrified circles.

For a broad discussion of the linkages between gender and musical instruments in respectable society see Richard Leppert, *Music and Image: Domesticity, Ideology and Socio-cultural Formation in Eighteenth-century England* (Cambridge, 1988), pp. 107–75. That string quartet playing was strongly associated with the leisure time of men is aptly illustrated by Ian Woodfield in his *Music of the Raj: a Social and Economic History of Music in Late Eighteenth-Century Anglo-Indian Society* (Oxford, 2000), pp. 127–30, 211–18.
8. Instances of women listening can be found in Brian Robins (ed.), *The John Marsh Journals: the Life and Times of a Gentleman Composer (1752–1828)* (Stuyvesant, NY, 1998); see, for example, p. 431.
9. The Mozart letter is quoted in Alec Hyatt King, *Mozart Chamber Music* (London, 1968), p. 31; the English quartet party, of November 1788, is described in Robins (ed.), *John Marsh Journals*, p. 441. There are many other such vignettes in these diaries.
10. Cited in Gerald Seaman, 'Amateur Music-making in Russia', *Music & Letters* 47 (1966), p. 252.
11. The passage can be found in Roger Fiske (ed.), *Michael Kelly: Reminiscences* (London, 1975), p. 122.
12. Jean Mongrédien, *French Music from the Enlightenment to Romanticism, 1789–1830*, Eng. trans. Sylvain Frémaux (Portland, OR, 1996), p. 292. Information on eighteenth-century print-runs and sales is tantalisingly elusive; but for insights into the Viennese publisher Artaria's dissemination of its publications of Mozart's works see Rupert M. Ridgewell, 'Mozart and the Artaria Publishing House: Studies in the Inventory Ledgers, 1784–1793' (diss., University of London, 1999).
13. Sometimes called *quatuors dialogués* or *quatuors concertants et dialogués*. The French repertoire is carefully outlined in Mongrédien, *French Music*, pp. 289–99.
14. Barbara R. Hanning, 'Conversation and Musical Style in the Late Eighteenth-century Parisian Salon', *Eighteenth-century Studies* 22 (1989), pp. 512–28. For an extended discussion of notions of conversation in the eighteenth-century quartet more generally see Mara Parker, *The String Quartet, 1750–1797:*

Four Types of Musical Conversation (Aldershot, 2002).

15. Sometimes called *quatuors d'airs variés*; on this genre see Mongrédien, *French Music*, pp. 297–8.

16. Simon McVeigh, *Concert Life in London from Mozart to Haydn* (Cambridge, 1993), p. 52. See also Woodfield, *Music of the Raj*, pp. 211–18, for an extended discussion of the desirability and practice of hiring a professional leader for an English quartet party.

17. Mary Sue Morrow, *Concert Life in Haydn's Vienna: Aspects of a Developing Musical and Social Institution* (Stuyvesant, NY, 1989), pp. 9–10. Schuppanzigh led the first performances of many of Beethoven's quartets, and was the dedicatee of Schubert's A minor quartet. For further discussion see the article on Schuppanzigh by K. M. Knittel in Sadie (ed.), *The New Grove Dictionary*, 2nd edn, vol. XXII, pp. 818–19.

18. On salons in Vienna see Morrow, *Concert Life*, pp. 1–3, 13–33; on those in Paris see Mongrédien, *French Music*, pp. 235–43 and Richard J. Viano, 'By Invitation Only: Private Concerts in France during the Second Half of the Eighteenth Century', *Recherches sur la musique française classique* 27 (1991–2), pp. 131–62.

19. Many French chamber music societies are well documented in Fauquet, *Les sociétés de musique*. Otto Biba ('Franz Schubert in den musikalischen Abendunterhaltungen der Gesellschaft der Musikfreunde', in Franz Grasberger and Othmar Wessely (eds.), *Schubert-Studien: Festgabe der Österreichischen Akademie der Wissenschaften zum Schubert-Jahr 1978* (Vienna, 1978), pp. 7–31) adds a Viennese perspective to modern coverage, while some documentation of London is in Christina Bashford, 'Public Chamber-Music Concerts in London, 1835–50: Aspects of History, Repertory and Reception' (diss., University of London, 1996). Several other societies can be traced in the articles on specific cities, and their bibliographies, in Sadie (ed.), *The New Grove Dictionary*, 2nd edn.

20. Ella's claim appears in his *Musical Sketches, Abroad and at Home* (London, 1869), p. 206. On adaptations of the concert hall for chamber music see Christina Bashford, 'Learning to Listen: Audiences for Chamber Music in Early-Victorian London', *Journal of Victorian Culture* 4 (1999), pp. 25–51.

21. Standing somewhat apart from the main body of nineteenth-century quartets, and yet similarly linked to technical prowess and performance opportunities, are the sparkling *quatuors brillants* (effectively violin concertos with lower-string accompaniment) that many

French player-composers (Rode, Kreutzer, Baillot) produced in the first three decades of the century. See Mongrédien, *French Music*, pp. 296–7.

22. Ensembles led by Josef Hellmesberger in Vienna, by Jules Armingaud in Paris and by Joseph Dando in London were of this sort.

23. Other packagings included the Musikalische Abendunterhaltungen in Vienna, where a string quartet tended to open proceedings, and a vocal quartet conclude them. In between came instrumental solos and songs: see Biba, 'Franz Schubert', pp. 10–11. In Florence, the Società Sbolci (established 1863) interspersed string quartets and concertante piano works with sung items, much in the manner of London, except that the vocal music was exclusively sacred. Some concert societies, for instance the Florentine Società del Quartetto, the Musical Union in London, and the Quartett Abenden in Berlin, focussed programmes solely on three instrumental ensemble works.

24. In London, programme notes were first supplied for the Musical Union concerts (from 1845), and later for the Quartett Association's concerts, Chappell's Popular Concerts and the South Place Sunday Concerts.

25. Pocket-sized scores of chamber works by Haydn, Mozart and Beethoven were issued by K. F. Heckel of Mannheim in the 1840s and 1850s and distributed widely (see Cecil Hopkinson, 'The Earliest Miniature Scores', *Music Review* 33 (1972), pp. 138–44); in Florence in the 1860s the music publisher Guidi issued small scores of the works being performed in the Società del Quartetto's annual concert series (see Fig. 1.3). The well-known miniature scores published by Eulenburg commenced publication in 1891. Piano-duet transcriptions of the central, Viennese repertoire, issued by such firms as Breitkopf & Härtel, appeared in significant numbers from mid-century; for a broad discussion see Thomas Christensen, 'Four-hand Piano Transcription and Geographies of Nineteenth-century Musical Reception', *Journal of the American Musicological Society* 52 (1999), pp. 255–98.

26. This was particularly the case at the (London) Musical Union; see Christina Bashford, 'John Ella and the Making of the Musical Union', *Music and British Culture, 1785–1914: Essays in Honour of Cyril Ehrlich* (Oxford, 2000), pp. 210–11.

27. Duisberg's concerts are highlighted in the survey of chamber music in Sandra McColl, *Music Criticism in Vienna 1896–1897: Critically Moving Forms* (Oxford, 1996), pp. 53–6. Basic documentation of the South Place initiative is in W. S. Meadmore, *The Story of a Thousand*

Concerts ([London], [1927]) and Frank V. Hawkins, *The Story of Two Thousand Concerts* (London, [1969]) and his *A Hundred Years of Chamber Music* (London, 1987). The extent to which the 'lower orders' penetrated chamber-music concerts awaits serious exploration, on both local and national levels; for an assessment of Samuel Midgley's attempts to establish cheap chamber concerts in Bradford in the early twentieth century see David Russell, 'Provincial Concerts in England, 1865–1914: a Case-Study of Bradford', *Journal of the Royal Musical Association* 114 (1989), pp. 43–55.

28. Mackenzie's views are in Walter Willson Cobbett (ed.), *Cobbett's Cyclopedic Survey of Chamber Music,* 2nd edn (London, 1963), s.v. 'Gramophone and Chamber Music, The'.

29. This repertoire can be traced in Compton Mackenzie's discography in the *Gramophone,* 2/11 (1925), pp. 406–11; the article was part of Mackenzie's serialised listing of chamber music records – 'as complete as I can make it'.

30. For a snapshot of the repertoire at this period see R. D. Darrell (comp.), *The Gramophone Shop Encyclopedia of Recorded Music* (New York City, 1936).

31. The BBC, for example, broadcast chamber-music concerts on the Home Service on Thursday evenings. Many artists and ensembles, including the Busch and Griller quartets, performed in them.

32. In the late 1920s and 1930s the *Gramophone* published much of this material in a series of articles entitled 'Chamber Music and the Gramophone'; more permanent music appreciation literature issued by Percy Scholes (*The First Book of the Gramophone Record* (London, 1924)) included quartets and chamber works. The true enthusiast's bible, however, was *Cobbett's Cyclopedic Survey of Chamber Music.*

33. Available recordings of quartets can be traced in issues of the *Gramophone Long Playing Classical Record Catalogue,* established in 1953. High-quality record reviewing can be found in issues of the *Gramophone* magazine and many other sister titles, as well as the general press; one notable permanent compilation is Edward Sackville-West and Desmond Shawe-Taylor's elegantly written and authoritative *The Record Guide* (London: Collins, 1951; rev. edn 1955). The growth of classical music listening in general is discussed in Day, *Century of Recorded Music,* pp. 58–141.

34. Their careers are explored in Nat Brandt, *Con Brio: Four Russians called the Budapest String Quartet* (New York and Oxford, 1993) and in Daniel Snowman, *The Amadeus Quartet: the Men and the Music* (London, 1981).

35. On all-female quartets before World War I see Marion M. Scott and Katharine E. Eggar,

'Women's Doings in Chamber Music', *Chamber Music* 3 (October 1913), pp. 12–15, and the discussion in Cyril Ehrlich, *The Music Profession in Britain since the Eighteenth Century: a Social History* (Oxford, 1985), pp. 160–1. Women players later emerged in the Quartetto Italiano, Hollywood Quartet, Aeolian Quartet, Allegri Quartet, Endellion Quartet and Kronos Quartet, among others. Late twentieth-century all-female ensembles include the Fairfield Quartet, Sorrel Quartet and Colorado Quartet. On the changing shape of the music profession in the twentieth century see Ehrlich, *ibid.,* pp. 164–232, passim.

36. See Cyril Ehrlich, 'The First Hundred Years', in Julia MacRae (ed.), *Wigmore Hall 1901–2001: a Celebration* (London, 2001), pp. 31–65 for this and other insights about artists, audiences and repertoire.

37. This point is made by Snowman, *The Amadeus Quartet,* p. 49, and by Brandt, *Con Brio,* p. 7.

38. For example, the Kolisch Quartet, back in the 1920s and 1930s, had championed the Second Viennese School, the Hungarian Quartet played many of the Bartók quartets and the Pro Arte took much Martinů, Milhaud and Honegger into its repertoire. The Juilliard Quartet, founded in 1946, made contemporary American works something of a priority, and the Fitzwilliam Quartet, established in 1968, specialised in Shostakovich.

39. For more on Cobbett see the article on him by Frank Howes (revised by Christina Bashford) in Sadie (ed.), *The New Grove Dictionary,* 2nd edn, vol. VI, pp. 70–1.

40. Coolidge is discussed in Brandt, *Con Brio,* pp. 17–18: she also underwrote the Berkshire and Coolidge quartets. Coolidge or her foundation commissioned many chamber works, including quartets (a list of commissioned composers is given in the article on her by Gustave Reese (revised by Cyrilla Barr) in Sadie (ed.), *The New Grove Dictionary,* 2nd edn, vol. VI, pp. 390–1).

41. See Brandt, *Con Brio,* pp. 12–19 for further discussion.

42. For a helpful discussion of canon in the postmodern age see Jim Samson, 'Canon (iii)', in Sadie (ed.), *The New Grove Dictionary,* 2nd edn, vol. V, pp. 6–7.

43. Theodor W. Adorno, 'Chamber Music', *Introduction to the Sociology of Music,* Eng. trans. E. B. Ashton (New York, 1976), pp. 85–103.

2 Developments in instruments, bows and accessories

1. See, for example, Louis Spohr, *Violinschule* (Vienna, [1832]), p. 15.

2. See, for example, John Hawkins, *A General History of the Science and Practice of Music*

(2 vols., London 1776. repr. 1853/R1963), vol. II, p. 688; and Georg Simon Löhlein, *Anweisung zum Violinspielen* (Leipzig and Züllichau, 1774), cited in W. H., A. F. and A. E. Hill, *Antonio Stradivari, His Life and Work (1644–1737)* (London, 1902, 2/1909/R1963), p. 253.
3. Some of the theories and experiments about modifications to stringed instruments are discussed in Antonio Bagatella, *Regole per la costruzione de' violini* (Padua, 1786); 'Noch etwas über den Bau der Geige', *Allgemeine musikalische Zeitung* (24 October, 1804), col. 49; 'Nochmalige Untersuchungen über den Bau der Violin', *Allgemeine musikalische Zeitung* (30 January, 1811), cols. 69–82; and Jacob Augustus Otto, *Ueber den Bau und die Erhaltung der Geige und aller Bogen-Instrumente* (Halle, 1817).
4. For details of the origins and early history of the violin and viola, see Robin Stowell, *The Early Violin and Viola: a Practical Guide* (Cambridge, 2001), pp. 28–34; the origins and early history of the cello are discussed by John Dilworth in Robin Stowell (ed.), *The Cambridge Companion to the Cello* (Cambridge, 1999), pp. 7–14.
5. The 'scraping' of certain instruments, particularly Guarneri violins, evidently became common practice. This process, for which the Mantegazza brothers of Milan were especially notorious, involved reducing the thickness of the table and back with the aim of making the instrument speak more readily.
6. Illustrations of the modified, as compared with the original, neck-setting are common. See, for example, David D. Boyden, *The History of Violin Playing from its Origins to 1761* (Oxford, 1965), Plate 26; Robin Stowell, *Violin Technique and Performance Practice in the Late Eighteenth and Early Nineteenth Centuries* (Cambridge, 1985), Fig. 7, p. 25.
7. The frontispiece of Leopold Mozart's *Versuch einer gründlichen Violinschule* (Augsburg, 1756) offers one eighteenth-century example, while Boyden's *The History of Violin Playing* includes various examples from earlier sources (see especially Plates 8, 9, 10, 11, 14, 20 and 23).
8. The customary position for the violin soundpost nowadays is directly in line with and slightly (*c.* 6–7 mm) *behind* the right-hand (treble side) foot of the bridge.
9. For an interesting comparison of various fittings from early violins and in particular of eight bass-bars extracted from instruments made between 1777 and 1894, see Gerhard Stradner, 'Eine Ausstellung: zur Entwicklung der Geige', in Vera Schwarz (ed.), *Violinspiel und Violinmusik in Geschichte und Gegenwart* (Vienna, 1975), pp. 314–23.

10. According to the Hill brothers, Stradivari's original violin fingerboards had varied in length from 19.05 cm to 21.59 cm. See W. H., A. F. and A. E. Hill, *Antonio Stradivari*, pp. 204–5.
11. Vincenzo Lancetti recorded (1823) that, about 1800, necks of Italian violins were being lengthened 'according to the fashion prevailing in Paris'. See George Hart, *The Violin, its Famous Makers and Imitators* (London, 1875), p. 151.
12. See 'Noch etwas über der Bau der Geige', *Allgemeine musikalische Zeitung* (24 October 1804), col. 50; 'Nochmalige Untersuchungen über den Bau der Violin', *Allgemeine musikalische Zeitung* (30 January 1811), cols. 69–82.
13. A Stradivari violin is listed in Viotti's will amongst his most valuable and prized possessions. See Arthur Pougin, 'Le Testament de Viotti', *Le Ménestrel* 68 (1902), p. 371.
14. 'Alto Viola' and 'Tenor Viola' parts were included in the Walsh edition (1734) of Handel's Concerto Op. 3 no. 1. Furthermore, three viola lines exploiting different registers were common in seventeenth-century French five-part ensembles; this is verified by the naming of the viola parts in Louis XIII's *24 Violons du Roi* as *haute-contre* or *haute-contre taille, taille*, and *quinte* or *cinquiesme*.
15. See John Dilworth, 'Unfinished Journey', *The Strad* 107 (1996), p. 484.
16. Dilworth (*ibid.*, p. 487) confirms that the success of smaller violas made in England, the Netherlands and elsewhere from the early 1700s influenced Italian makers such as Guadagnini, Storioni and Bellosio to produce violas of a length of 40.6 cm or less.
17. Notably Hermann Ritter's championing of Karl Hörlein's *viola alta*. See Robin Stowell, *The Early Violin and Viola: a Practical Guide* (Cambridge, 2001), pp. 177–8.
18. Martin Agricola, *Musica instrumentalis deudsch* (Wittenberg, 1528; 2/1529/R1969, rev. 6/1545), p. x.
19. For measurements of the Stradivari 'Forma B' cello, which is now an accepted standard (although dimensions of the body can still vary considerably), see Stowell (ed.), *The Cambridge Companion to the Cello*, p. 10.
20. An example of an Amati instrument of 1611 in this hybrid form is housed in the Ashmolean Museum, Oxford.
21. Robert Crome mentions a similar device (*c.* 1765).
22. High twist is a term coined by Ephraim Segerman (no such term is found in available primary sources) for a length of gut (treated, twisted and polished intestines of sheep, rams, or wethers) which is given as much twist as possible when wet and subjected to further twisting while it dries or slims. Such a string is more flexible, but weaker than plain gut. Catline

strings (variously called 'Katlyns', 'Cattelins'. 'Catlings' or 'Catlins') were made by twisting together two or more wet high-twist strings in a rope construction. They were thicker but more flexible than plain gut. See Djilda Abbot and Ephraim Segerman, 'Gut Strings', *Early Music* 4 (1976), pp. 430–7. For a contrary view re 'catline' strings, see Stephen Bonta, 'Catline Strings Revisited', *Journal of the American Musical Instrument Society* 14 (1988), pp. 38–60.

23. There were distinct national preferences for stringing in the eighteenth century. See Stowell, *The Early Violin and Viola*, p. 35.

24. In Howard Mayer Brown and Stanley Sadie (eds.), *Performance Practice* (2 vols., London, 1989), vol. II, p. 48.

25. Löhlein (*Anweisung*, p. 9) states that the violin G string was wound with silver. Pierre Baillot (*L'art du violon: nouvelle méthode* (Paris, 1835), p. 247) later cites either brass or silver, and Spohr (*Violinschule*, pp. 12–13) stipulates either plated copper or solid silver wire. Open-wound strings involved the gut core being wound, covered or overspun with tensioned metal (traditionally brass or silver) wire. If the core were visible between the windings, the strings were variously called 'open wound' or 'half-wound' ('half-covered' or 'half-overspun' were further alternatives), but when the winding was applied tightly and close together, 'close wound' was the usual description. See Segerman, 'Strings through the Ages', *The Strad* 99 (1988), p. 52.

26. Alberto Bachmann, *An Encyclopedia of the Violin* (New York, 1925/R1966), p. 150.

27. Segerman ('Strings through the Ages', pp. 195–201) has calculated string diameters and tensions, making reasonable assumptions as necessary from information (or lack of it) provided in a variety of sources from the early seventeenth century to the present.

28. Boyden, *The History*, pp. 321–2.

29. Sébastien de Brossard, 'Fragments d'une méthode de violon' (MS, *c.* 1712, Bibliothèque Nationale, Paris), p. 12.

30. Johann Joachim Quantz, *Versuch einer Anweisung die Flöte traversiere zu spielen* (Berlin, 1752, 3/1789/R1952); Eng. trans. Edward R. Reilly as *On Playing the Flute* (London, 1966), p. 215; Leopold Mozart, *A Treatise*, p. 16. See also Johann Reichardt, *Ueber die Pflichten des Ripien-Violinisten* (Berlin and Leipzig, 1776), p. 86. Of course, thicker strings lay high off the fingerboard and were more difficult to make respond.

31. François-Joseph Fétis, *Antoine Stradivari, luthier célèbre* (Paris, 1856; Eng. trans. John Bishop, London, 1864/R1964), p. 74, and Carl

Guhr, *Ueber Paganinis Kunst die Violine zu spielen* (Mainz, [1829]), p. 5; Spohr, *Violinschule*, p. 13.

32. This appears to have been very much a German trend. See also, for example, 'Anmerkungen über die Violin', *Musikalische Real-Zeitung* (11 October, 1788), col. 106; Bernhard Romberg, *A Complete Theoretical and Practical School for the Violoncello* (London, [1839]), p. 5.

33. Segerman ('Strings through the Ages', p. 198) considers that the most likely unit is the gauge system known as 'grades of millimeters' [sic] commonly employed in the nineteenth century and still used in Pirastro's string gauges (called PM or Pirastro Measure). In this system a mm is divided equally into twenty grades, each grade therefore measuring 0.05 mm.

34. Spohr, *Violinschule*, pp. 8–9.

35. Quantz, *On Playing*, pp. 233–4.

36. See Edward Heron-Allen, *Violin Making as It Was and Is* (London, 1884), p. 194, and Baillot, *L'art*, p. 223.

37. Baillot, *L'art*, p. 16.

38. Reported in the *Revue Musicale* (8, no. 14 (April 6, 1834), pp. 110–11) is a forerunner of the wolf-stop on the cello; described as a brass bracket which was attached to the tailpiece, it served the function of purifying the tone of individual notes, particularly the A and B. See Valerie Walden, *One Hundred Years of Violoncello* (Cambridge, 1998), p. 67.

39. Brown and Sadie (eds.), *Performance Practice*, vol. II, p. 49.

40. The Vega (or 'Bach') bow, promoted by Emil Telmányi in the 1950s to facilitate smooth sustained performances of polyphonic violin music, is not a reproduction of a Baroque model and enjoyed limited success.

41. Carel van Leeuwen Boomkamp and John Henry van der Meer, *The Carel van Leeuwen Boomkamp Collection of Musical Instruments* (Amsterdam, 1971), pp. 57–8.

42. Hawkins, *A General History*, vol. II, p. 782.

43. Boyden, *The History*, p. 209 and Plate 29d.

44. In his 'edition' of Leopold Mozart's violin treatise (1801), Woldemar illustrates one further type, used by Mestrino, which is similar to, though a little longer than, the Cramer model.

45. Fétis, *Antoine Stradivari*, Eng. trans., p. 124.

46. David Boyden, 'The Violin Bow in the Eighteenth Century', *Early Music* 8 (1980), p. 206.

47. Woldemar, *Grande Méthode*, p. 3.

48. François-Joseph Fétis (ed.), *Biographie universelle des musiciens et bibliographie générale de la musique* (Brussels 1835–44, 2/1860–5/R1963), vol. VII, p. 246. Boyden ('The Violin Bow in the Eighteenth Century', p. 210)

verifies that the measurement given conforms to that of Baillot's own Tourte bow preserved in the Library of Congress in Washington.

49. Fétis, *Antoine Stradivari*, Eng. trans., p. 117.
50. Franz Farga, *Violins and Violinists*, Eng. trans. E. Larsen (2nd rev. and enl. edn, London, 1969), p. 92. Jean-Baptiste Vuillaume (1798–1875) later proved that the unstrung stick could normally be expressed mathematically in terms of a logarithmic curve in which the ordinates increase in arithmetical progression while the abscissae increase in geometrical progression. See Fétis, *Antoine Stradivari*, Eng. trans., p. 124.
51. Spohr, *Violinschule*, p. 18.
52. Joseph Roda, *Bows for Musical Instruments of the Violin Family* (Chicago, 1959), p. 65.
53. Leopold Mozart, *A Treatise*, p. 97.
54. Michel Woldemar, *Méthode de violon par L. Mozart rédigée par Woldemar* (Paris, 1801), p. 5.
55. A review in *Les tablettes de Polymnie* (April, 1810, pp. 3–4) of the Paris Conservatoire Concerts highlights one particular attempt at achieving some uniformity in the bows employed.
56. Spohr, *Violinschule*, p. 17.
57. Roda, *Bows*, p. 53.
58. See Roger Millant, *J. B. Vuillaume: sa vie et son œuvre*, Eng. trans. (London, 1972), p. 108; Mark Reindorf, 'Authentic Authorship', *The Strad* 101 (1990), p. 548.
59. Octagonal sticks were largely favoured by Tourte.
60. Charles Beare (in Sadie (ed.), *New Grove Dictionary* 2nd edn, vol. VII, 417–18, s.v. 'John (Kew) Dodd') suggests that the improvements in bow construction implemented in France before 1800 came to England much later, perhaps only after 1815.
61. Charles Beare, in *ibid.*
62. For details of other attempts at 'improvement', some apparently quite ludicrous, see Heron-Allen, *Violin Making*, pp. 104–21; Jane Dorner, 'Fiddlers' Fancy', *The Strad* 94 (1983), pp. 180–5, 243–6.
63. See Chapter 6.
64. In Richard Dawes (ed.), *The Violin Book* (London, 1999), p. 61.
65. Current details of the Violin Octet and principal references to earlier work are provided in Carleen Hutchins, 'A 30-year Experiment in the Acoustical and Musical Development of Violin Family Instruments', *Journal of the Acoustical Society of America* 92 (1992), pp. 639–50.
66. See Hanno Graesser and Andy Holliman, *Electric Violins* (Frankfurt am Main, 1999) for an overview of modern developments in the violin family and details of methods and techniques for tuning, amplification, equalisation and special effects.

3 From chamber to concert hall
1. The significance of the Czech Quartet is discussed in Chapter 4.
2. See Chapter 2.
3. See Chapter 2.
4. See Chapter 4.
5. See Chapter 1.
6. See Chapter 13.
7. See also John W. Wagner, 'James Hewitt, 1770–1827', *Musical Quarterly* 58 (1972), pp. 259–76.

4 The concert explosion and the age of recording
1. See Daniel Snowman, *The Amadeus Quartet: the Men and the Music* (London, 1981); Suzanne Rozsa-Lovett, *The Amadeus: Forty Years in Pictures and Words* (London, 1988); and M. Nissel, *Married to the Amadeus* (London, 1998).
2. In Cobbett (ed.), *Cobbett's Cyclopedic Survey*, vol. I, p. 302.
3. David Blum, *The Art of Quartet Playing* (London, 1986).
4. This beautifully balanced group is featured in David Round, *The Four and the One: in Praise of String Quartets* (Lost Coast, 1999).

5 Playing quartets: a view from the inside
Throughout this chapter, the quartet members are referred to as 'he'. This has been done purely for the sake of convenience.
1. Letter of 15 October 1841, in Paul and Carl Mendelssohn Bartholdy (eds.), *F. Mendelssohn: Briefe aus den Jahren 1833 bis 1847* (Leipzig, 1863; Eng. trans. 1863), pp. 276–7.
2. See the section on blend, pp. 107–9.
3. Furthermore, as I have in mind quartets which exist over many years and are constantly rehearsing and performing, I shall think of their interpretations not as static, but as evolving with time and experience so that any performance, however convincing for the moment, is in retrospect only work in progress.
4. See pp. 121–3 for possible ways forward in cases where insoluble disagreement does occur.
5. This highlights again the vagueness of words in comparison to music.
6. Examples of this may be found in the ensuing discussion of specific aspects of quartet playing.
7. It is often, but not always, the highest voice, which may or may not be scored for the first violin.
8. There are, exceptionally, cases where the primary voice is not even played at the highest dynamic within the group e.g. the finale of Bartók's Sixth Quartet, b. 63; or the second

movement of Berg's *Lyric Suite*, bb. 66–8, where the *Hauptstimme* is explicitly marked at a lower dynamic than the cello. Sometimes a muted, still, highly characterised voice can gain the attention through a surrounding cacophony.

9. Of course, a quartet's range of possibilities of sonority depends to some extent on the compatibility of the instruments and bows the players choose, and even the type of strings they use.

10. The pressure throughout recent history to raise pitch to gain brilliance and clarity is making instruments shrill, putting them under too much pressure and sacrificing their mellower tones, as well as straining the voices of singers who have to collaborate with instrumentalists.

11. Letter of 24 October 1777, in Hans Mersmann (ed.), *Letters of Wolfgang Amadeus Mozart* (New York, 1972), pp. 38–42.

12. At times, the opposite happens as an over-reaction; rests, in particular, are easily clipped.

13. As an experiment, it is interesting for a quartet to listen to the slow beats of a metronome and then turn off the metronome and mentally count ten beats and clap the eleventh without looking at each other. It is rarely absolutely together.

14. The same is equally true of the rehearsal or training of an actor or a sportsman, as opposed to the description of their activities.

15. Some players find also that at the early stages of learning a piece it is better to experiment, and to allow things to remain fluid, listening and noticing, before fixing and defining too much.

16. The compatibility of a quartet's members has to extend not only to rehearsing and performing, but also to practical matters such as how to choose repertoire and plan programmes and itineraries, cope with publicity, accommodate the individuals' non-quartet engagements and commitments, look after their joint financial interests, and so on. In economic terms, quartet-players are self-employed business partners and need to be able to handle this very unmusical side of things.

17. So if Joachim chose his local partners well, his *ad hoc* quartets may well have given excellent performances.

6 Historical awareness in quartet performance

1. Two books are indispensable for general reference on matters of performance: Robin Stowell, *Violin Technique and Performance Practice in the Late Eighteenth and Early Nineteenth Centuries* (Cambridge, 1985), which is particularly useful for its inclusion of English translations of French, German and Italian texts; and Clive Brown, *Classical and Romantic Performing Practice 1750–1900* (Oxford, 1999).

2. See Chapter 2.

3. *Karl von Dittersdorfs Lebensbeschreibung, seinem Sohne in die Feder diktiert* (Leipzig, 1801); Eng. trans. A. D. Coleridge (1896/R1970), p. 90.

4. James Webster, 'The Bass Part in Haydn's Early Quartets', *The Musical Quarterly* 63 (1977), pp. 390–424.

5. Reginald Barrett-Ayres, *Joseph Haydn and the String Quartet* (London, 1974), p. 20.

6. Louis Spohr, *Selbstbiographie* (2 vols., Kassel and Göttingen, 1860–1; Eng. trans. 1865/R1969), vol. I, p. 281.

7. Pierre Baillot, *L'art du violon: nouvelle méthode* (Paris, 1835), p. 5.

8. Michel Woldemar, *Grande Méthode ou Etude Elémentaire pour le violon* (Paris, 1800), p. 3.

9. Baillot, *L'art*, p. 77.

10. Leopold Mozart, *Versuch einer gründlichen Violinschule* (Augsburg, 1756); Eng. trans. Editha Knocker as *A Treatise on the Fundamental Principles of Violin Playing* (London, 1948, 2/1951), pp. 100–1.

11. Francesco Galeazzi, *Elementi teorico-pratici di musica* (2 vols., Rome, 1791, 1796), vol. I, pp. 122–9; in Stowell, *Violin Technique*, pp. 117–25.

12. Baillot, *L'art*, pp. 146–9.

13. Carl Flesch, *The Memoirs of Carl Flesch*; Eng. trans. Hans Keller (London, 1957), p. 87.

14. Joseph Joachim and Andreas Moser, *Violinschule* (3 vols., Berlin 1902–5); Eng. trans. A. Moffat (London, 1905), vol. III, p. 9; Carl Flesch, *Die Kunst des Violinspiels* (2 vols., Berlin 1923–8); Eng. trans. Frederick H. Martens as *The Art of Violin Playing* (New York, 1924–9), vol. I, pp. 30–5.

15. Johann Wolfgang von Goethe, letter to Carl Friedrich Zelter, 9 November 1829, *Sämtliche Werke*, vol. XX.3, p. 1275 ('man hört vier vernünftige Leute sich untereinander unterhalten'); Baillot, *L'art*, pp. 268–9 ('le dialogue charmant semble être une conversation d'amis'); L. A. C. Bombet, trans. William Gardiner, *The Life of Haydn*, in Christopher Hogwood, *Haydn's Visits to England* (London, 1980), pp. 63–4 ('the conversation of four agreeable persons').

16. L. Mozart, *A Treatise*, p. 97; Wolfgang Mozart, letter to his father of 22 November 1777, re the violinist Ignaz Fränzl: 'er hat auch einen sehr schönen runden Thon; er fählt [sic] keine Note, man hört alles'. *Die Briefe W. A. Mozarts* (Georg Müller, 1914), vol. I, ed. Ludwig Schiedermair, p. 122.

17. See, for example, Daniel Gottlob Türk, *Klavierschule oder Anweisung zum Klavierspielen*

(Leipzig and Halle, 1789; enlarged
2/1802/R1967); Eng. trans. Raymond Haggh as
School of Clavier Playing (Lincoln, NE, 1982),
pp. 91 and 325–6, and Johann Schulz in Johann
Sulzer, *Allgemeine Theorie der schönen Künste*
(Leipzig, 1771–4), s.v. 'Takt', pp. 1130–8. The
subject is treated at length in Donald Trott,
'Accentuation in the Late Eighteenth Century'
(DMA diss., University of Oklahoma, 1984).
18. Jérôme-Joseph de Momigny, *La seule vraie
théorie de la musique* (Paris, 1821), pp. 111 and
112–13.
19. Hugo Riemann, 'Der Ausdruck in der
Musik', *Sammlung musikalischer Vorträge*, vol. I,
no. 50 (Leipzig, 1883), p. 47.
20. Richard Wagner, *Über das Dirigieren*
(Leipzig, 1869); Eng. trans. Edward Dannreuther
as *On Conducting* (London, 1887/R1976), p. 32.
Joachim and Moser, *Violinschule*, Eng. trans.
Alfred Moffat, vol. III, pp. 13 and 16.
21. L. Mozart, *A Treatise*, Preface, p. 7.
22. Brown, *Classical and Romantic Performing
Practice*, p. 268.
23. Charles Rosen, *The Classical Style* (London
and New York, 1971), p. 27.
24. Jean-Philippe Rameau, *Génération
Harmonique* (Paris, 1737), p. 104.
25. Momigny, *La seule vraie théorie*, p. 124;
Louis Spohr, *Violinschule* (Vienna, [1832]),
Preface for parents and teachers, p. 3, footnote
explaining 'absolute purity of intonation'.
26. In Patrizio Barbieri, 'Violin Intonation: a
Historical Survey', *Early Music* 19 (1991), p. 74
and n. 36 and 70.
27. *Ibid.*, p. 71 and n. 14. Demonstrated by the
French physicist Jacques-Alexandre Charles at
the Paris Conservatoire.
28. Anton Bemetzrieder, in Barbieri, 'Violin
Intonation', p. 82 and n. 50 ('the B of the second
string of the violin, which is tuned to the E of the
first string does not please the sensitive and
skilled ear in the chord of the sixth, which it
makes with the open D string'); Joachim and
Moser, *Violinschule*, Eng. trans. Moffat, vol. II,
pp. 17a, 18.
29. Flesch, *The Art of Violin Playing*, vol. I,
p. 22.
30. Bemetzrieder, in Barbieri, 'Violin
Intonation', p. 82 and n. 50; Bernhard Romberg,
Méthode de violoncelle (Paris, 1840), pp. 20, 127,
in Barbieri, 'Violin Intonation', p. 84 and n. 57.
31. Johann Joachim Quantz, *Versuch einer
Anweisung die Flöte traversiere zu spielen* (Berlin,
1752; 3rd edn, 1789/R1952); Eng. trans. Edward
R. Reilly as *On Playing the Flute* (London and
New York, 1966), Chapter XVI, § 7.
32. In Barbieri, 'Violin Intonation', p. 74, and
n. 27.

33. L. Mozart, *A Treatise*, p. 70; Francesco
Geminiani, *The Art of Playing on the Violin*
(London, 1751), p. 4 and Essempio II. 'The
Position of the Fingers marked in the first Scale
(which is that commonly practised) is a faulty
one; for two Notes cannot be stopped
successively by the same Finger without
Difficulty, especially in quick Time.'
34. Martin Agricola, *Musica instrumentalis
deudsch* (Wittenberg, 1545), fol. 42 v: sig. F2
('Auch schafft man mit dem zittern frey');
Leopold Auer, *Violin Playing as I Teach It* (New
York, 1921), p. 49.
35. Flesch, *The Art of Violin Playing*, vol. I,
pp. 35–40.
36. William C. Honeyman, *The Violin: How to
Master It* (55th edn, Newport, Fife, 1935),
pp. 78–9.
37. Flesch, *The Art of Violin Playing*, vol. I, p. 40.
38. Yehudi Menuhin, *Unfinished Journey*
(London, 1977), pp. 314–15.
39. Eric Coates, *Suite in Four Movements*
(London, 1953), p. 47.
40. Flesch, *The Memoirs*, p. 50.
41. Flesch, *Die Kunst des Violinspiels*, 2nd edn
(Berlin, 1929), vol. I, pp. 3 and 4.
42. Liza Honeyman, in William C. Honeyman,
The Violin: How to Master It, p. 106.
43. *Karl von Dittersdorfs Lebensbeschreibung*,
Eng. trans. pp. 54, 51–2.
44. Gustave Vallat, *Etudes d'histoire, de mœurs et
d'art musical: Alexandre Boucher et son temps*
(Paris, 1890), pp. 121, 122.
45. W. J. von Wasielewski, *Aus siebzig Jahren –
Lebenserinnerungen* (Leipzig, 1897), pp. 78–9.
Ten years later, during a performance of
Beethoven's Violin Concerto, Joachim dealt with
a broken E string in similar manner and, in
tropical heat, played the Bach Chaconne as an
encore (*ibid.*, pp. 80–2).
46. Flesch, *The Art of Violin Playing*, vol. I, p. 11.
47. Flesch, *Die Kunst des Violinspiels*, 2nd edn
(Berlin, 1929), vol. I, pp. 63–4.
48. Liza Honeyman, in William C. Honeyman,
The Violin: How to Master It, p. 106.
49. Türk, *Clavierschule*, ch. 1, para. 75.
50. Op. 18 no. 6/iv – Allegretto quasi Allegro:
dotted crotchet = 88
Op. 59 no. 2/iii – Allegretto: dotted minim = 69
51. Joseph Kerman, *The Beethoven Quartets*
(New York, 1967), p. 72.
52. H. Bertram Cox and C. L. E. Cox, *Leaves
from the Journals of Sir George Smart* (London,
1907), p. 114.
53. Brian Schlotel, 'Schumann and the
Metronome', in Alan Walker (ed.), *Robert
Schumann: the Man and his Music* (London,
1972), p. 116, n. 3.

54. Sandra Rosenblum, 'Two Sets of Unexplored Metronome Marks for Beethoven's Piano Sonatas', *Early Music* 16 (1988), p. 58.

55. William Malloch, 'Carl Czerny's Metronome Marks for Haydn and Mozart Symphonies', *Early Music* 16 (1988), p. 72.

56. *Ibid.*, p. 62.

57. Joachim and Moser, *Violinschule*, Eng. trans., vol. III, p. 10.

58. *30 berühmte Quartette* (edn Peters, 1918), Vorwort.

59. Joachim and Moser, *Violinschule*, Eng. trans., vol. I, p. 144, § 2, 'Of Grace-Notes and other Embellishments'.

60. Spohr, *Selbstbiographie*, Eng. trans., vol. II, p. 69.

61. Vallat, *Etudes d'histoire*, p. 159.

62. J. G. Prod'Homme, 'The Baron de Trémont: Souvenirs of Beethoven and Other Contemporaries', *The Musical Quarterly* 6 (1920), pp. 366–91.

63. Spohr, *Violinschule*, p. 246.

64. Dedication of *Sei Quartetti Opera X* (Artaria).

65. Baillot, *L'art*, pp. 156–62.

66. Spohr, *Selbstbiographie*, Eng. trans., vol. I, p. 31.

67. Jacob Augustus Otto, *A Treatise on the Structure and Preservation of the Violin and All Other Bow-instruments*, 2nd edn; Eng. trans. John Bishop (London, 1860), pp. 22–3, note.

68. Cox and Cox, *Leaves*, pp. 108–10.

69. See A. Ehrlich, *Das Streich-quartett in Wort und Bild* (Leipzig, 1898).

7 Extending the technical and expressive frontiers

1. See Ken Smith, 'Spicing up the Harmonies', *The Strad* 108 (1997), p. 27.

2. In his *Per la musica moderna e contemporanea* (Milan, 1977) Paolo Borciani makes a bold and laudable attempt 'to bring a modicum of order into a field where' he admits, 'anarchy reigns supreme' (Preface, p. V). See also Howard Risatti, *New Music Vocabulary: A Guide to Notational Signs for Contemporary Music* (Urbana, University of Illinois, 1975); Gardner Read, *Music Notation* (2nd edn, Boston, 1969).

3. In Sadie (ed.), *New Grove Dictionary*, 2nd edn, vol. VIII, p. 651, s.v. 'Feldman, Morton'.

4. H. Wiley Hitchcock, *Ives: a Survey of the Music* (Brooklyn, 1977), p. 62.

5. In James McCalla, *Twentieth-century Chamber Music* (New York, 1996), p. 203.

6. Elliott Carter, String Quartet No. 2, Prefatory Note.

7. Carter, String Quartet No. 4, Prefatory Note.

8. Supplement to the score published by Chester.

9. Ligeti, String Quartet No. 2 (Mainz, Schott, 1971), p. 18.

10. Alfred Schnittke, String Quartet (1965/66), Preface.

11. Carter, String Quartet No. 2, Prefatory Note.

12. Ferneyhough himself speaks of 'dense webs of organisation . . . becoming deliberately absorbed into a flickering interplay of surface gestures'.

13. Ives required each instrument to play alternately in a different rhythm much like a mensuration canon of the late fourteenth century.

14. See Else Stone and Curt Stone (eds.), *The Writings of Elliott Carter* (Bloomington, IN, 1977), pp. 274–9.

15. See 'Extra-musical Influences', pp. 169–71, and 'Music Theatre', pp. 171–2.

16. Performance notes as preface to the score, Edition Peters no. 7118.

17. Berio (*Sincronie*) also introduces symbols for various bowing considerations involving the contact-point of the bow on the string. See 'Variable Contact-point', pp. 165–6.

18. Carter, String Quartet No. 2, Prefatory Note.

19. In Sadie (ed.), *The New Grove Dictionary*, 2nd edn, vol. X, p. 631, s.v. 'Habá, Alois'.

20. *Ibid.*

21. Patricia and Allen Strange, *The Contemporary Violin: Extended Performance Techniques* (Berkeley, Los Angeles and London, 2001), p. 163.

22. Alvin Lucier, *Navigations* (Frankfurt, 1991), in Strange and Strange, *Contemporary Violin*, p. 164.

23. Ferneyhough (*Sonatas*) is one of a few composers to make a distinction.

24. Lucien Capet (*La Technique Supérieure de l'archet* (Paris, 1927)) wrote: 'the omission of the left-hand vibrato (at certain moments in the musical life of a work) is a means of discovering the abstract and inexpressible beauty of universal august art'. Quoted in Werner Hauck, Eng. trans. Kitty Rokos as *Vibrato on the Violin* (London, 1975), p. 22.

25. Carter, String Quartet No. 5, Prefatory Note.

26. Carter, String Quartet No. 2, Prefatory Note.

27. Ruth Crawford Seeger, Quartet No. 3, score.

28. This effect is discussed in detail in J. C. Schelleng, 'The Physics of the Bowed String', *Scientific American* 87 (1974), pp. 87–95.

29. The LaSalle Quartet, who premiered the work, failed to make this effect convincing.

30. See George Perle, 'The Secret Programme of the Lyric Suite', *Musical Times* 118 (1977), pp. 629–32, 709–13, 809.

31. A numerology underlying the entire work is reflected in the chanted numbers and in the work's arch structure, with its emphasis on 1, 7

and 13. The numerology revolves largely around the numbers 7 and 13, in various guises: sections may last 7 or 13 seconds, they may be 7 or 13 bars long, they may contain 7 or 13 notes, etc.

32. Stanley Sadie and H. Wiley Hitchcock (eds.), *The New Grove Dictionary of American Music* (4 vols., London, 1986), vol. I, s.v. 'Carter, Elliott'.

33. In Cobbett (ed.), *Cobbett's Cyclopedic Survey of Chamber Music* (2 vols., London, 1929–30; rev. 2/1963 (3 vols.) by C. Mason), vol. III, p. 182.

34. Paul Griffiths, *The String Quartet: a History* (London, 1983), p. 195.

35. In Dominic Gill (ed.), *The Book of the Violin* (Oxford, 1984), p. 151.

36. In the helicopters, each player can only hear himself through headphones; the players cannot hear each other.

8 The origins of the quartet

1. Georg August Griesinger, *Biographische Notizen über Joseph Haydn* (Leipzig, 1810). Modern translation by V. Gotwals, *Haydn: Two Contemporary Portraits* (Madison, 1968), p. 13.

2. See David Watkin, 'Corelli's Op. 5 Sonatas: "Violino e violone o cimbalo"?', *Early Music* 24 (1996), pp. 645–63.

3. Edward J. Dent, 'The Earliest String Quartets', *Monthly Musical Record* 33 (1903), pp. 202–4.

4. Charles Avison, *An Essay on Musical Expression* (2nd edn, London, 1753), pp. 141–2.

5. Eugene Wolf draws attention to this repertoire in *The Symphony 1720–1840*, Series A, vol. I, *Antecedents of the Symphony* (New York, 1983), pp. xv–xxix.

6. Wilhelm Fischer (ed.), *Denkmäler der Tonkunst in Österreich*, vol. XXXIX, *Wiener Instrumentalmusik vor und um 1750* (Vienna, 1912).

7. For a discussion of this broad repertoire see James Webster, 'Towards a History of Viennese Chamber Music in the Early Classical Period', *Journal of the American Musicological Society* 27 (1974), pp. 212–47.

8. U. Lehmann (ed.), *Das Erbe Deutscher Musik*, vol. XXIV, *Ignaz Holzbauer (1711–1783). Instrumentale Kammermusik* (Kassel, 1953).

9. An edition prepared from the five manuscript sources is given in *Musica Antiqua Bohemica*, vol. LXXI (Prague, 1969).

10. *Karl von Dittersdorfs Lebensbeschreibung* (Leipzig, 1801), Eng. trans. A. D. Coleridge (London, 1897), p. 90.

9 Haydn, Mozart and their contemporaries

1. For example, Mark Evan Bonds notes that many critics of the time were at least as inclined to stress the equality and interweaving of voices in the symphony as in the quartet. See 'The Symphony as Pindaric Ode', in Elaine Sisman (ed.), *Haydn and his World* (Princeton, 1997), pp. 144–6.

2. See Elaine Sisman, 'Learned Style and the Rhetoric of the Sublime in the "Jupiter" Symphony', in Stanley Sadie (ed.), *Wolfgang Amadè Mozart: Essays on his Life and Music* (Oxford, 1996), pp. 218–21.

3. Hans Keller, *The Great Haydn Quartets: Their Interpretation* (London, 1986), p. 6.

4. Leonard Ratner, for instance, writes of 'the imaginative distribution of important melodic material'. *Classic Music: Expression, Form, and Style* (New York, 1980), p. 126.

5. See Ludwig Finscher, *Studien zur Geschichte des Streichquartetts, I: Die Entstehung des klassischen Streichquartetts. Von den Vorformen zur Grundlegung durch Joseph Haydn* (Kassel, 1974), p. 285, and Paul Griffiths, *The String Quartet: A History* (London, 1983), p. 22.

6. A fine recent discussion of all issues connected with 'conversation' may be found in Hans-Joachim Bracht, 'Überlegungen zum Quartett-"Gespräch"', *Archiv für Musikwissenschaft* 51/3 (1994), pp. 169–89. For more on French associations with the concept, see Barbara R. Hanning, 'Conversation and Musical Style in the Late Eighteenth-century Parisian Salon', *Eighteenth-Century Studies* 22/4 (1989), pp. 512–28.

7. Of course, the cultural implications of the term are inappropriate; apart from anything else, North Germany was one of the few parts of Europe where quartet writing was hardly cultivated at the time. However, the label is a useful shorthand way of referring to an important possibility of quartet style.

8. For instance, Johann Ferdinand Ritter von Schönfeld noted in a musical almanac of 1796 that Haydn's quartets were 'full of bewitching harmonies'. *Jahrbuch der Tonkunst von Wien und Prag 1796*, in Sisman, *Haydn and his World*, p. 299.

9. Mary Hunter, 'Haydn's London Piano Trios and his Salomon String Quartets: Private vs. Public?', in Sisman, *Haydn and his World*, pp. 103–30, especially pp. 105–9.

10. Joseph Kerman makes a similar association with Fried in 'Beethoven Quartet Audiences: Actual, Potential, Ideal', in Robert Winter and Robert Martin (eds.), *The Beethoven Quartet Companion* (Berkeley and Los Angeles, 1994), p. 26.

11. See Warren Kirkendale, *Fugue and Fugato in Rococo and Classical Chamber Music*, revised and expanded 2nd edn, trans. Margaret Bent and the author (Durham, NC, 1979), p. 76. Several of the fugal finales of Ordoñez also end, exceptionally, with *perdendosi* markings. This is the case with Op. 1 no. 1 in A major, and Kirkendale draws

attention to the 'calando e sempre più piano' that is found at the end of the fugue in the Quartet E♭1; *Fugue and Fugato*, p. 76.

12. William Drabkin, *A Reader's Guide to Haydn's Early String Quartets* (Westport, CT, 2000), p. 11.

13. This is also noted by Philip G. Downs in *Classical Music: The Era of Haydn, Mozart and Beethoven* (New York, 1992), p. 149.

14. Giorgio Pestelli, *The Age of Mozart and Beethoven* (Cambridge, 1984), p. 134. Pestelli's phrase, it should be noted, refers to the polythematic construction of Boccherini's discourse.

15. Cited in Christian Speck, *Boccherinis Streichquartette: Studien zur Kompositionsgeschichte und zur gattungsgeschichtlichen Stellung* (Munich, 1987), p. 191 (my translation).

16. With Gassmann such canons are often first encountered in the dominant area of a movement. Nicole Schwindt-Gross points out that this was a common device of the time. See *Drama und Diskurs: Zur Beziehung zwischen Satztechnik und motivischem Prozeß am Beispiel der durchbrochenen Arbeit in den Streichquartetten Mozarts und Haydns* (Laaber, 1989), p. 44.

17. See Mara Parker, 'Friedrich Wilhelm II and the Classical String Quartet', *The Music Review* 54/3–4 (1993), pp. 161–82.

18. Dexter Edge points out that there were in fact several public playings of quartets in Vienna, although two of these were promotional concerts organised by the publisher Torricella in conjunction with the publication of sets by Hoffmeister and Pleyel. Edge, review of *Concert Life in Haydn's Vienna: Aspects of a Developing Musical and Social Institution* by Mary Sue Morrow, *Haydn Yearbook* 17 (1992), p. 130.

19. See Horst Walter, 'Haydn gewidmete Streichquartette', in Georg Feder, Heinrich Hüschen and Ulrich Tank (eds.), *Joseph Haydn: Tradition und Rezeption. Bericht über die Jahrestagung der Gesellschaft für Musikforschung, Köln 1982* (Regensburg, 1985), pp. 17–53.

20. See Philippe Oboussier, 'The French String Quartet, 1770–1800', in Malcolm Boyd (ed.), *Music and the French Revolution* (Cambridge, 1992), p. 74. This included of course arrangements, of which one type, the *quatuor d'airs variés*, even achieved its own identity in its working of popular theatrical tunes of the day.

21. Kofi Agawu, 'Prospects for a Theory-Based Analysis of the Instrumental Music', in Sadie (ed.), *Wolfgang Amadè Mozart*, p. 129.

22. Griffiths, *The String Quartet*, p. 57.

23. Julian Rushton, *Classical Music: A Concise History from Gluck to Beethoven* (London, 1986), p. 108.

24. For an account of Hoffmeister's structure see Hartmut Krones, 'Beobachtungen zur Sonatensatzform im Streichquartettschaffen einiger Zeitgenossen Joseph Haydns', *Haydn-Studien* 7/3–4 (1998), pp. 339–40.

25. Cited by Roger Hickman in the Preface to his edition of Kozeluch String Quartets, *Recent Researches in the Music of the Classical Era*, XLII, (Madison, 1994), p. vii.

26. Some or all of these may have been written by 1777, before the composer moved to Sweden to work in the service of Gustav III.

27. Cited in Speck, *Boccherinis Streichquartette*, p. 187.

28. See for example Drabkin, *Haydn's Early String Quartets*, p. 2, and James Webster, *Haydn's 'Farewell' Symphony and the Idea of Classical Style* (Cambridge, 1991), pp. 341–7.

29. See W. Dean Sutcliffe, *Haydn: String Quartets Op. 50* (Cambridge, 1992), for example pp. 71–2 and 94–5.

30. See Christian Esch, 'Haydns Streichquartett Op. 54/1 und Mozarts KV 465', *Haydn-Studien* 6/2 (1988), pp. 148–55.

31. See Wilhelm Seidel, 'Haydns Streichquartett in B-Dur Op. 71 Nr. 1 (Hob. III: 69): Analytische Bemerkungen aus der Sicht Heinrich Christoph Kochs', in Feder, Hüschen and Tank (eds.), *Joseph Haydn: Tradition und Rezeption*, pp. 3–13.

32. Cited in Horst Walter, 'Haydn gewidmete Streichquartette', in Feder, Hüschen and Tank (eds.), *Joseph Haydn: Tradition und Rezeption*, p. 25 (my translation).

33. See Rohan Stewart-MacDonald, 'Towards a New Ontology of Musical Classicism: Sensationalism, Archaism and Formal Grammar in the Music of Clementi, Hummel and Dussek, and Parallels with Haydn, Beethoven and Schubert' (diss., University of Cambridge, 2001), pp. 174–7.

10 Beethoven and the Viennese legacy

1. Alexander Weinmann, *Johann Traeg: Die Musikalienverzeichnisse von 1799 und 1804* (Beiträge zur Geschichte des alt-wiener Musikverlages, II/17) (Vienna, 1973), pp. 69–70.

2. See J. Yudkin, 'Beethoven's "Mozart" Quartet', *Journal of the American Musicological Society* 45 (1992), pp. 30–74.

3. It has provoked a variety of interpretations. See Lewis Lockwood, 'A Problem of Form: The "Scherzo" of Beethoven's String Quartet in F major, Op. 59, no. 1', *Beethoven Forum* 2 (1993), pp. 85–95; and the following response, Jonathan Del Mar, 'A Problem Resolved? The Form of the Scherzo of Beethoven's String Quartet in F: Op. 59, no. 1', *Beethoven Forum* 8 (2000), pp. 165–72.

4. James Webster, 'Traditional Elements in Beethoven's Middle-Period String Quartets' in

Robert Winter and B. Carr (eds.), *Beethoven, Performers, and Critics* (Detroit, 1980), pp. 94–133.

5. Translation from W. Senner, R. Wallace and W. Meredith (eds.), *The Critical Reception of Beethoven's Compositions by His German Contemporaries* (Lincoln, NE and London, 2001), vol. II, p. 53.

6. Letter (original lost), October 1816; Emily Anderson (ed. and trans.), *The Letters of Beethoven* (London, 1961), vol. II, p. 606.

7. Joseph Kerman, *The Beethoven Quartets* (London, 1967), p. 175. Kerman's comment relates to the beginning of the second movement but can be applied more generally.

8. For an exploration of the role of the cello see William Drabkin, 'The Cello Part in Beethoven's Late Quartets', *Beethoven Forum* 7 (1999), pp. 45–66.

9. Warren Kirkendale, *Fugue and Fugato in Rococo and Classical Chamber Music*, revised and expanded 2nd edn trans. M. Bent and the author (Durham, NC, 1979), p. 250.

10. For a probing exploration of movement types and cycle structures, and much else, in Op. 127, Op. 132 and Op. 130, see Daniel K. L. Chua, *The 'Galitzin' Quartets of Beethoven. Opp. 127, 132, 130* (Princeton, 1995).

11. The pedantic heritage that informs the fugue is revealed in Kirkendale, *Fugue and Fugato*, pp. 258–68.

11 The Austro-Germanic quartet tradition in the nineteenth century

1. Max Kalbeck, *Johannes Brahms* (Berlin, 1904–14, 3/1912–21/R1976), vol. I, p. 165.

2. See also Chapters 12 and 13, and for example, Association française pour le patrimoine musical (ed.), *Le quatuor à cordes en France de 1750 à nos jours* (Paris 1995), and Joël-Marie Fauquet, 'Chamber Music in France from Luigi Cherubini to Claude Debussy', in Stephen E. Hefling (ed.), *Nineteenth-Century Chamber Music* (New York, 1998, R/2003), pp. 287–314.

3. *Quartettsatz* is nothing more than the German for 'quartet movement', which has been adopted in English-speaking countries as well (it is also called simply 'the *Satz*').

4. For more detailed discussion of these and the later Schubert quartets, see Stephen E. Hefling and David S. Tartakoff, 'Schubert's Chamber Music', in Hefling (ed.), *Nineteenth-Century Chamber Music*, pp. 39–101.

5. Walter Gray, 'Schubert the Instrumental Composer', *Musical Quarterly* 64 (1978), pp. 488 and 492–3.

6. Concerning the topical associations of the descending tetrachord, see Ellen Rosand, 'The Descending Tetrachord: An Emblem of Lament', *Musical Quarterly* 65 (1979), pp. 346–59.

7. For further discussion of this topical tradition see Timothy L. Jackson, 'The Tragic Reversed Recapitulation in the German Classical Tradition', *Journal of Music Theory* 40 (1996), pp. 61–111.

8. Otto Erich Deutsch, *The Schubert Reader: a Life of Franz Schubert in Letters and Documents*, Eng. trans. Eric Blom (New York, 1951), p. 339; see also Sadie (ed.), *The New Grove Dictionary* 2nd edn, vol. XXII, s.v. 'Schubert, Franz', p. 668.

9. Further on this, see Hefling and Tartakoff, 'Schubert's Chamber Music', pp. 79–81.

10. The theme comes from the entracte before act IV of *Rosamunde*; while no copies of the play are known to survive, a long review of it reveals that in the fourth act Rosamunde appears among her flocks in an idyllic valley, having been previously released from arrest brought on by false accusation (see Deutsch, *The Schubert Reader*, p. 312, and *Neue Schubert Ausgabe* VI/5, *Streichquartette*, vol. III, pp. x–xi).

11. See Jonathan Bellman, *The 'Style Hongrois' in the Music of Western Europe* (Boston, 1993), especially ch. 7, and Hefling and Tartakoff, 'Schubert's Chamber Music', pp. 72 ff.

12. See Hefling and Tartakoff, 'Schubert's Chamber Music', pp. 85, 132–3, nn. 117–20.

13. Peter Gülke, *Franz Schubert und seine Zeit* (Laaber, 1991), p. 212.

14. Carl Dahlhaus, 'Sonata Form in Schubert: The First Movement of the G-Major String Quartet, Op. 161 (D. 887)', Eng. trans. Thilo Reinhard, in Walter Frisch (ed.), *Schubert: Critical and Analytical Studies* (Lincoln, NE, 1986), pp. 1, 8. Dahlhaus proceeds from Theodor Adorno's notions of musical epic, novel, and remembrance discussed in his *Mahler: A Musical Physiognomy* [1960], Eng. trans. Edmund Jephcott (Chicago, 1992).

15. Two additional late quartets from 1856–7 (WoO 41–2) remain unpublished; the second of these was Spohr's last completed composition; see Clive Brown (ed), *Selected Works of Louis Spohr*, vol. IX, *Chamber Music for Strings* (New York, 1987), p. vii.

16. *Allgemeine musikalische Zeitung* 12 (1809/10), col. 515.

17. Louis Spohr, *Lebenserinnerungen*, ed. Folker Göthel (Tutzing, 1968), I, p. 119.

18. Clive Brown, *Louis Spohr: A Critical Biography* (Cambridge, 1984), p. 44.

19. For example, in the first movement of Op. 4 no. 1, the move to a third-related tonality (E♭) for the second subject is probably inspired by Haydn's Op. 76 no. 3, Op. 77 no 2, and Beethoven's Op. 18 nos. 1 and 3. In the first movement of Spohr's Op. 4 no. 2, the pedal-point closing material in the exposition and recapitulation is derived from several Mozartian models, probably including the first

movements of the 'Dissonance' Quartet, K. 465,
the D major Quartet, K. 575, and the first
movement of the Divertimento for string trio
K. 543, whereas the turn to major for the
conclusion of the movement stems from Haydn
(Op. 74 no. 3). In the Poco Adagio movement of
Op. 4 no. 2, the transition to the reprise
(bb. 52ff.) is borrowed from the similar passage
(bb. 39 ff.) in the Andante cantabile of Mozart's
'Dissonance' (cf. also Brown, p. 45). Both the
treading repeated crotchets and the unusual
half-diminished supertonic chord (b. 14) in the
scherzo of Op. 4 no. 2 stem from the minuet of
Mozart's A major Quartet K. 464 (esp. b. 42).
The fugato material in the rondo finale (bb. 46
and 153ff.) follows a Viennese custom dating
from the time when Haydn (contemporaneously
with several other composers) incorporated
fugues into the finales of his Op. 20; the
tradition continued in Haydn's Op. 55, Mozart's
K. 387, and Beethoven's Op. 18 no. 1. Spohr
admits in his autobiography that in seeking to
develop his compositional talents he made
'many imitations of Mozart's masterpieces'
(*Lebenserinnerungen*, vol. I, p. 127).
20. Brown, *A Critical Biography*, p. 44.
21. Cf. also *ibid.*, p. 52.
22. *Allgemeine musikalische Zeitung* 19 (1817),
col. 154.
23. Brown, *A Critical Biography*, p. 93.
24. *Neue Zeitschrift für Musik* 32 (1850), p. 209,
cited by Brown, *A Critical Biography*, p. 315.
25. See Brown, *A Critical Biography*, pp. 97–9.
26. Carl Dahlhaus, *Nineteenth Century Music*,
Eng. trans. J. Bradford Robinson (Berkeley,
1989), pp. 168–78, especially pp. 169–70.
27. *Neue Berliner Musikzeitung* 13 (1859), p.
345, cited by Brown, *A Critical Biography*, p. 341.
28. Sadie (ed.), *The New Grove Dictionary*, 2nd
edn, vol. XXIV, p. 202. s.v. 'Spohr, Louis'.
29. See R. Larry Todd, 'The Chamber Music of
Mendelssohn', in Hefling (ed.),
Nineteenth-Century Chamber Music, p. 170, and
Sadie (ed.), *The New Grove Dictionary*, 2nd edn,
vol. XVI, s.v. 'Mendelssohn, Felix', pp. 404–6.
30. Johann Christian Lobe, 'Conversations with
Felix Mendelssohn', Eng. trans. Susan Gillespie,
in R. Larry Todd (ed.), *Mendelssohn and His
World* (Princeton, 1991), p. 193.
31. Robert Schumann, 'Trios für Pianoforte mit
Begleitung (1840)', in Martin Kreisig (ed.),
*Gesammelte Schriften über Musik und Musiker
von Robert Schumann* (Leipzig, 1914), vol. I,
p. 500.
32. For a brief discussion of this piece, see Todd,
'The Chamber Music of Mendelssohn', in
Hefling (ed.), *Nineteenth-Century Chamber
Music*, p. 174.

33. Although Beethoven's Op. 132 was
apparently performed in Berlin in 1826, it was
not issued by the Berlin publisher Schlesinger
until September 1827; however, Schlesinger had
also published music by Mendelssohn and may
have allowed him access to a manuscript of the
work (see Maynard Solomon, *Beethoven* (2nd
rev. edn, New York, 1998), pp. 416–17, and
Thayer's Life of Beethoven, rev. and ed. Elliot
Forbes (Princeton, 1967), p. 970).
34. See, for example, Joscelyn Godwin, 'Early
Mendelssohn and Late Beethoven', *Music and
Letters* 55 (1974), pp. 272–85, and Todd,
'Mendelssohn's Chamber Music', pp. 185–8, who
provides a fuller discussion of this quartet.
35. Letter of *c.* February 1828, in Adolf Fredrik
Lindblad, *Bref till Adolf Fredrik Lindblad fran
Mendelssohn . . . och andra* (Stockholm, 1913),
pp. 20; see also Todd, 'Mendelssohn's Chamber
Music', p. 185.
36. See also Friedhelm Krummacher,
*Mendelssohn – der Komponist: Studien zur
Kammermusik für Streicher* (Munich, 1978),
pp. 161–7.
37. Lindblad, *Bref*, p. 20.
38. Todd, 'Mendelssohn's Chamber Music',
p. 188.
39. Beethoven's 'Harp' Quartet, Op. 74 (also in
E♭) is often said to have provided the model for
Mendelssohn's first movement, but the
connections do not extend beyond two rhythmic
gestures in the slow introduction and some
showy arpeggio passagework for the first violin
in the coda (bb. 212ff.); see also Krummacher,
Mendelssohn – der Komponist, pp. 166–8, who
observes that the main theme of Op. 127, albeit
in 3/4, is closer in *ambitus* and texture to
Mendelssohn's principal melodic idea than any
of the material in Op. 74. (Op. 127 had been in
print since 1826.)
40. See 'From the Memoirs of Ernst Rudorff',
trans. and ed. Nancy B. Reich, in Todd (ed.),
Mendelssohn and His World, pp. 259ff., especially
pp. 265–9 (quotation from 268).
41. The finale of Schubert's Piano Trio in E♭
major, Op. 100, published in 1828, is an unusual
block-like form that quotes extensively from the
work's haunting C minor slow movement (see
Hefling and Tartakoff, 'Schubert's Chamber
Music', pp. 119–20). Mendelssohn's
tarantella-style triplets (especially in bb. 44–9
and 157–64) seem to recall the finale of
Schubert's 'Death and the Maiden' Quartet;
although it was not published until 1831,
Mendelssohn might have obtained a manuscript
copy.
42. However, Krummacher (*Mendelssohn – der
Komponist*, pp. 476 et passim) argues that

Mendelssohn was simply drawing conclusions from his earlier engagement with Beethoven and, taking Beethoven for granted, distancing himself to find his own *modus operandi*.

43. Letter of 17 February 1835 in *The Letters of Fanny Hensel to Felix Mendelssohn*, ed. and trans. Marcia J. Citron (Stuyvesant, NY, 1987), 174 and 490 (translation modified).

44. See Todd, 'The Chamber Music of Mendelssohn', p. 190.

45. Todd regards the scherzo as 'the summit of Op. 44' and provides a useful analytical discussion of it ('The Chamber Music of Mendelssohn', p. 190).

46. The shape of the movement is perhaps closest to what James Webster terms 'A|BA form' in Sadie (ed.), *The New Grove Dictionary*, 2nd edn, vol. XXIII, p. 690, s.v. 'Sonata Form'.

47. The history of the *furiant* in the early nineteenth century is not entirely clear (see Sadie, *The New Grove Dictionary*, 2nd edn, vol. IX, pp. 350–1, s.v. 'Furiant').

48. For example, in the finales of the B♭ String Quartet Op. 67 and the Clarinet Quintet Op. 115.

49. See Friedhelm Krummacher, 'Mendelssohn's Late Chamber Music: Some Autograph Sources Recovered', in Jon W. Finson and R. Larry Todd (eds.), *Mendelssohn and Schumann: Essays on Their Music and Its Context* (Durham, NC, 1984), pp. 82–4.

50. At the time of his death Mendelssohn was apparently working on another quartet, for which a set of variations in E major (Andante sostenuto) and a scherzo in A minor survive. These movements were subsequently combined with two earlier isolated movements for string quartet, a Capriccio in E minor (1843) and an early fugue in E♭ (1827), and published as the String Quartet Op. 81 in 1850.

51. Gustav Jansen (ed.), Schumann: *Briefe, Neue Folge*, 2nd edn (Leipzig, 1904), no. 450.

52. Schumann, 'Rückblick auf das Leipziger Musikleben im Winter 1837–1838', in *Gesammelte Schriften*, vol. I, p. 380.

53. John Daverio, 'The Chamber Music of Robert Schumann', in Hefling (ed.), *Nineteenth-Century Chamber Music*, p. 215; Jansen (ed.), *Briefe, Neue Folge*, no. 101 (30 June 1839). See also Nicholas Marston, 'Schumann's Monument to Beethoven', *19th Century Music* 14 (1991), pp. 248–53.

54. Daverio, 'Chamber Music', pp. 216–17; John Daverio, *Robert Schumann: Herald of a 'New Poetic Age'* (Oxford, 1997), pp. 247–9.

55. Schumann, 'Erster Quartettmorgen' (1838), in *Gesammelte Schriften*, vol. I, p. 335.

56. Max Hecker (ed.), *Briefwechsel zwischen Goethe und Zelter 1799–1832*, 3 vols. (Frankfurt am Main, 1987), vol. III, p. 246.

57. Schumann, 'Zweiter Quartettmorgen' (1838), in *Gesammelte Schriften*, vol. I, pp. 338–9, and 'Streichquartette' (1842), *Gesammelte Schriften*, vol. II, p. 75.

58. Schumann, 'Streichquartette', *Gesammelte Schriften*, vol. II, pp. 75–6, and 'Preisquartett von Julius Schapler' (1842), *Gesammelte Schriften*, vol. II, pp. 71–2.

59. Schumann, 'Zweiter Quartettmorgen' (1838), in *Gesammelte Schriften*, vol. I, pp. 338–9, and 'Streichquartette' (1842), *Gesammelte Schriften*, vol. II, p. 75.

60. Schumann, *Gesammelte Schriften*, vol. II, pp. 71, 75.

61. See Daverio, *Robert Schumann*, 252, and Daverio, 'Chamber Music', p. 218. Daverio also suggests that the juxtaposition of A minor and F major is derived from the first-movement exposition of Beethoven's Op. 132. But sonata forms based on third relations date back at least to Beethoven's Piano Sonata, Op. 31 no. 1, whereas third-relations between movements of a quartet crop up in Haydn, Opp. 74, 76, and 77, as well as Beethoven, Op. 18 no. 3.

62. The fifth of these units is extended to ten bars in a full close on the tonic (b. 75).

63. Bb. 101ff. in the exposition approximate bb. 177ff. and 207ff. in the development; bb. 117ff. approximate bb. 145ff. and 193ff. On sequential block developments, see Joel Lester, 'Robert Schumann and Sonata Forms', *19th Century Music* 18 (1995), pp. 206 *et passim*.

64. Paul Griffiths (*The String Quartet* (New York, 1983), p. 121) suggests that such a 'heroically orthodox procedure' may reflect the influence of nineteenth-century textbook formulations of sonata form.

65. See Daverio, 'Schumann's "Im Legendenton" and Friedrich Schlegel's *Arabeske*', *19th Century Music* 11 (1987), pp. 150–63.

66. Schumann's metronome marking of crotchet = 126 is precisely the standard pace of this dance; see Sadie (ed.), *The New Grove Dictionary*, 2nd edn, vol. IX, pp. 481–2, s.v. 'Galop'.

67. It has long been assumed that the motto motive is a musical cipher for Schumann's wife Clara, and indeed the work is popularly known as the 'Clara' Quartet. This is, however, a fictitious assumption for which there is no authentic substantiation. (I am grateful to Schumann specialist John Daverio for confirming this via personal communication.)

68. The broad ABABA slow-movement design has precedents in Schubert's sonatas. While

Beethoven's Adagio ma non troppo in the E♭ Quartet Op. 74 may have provided inspiration, that movement incorporates a contrasting 'C' section and varies both melody and accompaniment of its principal subject at each recurrence. Schumann's dialogue between first violin and viola in this Adagio molto recalls the Andante of Mozart's Quintet in C K. 515, essentially a love duet for those two instruments.

69. Daverio, *Robert Schumann*, p. 253.

70. Bach's Sixth French Suite may have provided the model; see George Grove (ed.), *A Dictionary of Music and Musicians*, 4 vols. (London, 1879–89), vol. IV, p. 414, s.v. 'Schumann, Robert'.

71. Anthony Newcomb, 'Schumann and Late Eighteenth-Century Narrative Strategies', *19th Century Music* 11 (1987), pp. 170–4.

72. Schumann, *Gesammelte Schriften*, vol. II, pp. 301–2.

73. Kalbeck, *Johannes Brahms*, vol. II, p. 440.

74. Richard Heuberger, *Erinnerungen an Johannes Brahms: Tagebuchnotizen aus den Jahren 1875 bis 1897*, ed. Kurt Hofmann (Tutzing, 1971), pp. 60–1.

75. See also Michael Musgrave, *The Music of Brahms* (Oxford, 1994), p. 111, and Walter Frisch, *Brahms and the Principle of Developing Variation* (Berkeley, 1984), p. 110. On the origins of the Op. 51 quartets, see Musgrave and Robert Pascall, 'The String Quartets Op. 51, No. 1 in C minor and No. 2 in A minor: A Preface', in Musgrave (ed.), *Brahms 2: Biographical, Documentary, and Analytical Studies* (Cambridge, 1987), pp. 137–43.

76. Malcolm MacDonald, *Brahms* (New York, 1990), p. 210; see also Donald Francis Tovey, 'Brahms's Chamber Music', *The Main Stream of Music and Other Essays* (New York, 1949), pp. 251–2.

77. Frisch, *Brahms*, p. 111; on the influence of Schubert, see James Webster, 'Schubert's Sonata Form and Brahms's First Maturity', *19th Century Music* 2 (1978), pp. 18–35; 3 (1979), pp. 52–71.

78. Schubert's *Quartettsatz* was first published in 1870, edited (anonymously) by Brahms, who had owned the autograph manuscript since at least 1867 (see *Johannes Brahms Briefwechsel*, vol. XIV: *Breitkopf & Härtel, Bartolf Senff . . .* [et al.] (Berlin, 1920), p. 146). Further on the *Quartettsatz*, see above, pp. 229–30.

79. The descending viola line is completed via register transfer to b♮¹ in bar 7 (second violin). The tetrachord was frequently embellished by passing chromaticism, as it is in later passages of Brahms' first movement.

80. See, for example, Allen Forte, 'Motivic Design and Structural Levels in the First Movement of Brahms' String Quartet in C

minor', *Musical Quarterly* 69 (1983), pp. 471–502, reprinted in Musgrave (ed.), *Brahms 2*, pp. 165–96, as well as Peter H. Smith, 'Brahms's Recapitulatory Overlaps', *19th Century Music* 17 (1994), pp. 241–3.

81. On the 'omnibus', see Robert W. Wason, *Viennese Harmonic Theory from Albrechtsberger to Schenker and Schoenberg* (Ann Arbor, 1985), pp. 15–19, and Hefling and Tartakoff, 'Schubert's Chamber Music', p. 86.

82. See also Smith, 'Brahms's Recapitulatory Overlaps', pp. 243–7.

83. See also Musgrave, *The Music of Brahms*, p. 115 *et passim*, and MacDonald, *Brahms*, pp. 211–13.

84. Kalbeck, *Johannes Brahms*, vol. II, p. 445. An explicit linking of the two mottos is reserved for the coda (bb. 301–3, second violin leading).

85. Schoenberg treats this movement as a *locus classicus* of developing variation in 'Brahms the Progressive', *Style and Idea*, ed. Leonard Stein, Eng. trans. Leo Black (New York, 1975), pp. 429ff.

86. Especially the slow movements of the G major String Quartet (D. 887), the B♭ major Piano Trio (D. 898) and the C major String Quintet (D. 956). Brahms, however, adds the learned touch of canon at the fifth for first violin and cello.

87. See Margaret Notley, 'The Chamber Music of Brahms', in Hefling (ed.), *Nineteenth-Century Chamber Music*, pp. 256–8.

88. Further on this topic, see Arnold Whittall, 'Two of a Kind? Brahms's Op. 51 Finales', in Musgrave (ed.), *Brahms 2*, p. 155.

89. See also MacDonald, *Brahms*, pp. 214–15, and Musgrave, *The Music of Brahms*, pp. 114–16; the 'Rondo alla Zingarese' of the G minor Piano Quartet Op. 25, although in 2/4, also moves in three-bar phrases.

90. Griffiths, *The String Quartet*, p. 131.

91. MacDonald, *Brahms*, p. 250.

92. Musgrave, *Brahms*, p. 179.

93. MacDonald, *Brahms*, p. 251.

94. George Henschel, *Personal Recollections of Johannes Brahms* (Boston, 1907, R/1978), pp. 50–1.

95. See, for example, Griffiths, *The String Quartet*, p. 132.

96. In Cobbett (ed.), *Cobbett's Cyclopedic Survey of Chamber Music* (London, 1929, R/1963), vol. I, p. 449.

97. Dahlhaus, *Nineteenth-Century Music*, pp. 2, 334ff.

98. See Walter Frisch, 'The Brahms Fog: On Analyzing Brahmsian Influences at Fin de Siècle', in Frisch (ed.), *Brahms and His World* (Princeton, 1990), pp. 81–99, especially p. 91.

99. Griffiths, *The String Quartet*, p. 156.
100. Dahlhaus, *Nineteenth-Century Music*, p. 339.
101. John Daverio, 'Fin de Siècle Chamber Music and the Critique of Modernism', in Hefling (ed.), *Nineteenth-Century Chamber Music*, p. 364.

12 Traditional and progressive nineteenth-century trends: France, Italy, Great Britain and America

1. For a detailed discussion, see Michelle Garnier-Butel, 'La naissance du quatuor à cordes français au siècle des lumières', in *Le quatuor à cordes en France de 1750 à nos jours* (Paris, 1995), especially pp. 25–6, 50–1, 57.
2. See, for example, Brigitte François-Sappey, 'Les quatuors à cordes dans le premier tiers du XIXe siècle', in *Le quatuor à cordes en France de 1750 à nos jours* (Paris, 1995), p. 77.
3. See Jeffrey Cooper, *The Rise of Instrumental Music and Concert Series in Paris, 1828–1871* (Ann Arbor, 1983) and Joël-Marie Fauquet, *Les sociétés de musique de chambre de la Restauration à 1870* (Paris, 1986).
4. Jérôme-Joseph de Momigny, *Cours complet d'harmonie et de composition* (Paris, 1806), vol. II, pp. 693–4. Reicha (1770–1836) was himself a prolific composer of chamber music and wrote for numerous combinations of instruments, including the string quartet.
5. In Sadie (ed.), *The New Grove Dictionary*, 2nd edn, vol. XX, p. 905, s.v. 'Reber, Napoléon-Henri'.
6. In Cobbett, *Cobbett's Cyclopedic Survey*, vol. II, p. 148.
7. In Sadie (ed.), *The New Grove Dictionary*, 2nd edn, vol. XXV, p. 403, s.v. 'Thomas, Ambroise'.
8. *Ibid.*, vol. VII, p. 47, s.v. 'David, Félicien'.
9. See R. Hayes, 'Onslow and Beethoven's Late Quartets', *Journal of Musicological Research* 5 (1985), pp. 273–96.
10. See V. Niaux, 'Les quatuors à cordes de George Onslow', in B. Crozier (ed.), *Le Quatuor à cordes en France de 1750 à nos jours* (Paris, 1995), pp. 63–74.
11. See Vincent D'Indy, *César Franck* (Paris, 1906), pp. 167–70. D'Indy gives a detailed analysis of the work in Cobbett (ed.), *Cobbett's Cyclopedic Survey*, vol. I, pp. 426–9.
12. In Cobbett (ed.), *Cobbett's Cyclopedic Survey*, vol. II, p. 325.
13. See J. Barrie Jones (ed. and trans.), *Gabriel Fauré: a Life in Letters* (London, 1989), p. 202.
14. Cited by Florence Nash in the booklet for the CD by the Stanford Quartet, Music and Arts CD-823.
15. Paganini's three string quartets in D minor, Eb major and A minor (*c.* 1815), dedicated to the King of Sardinia and left in manuscript, are available in an edition by Federico Mompellio (Rome, 1976).
16. Ferruccio Busoni, *Collected Letters*, Eng. trans. and ed. Antony Beaumont (London, 1987), p. 26.
17. *Ibid.*, p. 101.
18. Ellerton was actually born John Lodge and adopted the additional name in the late 1830s.
19. Dunhill achieved little of note in string quartet composition, but he founded (1907) a series of chamber concerts devoted to the works of British composers and was the first recipient of the Cobbett Chamber Music Medal (1924).
20. Ireland's two Brahmsian string quartets of 1897 were suppressed throughout his lifetime.
21. See Stephen Banfield, 'British Chamber Music at the Turn of the Century: Parry, Stanford, Mackenzie', *The Musical Times* 115 (1974), pp. 211–13.
22. Parry, Professor of Music at the University College, Aberystwyth and later at University College, Cardiff, composed the hymn tune 'Aberystwyth', the male-voice partsong 'Myfanwy' and the opera *Blodwen*.
23. *Cobbett's Cyclopedic Survey of Chamber Music* remains a monument to his outstanding contribution to chamber music.
24. For example, the American Musical Fund Society (1852), the American Music Association (1856) and the Metropolitan Music Association (1859), all in New York.
25. In addition to his quartets in C minor and A minor, Fry also left several incomplete works in the genre.
26. In Cobbett (ed.), *Cobbett's Cyclopedic Survey*, vol. I, p. 237.
27. *Ibid.*, vol. II, p. 529.
28. François-Joseph Fétis, *Biographie Universelle* (2nd edn, Paris, 1866–70), vol. I, p. 149.

13 Nineteenth-century national traditions and the string quartet

1. Both Smetana's string quartets are strongly autobiographical, although only the first, 'From my Life', has an explicit programme.
2. Tchaikovsky's Third Quartet in Eb minor was dedicated to the memory of Ferdinand Laub, and Arensky's A minor quartet was dedicated: 'à la mémoire de P. Tchaikovsky'.
3. See Richard Taruskin, *Defining Russia Musically* (Princeton, NJ, 1997), p. 199. Glinka also wrote a set of piano variations on the song.
4. See David Brown, *Mikhail Glinka – A Biographical and Critical Study* (London, 1974), p. 53.
5. See Francis Maes, *A History of Russian Music from Kamarinskaya to Babi Yar* (Berkeley, CA, 2002), p. 172.

6. See *ibid.*, p. 172.

7. See David Brown (ed.), miniature score of Borodin's String Quartet no. 1 in A major (London, 1976), introduction.

8. *Ibid.*

9. *Ibid.*

10. See Maes, *A History of Russian Music*, p. 72.

11. Brown (ed.), miniature score of Borodin's String Quartet No. 1, introduction.

12. See Maes, *A History of Russian Music*, p. 72.

13. David Brown, *Tchaikovsky: to the Crisis – 1840–1878* (2 vols., London, 1992), vol. I, p. 217.

14. *Ibid.*, vol. I, p. 298.

15. *Ibid.*, vol. II, p. 61.

16. See Maes, *A History of Russian Music*, p. 193.

17. See Knud Ketting, liner notes to Niels Gade, *String Quartets*, BIS-CD-516, The Kontra Quartet.

18. By Asger Lund Christiansen; a premiere of this edition was given in 1963 by the Copenhagen String Quartet with whom Christiansen was the cellist (see Ketting, liner notes).

19. A quartet in D minor was written, along with a fugue for the same combination, during his studies in Leipzig and then subsequently lost. Grieg himself described the work as derivative of Schumann, Gade and Mendelssohn (see John Horton, *Grieg* (London, 1974), p. 9).

20. See Edward Lockspeiser, *Debussy* (London, rev. edn, 1963), pp. 235–6, and Roger Nichols (ed.), *Debussy Remembered* (London, 1992), pp. 99 and 166.

21. Notably Gerald Abraham in Gerald Abraham (ed.), *Grieg: A Symposium* (London, 1948), p. 8, and Nils Grinde, in Sadie (ed.), *The New Grove Dictionary*, 2nd edn, vol. X, p. 408, s.v. 'Grieg'.

22. See Finn Benestad and Dag Schjelderup-Ebbe, *Edvard Grieg, mennesket og kunsteren* [Edvard Grieg, Man and Artist] (Bergen, 1962), pp. 189–90.

23. Abraham (ed.), *Grieg: A Symposium*, p. 8.

24. List derived from David Fanning, in Sadie (ed.), *The New Grove Dictionary*, 2nd edn, vol. XVII, p. 895, s.v. 'Nielsen'.

25. See Charles M. Joseph's very useful consideration of Nielsen's string quartets: 'Structural Pacing in the Nielsen String Quartets', in Mina Miller (ed.), *The Nielsen Companion* (London, 1994), pp. 460–1.

26. *Ibid.*, p. 462.

27. in Sadie (ed.), *The New Grove Dictionary*, 2nd edn, vol. XVII, p. 891.

28. See Erik Tawaststjerna, *Sibelius vol. I: 1865–1905*, Eng. trans. Robert Layton (London, 1976), p. 24.

29. *Ibid.*, pp. 47–8.

30. Robert Layton, *Sibelius* (London, 1965), p. 6.

31. Tawaststjerna, *Sibelius vol. I:1865–1905*, p. 55.

32. Robert Layton recounts that there were reports of Sibelius working on two quartets when he was composing the Fourth Symphony. See Layton, *Sibelius*, p. 139.

33. See *ibid.*, p. 140.

34. Donald Francis Tovey, *Essays and Lectures on Music* (London, 1949), pp. 307–8.

35. In a letter to Eusebius Mandyczewski in Milan Kuna (ed.), *Antonín Dvořák: korespondence a dokumenty; korespondence odeslaná* [Antonin Dvořák: Correspondence and Documents; Correspondence Sent], vol. IV (Prague, 1995), pp. 112–13. It is also interesting that in this letter, to the editor of the Schubert complete edition, there is no reference to Schubert, who is considered by many commentators to be a major influence on Dvořák at an early stage; see Jan Smaczny, 'The Schubertian Inheritance among Czech Composers in the Mid-Nineteenth Century', in *Internationales Franz Schubert Institut, Mitteilungen 21/ Sondernummer* (Tutzing, June 1998), pp. 61–75; also Jan Smaczny, '"Biding His Time" – Schubert among the Bohemians', in Brian Newbould (ed.), *Schubert Studies* (Aldershot, 1998), pp. 153–65.

36. The only other instance of a folksong quotation is in the incidental music to Samberk's play *J. K. Tyl*, Op. 62 (B 125) where the use of the melody 'Na tom nasem dvore' is prompted by the text.

37. The Andante religioso was used again in the first version of the string Quintet in G major Op. 77 (B 49), and further arranged for string orchestra as the Notturno Op. 40 (B 47), also for violin and piano (B 48a), and piano four hands (B 48b).

38. See, for example, the first movements of the Piano Trio in B♭ major Op. 21 (B 51) and the second Piano Quintet in A major Op. 81 (B 155).

39. A convincing conclusion to the work by Jarmil Burghauser is to be found in the Dvořák complete edition, vol. IV/5 (Prague, 1982).

40. The quartet was unpublished during Fibich's lifetime, but the polka movement was frequently played as a separate item.

41. František Bartoš (ed.), *Bedřich Smetana ve vzpomínkách a dopisech* [Bedrich Smetana: in Reminiscences and Letters] (Prague, 1939), p. 142. All Czech translations are by the author.

42. *Ibid.*

43. *Ibid.*, pp. 142–3.

44. A private performance was given in Srb-Debrnov's house in April 1878 with Dvořák playing the viola part. See John Clapham, *Smetana* (London, 1972), p. 68, n. 1.

45. See Milan Kuna, 'Dvořák's Slavic Spirit' in David Beveridge (ed.), *Rethinking Dvořák: Views from Five Countries* (Oxford, 1996), pp. 146–7.

46. Dvořák entitled these arrangements of Cypresses, B 152 (originally composed 1865), 'Echo of songs'.

47. Not least the Te Deum Op. 103 (B 176), composed just before Dvořák set out for the United States. Pentatonic writing is apparent in Dvořák's music from his earliest efforts (String Quartet No. 1) to his later maturity. The 'American' style, as described in the text, could also appear in works written well before he had any idea that he would one day be working in New York, notably the scherzo of the Terzetto in C major Op. 74 (B 148).

14 The string quartet in the twentieth century

1. This chapter can only be selective in the repertory that it covers. For information about the wider repertory the reader is referred to Ian Lawrence, *The Twentieth-Century String Quartet* (London, 2001), which catalogues more than 10,000 works with details of publishers and recordings.

2. Arnold Schoenberg, 'Brahms the Progressive', in Leonard Stein (ed.), *Style and Idea: Selected Writings of Arnold Schoenberg* (London, 1984).

3. *Ibid.*, p. 402, Ex. 3.

4. Arnold Whittall, *Schoenberg Chamber Music* (London, 1972), p. 7.

5. Hans Werner Henze, liner notes to recording of string quartets, Wergo, WER 60114–50.

6. *Ibid.*

7. For more extended discussion of this work, see Carola Nielinger-Vakil, 'Quiet Revolutions: Hölderlin Fragments by Luigi Nono and Wolfgang Rihm', *Music & Letters* 81 (2000), pp. 245–74.

8. As well as the four numbered quartets, Bridge also composed some works in the medium with descriptive titles, including *Scherzo Phantastick* (1901), *Phantasie Quartet* (1905), *Three Idylls* (1906) and *An Irish Melody* (Londonderry Air) (1908).

9. Peter Evans, 'Chamber Music I', in Stephen Banfield (ed.), *Music in Britain: The Twentieth Century* (Oxford, 1995), p. 240.

10. Arnold Whittall, *The Music of Britten and Tippett: Studies in Themes and Techniques* (Cambridge, 1990), pp. 108–9.

11. *Ibid.*, p. 31.

12. For an extended analytical discussion of this movement, see Derrick Puffett, 'The Fugue from Tippett's Second String Quartet', *Music Analysis* 5 (1986), pp. 233–64.

13. Whittall, *The Music of Britten and Tippett*, p. 90.

14. Elizabeth Maconchy, liner notes to 'The Complete String Quartets Vol. I', Unicorn-Kanchana, DKP(C) 9080.

15. *Ibid.*

16. Preface to score.

17. For further discussion, see Wolfgang Schwinger, *Krzysztof Penderecki: his Life and Work* (London, 1989), pp. 128–9.

18. There are also works by Cage for unspecified or variable forces which could be performed by a string quartet. A most obvious possibility would be $59\frac{1}{2}''$ for any four string instruments (1953).

19. David Schiff, *The Music of Elliott Carter* (London, 1983), p. 197.

20. *Ibid.*

21. See *ibid.*

15 The string quartet as a foundation for larger ensembles

1. Cobbett (ed.), *Cobbett's Cyclopedic Survey*, vol. I, p. 136, where he clearly regards Boccherini as the first composer in the mature classical style. 'Spohr, writing of Baillot, remarks: "He plays Boccherini's quintets frequently and with pleasure. It is curious . . . to note how his interpretation makes one forget the mediocrity of the works."' See Cobbett, *Cyclopedic Survey*, vol. I, p. 141.

2. Karel Padrta's recent thematic catalogue of Franz Krommer's works (Prague, 1997) reveals a large body of quartet-based material, including thirty-five string quintets, eight flute quintets and two oboe quintets.

3. Eduard Hanslick, *Geschichte des Concertwesens in Wien* (2 vols., Vienna, 1869–70), vol. II, p. 397.

4. George Grove, *A Dictionary of Music and Musicians* (London, 1889), vol. IV, p. 426. Of many favourable responses to the work, one of the most illuminating came from Theodor Helm, who witnessed the first performances in 1892 of both Bruckner's Eighth Symphony and Brahms' Clarinet Quintet. Describing the latter as masterly, he nevertheless wrote in the *Deutsche Zeitung* of 28 December: 'What does even the most beautiful "chamber piece" signify – a genre that is effective only in a small space and therefore addresses itself to narrow circles – in comparison with a symphony like the latest by Bruckner, whose thrillingly all-powerful tonal language . . . is capable of inspiring thousands upon thousands who have ears to hear and a heart to hear what is heard.'

5. Florence May, *The Life of Brahms* (London, 1905), vol. II, pp. 249–50.

6. Walter Frisch, *Brahms and the Principle of Developing Variation* (Berkeley and Los Angeles, 1984), p. xiii.

7. Schumann's step-brother-in-law Woldemar Bargiel studied with Rietz and Gade at the Leipzig Conservatoire from 1846, some four years after its foundation by Mendelssohn. His Octet dates from student days, and achieved a considerable success. The octet established itself as an occasional genre at the hands of Gade, Svendsen and Raff, to be followed in the twentieth century by Eugene Goossens, Shostakovich and Milhaud, amongst others. Shostakovich's Octet Op. 11 is an inventive and experimental student work. Extraordinarily, Milhaud's Octet Op. 291 is made up of simultaneous performance of his Quartets nos. 14 and 15.

8. Other Romantic composers for this combination include Cherubini and Joseph Miroslav Weber. The list also contains a number of later British composers, including Imogen Holst, Ethel Smyth, Arnold Bax and McEwen and the Swiss Frank Martin. Amongst works for related ensembles is the sextet for three violins, viola and two cellos by Eugene Goossens.

9. *Allgemeine musikalische Zeitung* 22 (1820), p. 239. For musical illustrations of this quintet, see Brown, *Louis Spohr: a Critical Biography*, pp. 88–92.

10. In Brown's commendably forthright appraisal of Spohr's chamber works, he includes the Piano Quintet of 1845 as one of those works which to some extent show evidence of creative exhaustion.

11. *The Musical World* 28 (1853), p. 443.

12. Michael Musgrave (*The Music of Brahms* (Oxford, 1985), p. 92) admits that Brahms may have found Spohr's Sextet a possible stimulus, while claiming that Spohr offered no model, even though Brahms admired him and would have known much about him from Joachim and his acquaintances at Detmold. The role of counterpoint in Brahms' developing language is an important point of difference between the two composers.

13. Eduard Speyer, *Wilhelm Speyer der Liederkomponist* (Munich, 1925), p. 67.

14. Musgrave, *The Music of Brahms*, p. 92.

15. *Ibid.*

16. The string quintet with two violas was cultivated by a variety of later composers, notably Ysaÿe, Vaughan Williams, Bax, Martinů, Milhaud and Sessions, amongst many others.

17. Occasional later writers for this combination include works by such diverse figures as Reger and Milhaud.

18. Alec Robertson, *Dvořák* (London, 1945), p. 189.

19. Frank Howes, *The English Musical Renaissance* (London, 1966), p. 59.

20. See Colin Lawson, *Brahms: Clarinet Quintet* (Cambridge, 1998), pp. 84–5.

21. Arthur Bliss, *As I Remember* (London, 1970), p. 91.

22. Stephen Banfield, *Gerald Finzi* (London, 1997), p. 201. Many works for woodwind and strings remain little known outside specialist circles, such as oboe quartets by Arnold, Lennox Berkeley, Cooke, Françaix (for cor anglais), Jacob, Moeran and Rawsthorne. The bassoon repertory includes quintets by Reicha, Almenraeder and Vogt, a mid-nineteenth-century sextet by Gustav Satter (with two cellos) and later quintets by Holbrooke, Hans Lange, Françaix, Searle, Villa Lobos and Vintner. Post-war flute quintets include an example by Walter Piston.

23. Basil Smallman, *The Piano Quartet and Quintet: Style, Structure and Scoring* (Oxford, 1994), p. 12.

24. The genre of the piano quartet established by Mozart gave rise to many distinguished successors, such as Beethoven, Weber, Mendelssohn, Schumann, Brahms, Dvořák, Fauré, D'Indy, Chausson, Taneyev, Strauss, Reger, Martinů and Copland.

25. Smallman, *The Piano Quartet and Quintet*, p. 47. Schumann's majestic, lyrical quintet was followed by a more energetic and contrapuntal Piano Quartet Op. 47, also in E♭.

26. Smallman (*ibid.*, p. 111) remarks that 'D'Indy's Quintet, for all its merits, reveals a romantic ripeness of style which, by 1924, had already turned largely to decay.'

27. Smallman (*ibid.*, p. 104) notes the Brahmsian style in England of Parry and Stanford; in Italy, Sgambati and Martucci; in Scandinavia, Sinding and Sibelius; in Russia, Arensky and Taneyev; in Switzerland, Frank Martin; and in Spain, Granados and Turina. Other composers for quintet (in alphabetical order) include Bacewicz (1952, 1965), Badings (1952), Amy Beach (1909), Bridge (1904–12), Busch (1927), Castelnuovo-Tedesco (1932, 1951), Enesco (1895, 1940), Fricker (1971), Ginastera (1963), Goossens (1918), Granados (1898), Gubaidulina (1957), Hahn (1923), Hoddinott (1972), Hovhaness (1927/R1962, 1953/R1963), Korngold (1920), Leighton (1962), Malipiero (1957), Medtner (1950),

Migot (1920), Milhaud (1951), Novák (1904), Persichetti (1954), Pfitzner (1908), Pierné (1917), Rawsthorne (1968), Reizenstein (1948), Riegger (1951), Rózsa (1928), Rubbra (1947), Saint-Saëns (1855), Schmidt (1926), Schmitt (1910), Scott (1925), Sorabji (1920), Suk (1893), Szell (1911), Tcherepnin (1927), Toch (1938), Vierne (1924), Widor (c. 1890, 1896), Williamson (1968).

28. Smallman (*ibid.*, p. 132) notes that Martinů provides the strings with his most idiomatic writing, his piano parts light and open in texture and never dominating in the manner of certain contemporaries.

29. *Ibid.*, p. 141.

30. Alexander Ivashkin and Gidon Kremer, 'Masterclass: Schnittke's Piano Quintet', *BBC Music Magazine,* May 2001, pp. 48–9.

Select bibliography

Abbot, Djilda, and Segerman, Ephraim, 'Gut Strings', *Early Music* 4 (1976), pp. 430–7

Abraham, Gerald (ed.), *Grieg: A Symposium* (London, 1948)

Adorno, Theodor W., *Alban Berg*, Eng. trans. Julianne Brand and Christopher Hailey (Cambridge, 1991)

Altmann, Wilhelm, *Handbuch für Streichquartettspieler* (4 vols., Berlin, 1928–31, 2/1972–4)

Antokoletz, Elliott, *The Music of Béla Bartók: a Study of Tonality and Progression in Twentieth-Century Music* (Berkeley, 1984)

Archibald, Bruce, 'Berg's Development as an Instrumental Composer', in Douglas Jarman (ed.), *The Berg Companion* (Boston, 1989), pp. 91–122

Association française pour le patrimoine musical (ed.), *Le Quatuor à cordes en France de 1750 à nos jours* (Paris, 1995)

Aulich, Bruno, and Heimeran, Ernst, *Das stillvergnügte Streichquartett* (Munich, 1936); Eng. trans. D. Millar Craig as *The Well-tempered String Quartet* (London, 1938)

Baillot, Pierre, *L'art du violon: nouvelle méthode* (Paris, 1835)

Banfield, Stephen (ed.), *Music in Britain: The Twentieth Century* (Oxford, 1995)

Baron, John Herschel, *Chamber Music: a Research and Information Guide* (New York, 1987)

   Intimate Music: A History of the Idea of Chamber Music (Stuyvesant, New York, 1998)

Barrett-Ayres, Reginald, *Joseph Haydn and the String Quartet* (London, 1974)

Bashford, Christina, 'Public Chamber-music Concerts in London, 1835–50: Aspects of History, Repertory and Reception' (diss., University of London, 1996)

   'Learning to Listen: Audiences for Chamber Music in Early-Victorian London', *Journal of Victorian Culture* 4 (1999), pp. 25–51

Bayley, Amanda (ed.), *The Cambridge Companion to Bartók* (Cambridge, 2001)

Beckerman, Michael (ed.), *Dvořák and his World* (Princeton, NJ, 1993)

Benson, Mark, 'Schoenberg's Private Program for the String Quartet in D minor, Op. 7', *Journal of Musicology* 11 (1993), pp. 374–95

Berger, M., *Guide to Chamber Music* (New York, 1985)

Beveridge, David (ed.), *Rethinking Dvořák: Views from Five Countries* (Oxford, 1996)

Blum, D., *The Art of Quartet Playing* (London, 1986)

Bonnerot, Jean, *Camille Saint-Saëns* (Paris, 1922)

Bonta, Stephen, 'Catline Strings Revisited', *Journal of the American Musical Instrument Society* 14 (1988), pp. 38–60

Boomkamp, Carel van Leeuwen, and Meer, John Henry van der, *The Carel van Leeuwen Boomkamp Collection of Musical Instruments* (Amsterdam, 1971)

Boyden, David D., *The History of Violin Playing from its Origins to 1761* (London, 1965)

'The Violin Bow in the Eighteenth Century', *Early Music* 8 (1980), pp. 199–212

Brandt, Nat, *Con Brio: Four Russians called The Budapest String Quartet* (New York, 1993)

Brown, Clive, *Louis Spohr: A Critical Biography* (Cambridge, 1984)

Classical and Romantic Performing Practice 1750–1900 (Oxford, 1999)

Brown, David, *Tchaikovsky: to the Crisis – 1840–1878* (2 vols., London, 1992)

Brown, Howard Mayer, and Sadie, Stanley (eds.), *Performance Practice* (2 vols., London, 1989)

Burghauser, Jarmil, *Antonín Dvořák* (Prague, 1964–7)

Burkholder, J. Peter, *Charles Ives: the Ideas behind the Music* (New Haven, CT, 1985)

All Made of Tunes: Charles Ives and the Uses of Musical Borrowing (New Haven, CT, 1995)

Chua, Daniel K. L., *The 'Galitzin' Quartets of Beethoven. Opp. 127, 132, 130* (Princeton, NJ, 1995)

Clapham, John, *Dvořák* (New York, 1979)

Smetana (London, 1972)

Cobbett, Walter Willson (ed.), *Cobbett's Cyclopedic Survey of Chamber Music* (2 vols., London, 1929; rev. C. Mason, 3 vols. 2/1963/R)

Coolidge, Richard A., 'Form in the String Quartets of Franz Schubert', *Music Review* 32 (1971), pp. 309–25

Cooper, Jeffrey, *The Rise of Instrumental Music and Concert Series in Paris, 1828–1871* (Ann Arbor, 1983)

Day, Timothy, *A Century of Recorded Music: Listening to Musical History* (London, 2000)

Dent, Edward J., 'The Earliest String Quartets', *Monthly Musical Record* 33 (1903), pp. 202–4

Drabkin, William, 'The Cello Part in Beethoven's Late Quartets', *Beethoven Forum* 7 (1999), pp. 45–66

A Reader's Guide to Haydn's Early String Quartets (Westport, CT, 2000)

Ehrlich, A. [Payne, Albert] (ed.), *Das Streich-quartet in Wort und Bild* (Leipzig, 1898)

Ehrlich, Cyril, *The Music Profession in Britain since the Eighteenth Century: a Social History* (Oxford, 1985)

Farish, Margaret K., *String Music in Print* (New York, 1965; supplement 1968)

Fauquet, Joël-Marie, *Les sociétés de musique de chambre à Paris de la Restauration à 1870* (Paris, 1986)

Ferguson, Donald N., *Image and Structure in Chamber Music* (Minneapolis, 1964)

Finscher, Ludwig, 'Zur Sozialgeschichte des klassischen Streichquartetts', *Gesellschaft für Musikforschung: Kongress-Bericht* (Kassel, 1962), pp. 37–9

'Zur Geschichte des Streichquartetts als musikalische Gattungsgeschichte', in Vera Schwarz (ed.), *Violinspiel und Violinmusik* (Graz, 1972), pp. 80–9

   Studien zur Geschichte des Streichquartets, vol. I: *Die Entstehung des klassischen
      Streichquartetts: von den Vorformen zur Grundlegung durch Joseph Haydn*
      (Kassel, 1974)
Finson, Jon W., and Todd, R. Larry (eds.), *Mendelssohn and Schumann: Essays on
      their Music and its Context* (Durham, NC, 1984)
Flesch, Carl, *The Memoirs of Carl Flesch*; Eng. trans. Hans Keller (London, 1957)
   Die Kunst des Violinspiels (2 vols., Berlin, 1923–8); Eng. trans. Frederick H.
      Martens as *The Art of Violin Playing* (New York, 1924–9)
François-Sappey, Brigitte, *Alexandre P. F. Boëlly, 1785–1858* (Paris, 1989)
Frank, Alan, *see* Stratton, George
Frisch, Walter, *The Early Works of Arnold Schoenberg, 1893–1908* (Berkeley, 1993)
Frisch, Walter (ed.), *Schubert: Critical and Analytical Studies* (Lincoln, NE, 1986)
   Brahms and his World (Princeton, 1990)
Gallois, Jean, *Chausson* (Paris, 1994)
Geminiani, Francesco, *The Art of Playing on the Violin* (London, 1751/R1952)
Gillespie, Don (ed.), *George Crumb: Profile of a Composer* (New York, 1986)
Gillett, Judy, 'The Problem of Schubert's G Major String Quartet (D. 887)', *Music
      Review* 35 (1974), pp. 281–92
Gillies, Malcolm (ed.), *The Bartók Companion* (London, 1993)
Graesser, Hanno, and Holliman, Andy, *Electric Violins* (Frankfurt am Main, 1999)
Griffiths, Paul, *The String Quartet: a History* (London and New York, 1983)
   György Ligeti (London, 1983)
Gruhle, W., *Streichquartett-Lexikon: Komposition, Werke, Interpretation*
      (Gelnhausen, 1996, 2/1999)
Gut, Serge, and Pistone, Danièle, *La musique de chambre en France de 1870 à 1918*
      (Paris, 1978)
Hanning, Barbara R., 'Conversation and Musical Style in the Late
      Eighteenth-Century Parisian Salon', *Eighteenth-century Studies* 12 (1989),
      pp. 512–28
Hawkins, Frank V., *The Story of Two Thousand Concerts* (London, [1969])
   A Hundred Years of Chamber Music (London, 1987)
Hefling, Stephen E. (ed.), *Nineteenth-century Chamber Music* (New York, 1998,
      R/2003)
Heimeran, Ernst, *see* Aulich, Bruno
Hickman, Roger, 'Six Bohemian Masters of the String Quartet in the Late
      Eighteenth Century' (diss., University of California, Berkeley, 1979)
   'The Nascent Viennese String Quartet', *Musical Quarterly* 67 (1981), pp. 193–212
   'The Flowering of the Viennese String Quartet in the Late Eighteenth Century',
      Music Review 1 (1989), pp. 157–80
Hinson, Maurice, *The Piano in Chamber Ensemble: an Annotated Guide*
      (Bloomington, IN, 1978)
Hitchcock, H. Wiley, *Ives: a Survey of the Music* (London, 1977)
   Music in the United States: A Historical Introduction (3rd edn, Englewood Cliffs,
      NJ, 1988)
   see also Sadie, Stanley
Hollander, Hans, *Leos Janáček. His Life and Work*; Eng. trans. Paul Hamburger
      (London, 1963)

Holliman, Andy, *see* Graesser, Hanno

Horton, John, *Grieg* (London, 1974)

Howes, Frank, *The English Musical Renaissance* (London, 1966)

Hyatt King, Alec, *Chamber Music* (London, 1948)

Jacobson, Bernard, *A Polish Renaissance* (London, 1996)

Joachim, Joseph, and Moser, Andreas, *Violinschule* (3 vols., Berlin, 1902–5); Eng.
    trans. Alfred Moffat (London, 1905)

Jones, John Barrie (ed. and trans.), *Gabriel Fauré: a Life in Letters* (London, 1989)

Kárpáti, János, *Bartók's String Quartets*; Eng. trans. Fred MacNicol (Budapest,
    1975)

Keller, Hans, *The Great Haydn Quartets: Their Interpretation* (London, 1986)

Kemp, Ian, *Tippett: The Composer and his Music* (London, 1984)

Kemp, Ian (ed.), *Michael Tippett: a Symposium on his 60th Birthday* (London, 1965)

Kerman, Joseph, *The Beethoven Quartets* (New York, 1967)

Kilburn, N., *The Story of Chamber Music* (London, 1904, 2/1932 with G. E. H.
    Abraham as *Chamber Music and its Masters in the Past and in the Present*)

Kirkendale, Warren, *Fugue and Fugato in Rococo and Classical Chamber Music*, rev.
    and enlarged M. Bent and W. Kirkendale (Durham, NC, 1979)

Konold, W., *Das Streichquartett, von den Anfängen bis Franz Schubert*
    (Wilhelmshaven, 1980; Eng. trans. Susan Hellauer, New York, 1983)

Kornstein, E., 'How to Practise a String Quartet', *Music and Letters* 3 (1922),
    pp. 329–44

Kramarz, J., *Von Haydn bis Hindemith: das Streichquartett in Beispielen*
    (Wolfenbüttel, 1961)

Krummacher, Friedhelm, *Das Streichquartett* [= *Handbuch der musikalischen
    Gattungen*, vol. VI/1] (Laaber, 2001)

Large, Brian, *Smetana* (London, 1970)

Lawrence, Ian, *The Twentieth-Century String Quartet* (London, 2001)

Lawson, Colin, *Brahms: Clarinet Quintet* (Cambridge, 1998)

Lawson, Colin, and Stowell, Robin, *The Historical Performance of Music: an
    Introduction* (Cambridge, 1999)

Layton, Robert, *Sibelius* (London, 1965)

Léner, Jenö, *The Technique of String Quartet Playing* (London, 1935)

Leppert, Richard, *Music and Image: Domesticity, Ideology and Socio-Cultural
    Formation in Eighteenth-Century England* (Cambridge, 1988)

Levy, Janet M., *Beethoven's Compositional Process* (Philadelphia, 1982)

MacDonald, Malcolm, *Brahms* (New York, 1990)

MacRae, Julia (ed.), *Wigmore Hall 1901–2001: a Celebration* (London, 2001)

Maes, Francis, *A History of Russian Music* (Berkeley, CA, 2002)

Mahling, C.-H. (ed.), *Schloss Engers Colloquia zur Kammermusik*, vol. I: *Aspekte der
    Kammermusik vom 18. Jahrhundert bis zur Gegenwart* (Mainz, 1998)

Martin, Robert, *see* Winter, Robert

McCalla, James, *Twentieth-Century Chamber Music* (New York, 1996)

McFarlane, Meredith, 'The String Quartet in Late Eighteenth-century England: a
    Contextual Examination' (diss., Royal College of Music, London, 2002)

McVeigh, Simon, *Concert Life in London from Mozart to Haydn* (Cambridge,
    1993)

Meer, John Henry van der, *see* Boomkamp, Carel van Leeuwen

Miller, Mina (ed.), *The Nielsen Companion* (London, 1994)

Moldenhauer, Hans, *Anton von Webern* (London, 1978)

Momigny, Jérôme-Joseph de, *La seule vraie théorie de la musique* (Paris, 1821)

Mongrédien, Jean, *French Music from the Enlightenment to Romanticism, 1789–1830*, Eng. trans. Sylvain Frémaux (Portland, OR, 1996)

Morrow, Mary Sue, *Concert Life in Haydn's Vienna: Aspects of a Developing Musical and Social Institution* (Stuyvesant, NY, 1989)

Moser, Andreas, *see* Joachim, Joseph

Mozart, Leopold, *Versuch einer gründlichen Violinschule* (Augsburg, 1756); Eng. trans. Editha Knocker as *A Treatise on the Fundamental Principles of Violin Playing* (London, 1948, 2/1951)

Musgrave, Michael, *The Music of Brahms* (Oxford, 1994)

Nicholls, David (ed.), *The Cambridge History of American Music* (Cambridge, 1998)

Nichols, Roger, *Ravel* (London, 1977)

Nichols, Roger (ed.), *Debussy Remembered* (London, 1992)

Norris, Christopher (ed.), *Shostakovich: the Man and his Music* (London, 1982)

Norton, M. D. Herter, *The Art of String Quartet Playing* (New York, 1925, 2/1962/R as *The Art of String Quartet Playing: Practice, Technique and Interpretation*)

Oboussier, Philippe, 'The French String Quartet, 1770–1800', in Malcolm Boyd (ed.), *Music and the French Revolution* (Cambridge, 1992), pp. 74–92

Orledge, Robert, *Gabriel Fauré* (2nd edn, London, 1983)

Otto, Jacob Augustus, *A Treatise on the Structure and Preservation of the Violin and All Other Bow-instruments*, 2nd edn, Eng. trans. John Bishop (London, 1860)

Page, Athol, *Playing String Quartets* (London, 1964)

Parker, Mara, 'Friedrich Wilhelm II and the Classical String Quartet', *The Music Review* 54/3–4 (1993), pp. 161–82

Perle, George, 'The Secret Programme of the *Lyric Suite*', *Musical Times* 118 (1977), pp. 629–32, 709–13, 809–13

Pincherle, Marc, 'On the Origins of the String Quartet'; Eng. trans. M. D. Herter Norton, *Musical Quarterly* 15 (1929), pp. 77–87

Pistone, Danièle, *see* Gut, Serge

Pochon, A., *A Progressive Method of String-Quartet Playing* (New York, 1924)

Potter, Caroline, *Henri Dutilleux: His Life and Works* (Aldershot, 1997)

Quantz, Johann Joachim, *Versuch einer Anweisung die Flöte traversiere zu spielen* (Berlin, 1752; 3rd edn, 1789/R1952); Eng. trans. Edward R. Reilly as *On Playing the Flute* (London and New York, 1966)

Rae, Charles Bodman, *The Music of Lutoslawski* (London, 1999)

Risatti, Howard, *New Music Vocabulary: A Guide to Notational Signs for Contemporary Music* (Urbana, IL, 1975)

Robertson, Alec (ed.), *Chamber Music* (Harmondsworth, 1957)

Roda, Joseph, *Bows for Musical Instruments of the Violin Family* (Chicago, 1959)

Sadie, Stanley (ed.), *The New Grove Dictionary of Music and Musicians*, 2nd edn (29 vols., London, 2001)

Sadie, Stanley, and Hitchcock, H. Wiley (eds.), *The New Grove Dictionary of American Music* (London, 1986)

Salmen, Walter, *Haus- und Kammermusik: Privates Musizieren im gesellschaftlichen Wandel zwischen 1600 und 1900*, Musikgeschichte in Bildern, vol. IV/3 (Leipzig, 1969)

Samson, Jim, *The Music of Szymanowski* (London, 1981)

Schelleng, John, 'The Physics of the Bowed String', *Scientific American* 230 (1974), pp. 87–95

Schiff, David, *The Music of Elliott Carter* (London, 1983)

Schneider, Herbert, 'Das Streichquartett Op. 45 von Vincent D'Indy als Exemplum des zyklischen Sonate', in *Studien zur Musikgeschichte: ein Festschrift für Ludwig Finscher* (Kassel, 1995)

Schwinger, Wolfgang, *Krzysztof Penderecki: his Life and Work* (London, 1989)

Seaman, Gerald, 'The First Russian Chamber Music', *Music Review* 26 (1965), pp. 326–37

'Amateur Music-Making in Russia', *Music and Letters* 47 (1966), pp. 249–59

Segerman, Ephraim, 'Strings through the Ages', *The Strad* 99 (1988), pp. 52–5, 195–201, 295–9

see also Abbot, Djilda

Smallman, Basil, *The Piano Quartet and Quintet: Style, Structure and Scoring* (Oxford, 1994)

Smith, Joan Allen, *Schoenberg and his School* (New York, 1986)

Snowman, Daniel, *The Amadeus Quartet: the Men and the Music* (London, 1981)

Solomon, Maynard, 'Schubert and Beethoven', *19th Century Music* 3 (1979), pp. 114–25

Šourek, Otakar, *The Chamber Music of Antonín Dvořák*, Eng. trans. Roberta Finlayson Samsour (Prague, 1956)

Spohr, Louis, *Violinschule* (Vienna, [1832])

Selbstbiographie, vols. I–II (Kassel, 1860–1; Eng. trans., 1865/R, 2/1878/R)

Stein, Leonard (ed.), *Style and Idea: Selected Writings of Arnold Schoenberg* (London, 1984)

Stevens, Halsey, *The Life and Music of Béla Bartók* (3rd edn, ed. Malcolm Gillies, Oxford, 1993)

Stowell, Robin, *Violin Technique and Performance Practice in the Late Eighteenth and Early Nineteenth Centuries* (Cambridge, 1985)

The Early Violin and Viola: a Practical Guide (Cambridge, 2001)

Stowell, Robin (ed.), *The Cambridge Companion to the Violin* (Cambridge, 1992)

The Cambridge Companion to the Cello (Cambridge, 1999)

see also Lawson, Colin

Strange, Patricia, and Strange, Allen, *The Contemporary Violin: Extended Performance Techniques* (London, Berkeley and Los Angeles, 2001)

Stratton, George, and Frank, Alan, *The Playing of Chamber Music* (London, 1935)

Stucky, Stephen, *Lutoslawski and his Music* (Cambridge, 1981)

Sutcliffe, W. Dean, *Haydn: String Quartets Op. 50* (Cambridge, 1992)

Taruskin, Richard, *Defining Russia Musically: Historical and Hermeneutical Essays* (Princeton, NJ, 1997)

Tawaststjerna, Erik, *Sibelius*, Eng. trans. Robert Layton (London, 1976–97)

Todd, R. Larry, *see* Finson, Jon W.

Truscott, Harold, 'Schubert's D minor String Quartet', *Music Review* 19 (1958), pp. 27–36
  'Schubert's String Quartet in G Major', *Music Review* 20 (1959), pp. 119–45
Ulrich, H., *Chamber Music: the Growth and Practice of an Intimate Art* (New York, 1948, 2/1966)
Viano, Richard J., 'By Invitation Only: Private Concerts in France during the Second Half of the Eighteenth Century', *Recherches sur la musique française classique* 27 (1991–2), pp. 131–62
Vidal, Louis-Antoine, *Les instruments à archet: . . . les joueurs d'instruments, leur histoire sur le continent européen, suivi d'un catalogue général de la musique de chambre* (3 vols., Paris, 1876–78)
Walden, Valerie, *One Hundred Years of Violoncello* (Cambridge, 1998)
Walsh, Stephen, *Bartók Chamber Music* (London, 1982)
Walthew, Richard, *The Development of Chamber Music* (London and New York, [1909])
Wasielewski, W. J. von, *Die Violine und ihre Meister* (Leipzig, 1869)
Way-Sullivan, Elizabeth, 'German Nationalism and the Reception of the Czech String Quartet in Vienna', in Jim Samson and Bennett Zon (eds.), *Nineteenth-century Music: Selected Proceedings of the Tenth International Conference* (Aldershot, 2001)
Weber, Horst, *Alexander Zemlinsky* (Vienna, 1977)
Webster, James, 'The Bass Part in Haydn's Early String Quartets and in Austrian Chamber Music, 1750–1780' (diss., Princeton University, 1973)
  'The Bass Part in Haydn's Early String Quartets', *Musical Quarterly* 63 (1977), pp. 390–424
  'Towards a History of Viennese Chamber Music in the Early Classic Period', *Journal of the American Musicological Society* 27 (1974), pp. 212–47
  'Violoncello and Double Bass in the Chamber Music of Haydn and his Viennese Contemporaries', *Journal of the American Musicological Society* 29 (1977), pp. 413–38
Whittall, Arnold, *Schoenberg Chamber Music* (London, 1972)
  The Music of Britten and Tippett; Studies in Themes and Techniques (Cambridge, 1990)
Wightman, Alistair, *Karol Szymanowski: His Life and Work* (Aldershot, 1999)
Winter, Robert, and Carr, B. (eds.), *Beethoven, Performers and Critics* (Detroit, 1980)
Winter, Robert, and Martin, Robert (eds.), *The Beethoven Quartet Companion* (London, 1994)
Yudkin, Jeremy, 'Beethoven's "Mozart" Quartet', *Journal of the American Musicological Society* 45 (1992), pp. 30–74
Zaimont, J. L., 'String Quartets by Women: Report on Two Conferences', *The Musical Woman: an International Perspective*, vol. II (New York, 1987), pp. 378–87
Zukofsky, Paul, 'On Violin Harmonics', in Benjamin Boretz and E. T. Cone (eds.), *Perspectives on Notation and Performance* (New York, 1976), pp. 145–53

Index